THE TIMES

COMPACT
HISTORY
OF THE
WORLD

THE TIMES

COMPACT
HISTORY
OF THE
WORLD

Edited by Geoffrey Parker

TIMES BOOKS
London

Times Books, London
77-85 Fulham Palace Road,
Hammersmith, London W6 8JB

First published by Times Books (as *The Times
Compact Atlas of World History*) 1995
Second edition 1997
Third edition 2001
Updated and reprinted 2002
Fourth Edition 2005

Printed and bound in Hong Kong

British Library Cataloguing in Publication Data
A catalogue record for this book is available
from the British Library

ISBN-10 0-00-721411-1
ISBN-13 978-0-00-721411-2

Times Atlas set ISBN-10 0-00-721354-9
              ISBN-13 978-0-00-721354-2

EDITOR

GEOFFREY PARKER
Andreas Dorpalen
Distinguished Professor
of History
The Ohio State University

Editorial Consultants

Chris Scarre
McDonald Institute
University of Cambridge

Richard Overy
Professor of Modern History
King's College
University of London

Editorial Direction

Philip Parker

Cartographic Direction and Design

Martin Brown

Cartographers

Cosmographics, Watford
Bartholomew Mapping Services,
Glasgow

Designer

Colin Brown

Place-names Consultant, Index

Pat Geelan

Contents

PART THREE

The Rise of
the West

Introduction

This volume, like *The Times Complete History of the World*, which has sold over two million copies in 14 languages worldwide since its first publication in 1978, attempts to cover the whole story of humankind from its origins, when our ancestors first emerged from the tropical forests of Africa, to the complex, highly articulated world in which we now live.

It differs, however, from the original *History of the World* in three important ways. First, as its name makes clear, it presents the data in a more compact form. Although it includes 80 spreads each contains fewer, simpler maps and (proportionately) more text. Second, every map has been reviewed in order to highlight the salient trends and facts it features. Third, the topics selected for treatment include far more material from the modern period: 24 spreads concentrate on the period since 1914 and no fewer than 17 of them cover the world since 1945.

Nevertheless, although the present volume incorporates new material and differs in several ways from its predecessor, it rests upon the same principles. Above all, it tries to break away from a concentration on Europe and to offer instead a view of history that is world-wide in conception and presentation and which does justice, without prejudice or favour, to the achievements of all peoples, in all ages and in all quarters of the globe. It thus remains true to the vision of the late Geoffrey Barraclough, who planned and edited the *History*.

'When we say this is an atlas of world history, we mean that it is not simply a series of national histories loosely strung together. In other words, it is concerned less with particular events in the history of particular countries than with broad movements – for example the spread of the great world religions spanning whole continents... In singling out topics for inclusion we have adhered to the principle of selecting what was important then rather than what seems important now'

The essence of history, as Geoffrey Barraclough realized, is change and movement over time; and the historian's principal mission is therefore to discern the static from the dynamic, the aberration from the trend, and the contingent from the constant. So instead of presenting a series of individual snapshots, The *The Times Compact History of the World* emphasizes change, expansion and contraction. It aims to convey a sense of the past as a continuing process and thus to provide a fresh perspective on today's world which will meet the requirements and interests of present-day readers in all parts of the globe.

This new edition incorporates several distinctive features. First, we have updated all the later spreads – both maps and text – and added four new spreads to cover developments down to March 2005. Second, other maps have been revised and provided with physical bases. Third the volume includes over 80 images and numerous new tables. Finally, we have corrected errors brought to our attention by readers.

GEOFFREY PARKER
March 2005

ONE

The Ancient World

About 6000 years ago, in a few areas of particularly intensive agriculture, the dispersed villages of Neolithic peoples gave way to more complex societies. These were the first civilizations, and their emergence marks the start of a new phase of world history. They arose, apparently independently, in four widely dispersed areas (the early civilizations of America emerged considerably later): the lower Tigris and Euphrates valleys; the valley of the Nile; the Indus valley around Harappa and Mohenjo-Daro; and the Yellow River around An-yang. The characteristic feature of them all was the city, which now became an increasingly dominant social form, gradually encroaching on the surrounding countryside, until today urban civilization has become the criterion of social progress. But the city possessed other important connotations: a complex division of labour; literacy and a literate class (usually the priesthood); monumental public buildings; political and religious hierarchies; a kingship descended from the gods.

Statue of the pharaoh Ramesses II
Great Temple of Abu Simbel, c. 1257 BC

Human origins

The earliest known hominine fossils come from the Afar region of Ethiopia and are 4.5 million years old. Between three and four million years ago, skeletal and fossilized footprints of *Australopithecus afarensis* indicate a serviceable if not fully bipedal gait, hands still partly adapted for specialized tree climbing and a brain approximately one-third the size of ours. This species is the probable ancestor both of the robustly built Australopithecines ('southern apes'), all with large teeth and herbivorous diets, and of our genus *Homo* ('man'). These

closely related but nonetheless distinct species not only lived at the same time but side by side in the same habitats.

About three million years ago, *Homo* began to undergo important evolutionary trends, acquiring a larger brain and full bipedalism. As larger brains need better diets to sustain them, the increase in

brain size must have been accompanied by a move towards an energy-rich diet including animal proteins. And indeed the earliest-known stone tools, found in Gona, Ethiopia, suggest that 2.5 million years ago meat was a central part of hominines' diet. The sharpened stones were used to cut flesh and pound marrow-rich bones from carcasses either scavenged or hunted and then defended against other carnivores. Burnt bones found in southern Africa indicate that by 1.5 million years ago hominines had learned to cook their food, a development which would have aided digestion by breaking down animal proteins before eating.

This pattern of development was the basis for the colonization by *Homo erectus* of areas outside sub-Saharan Africa around 1.8 million years ago. Then, a million years ago *Homo heidelbergensis* migrated into North Africa and the Near East, reaching northern Europe about 500,000 years ago. Both *erectus* and *heidelbergensis* probably shared a common African ancestor,

A hand-axe from Olduvai Gorge, Tanzania. Handaxes, which are more efficient butchery tools than stone flakes, began to appear around 1.5 million years ago. This probably coincided with an increase in active hunting – as opposed to scavenging – for meat.

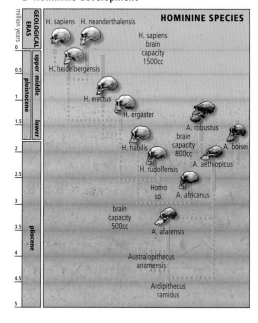

Homo ergaster, best known from the Nariokotome skeleton. All three had brains of about 1,000 cubic centimetres and an adaptable stone technology: the weight and careful shaping of the edges of their distinctive handaxes, whether pointed or oval, made them effective butchery tools.

Stone technology in itself did not play a part in the evolutionary pressures that led to larger brains. The importance of *Homo*'s larger brain had less to do with the food quest than with allowing hominines to remember, to manipulate, to support and to organize others in more complex ways. This in turn allowed them to colonize harsher barrier habitats such as the Sahara at the margins of their homelands from where they could spread into more temperate areas beyond.

From about 500,000 years ago, this early burst of colonization came to a halt. There followed a period during which, through many dispersals of populations and much intermingling of genes, regional populations such as the Neanderthals developed, living side by side with other groups. But from 100,000 years ago, a second major dispersal began when anatomically modern people – *Homo sapiens sapiens* – emigrated from sub-Saharan Africa. By 50,000 years ago, Australia had been reached by boat; 33,000 years ago, the western Pacific islands were colonized; 15,000 years ago, the Americas were reached. Major expansion into the Arctic began about 4500 years as the continental ice sheets retreated. Finally, 2000 years ago, humans began to settle the deep Pacific islands from where they reached New Zealand around 1200 years ago, 1000 years before the island's discovery by Captain Cook.

2 Hominine development

13

The spread of modern humans

DNA studies have revealed that the first anatomically modern humans (*Homo sapiens sapiens*) arose in Africa between 200,000 and 140,000 years ago. The earliest modern-looking human skulls yet found are about 130,000 years old and come from the Omo basin in Ethiopia and Klasies River Mouth in southern Africa. Around 100,000 years ago, these early populations began to migrate northwards out of Africa.

Archaeological and genetic evidence then point to a further rapid expansion of modern human populations and settlements about 50,000 years ago. There is evidence of lighter, multi-component weapons and of textiles and baskets. Camp sites became more orderly and included cold-weather dwellings and underground food stores. Trading networks also expanded dramatically and raw materials, particularly stone, which had previously been traded over distances of less than 50 miles, were now traded over many hundreds of miles.

Human colonisation of the Old World took place against the background of the Ice Ages. There have been eight Ice Ages in the last 800,000 years, alternating with warmer periods of about 10,000 years known as interglacials. During the Ice Ages, ice sheets advanced across the frozen wastes of the northern hemisphere and temperatures fell by up to 15 degrees centigrade. With so much of the earth's water locked into the ice sheets, sea levels fell,

opening up land bridges, but half the area between the tropics became desert as rainfall diminished. Animals withdrew to warmer latitudes during cold phases and humans, too, must have migrated with these changing climates, although they could also adapt to the cold through the mastery of fire, the invention of clothing, and new social and communication skills.

For many thousands of years, *Homo sapiens sapiens* shared the world with *Homo erectus* in East Asia and with Neanderthals in Europe and West Asia, both groups in many ways as sophisticated and successful in their mastery of their environments as *Homo sapiens sapiens*. The similarities between these contemporary hominine species are in most respects more striking than the differences. Nonetheless, the greater social sophistication of *Homo sapiens sapiens* proved decisive in allowing them to colonize a much wider range of habitats than any previous hominine.

By 12,000 years ago, the last Ice Age was drawing to a close. As temperatures rose, vegetation spread and animals re-colonized the cold northern wastes. With them went hunters and gatherers. Meanwhile, in South-West Asia, people had begun to move beyond their existing resources and to investigate new ways of producing food and manipulating plants and animals in the first experiments in farming.

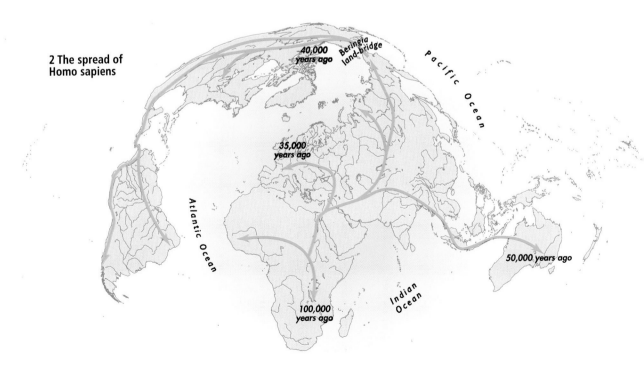

2 The spread of Homo sapiens

40,000 years ago

Beringia land-bridge

Pacific Ocean

35,000 years ago

Atlantic Ocean

50,000 years ago

Indian Ocean

100,000 years ago

Kanto Plain

Sokchang-Ni

Zhoukoudian Upper Cave

SIBERIA

...gia land-bridge

Arctic Ocean

Salawusu   Tongliang

Malta Buret

Shestakovo   Shlenka

Anyi

SUNDA

Sokchang-Ni   Kanto Plain

Pacific Ocean

Laharia-Dih

SUNDA   SAHUL

Nawamoyn

Pushkari   Kostienki
Amvrosievka

Krakow Spadzista

EUROPE   WEST ASIA

INDIA

Puritjarra

AUSTRALIA
Lake Mungo   Murray

Koonalda

Grotta dei
Fanciulli   Kastritsa

Lascaux   Kebara Cave   Wadi Al-Hammeh

Altamíra   Paglicci   Wadi Jilat

...a Morin   Kutikina

Parpalló   Tamar Hat   Haua Fteah

Taforalt   Wadi Kubbaniya

Nile

Sahara

AFRICA

Omo

Indian Ocean

Ishango   Nasera

A bison from the caves at Altamíra, near Santander in northern Spain. This 14,000-year-old masterpiece comes from the painted ceiling of a chamber covered with depictions of animals. The painters used more than one colour and exploited the natural contours of the ceiling to give a number of the creatures three-dimensional form. It remains among the most potent and vivid images created by the artists of the late Ice Age in Europe.

Depression Cave   Sehonghong

Klasies River Mouth
Boomplaas
Nelson Bay Cave

15

The origins of agriculture

The period 10,000 to 4000 BC witnessed three critical developments: the origins of settled life; the first farming; and the first cities. The origin of agriculture is often termed the 'Neolithic revolution', but archaeology reveals only gradual changes in techniques of food acquisition over thousands of years until present-day climatic conditions began to prevail, around 8000 BC.

Until then, humankind consisted of bands of hunters and gatherers who, although more numerous than ever before, pursued a lifestyle that differed little from that of their predecessors. In China and west Asia, however, new lifestyles began to develop, based on cultivation rather than collecting plant foods. Within the next 2,000 years substantial villages appeared in certain regions; and 5,000 years later there were towns and cities.

This decisive quickening in the pace of human development stemmed largely from the beginning of agriculture: the deliberate alteration of natural systems to promote the abundance of an exploited species or set of species. Many parts of the globe, especially those between latitude 10° South and 50° North, have contributed to the present-day repertory of domesticated plants and animals (map 1). Among the earliest and most important centres of cereal cultivation were South-West Asia, where the wild ancestors of wheat and barley grew; China and South-East Asia, where millet and rice thrived; and Mesoamerica, which developed maize as a staple crop. In Africa, people in the lands south of the Sahara and in the high grasslands of North-East Africa domesticated a wide variety of native plant species. Generally, cereal cultivation characterized temperate regions while root or tree crop cultivation – potatoes, yams, bananas – predominated in tropical zones.

At the same time, useful local animal species were domesticated to provide meat, milk, hides or wool, and (except in the Americas, which lacked suitable animals) an important source of power for ploughing and other agricultural tasks. On the steppe-lands of central Eurasia, animal-keeping prevailed over plant cultivation, and the domestication of the horse facilitated a specialized life-style based on nomadic herding.

The exact origins of agriculture remain unknown, but once chosen, farming developed a momentum of its own: there was no easy turning back, and the very success of the new lifestyle induced other fundamental changes. The ensuing increase in food resources made possible a spectacular growth of human population between 8000 and 4000 BC. It also required cooperative effort, particularly after the introduction of

MESOAMERICA

Cereals	Pulses
Maize	Common bean
Teosinte	Runner bean
	Tepary bean

Fruits	Other Crops
Avocado	Chilli pepper
Tomato	Squashes

MESOAMERI

Tur

NORTHERN SOUTH AMERICA

Pulses	Root Crops
Common bean	Manioc
Lima bean	Potato
	Sweet Potato
	Yam

Fruits	Other Crops
Guava	Cashew
Pineapple	Chili pepper
Soursop	Cocoa
Sweetsop	Peanut
	Quinoa
	Squashes

ANDES

LOWLAN

Guinea pig

Llama

Alpaca

African rock art painting
From around 9000 BC to 3000 BC the climate in the Sahara was much more favourable than today. Rock art paintings depict a great variety of plants and animals such as elephant, lion and buffalo as well as, from about 6000 BC, domesticated cattle.

irrigation led to the establishment of settled organized societies, at first in villages and later in towns and cities, and the development of new technologies, social systems and ideologies.

The transformation from hunting and gathering to agriculture, from a migratory to a sedentary life, was a decisive event in world history. Hunters and gatherers survived but, as farming spread, they retreated to the marginal world environments where agriculture could not secure a foothold (map 2). Both absolutely and relatively, their numbers declined until today their representatives survive only in hot deserts (the Kalahari and central Australia), in the dense rain forests of the Amazon basin, central Africa and South-East Asia, and in the frozen Arctic. Even there, traditional lifestyles – followed by mankind for millennia – now face the threat of extinction.

2 The decline of hunting and gathering

world distribution of hunter-gathering peoples

15,000 BC
world population: 10 million
% hunters: 100

AD 1500
world population: 350 million
% hunters: 1.0

1960
world population: 3 billion
% hunters: 0.001

1 The origins of domestic plants and animals to 4000 BC

the origins of domestic plants and animals to 4000 BC

Pacific Ocean

NORTH AMERICA

Atlantic Ocean

SOUTH WESTERN STEPPES

CENTRAL ASIA

CHINA

Reindeer

Pig

Horse

Bactrian Camel

Yak

Chicken

Cattle

Pig

Cattle

Sheep

INDUS

Water Buffalo

SOUTHEAST ASIA

Goat

SOUTHWEST ASIA

Zebu

Pig

Ass

Dromedary

S A H A R A

NORTHERN TROPICAL AFRICA

CHINA AND SOUTHEAST ASIA

Cereals	Pulses	Root Crops
Asian rice	Mung bean	Taro
Common millet	Soybean	Yams
Foxtail millet		

Fruits	Other Crops
Apricot	Aubergine
Banana	Coconut
Citrus fruits	Sago palm
Mango	Tea
Peach	

SOUTHWEST AND CENTRAL ASIA

Cereals	Pulses	Root Crops
Barley	Broad bean	Carrot
Oats	Chickpea	Parsnip
Rye	Grasspea	Radish
Wheats	Lentil	
	Pea	

Fruits	Other Crops
Apple	Garlic
Date	Onion
Fig	Safflower
Grape	
Olive	
Pear	

NORTHERN TROPICAL AFRICA

Cereals	Pulses	Root Crops
African rice	Cowpea	Yams
Finger millet	Pigeon pea	
Pearl millet		
Sorghum		

Fruits	Other Crops
Tamarind	Coffee
Watermelon	Oil palm
	Sesame

17

The first farmers of Asia

The first economies to be based on the husbandry of animal and plant staples came into being in South-West Asia. In the upland areas around the Zagros and Taurus mountains, and in Palestine, moister conditions led to the spread of large-seeded grasses – the ancestors of modern wheat and barley – which early hunters quickly appreciated for their nutrition and ease of storage. By 10,000 BC small villages of circular stone-walled huts developed, whose inhabitants lived from both the hunting and herding of gazelle and the harvesting of wild wheat. About 9000 BC, in northern Syria, some communities began to cultivate cereals outside their natural habitat while sheep were domesticated in Mesopotamia. By 7000 BC wheat and barley cultivation was established, as was the herding of goats, from Anatolia to the Zagros mountains, and this agricultural revolution spread shortly afterwards to Greece.

In the 7th and 6th millennia BC, developed Neolithic villages appeared over much of the landscape. Their economies depended on domesticated plants and animals, and on technological developments. Excavations at Çatal Hüyük, 32 acres in area, revealed extensive evidence of wealth (obsidian and semi-processed stones) and house fittings bore elaborate ornaments (including wall paintings and the plastered skulls of wild cattle). Much of the lowland area, however, remained too dry for cultivation. Only the development of irrigation – by spreading water from the rivers that drained from the mountains – allowed settlements to extend to the Mesopotamian plain in the 6th and 5th millennia. Sedentary farming began in South Asia on the Kachi Plain of Pakistan around 7000 BC. The early settlers cultivated barley and wheat, domesticated sheep, cattle and goats, and buried their dead with elaborate grave goods. From 6000 BC onwards, mud-brick storehouses divided into small compartments served as the focal point for food, tools and trade goods.

Plants and animals were independently domesticated in many other parts of the world. In northern China the cultivation of millet, another cereal, began on the great loess plain around the Yellow River and its tributaries around 7000 BC. It remained the staple crop of the region for many centuries. Further south the principal cereal was rice, first cultivated in the Yangtze valley before 6000 BC (map 2). Villages acquired defensive walls, from 8000 BC in the Near East (the first fortified community being Jericho) and from around 3500 BC in China.

Terracotta figurine
Characteristic products of the earliest farming villages are small terracotta figurines of women, with emphasis on their sexual characteristics. This small cult statuette, only 6.5 inches high, came from Çatal Hüyük in south-central Turkey.

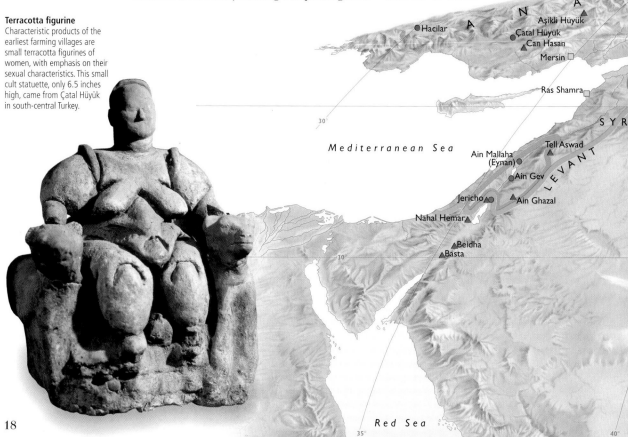

In addition, the ox-drawn plough began to be adapted throughout much of Eurasia, enlisting animal traction to increase the efficiency of farming.

The greater size and permanence of farming settlements stemmed from three major factors: firstly, the exceptional productivity of the principal cultivated species could feed large concentrations of people all year round – something hunting and gathering can never do; secondly, plant foods could survive storage over many months, allowing the community to stay in one place and live off the previous harvest while a new crop grows and ripens. Finally, farmers need to live near their fields, both to protect them against human and animal predators and to minimize the travel and transport involved in preparing the ground, in weeding, and in harvesting.

Hunters and gatherers keep their possessions to a minimum, since they must carry everything around; but sedentary communities can produce and accumulate a wide range of items, both utilitarian and for ritual and pleasure – pottery and tools, ornaments and display items. Village farming communities became larger and more differentiated, with specialist craftspeople producing fine ceramics and metalwork. As complexity increased, new forms of social organisation developed, leading around 3000 BC to the first cities.

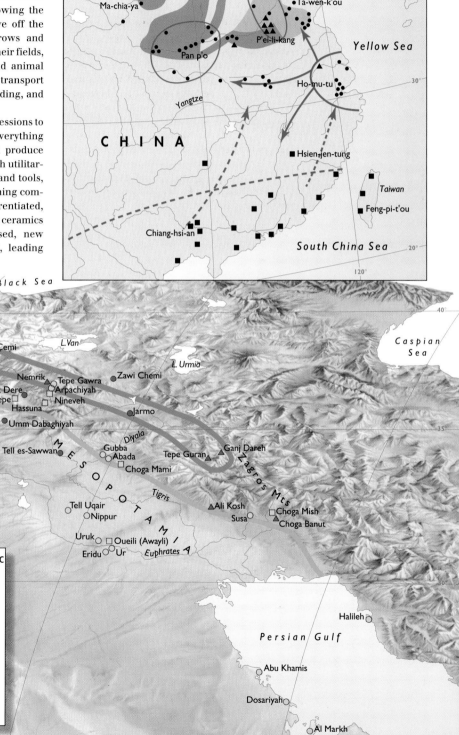

2 Early Chinese agriculture

- area of loess soil
- redeposited loess
- —— early millet cultivation
- - - - approximate northern limit of wild rice distribution
- —— early wet rice cultivation

Chinese settlement
- ▲ 6000–5000 BC
- ■ 6000–4000 BC
- ● 5000–2500 BC

Ma-chia-ya • Tz'u-shan • Ta-wen-k'ou • Po Hai • KOREA
Yellow River • P'ei-li-kang • Yellow Sea
Pan p'o • Ho-mu-tu
Yangtze • CHINA • Hsien-jen-tung
Chiang-hsi-an • Taiwan • Feng-pi-t'ou
South China Sea

1 The ancient Near East, 12,000–3100 BC

- natural habitat of wild emmer
- natural habitat of wild einkorn and emmer
- southern limit of rain-fed agriculture (300mm average annual rainfall)

ancient sites:
- ● epipalaeolithic, 12,000–9000 BC
- ▲ pre-pottery Neolithic, 9000–6500 BC
- ● pottery Neolithic, 6500–5500 BC
- ○ Chalcolithic
   'Ubaid period, 5500–4200 BC
   Uruk period, 4200–3100 BC
- □ multi-period Neolithic-Chalcolithic sites

Black Sea
Değirmentepe • Cafer Hüyük • Çayönü • Hallan Çemi • L. Van • L. Urmia • Caspian Sea
Nevali Çori • Chagar Bazar • Nemrik • Tepe Gawra • Zawi Chemi
Tell Abr • Sabi Abyad • Tell Brak • Qermez Dere • Arpachiyah • Nineveh
Mureybet • Yarim Tepe • Hassuna • Jarmo
Abu Hureyra • Umm Dabaghiyah
Bouqras • Tell es-Sawwan • Gubba • Abada • Tepe Guran • Ganj Dareh
Choga Mami • Zagros Mts
Tigris • Ali Kosh • Choga Mish
Tell Uqair • Susa • Choga Banut
Nippur • MESOPOTAMIA
Uruk • Oueili (Awayli) • Euphrates
Eridu • Ur
Halileh
Persian Gulf
Abu Khamis
Dosariyah
Al Markh
Ain Qannas

The rise of civilization

The first civilizations arose in the alluvial basins of four major rivers which drain from the mountain fringes where agriculture began: the Tigris and Euphrates in Mesopotamia, the Nile in Egypt, the Indus in India, and the Yellow River in China. Each proved capable of supplying the high, regular yields needed to support large urban populations. Cities of thousands, and then tens of thousands, evolved. In Mesopotamia, cities already existed by 3500 BC. Egypt adopted urban civilization in about 3200 BC and the Harappan civilization arose in the Indus plain from about 2500 BC. Civilization in north China appears to have developed, again wholly or largely independently, around 1800 BC.

These societies shared many common features: the development of cities; writing; large public buildings; and the political apparatus of a

state. The large agricultural surpluses produced by irrigation – some Mesopotamian communities harvested 60, 70 or even 80 grains for each grain sown – made it possible to employ a significant segment of society in activities other than farming, such as manufacture and trade. This in turn led to the emergence of a ruling class which accumulated wealth through the exploitation of labour and the imposition of taxes. In Mesopotamia the ruler was also the chief priest and the temple centre provided a vital element of the political system, its monumental structure

1 The rise of civilization

- fertile land
- centres of urban civilization
- areas of pastoral nomadism

Arctic

Ural Mts

Ural

Volga

Dnieper

STEPP

Aral Sea

Syr Dayra

KAZAKHSTAN
early horse-based pastoralism and metallurgy

Caspian Sea

Amu Darya

Hindu Kush

ANATOLIA
farming communities sophisticated bronze-use and incipient urbanization

Black Sea

Caucasus Mts

TURKESTAN
walled cities and irrigated agriculture villages

Indus

Hattushash
Tell Brak
Tepe Gawra
•Troy
Taurus Mts
Habuba
MESOPOTAMIA
Ashur
Çatal Hüyük
•Tarsus
•Ebla
Tell Asmar
Zagros Mts

IRANIAN PLATEAU
scattered cities supported by long-distance trade and irrigated agriculture

Mundigak•
Rahman Dheri
•Mycenae
Ugarit
Mari
Euphrates
Tigris
Shuruppak
Rana Ghundai•
Har

Crete
Knossos
Cyprus
Babylon
Umma
•Susa

Mediterranean Sea
Nippur
Abu Salabikh
Uruk Ur
Eridu
•Lagash

Mohenjo Daro•
•Kot Di
Memphis •Heliopolis
Nindowari
•Amri

Sutkagen Dor •
INDUS PLA

Kahun•
DESERT NOMADS
Balakot•
Allahdino
Surkot

Abydos•
EGYPT
Desalpur•
L

Thebes•
Rang

Hieraconpolis•
•Edfu

Elephantine•

ARABIA
maritime trading cities in contact with Mesopotamia and the Indus Valley

Buhen•

Nile

Red Sea

Arabian Sea

30
50
70

forming a visual reminder to all citizens of the power that governed their daily life. The centralized control found in these societies fostered a special legal system, a standing army, a permanent bureaucracy, and the division of society into distinct classes. The state also supported scribes, who were usually trained and employed within the temples and palaces. The earliest writing was used as a means of keeping track of commodities, wages and taxes; but it soon served other purposes: to preserve religious traditions, which thereby became sacred books; to register social customs, which thereby became codes of law; and to record myths, which thereby developed into history and literature.

Since, apart from agricultural produce, the alluvial plains lacked most other natural resources, an extensive trading activity exchanged luxury goods and raw materials from other areas with the textiles and other manufactured goods of the cities and thus helped to develop other trading centres in a great arc from the eastern Mediterranean to the Indus valley and in China. The cities therefore exercised an influence out of all proportion to their comparatively small geographical extent. True, not all areas were affected: Australia, Africa, Europe and large parts of Asia had no cities; the first civilizations of the Americas did not emerge until about 1500 BC (and, when they did, owed nothing to ideas introduced from outside). Nevertheless the growth of the first urban centres, with their technology, literacy, and class divisions began a new phase in the development of human society.

The Royal standard of Ur from the largest of the royal tombs at Ur. It has panels on each side depicting the activities of the king in peace and war. The war side shows helmeted infantry, four-wheeled battle wagons pulled by asses or onagers, and prisoners being presented to the king.

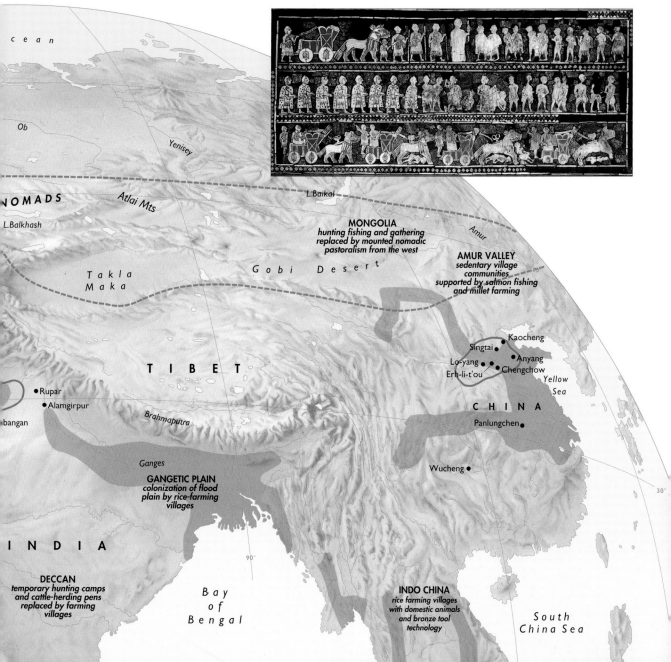

West Asia and Egypt

The earliest of all known civilizations, Sumer, rested upon some 12 city-states in southern Mesopotamia, the largest of them covering about 100 hectares, defended by a wall, and housing perhaps 30,000 people. At first, pre-eminence passed from one city to another, but towards the end of the 3rd millennium powerful leaders established hegemony over ever-wider areas. The first was Sargon (c. 2296-2240 BC), who created a new political centre at Agade (also known as Akkad) before conquering the cities of southern Mesopotamia and claiming authority as far west as Byblos. Sargon's grandson Naram-Sin (2213-2176 BC) enlarged the empire further, but within a generation it disappeared as subject cities asserted their independence. The rise of Agade had long-lasting effects on the region, with Akkadian (whose variants included Babylonian and Assyrian) replacing Sumerian as the main language of Mesopotamia.

Around 2000 BC, a new empire arose around Ur, its hegemony stretching from the Persian Gulf to Nineveh, but Ur also fell after about a century, and a kaleidoscope of shifting alliances brought new cities to prominence, most notably Mari and Babylon on the Euphrates. Under its powerful king Hammurabi (1728-1686 BC), Babylon created another empire that covered the whole of southern Mesopotamia; but, once more, it did not long survive the death of its founder (map 1).

Even before Sargon unified Mesopotamia, Egypt

came under the sway of a single ruler. The harnessing of the Nile's annual floods to irrigate the fields on its banks made possible a civilization that lasted for over 25 centuries. Around 3000 BC an Upper Egyptian ruler conquered the Nile delta and established a new capital at Memphis, which for almost 2000 years served as the administrative centre for a densely

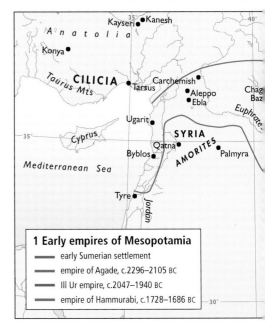

1 Early empires of Mesopotamia
— early Sumerian settlement
— empire of Agade, c.2296–2105 BC
— III Ur empire, c.2047–1940 BC
— empire of Hammurabi, c.1728–1686 BC

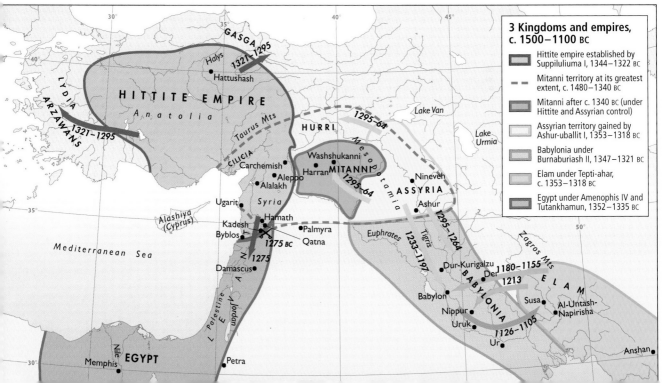

3 Kingdoms and empires, c. 1500–1100 BC

- Hittite empire established by Suppiluliuma I, 1344–1322 BC
- Mitanni territory at its greatest extent, c. 1480–1340 BC
- Mitanni after c. 1340 BC (under Hittite and Assyrian control)
- Assyrian territory gained by Ashur-uballit I, 1353–1318 BC
- Babylonia under Burnaburiash II, 1347–1321 BC
- Elam under Tepti-ahar, c. 1353–1318 BC
- Egypt under Amenophis IV and Tutankhamun, 1352–1335 BC

populated region of some 15,000 square miles running from the first cataract at Aswan to the Mediterranean coast (map 2). At about the same time, writing in hieroglyphic script commenced. During the 'Old Kingdom' period (2685-2180 BC) the rulers of Egypt built a series of massive pyramid-tombs along the desert edge opposite Memphis which emphasised their power and prestige. Then, after a century of invasion and anarchy, the Egyptian state entered a second period of cultural achievement under the able rulers of the Middle Kingdom (2040-1783 BC); and another era of expansion under the XVIIIth and XIXth dynasties (1570-1200 BC). At home they undertook vast building projects, like the rock-cut temple at Abu Simbel created by Ramesses II (1290-1224 BC); abroad they advanced through Palestine into Syria and created an empire that extended almost to the Euphrates.

The continuity of Ancient Egyptian language, religion and culture stood in marked contrast to developments in Mesopotamia. The two civilizations also differed in other respects. First, because of the annual Nile flood, Egypt did not depend to the same extent on irrigation canals and dams; second, although it possessed some cities, they lacked the geographical concentration found in southern Mesopotamia, so that Egypt was more a territorial unit than an agglomeration of city-states. Third, and most important, Egypt rarely suffered foreign invasion. Admittedly the Hyksos, an Asiatic people, overran most of the country in the 18th century BC, but a new native dynasty expelled them c.1570 BC and then pursued the invaders northwards to the upper Euphrates. Egypt's Asiatic empire lasted until about 1200 BC when the 'Sea Peoples', marauders from the Aegean and Asia Minor, attacked all the major powers of the East Mediterranean and initiated a 'Dark Age', concerning which very few historical sources survive, until about 900 BC and the emergence of Assyria.

Babylon and Assyria weathered the storm of the 12th and 11th centuries with greatly reduced territory, and the 10th century saw the beginnings of an Assyrian recovery. In the following century Ashurnasirpal II (883-859 BC) sent his armies north and west and used the wealth they gained to build a spectacular new palace at Nimrud. Even greater gains were made by Tiglath-pileser III (744-727 BC) and Sargon II (721-705 BC) who annexed Babylonia and conquered the Phoenician cities on the Mediterranean coast. Egyptian weakness allowed Esarhaddon (680-669 BC) and Ashurbanipal (668-627 BC) to capture Memphis and Thebes, although the Assyrians did not attempt to formalize their control over Egypt.

To the Old Testament prophets, the Assyrians appeared invincible; yet their control over Babylonia was never secure: the Babylonian king Nabopolassar (626-605 BC) rebelled and, aided by the Medes, sacked the major Assyrian cities including Ashur and Nineveh. The Babylonians then inherited the Assyrian empire, but they too had to fight to keep it. In 605 BC the Egyptians attempted to annex Syria, but were defeated at Carchemish and Hamath. Nebuchadnezzar (604-562 BC) consolidated Babylonian rule, but his successors were unable to maintain their gains and Babylon fell to the Persians in 539 BC.

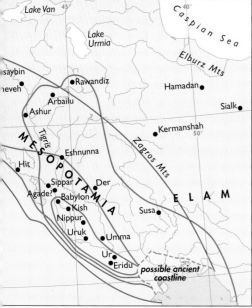

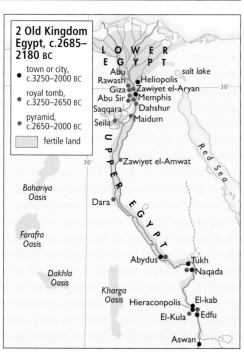

2 Old Kingdom Egypt, c.2685–2180 BC

- town or city, c.3250–2000 BC
- royal tomb, c.3250–2650 BC
- pyramid, c.2650–2000 BC
- fertile land

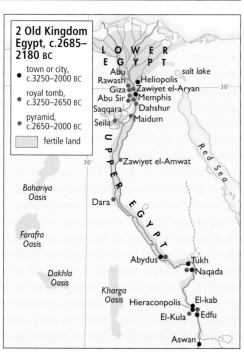

A Limestone stela, now in the Louvre, of Naram-Sin of Agade (2213-2176 BC) depicting his victory over the Lullubu of the Zagros mountains. Naram-Sin led many successful campaigns in his reign, leaving rock-reliefs commemorating his achievements near Diyarbakir in Turkey and in the Zagros.

The Americas

The Americas were colonized from Asia late in the last Ice Age, when lowered sea levels turned the Bering Strait into dry land. The subsequent melting of the ice cut off the continent from Eurasia (page 14). It is one of the remarkable facts of human history that despite their geographical separation, development in Old and New Worlds followed much the same path: the adoption of agriculture; the creation of cities and empires; the invention of writing. These two geographical zones continued on parallel paths until the New World was invaded by Europeans after 1492 (page 86). The New World civilizations were highly inventive in their own right, and in some ways in advance of their western counterparts. They produced – quite independent of the Old World – magnificent art, remarkable mathematical and astronomical skills, and monumental architecture.

The inhabitants of Mesoamerica and the central Andes began to experiment with plant cultivation around 7000 BC and farming soon allowed a rapid increase in population. By 800 BC the Olmec on the Gulf of Mexico, the Zapotec at Monte Albán, and the people of Chavín in Peru had developed complex societies with populations that numbered tens of thousands, boasting a hierarchy of social classes, an efficient civil service, a professional priesthood, and specialists in all kinds of tasks, from manufacturing to commerce and government.

Around and between these civilizations, other communities remained at the chiefdom level. Maize, beans and squash cultivation spread from Mexico to north America, and their arrival initiated a period of rapid development. In Ohio and Illinois, between 300 BC and AD 550, Hopewell chiefs built elaborate burial mounds and maintained trade contacts from Florida to the Rockies. Most American chiefdoms were agricultural, based on plant cultivation, but along the north-west coast rich fishing grounds and an abundance of whales and seals supported large villages and a complex ceremonial life by hunting, fishing and gathering alone. Towards the extremities of the continent, however, harsh conditions precluded farming, settlement remained sparse, and nomadic lifestyles persisted (map 1).

The sudden rise of Teotihuacán about AD 100 eclipsed earlier developments in Mesoamerica. Laid out in a precise grid plan and covering 8 square miles (20 km²), its population grew eventually to some 200,000. The nature of the city's economy remains uncertain but the centre, with two mighty pyramids, was planned for rites that included human sacrifice. Whether or not in association with trade, the Teotihuacanos' influence spread widely. They colonized some neighbouring districts and possibly sponsored new towns further afield.

At the same time, the powerful lowland kingdoms of the Maya flourished. Their capitals were

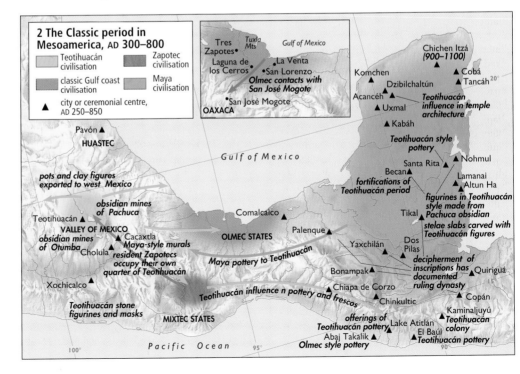

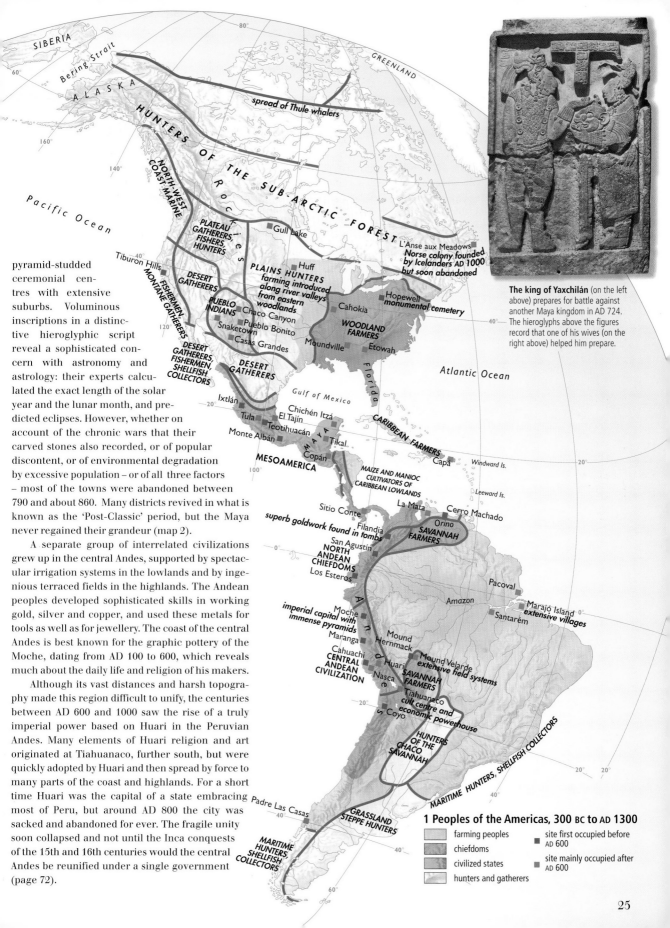

pyramid-studded ceremonial centres with extensive suburbs. Voluminous inscriptions in a distinctive hieroglyphic script reveal a sophisticated concern with astronomy and astrology: their experts calculated the exact length of the solar year and the lunar month, and predicted eclipses. However, whether on account of the chronic wars that their carved stones also recorded, or of popular discontent, or of environmental degradation by excessive population – or of all three factors – most of the towns were abandoned between 790 and about 860. Many districts revived in what is known as the 'Post-Classic' period, but the Maya never regained their grandeur (map 2).

A separate group of interrelated civilizations grew up in the central Andes, supported by spectacular irrigation systems in the lowlands and by ingenious terraced fields in the highlands. The Andean peoples developed sophisticated skills in working gold, silver and copper, and used these metals for tools as well as for jewellery. The coast of the central Andes is best known for the graphic pottery of the Moche, dating from AD 100 to 600, which reveals much about the daily life and religion of his makers.

Although its vast distances and harsh topography made this region difficult to unify, the centuries between AD 600 and 1000 saw the rise of a truly imperial power based on Huari in the Peruvian Andes. Many elements of Huari religion and art originated at Tiahuanaco, further south, but were quickly adopted by Huari and then spread by force to many parts of the coast and highlands. For a short time Huari was the capital of a state embracing most of Peru, but around AD 800 the city was sacked and abandoned for ever. The fragile unity soon collapsed and not until the Inca conquests of the 15th and 16th centuries would the central Andes be reunified under a single government (page 72).

The king of Yaxchilán (on the left above) prepares for battle against another Maya kingdom in AD 724. The hieroglyphs above the figures record that one of his wives (on the right above) helped him prepare.

1 Peoples of the Americas, 300 BC to AD 1300

- farming peoples
- chiefdoms
- civilized states
- hunters and gatherers
- site first occupied before AD 600
- site mainly occupied after AD 600

25

Prehistoric Africa and Australasia

Both Australia and Sub-Saharan Africa have been largely isolated from the rest of the Old World for the last 10,000 years, the former by sea, the latter by desert. Although the inhabitants of North Africa began the transition from hunting and gathering to farming around 8000 BC, the desiccation of the Sahara after about 4000 BC cut off Africa south of the Equator for centuries.

In Australia, the aborigines mostly remained hunters and gatherers adapted to living in a large range of environments from tropical forest to harsh desert. They enjoyed a rich symbolic life, as evidenced by the marking of their sacred places with rock art from at least 25,000 years ago. The colonization of the Melanesian islands occurred considerably later, when settlers from New Guinea, associated with the distinctive Lapita pottery, reached Fiji around 1300 BC and then made their way into Polynesia via Tonga and Samoa, reaching the Marquesas islands in about 150 BC (map 1). From there they spread north to Hawaii (c. AD 400)

and south-west via the Cook islands to New Zealand between AD 750 and 1300. When the Europeans arrived in the 18th century, at least 750,000 aborigines inhabited Australia and up to 150,000 Maoris lived in New Zealand

The geographical isolation of southern Africa was never complete. In the east settlers spread down the Rift Valley from Ethiopia during the first millennium BC, while trans-Saharan trade increased in importance after the introduction of the camel from Asia, around 100 BC. Iron came into use in parts of sub-Saharan Africa after 750 BC. Aided by the new technology, Bantu-speaking farmers and cattle-herders began to colonize southern Africa in the early centuries AD. By the 13th century powerful Bantu chiefdoms had emerged, such as that centred on Great Zimbabwe, and on cattle-raising communities. These engaged in long-distance trade, long before the Portuguese arrived off both the south-east and south-west coasts of the continent at the close of the 15th century

Rock art became common in Australia 25,000 years ago. This more recent painting shows the two 'Lightning Brothers', ancestral spirits of the Wardaman Aboriginal people from northwestern Australia.

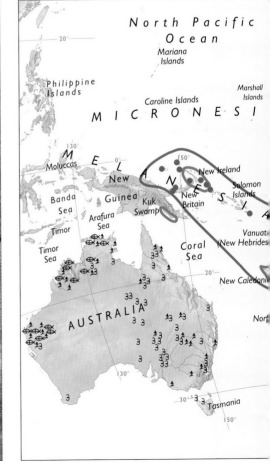

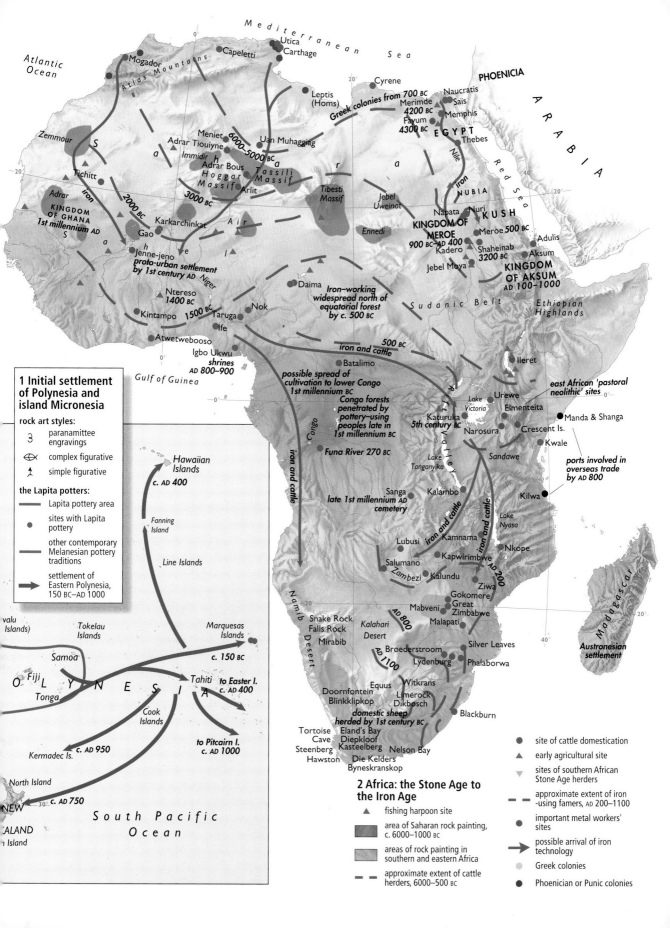

1 Initial settlement of Polynesia and island Micronesia

rock art styles:
- paranamittee engravings
- complex figurative
- simple figurative

the Lapita potters:
- Lapita pottery area
- sites with Lapita pottery
- other contemporary Melanesian pottery traditions
- settlement of Eastern Polynesia, 150 BC–AD 1000

2 Africa: the Stone Age to the Iron Age
- fishing harpoon site
- area of Saharan rock painting, c. 6000–1000 BC
- areas of rock painting in southern and eastern Africa
- approximate extent of cattle herders, 6000–500 BC
- site of cattle domestication
- early agricultural site
- sites of southern African Stone Age herders
- approximate extent of iron-using famers, AD 200–1100
- important metal workers' sites
- possible arrival of iron technology
- Greek colonies
- Phoenician or Punic colonies

South and South East Asia

The first great Indian civilization emerged in the Indus valley in the 3rd millennium with complex urban societies at Harappa and Mohenjo-Daro, which developed a pictographic writing system (as yet not definitively deciphered) and traded as far afield as Mesopotamia (map 1). Around 1500 BC, for reasons that remain obscure, the major Indus valley cities suddenly collapsed

When the picture becomes clear once again the population of northern India had been transformed, with a Hindu religion, a Sanskrit literature, a caste system and (by about 800 BC) iron working, which enabled the spread of farming communities eastward into the rich plain of the Ganges. By 600 BC at least 16 political units had grown up along the Ganges, the subcontinent's new centre of gravity. By 400 BC war had reduced the states to four, and no doubt the resulting social tensions helped to spread new ethical and religious systems, for in the 6th century Gautama (Buddha), founder of Asia's most pervasive religion, was born in one of these states (see

page 34), while in another Mahavira formulated the teaching of Jainism.

A further turning point came in 320 BC when Chandragupta Maurya seized the state of Magadha on the lower Ganges, and occupied large parts of central India, and in 305 BC annexed the province of Trans-Indus from the successors of Alexander the Great (see page 32). Chandragupta's grandson Ashoka (273-232 BC) expanded this Mauryan empire southwards, bringing the greater part of the sub-continent under his rule and inscribing edicts on pillars and rock-faces all over India as a permanent reminder of his power (map 2). Ashoka's death introduced a troubled period, punctuated by invasions of both Greeks and nomads who founded states in the north-west, such as the Kushan empire, where Hellenistic and Indian influences mingled. Further south, the Satavahanas of the Deccan ruled a state that straddled the peninsula by AD 150. Then, in the 4th century, the Gupta dynasty, created an empire which by AD 400 extended from the Indus to the bay

1 The Indus civilizations of Harappa and Mohenjo-Daro, c. 2500–1750 BC

○ pre-Harappan settlements

● principal sites of Harappan civilization

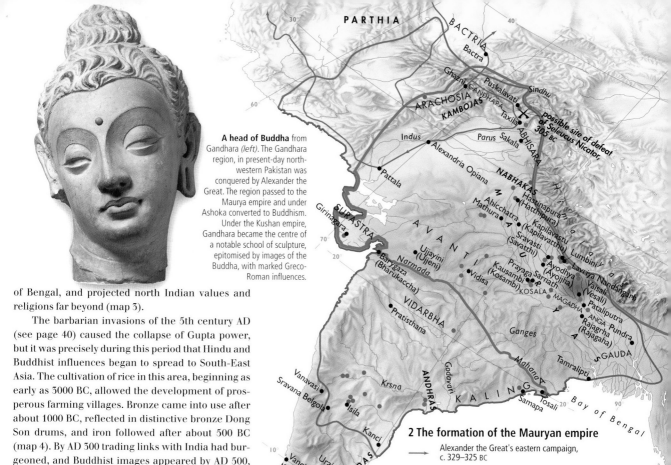

A head of Buddha from Gandhara *(left)*. The Gandhara region, in present-day north-western Pakistan was conquered by Alexander the Great. The region passed to the Maurya empire and under Ashoka converted to Buddhism. Under the Kushan empire, Gandhara became the centre of a notable school of sculpture, epitomised by images of the Buddha, with marked Greco-Roman influences.

of Bengal, and projected north Indian values and religions far beyond (map 3).

The barbarian invasions of the 5th century AD (see page 40) caused the collapse of Gupta power, but it was precisely during this period that Hindu and Buddhist influences began to spread to South-East Asia. The cultivation of rice in this area, beginning as early as 3000 BC, allowed the development of prosperous farming villages. Bronze came into use after about 1000 BC, reflected in distinctive bronze Dong Son drums, and iron followed after about 500 BC (map 4). By AD 300 trading links with India had burgeoned, and Buddhist images appeared by AD 500, notably in Burma, Cambodia, and Java. By AD 700 the construction of Hindu temples in the same three areas had begun.

2 The formation of the Mauryan empire

→ Alexander the Great's eastern campaign, c. 329–325 BC

— Mauryan empire under Chandragupta, c. 297 BC

— Mauryan empire under Ashoka, c. 260 BC

▨ ancestral home of the Mauryas

• site of Ashokan inscriptions

• site of Mauryan-age Buddhist stupa

ANGA regions *CODAS* dynasties
(place names in brackets are Prakrit forms)

3 The Gupta-Vakataka imperial formation, AD 300–550

▨ Gupta core area   ▨ Vakataka core area

— maximum extent of Gupta empire

— limit of areas at some time under Vakataka rule

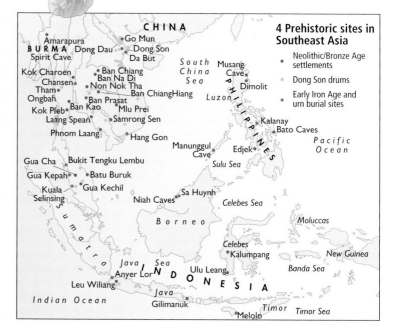

4 Prehistoric sites in Southeast Asia

• Neolithic/Bronze Age settlements

○ Dong Son drums

○ Early Iron Age and urn burial sites

Early Europe

Farming spread from West Asia to Europe about 6500 BC, beginning with the Balkans. Agriculture in these regions involved wheat and barley, sheep and goats, just as in western Asia; but as farming spread beyond into more temperate zones, major adjustments became necessary. New, more robust types of cereal developed, and cattle and pigs became the dominant livestock. By about 5500 BC agricultural communities had developed along the Danube valley, and their descendants spread northwest from there until they reached the Paris basin around 4750 BC. After a brief pause, the final phase saw the spread of farming to the northern fringes of Europe, including Scandinavia and the British Isles, where existing hunter-gatherer communities adopted it by about 4000 BC (map 1).

There has been much debate about whether the spread of agriculture was due to the expansion of colonizing populations from the southeast or to the adoption of the new way of life by existing foragers. Current evidence from archaeology and the analysis of the DNA of modern populations suggests that there was a colonizing element, probably associated with the expansion through the Balkans and the loess lands of central Europe, but that in most of Europe the dominant process was the adoption of agriculture and its material attributes by existing populations, perhaps in part because of the prestige of the new way of life.

Meanwhile, beginning in the Balkans, copper-working spread after c. 4500 BC and by 2500 BC it had become common to alloy the copper with tin to produce bronze. The need for these two raw materials stimulated the development of extensive trade networks, which also conveyed other materials, such as amber from the Baltic. Amber is found as far afield as Mycenae in southern Greece, where graves filled with sumptuous funerary offerings of gold and jewellery appeared from 1600 BC.

Mycenae was not the earliest European state: that honour belongs to the island of Crete where from about 2000 BC 'Minoan' culture, based on palaces decorated with colourful frescoes and equipped with sanitary and drainage systems, developed. Bureaucracy and trade flourished, and a script known as Linear A developed around 1600 BC. Two centuries later, however, the Mycenaeans (named after the fortress of Mycenae in the eastern Peloponnese) took control of Crete and became the principal military and economic power in the

Aegean (see map 2). They adapted the Minoan culture, including its script which they modified (to a form known as Linear B, an early version of Greek) and used to administer their own lands. Mycenaean Greece was divided among a number of independent leaders, each of whom ruled a small kingdom, in much the same way as Greece in the Classical period was divided into city-states (see page 32). The legend of the Trojan War, recorded centuries later in Homer's *Iliad*, is thought to recall a Mycenaean campaign of c. 1250 BC against the city of Troy, strategically situated at the entrance to the Dardanelles, and controlling access to the trade of the Black Sea. But this success, if indeed it occurred, must have been the final fling of the Mycenean warlords because by 1200 BC their palaces lay in ruins, overthrown perhaps by rebellion or by outside attack, and a 'Dark Age' which left very few records ensued all over Greece for the next four centuries.

Snake handler from Knossos
This faience statuette, dating from c.1700 BC, possibly represents a household goddess. Little is known about Minoan divinities, but most appear to be female.

1 The spread of agricultural settlement

→ main routes of agrarian expansion

dates of agricultural settlement
(based on tree-ring corrected radiocarbon dating)

	by 7000 BC
	7000–6000 BC
	6000–5000 BC
	5000–3000 BC
	3000–2000 BC

bowl cultures early farming groups

● Hembury site of excavated farming village

SPAIN modern state names

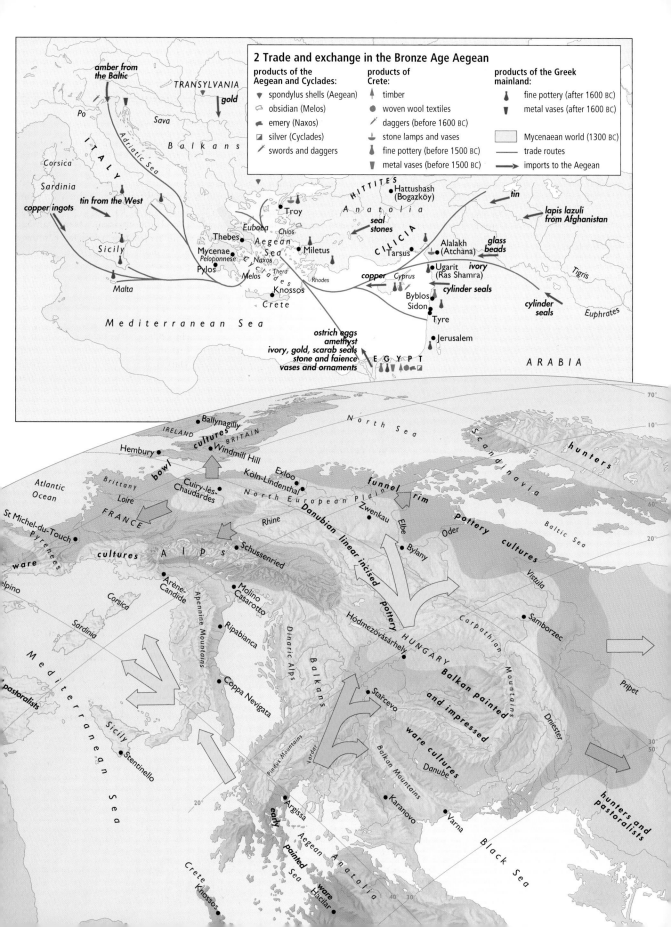

The Greek world

The Acropolis (below). Acting
as the defensive strong point for
Athens since the Mycenaean
period, the acropolis was also an
important religious sanctuary. Its
most famous temple was the
Parthenon, begun in 447 BC.

The Greek heartland is an area of islands and plains
divided by mountains. After the collapse of the
Mycenaean palace system, the *polis* or city-state
emerged and soon became the dominant form of
political organization in the Mediterranean world.

The 8th century BC was a period of great trans-
formations in Greece. It saw the appearance of the
first monumental public buildings, changes in
burial practices and new artistic styles. At the same
time, literacy re-emerged, with a new alphabet.
Though contact with the wider world had not totally
disappeared in previous centuries, it now increased
dramatically, above all on the island of Euboea,
perhaps as the result of Phoenician exploration and
settlement.

From the middle of the century, following in the
wake of the Phoenicians, groups of Greeks created
settlements around the Mediterranean, first in Italy
and Sicily, but by the middle of the 6th century also
in north Africa and, to the east, along the Black
Sea coast. These included many cities that have
remained famous to the present, such as Marseilles
and Naples (see map 1). In the central Mediterranean,
the Greeks came into conflict with the Carthaginians,
who for many centuries disputed control of Sicily
with them.

In Asia Minor, however, the Greeks came up
against the Persian empire, which first sought to
annex the city-states of the Aegean coast and in 490
and 480-479 BC invaded Greece itself. The Persians
met with defeat and the next 50 years marked the
great age of Greek culture: the tragic drama of
Aeschylus, Sophocles and Euripedes; the comedy of
Aristophanes; the histories of Herodotus and
Thucydides; the splendour of the Parthenon; the
sculptures of Phidias. Athens also built up a formidable fleet and used it to create an Aegean empire
which the cities of the Peloponnese, led by Sparta,
saw as a threat. In 431 BC, Sparta declared war on

3 The campaigns of Alexander
→ Alexander, 334–23 BC   → Nearchus, 325–24 BC

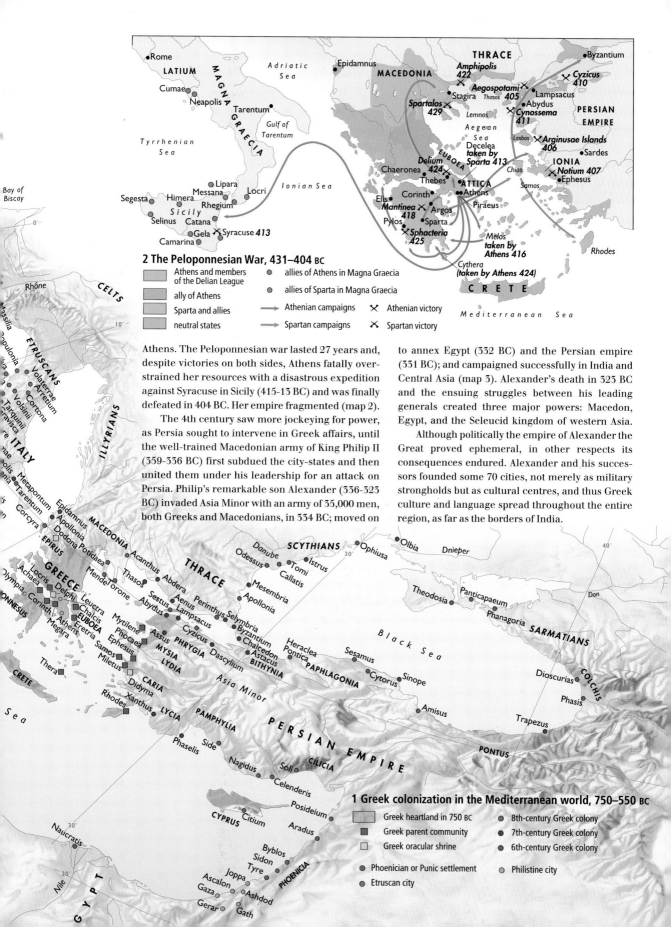

2 The Peloponnesian War, 431–404 BC

- Athens and members of the Delian League
- ally of Athens
- Sparta and allies
- neutral states
- allies of Athens in Magna Graecia
- allies of Sparta in Magna Graecia
- Athenian campaigns
- Spartan campaigns
- ✕ Athenian victory
- ✕ Spartan victory

Athens. The Peloponnesian war lasted 27 years and, despite victories on both sides, Athens fatally overstrained her resources with a disastrous expedition against Syracuse in Sicily (415-13 BC) and was finally defeated in 404 BC. Her empire fragmented (map 2).

The 4th century saw more jockeying for power, as Persia sought to intervene in Greek affairs, until the well-trained Macedonian army of King Philip II (359-336 BC) first subdued the city-states and then united them under his leadership for an attack on Persia. Philip's remarkable son Alexander (336-323 BC) invaded Asia Minor with an army of 35,000 men, both Greeks and Macedonians, in 334 BC; moved on

to annex Egypt (332 BC) and the Persian empire (331 BC); and campaigned successfully in India and Central Asia (map 3). Alexander's death in 323 BC and the ensuing struggles between his leading generals created three major powers: Macedon, Egypt, and the Seleucid kingdom of western Asia.

Although politically the empire of Alexander the Great proved ephemeral, in other respects its consequences endured. Alexander and his successors founded some 70 cities, not merely as military strongholds but as cultural centres, and thus Greek culture and language spread throughout the entire region, as far as the borders of India.

1 Greek colonization in the Mediterranean world, 750–550 BC

- Greek heartland in 750 BC
- Greek parent community
- Greek oracular shrine
- Phoenician or Punic settlement
- Etruscan city
- 8th-century Greek colony
- 7th-century Greek colony
- 6th-century Greek colony
- Philistine city

World religions

Before the 1st millennium BC, polytheism was the dominant form of religious belief throughout Eurasia, with individual communities worshipping their own gods. As the empires of the ancient world emerged, a number of major religions, each characterized by a single doctrine and claims to universality, largely replaced these myriad cults, although elsewhere innumerable other creeds survived without making the transition to world religions.

All the great world religions originated in Asia, and three of them – Judaism, Christianity and Islam – developed in the same small region. Moreover, several were either established or radically reformulated at much the same time: the outstanding prophets and reformers of Hinduism, Buddhism, Judaism, Confucianism and Taoism all lived in the 6th century BC. Their appearance perhaps reflected a need in the rising empires for more universal creeds than local deities could provide, and their diffusion – particularly the spread of the great missionary religions, Buddhism and Christianity – played an important role in linking the different areas. The new religions also spread the values of those advanced cultures to people living beyond the frontiers.

All the world religions shared, to some degree, a belief in a single spiritual reality. Hinduism, the oldest of them, although it reveres

1 The diffusion of religions

- dispersion of Jews to AD 500
- spread of Christianity
- area converted to Christianity by AD 600
- spread of Buddhism
- first area of Buddhist missionary activity
- area of rise of Mahayana Buddhism
- Buddhist sites
- area of Hinduism
- area of Daoism and Confucianism
- area of Shintoism
- area of Zoroastrian
- spread of Mithraism
- Mithraic sites

A reclining Buddha from Polonnaruwa in Sri Lanka. The importance of Buddism grew after it was adopted by Mauryan emperor Ashoka and it spread throughout India. Missionary activity then brought Buddhist ideas to many places in south and east Asia. Buddhism reached Sri Lanka in the late third century BC.

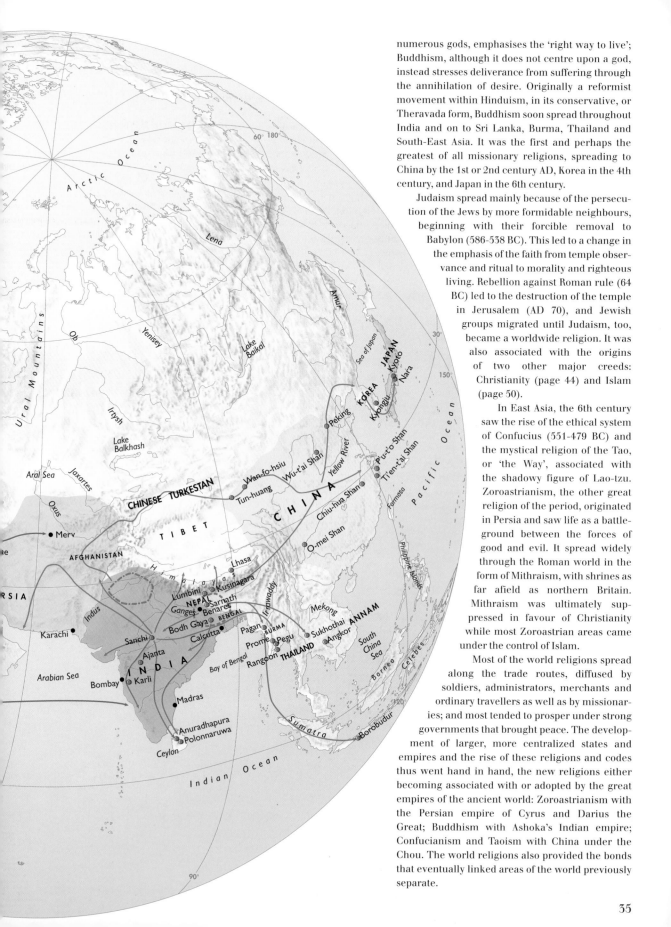

numerous gods, emphasises the 'right way to live'; Buddhism, although it does not centre upon a god, instead stresses deliverance from suffering through the annihilation of desire. Originally a reformist movement within Hinduism, in its conservative, or Theravada form, Buddhism soon spread throughout India and on to Sri Lanka, Burma, Thailand and South-East Asia. It was the first and perhaps the greatest of all missionary religions, spreading to China by the 1st or 2nd century AD, Korea in the 4th century, and Japan in the 6th century.

Judaism spread mainly because of the persecution of the Jews by more formidable neighbours, beginning with their forcible removal to Babylon (586-538 BC). This led to a change in the emphasis of the faith from temple observance and ritual to morality and righteous living. Rebellion against Roman rule (64 BC) led to the destruction of the temple in Jerusalem (AD 70), and Jewish groups migrated until Judaism, too, became a worldwide religion. It was also associated with the origins of two other major creeds: Christianity (page 44) and Islam (page 50).

In East Asia, the 6th century saw the rise of the ethical system of Confucius (551-479 BC) and the mystical religion of the Tao, or 'the Way', associated with the shadowy figure of Lao-tzu. Zoroastrianism, the other great religion of the period, originated in Persia and saw life as a battleground between the forces of good and evil. It spread widely through the Roman world in the form of Mithraism, with shrines as far afield as northern Britain. Mithraism was ultimately suppressed in favour of Christianity while most Zoroastrian areas came under the control of Islam.

Most of the world religions spread along the trade routes, diffused by soldiers, administrators, merchants and ordinary travellers as well as by missionaries; and most tended to prosper under strong governments that brought peace. The development of larger, more centralized states and empires and the rise of these religions and codes thus went hand in hand, the new religions either becoming associated with or adopted by the great empires of the ancient world: Zoroastrianism with the Persian empire of Cyrus and Darius the Great; Buddhism with Ashoka's Indian empire; Confucianism and Taoism with China under the Chou. The world religions also provided the bonds that eventually linked areas of the world previously separate.

Rome

Rome, a city-state governed by aristocratic families leading an army of peasant soldiers, came to control an empire that stretched from the Atlantic to the Euphrates and from the English Channel to the Sahara. But military success brought social disorder; rivalries between warlords led to civil war; and republican institutions became an autocracy.

In the 6th century BC Rome was just a small fortress-town in central Italy commanding both the lowest crossing point on the river Tiber and a salt route between the mountains and the sea. By exploiting quarrels with its neighbours, the Roman Republic emerged as the dominant power first in central Italy and then in the whole peninsula. By 264 BC Rome controlled the whole of Italy and challenged the other major power in the western Mediterranean: Carthage. After three savage wars Rome defeated Carthage to acquire Sicily (241 BC), Spain (206 BC) and North Africa (146 BC). At the same time, conflict with the Hellenistic kingdoms further east resulted in the conquest of Macedon, Greece and Western Anatolia. In this way, almost by accident, Rome became an imperial power with far-flung possessions.

Administration of these provinces overstrained the Roman constitution, which had not been designed to manage an overseas empire, and the Republic finally collapsed in a series of civil wars. The last of these brought to power Octavian, who established himself as *Princeps* ('first citizen'), accepted the title Augustus (in 27 BC), reshaped the constitution, and extended and strengthened the frontiers (map 1).

While maintaining undivided power in his own hands, Augustus allowed the Senate – the traditional government of Rome – to take a share in running the empire, with responsibility for several provinces. Thus, in theory, the Republican forms endured, and administration remained in civilian not military hands. Under his successors, Roman rule expanded further still, but the Senate lost most of its power. Nevertheless, strong central control ensured peace for over two centuries and population expanded, trade flourished and cities grew. In the mid-3rd century AD, however, Germanic invasions in the west and Persian victories in the east brought the empire temporarily to its knees. A series of strong emperors between AD 268 and AD 284 restored a semblance of orderly government to the empire, but Diocletian (AD 284-305) realized that a single ruler could no longer hold the whole edifice together. He divided power between himself and a joint Augustus,

An equestrian statue of the emperor Marcus Aurelius (161-80). Preoccupied for much of his reigns with wars against the Parthians and the Germans (who in 170 invaded Italy), Marcus Aurelius maintained, but did not expand the Roman frontiers. He was the author of the *Meditations*, espousing stoicism as his philosophy in the face of adversity.

with two deputies (Caesars), and split the empire into four prefectures and twelve dioceses (map 2). By now the military had triumphed over the civilian, and a new basis had to be found for imperial authority. Under the influence of eastern ideas, the *Princeps* became *Dominus* (lord), an absolute ruler, at the head of a vast bureaucracy. Gradually the centre of Roman power shifted eastwards: Diocletian's successor Constantine (305-37) established a new capital at Byzantium (330), which he renamed Constantinople.

Although theoretically governed by joint rulers, the empire gradually broke into eastern and western halves, and when the western provinces crumbled before a new wave of Germanic invaders in the early 5th century, little help arrived from the east. Rome itself was sacked in 410 and 455, and the Ostrogoths created their own kingdom in Italy in 493. Justinian (AD 527-565) briefly recovered some of the western provinces but failed to reunite the empire.

Nevertheless, the Byzantine (East Roman) empire survived for another millennium, and many Roman traditions continued in the West. The Latin tongue, although developing into the derivative 'Romance' languages, long remained the language of churchmen and scientists; Roman Law forms the basis of most modern Western legal systems; many feats of Roman engineering genius survive to this day; and the Roman church lives on as a direct link with the past.

2 The Roman empire, AD 305–565

- – – frontier of the Roman empire, AD 305
- —— boundary of dioceses under Diocletian
- /// territory reconquered by Justinian, 533–54

Praetorian prefectures, c. 405:
- Praefectus Praetorio Galliarum
- Praefectus Praetorio Illyrici, Italiae, Africae
- Praefectus Praetorio per Illyricum
- Praefectus Praetorio per Orientem

1 The Roman empire, 31 BC–c. AD 250
- under administration of the Senate
- imperial provinces
- public provinces
- provinces added after AD 14, with date
- – – – later subdivisions of provinces, with dates

China: the first empires

From the 16th to the 11th century BC China's first historical dynasty, the Shang, presided over a confederation of clans in the Yellow River valley. Around 1027 BC the Chou replaced them and extended their authority over the Yangtze valley as well, investing their supporters with fiefs to create a feudal hierarchy sustained by the services, food and clothes produced by peasant communities. Then in 771 BC western invaders sacked the Chou capital, and the feudatories seized the opportunity to break away. Over 100 belligerent political units sprang up. In the 5th century BC, however, bronze technology gave way to iron, animal power and irrigation transformed agriculture, increasing both food production and population, while warfare reduced the number of states. By 300 BC seven states still competed for hegemony; by 221 BC only one of them remained – Ch'in.

The Ch'in organized their subjects into groups which bore collective responsibility to maintain public order, and to provide manpower both for construction works (above all roads, canals and fortifications) and for the army (which was composed primarily of infantry). The defeated nobles suffered demotion and, instead of performing labour services to their lord, the peasants now paid taxes to the conqueror. A savage penal code, administered by a professional bureaucracy, enforced the new system.

In 221 BC Prince Cheng of Ch'in, took the title Shih Huang-ti (meaning 'first emperor'); ordered the construction of a national network of roads and canals, centered on his new capital at Hsieng-yang; rebuilt and strengthened the Great Wall; introduced a uniform coinage whose distinctive shape (circular with a square hole in the centre) remained standard until 1911; and took steps to standardize the written language throughout the empire. Small wonder that his dynasty gave 'China' its name.

The burdens imposed by the autocratic first emperor provoked civil war shortly after his death in 206 BC; but before long a new dynasty, the Han, reunited China. At first they worked through feudal principalities allocated to their family and supporters, but by 100 BC the fiefs had again come under strong central control. The Han also extended the Great Wall far to the north-west, undertook several military expeditions against the nomad Hsiung-nu in the north, invaded northern Vietnam and Korea, and for a brief period after 59 BC controlled the Tarim basin. They also eliminated the Min-Yüeh kingdoms of the south-east coast. A lively export trade, mainly in silk, began to Parthia and to the Roman empire.

Terracotta warriors from Sian (Xian). Discovered in 1974, close to the mausoleum of the first Ch'in emperor, thousands of terracotta warriors have since been excavated. Each figure was individually produced, and the varying uniforms, badges, weaponry and styles of armour provide information on the organization of the Ch'in army. By around 250 BC the Ch'in state was as large as all the other Chinese states put together. By 221 BC all the remaining states were absorbed by the Ch'in creating, for the first time, a unified China under Shih Huang-ti (the 'first emperor'). Although Ch'in rule collapsed in 206 BC, the Han dynasty inherited their unified kingdom.

Map labels:
Lake Balkhash
to Sogdiana (K'ang-chu)
centre of Former Han protectorate 59 BC–AD 23
Issyk Qul
to Ferghana
Kuc
Kashgar (Shu-le)
Takla Makan D
Yarkand (Sha-ch'e)
Cherc
Guma (P'i-shan)
(Chie
to Bactria (Ta-hsia)
Khotan (Ho-t'ier

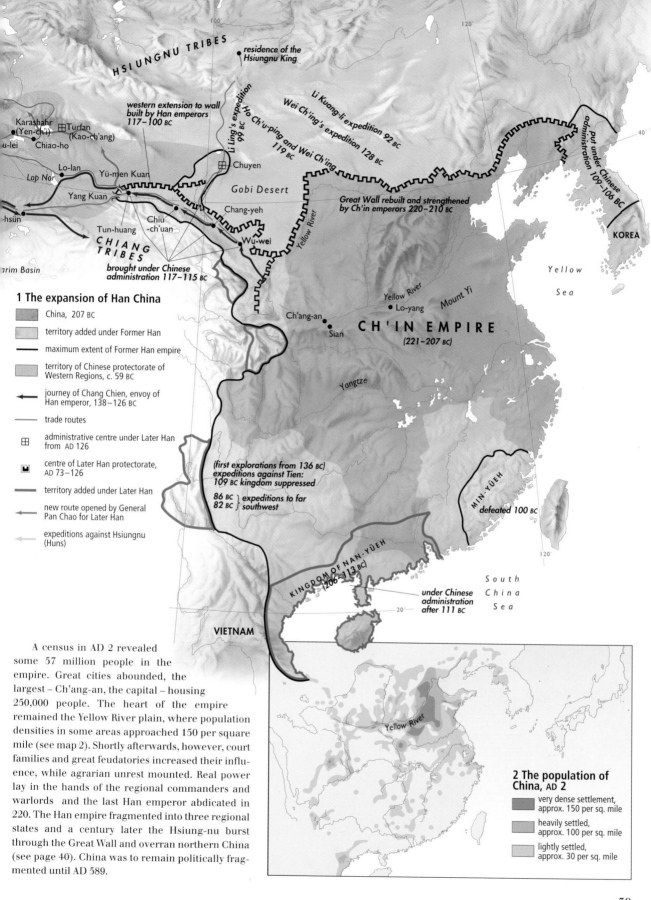

1 The expansion of Han China

- China, 207 BC
- territory added under Former Han
- maximum extent of Former Han empire
- territory of Chinese protectorate of Western Regions, c. 59 BC
- journey of Chang Chien, envoy of Han emperor, 138–126 BC
- trade routes
- ⊞ administrative centre under Later Han from AD 126
- ⊡ centre of Later Han protectorate, AD 73–126
- territory added under Later Han
- new route opened by General Pan Chao for Later Han
- expeditions against Hsiungnu (Huns)

HSIUNGNU TRIBES

residence of the Hsiungnu King

western extension to wall built by Han emperors 117–100 BC

Li Ling's expedition 99 BC

Ho Ch'u-ping and Wei Ch'ing 119 BC

Li Kuang-li expedition 92 BC

Wei Ch'ing's expedition 128 BC

Karashahr (Yen-ch'i) ⊞ Turfan (Kao-ch'ang)

u-lei   Chiao-ho

Lo-lan

Lop Nor   Yü-men Kuan

Yang Kuan

-hsün   Tun-huang

CHIANG TRIBES

Chuyen

Gobi Desert

Chang-yeh

Chiu -ch'uan

Wu-wei

Yellow River

Great Wall rebuilt and strengthened by Ch'in emperors 220–210 BC

put under Chinese administration 109–106 BC

40

KOREA

Yellow Sea

brought under Chinese administration 117–115 BC

arim Basin

Ch'ang-an   Lo-yang   Mount Yi

Sian   Yellow River

CH'IN EMPIRE (221–207 BC)

Yangtze

(first explorations from 136 BC) expeditions against Tien: 109 BC kingdom suppressed

86 BC } expeditions to far 82 BC } southwest

MIN-YÜEH

defeated 100 BC

KINGDOM OF NAN-YÜEH (206–113 BC)

under Chinese administration after 111 BC

South China Sea

120

20

VIETNAM

A census in AD 2 revealed some 57 million people in the empire. Great cities abounded, the largest – Ch'ang-an, the capital – housing 250,000 people. The heart of the empire remained the Yellow River plain, where population densities in some areas approached 150 per square mile (see map 2). Shortly afterwards, however, court families and great feudatories increased their influence, while agrarian unrest mounted. Real power lay in the hands of the regional commanders and warlords and the last Han emperor abdicated in 220. The Han empire fragmented into three regional states and a century later the Hsiung-nu burst through the Great Wall and overran northern China (see page 40). China was to remain politically fragmented until AD 589.

Yellow River

2 The population of China, AD 2

- very dense settlement, approx. 150 per sq. mile
- heavily settled, approx. 100 per sq. mile
- lightly settled, approx. 30 per sq. mile

AD 300-600
The transformation of the ancient world

By the 3rd century AD, a continuous web of large states stretched across the southern half of the continents of Europe and Asia. In the West, Rome controlled the whole Mediterranean world and much of Europe; in China, the Han ruled a state that equalled the Roman empire in population and extended from the Pacific to the Takla Makan desert in central Asia; in between lay the Persian empire. The co-existence of these great states brought to vast areas of the Old World internal peace and centralised government, conditions that made possible commercial and cultural interchange on an unprecedented scale.

But this 'imperial zone' formed only a narrow corridor, flanked to the north by the domain of nomadic tribes, expert horsemen who possessed in war a speed and striking power that their sedentary neighbours could rarely match. In the 4th and 5th centuries AD, numerous nomad groups launched devastating attacks against all the major civilizations. A confederation known as the Hsiung-nu from Mongolia broke through the Great Wall of China in AD 304 and within a decade reached the Yellow River, sacking the ancient Han capital Ch'ang-an (AD 316). A succession of invaders from the steppes dominated northern China for the next three centuries.

Atlantic Ocean

Picts and Scots attack Hadrian's wall

Angles, Saxons, Jutes Hadrian's Wall

defeat of Huns 451

562 Avars invade Frankish lands

Châlons ✕ GERMANY

EUROPE

from 370 Goths displaced by Huns, settle in West Roman empire Volga

370 Black Huns appear in Europe

Ural Mts.

Alps

Vandals conquer North Africa (430s) ITALY

Rome sacked 410 by ✕ Visigoths

378 Visigoths defeat Romans at Adrianople Don

Black Sea

Caspian Sea

Aral Sea

North African limes

Carthage

Constantinople

Athens ASIA MINOR Anatolia

Berbers, attack Roman empire in North Africa

Mediterranean Sea

Syrian limes Tigris

Zagros M.

Euphrates

Oxus (Amu Darya)

484 White Huns (Ephthalites) kill Sassanian emperor, Persian empire surv

PERSIA

Alexandria EGYPT

Sahara Desert

AFRICA

Nile

Persian Gulf

Red sea

Arabian Desert

Indian Ocean

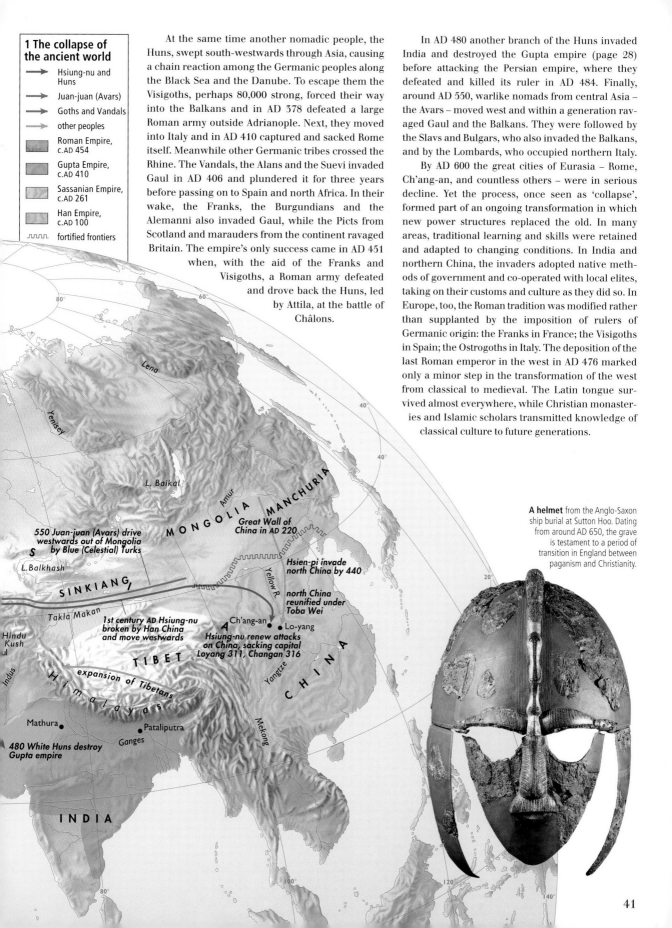

1 The collapse of the ancient world

→ Hsiung-nu and Huns
→ Juan-juan (Avars)
→ Goths and Vandals
→ other peoples

Roman Empire, c.AD 454
Gupta Empire, c.AD 410
Sassanian Empire, c.AD 261
Han Empire, c.AD 100

ᴗᴗᴗᴗ fortified frontiers

At the same time another nomadic people, the Huns, swept south-westwards through Asia, causing a chain reaction among the Germanic peoples along the Black Sea and the Danube. To escape them the Visigoths, perhaps 80,000 strong, forced their way into the Balkans and in AD 378 defeated a large Roman army outside Adrianople. Next, they moved into Italy and in AD 410 captured and sacked Rome itself. Meanwhile other Germanic tribes crossed the Rhine. The Vandals, the Alans and the Suevi invaded Gaul in AD 406 and plundered it for three years before passing on to Spain and north Africa. In their wake, the Franks, the Burgundians and the Alemanni also invaded Gaul, while the Picts from Scotland and marauders from the continent ravaged Britain. The empire's only success came in AD 451 when, with the aid of the Franks and Visigoths, a Roman army defeated and drove back the Huns, led by Attila, at the battle of Châlons.

In AD 480 another branch of the Huns invaded India and destroyed the Gupta empire (page 28) before attacking the Persian empire, where they defeated and killed its ruler in AD 484. Finally, around AD 550, warlike nomads from central Asia – the Avars – moved west and within a generation ravaged Gaul and the Balkans. They were followed by the Slavs and Bulgars, who also invaded the Balkans, and by the Lombards, who occupied northern Italy.

By AD 600 the great cities of Eurasia – Rome, Ch'ang-an, and countless others – were in serious decline. Yet the process, once seen as 'collapse', formed part of an ongoing transformation in which new power structures replaced the old. In many areas, traditional learning and skills were retained and adapted to changing conditions. In India and northern China, the invaders adopted native methods of government and co-operated with local elites, taking on their customs and culture as they did so. In Europe, too, the Roman tradition was modified rather than supplanted by the imposition of rulers of Germanic origin: the Franks in France; the Visigoths in Spain; the Ostrogoths in Italy. The deposition of the last Roman emperor in the west in AD 476 marked only a minor step in the transformation of the west from classical to medieval. The Latin tongue survived almost everywhere, while Christian monasteries and Islamic scholars transmitted knowledge of classical culture to future generations.

550 Juan-juan (Avars) drive westwards out of Mongolia by Blue (Celestial) Turks

Great Wall of China in AD 220

Hsien-pi invade north China by 440

north China reunified under Toba Wei

1st century AD Hsiung-nu broken by Han China and move westwards

Hsiung-nu renew attacks on China, sacking capital Loyang 311, Changan 316

expansion of Tibetans

480 White Huns destroy Gupta empire

Mathura
Pataliputra
Ganges

L. Baikal
Amur
MONGOLIA   MANCHURIA
Yellow R.
Ch'ang-an • • Lo-yang
Yangtze
CHINA
Mekong

Lena
Yenisey

L. Balkhash
SINKIANG
Takla Makan
TIBET
Himalayas
Hindu Kush
Indus

INDIA

A **helmet** from the Anglo-Saxon ship burial at Sutton Hoo. Dating from around AD 650, the grave is testament to a period of transition in England between paganism and Christianity.

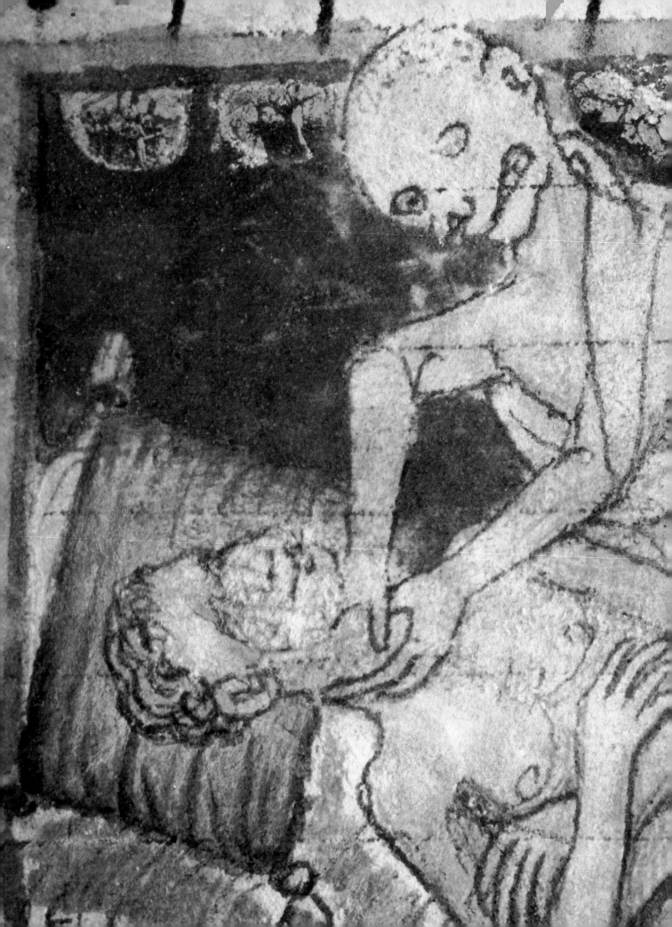

TWO
The World Fragmented

After AD 500 the narrow chain of empires extending from Rome to China crumbled under attacks from nomads from the Asian steppes. Contacts between China and the West, between north Africa and Italy and between Byzantium and western Europe dwindled as each region fell back on its own resources and had to fend for itself.

In Eurasia, two phenomena dominated: the expansion of Islam after 632; and the emergence of the Mongol empire after 1206. Meanwhile, the Maya, Aztec and Inca civilizations appeared in America, the empires of Sri Vijaya and Majapahit grew in southeast Asia, and the empires of Ghana, Mali and Songhay developed in Africa. Europe, by comparison, remained backward until, in the second half of the 15th century, a series of path-breaking voyages of exploration laid the foundations for overseas expansion. Even then, however, Europe's achievements remained overshadowed and threatened by the expanding power of the Ottoman Turks for another century.

Death strangling a plague victim,
from the 14th-century Stiny Codex (Prague University)

The spread of Christianity

Christianity began as a Jewish splinter movement in Roman Palestine. Its founder, Jesus of Nazareth, claimed to be the Messiah, or Saviour, sent to prepare the Jews for 'the kingdom of God' but, after an initial, short-lived success, he was executed as a revolutionary (AD 29). Jewish orthodoxy rejected his message, but his followers turned instead to the conversion of non-Jews and by AD 200, despite repression and persecution, communities of Christians (as the followers of Jesus came to be called) flourished in several cities of the Roman empire (especially Antioch and Edessa). In AD 313 the Emperor Constantine granted the new faith toleration and in AD 325 at Nicaea presided over the first ecumenical council, representing the whole church, which defined beliefs for all Christians. A full ecclesiastical organization developed, with a hierarchy of bishops and a framework of patriarchates, provinces and dioceses throughout the empire (map 1).

The council of Chalcedon (451) attempted to enforce orthodoxy on the Christian world, but instead alienated the Monophysite (or Coptic) Christians of Egypt, Syria and Armenia, and the Nestorians who, expelled from Edessa, took refuge in Persia. Meanwhile the disintegration of the Roman empire in the West (page 36) undermined the position of the church. But salvation came from the periphery. The Coptic church of Egypt, with a strong monastic tradition, sent missionaries down the Nile from the 4th century, converting the peoples of Nubia and Ethiopia; while from the 7th century, the Nestorians of Persia expanded south into Arabia and east to China. In the west, the impetus for revival came from the monastic missionary church of Ireland, which evangelized first its Celtic neighbours in Britain and Brittany, and then in the 7th and 8th centuries the pagan tribes of continental Europe (map 2).

As the Muslim onslaught devastated the Christian Mediterranean (page 50), both Rome and Constantinople launched missions northwards among the Slavs. Russia opted for Orthodox Christianity, and in 988 the Russian prince Vladimir was baptized, while Poland (966) and Hungary (1001) chose Catholic Christianity. Although rivalry between the two patriarchates resulted after 1054 in schism, the popes increased their authority by sponsoring Christian counter-offensives in Iberia, the Baltic and West Asia: the crusades (page 48). The attempt to restore Christianity to Palestine proved a costly failure, but the crusades made great advances elsewhere. Meanwhile, within Europe, monks and (from the 13th century) friars joined the expanding network of parish clergy in Christianizing the countryside and combating heresy. In 1387 Lithuania, the last remaining pagan state in Europe, converted to Catholicism, just as persecution by Timur and other rulers (page 60) extinguished the faith in Asia, the continent of its birth.

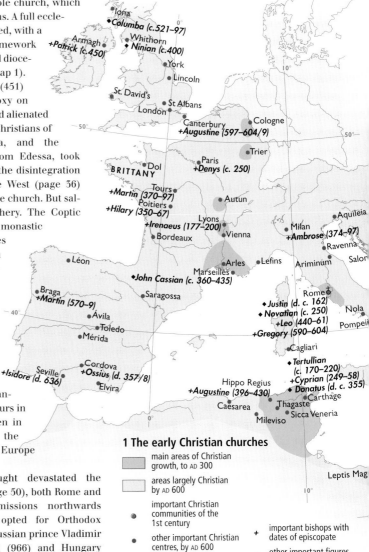

1 The early Christian churches

main areas of Christian growth, to AD 300

areas largely Christian by AD 600

● important Christian communities of the 1st century

● other important Christian centres, by AD 600

⚲ the five patriarchates

+ important bishops with dates of episcopate

◆ other important figures, with dates

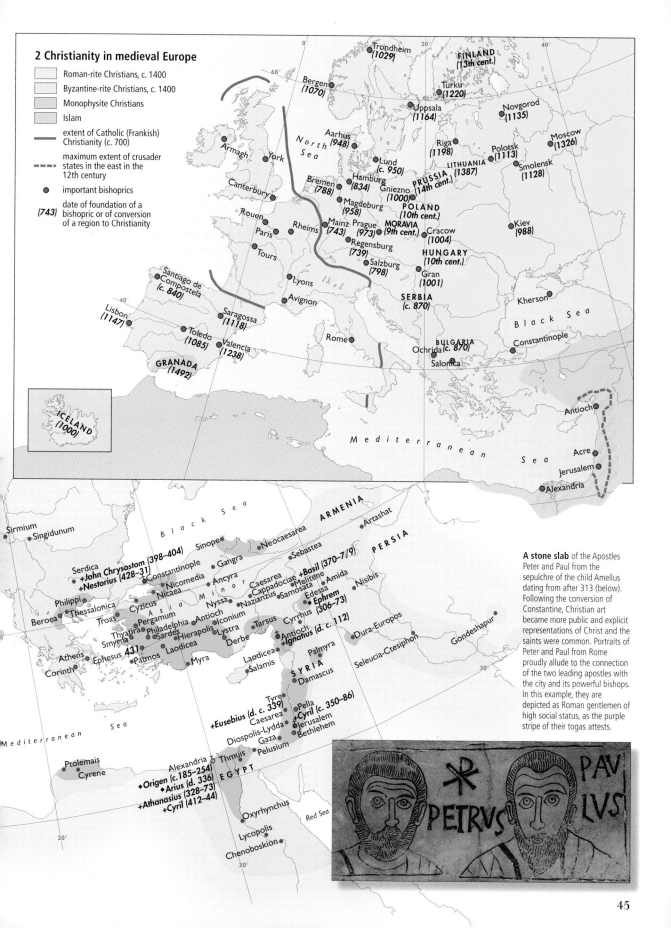

2 Christianity in medieval Europe

- Roman-rite Christians, c. 1400
- Byzantine-rite Christians, c. 1400
- Monophysite Christians
- Islam
- ——— extent of Catholic (Frankish) Christianity (c. 700)
- – – – maximum extent of crusader states in the east in the 12th century
- ● important bishoprics
- (743) date of foundation of a bishopric or of conversion of a region to Christianity

Trondheim (1029)
FINLAND (13th cent.)
Bergen (1070)
Turku (1220)
Uppsala (1164)
Novgorod (1135)
Aarhus (948)
Riga (1198)
Moscow (1326)
Armagh
York
Lund (c. 950)
Polotsk (1113)
Smolensk (1128)
North Sea
LITHUANIA (1387)
Canterbury
Hamburg (834)
PRUSSIA (14th cent.)
Bremen (788)
Gniezno (1000)
Kiev (988)
Rouen
Magdeburg (958)
POLAND (10th cent.)
Paris
Rheims
Mainz (743)
Prague (973)
MORAVIA (9th cent.)
Cracow (1004)
Tours
Regensburg (739)
HUNGARY (10th cent.)
Kherson
Salzburg (798)
Lyons
Gran (1001)
Santiago de Compostela (c. 840)
Avignon
SERBIA (c. 870)
Black Sea
Lisbon (1147)
Saragossa (1118)
Rome
BULGARIA (c. 870)
Constantinople
Toledo (1085)
Valencia (1238)
Ochrida (c. 870)
Salonica
GRANADA (1492)
ICELAND (1000)
Mediterranean Sea
Antioch
Acre
Jerusalem
Alexandria

Sirmium
Singidunum
Black Sea
ARMENIA
Artashat
Serdica
+John Chrysostom (398–404)
Sinope
Neocaesarea
Sebastea
PERSIA
+Nestorius (428–31)
Constantinople
Gangra
Nicomedia
Ancyra
Caesarea
+Basil (370–7/9)
Philippi
Nicaea
Asia Minor
Cappadociae
Melitene
Amida
Nisibis
Thessalonica
Cyzicus
Nyssa
Nazianzus
Samosata
Edessa
+Ephrem (306–73)
Beroea
Troas
Pergamum
Antioch
Iconium
Cyrrhus
Thyatira
Philadelphia
Hierapolis
Lystra
Antioch
+Ignatius (d. c. 112)
Athens
Smyrna
Sardes
Derbe
Tarsus
Dura-Europos
Ephesus 431
Laodicea
Palmyra
Gondeshapur
Corinth
Patmos
Myra
SYRIA
Seleucia-Ctesiphon
Laodicea
Salamis
Damascus
Mediterranean Sea
Tyre
Pella
+Eusebius (d. c. 339)
Caesarea
+Cyril (c. 350–86)
Diospolis-Lydda
Jerusalem
Ptolemais
Gaza
Bethlehem
Cyrene
Alexandria +
Thmuis
Pelusium
+Origen (c.185–254)
+Arius (d. 336)
EGYPT
+Athanasius (328–73)
+Cyril (412–44)
Oxyrhynchus
Red Sea
Lycopolis
Chenoboskion

A stone slab of the Apostles Peter and Paul from the sepulchre of the child Amellus dating from after 313 (below). Following the conversion of Constantine, Christian art became more public and explicit representations of Christ and the saints were common. Portraits of Peter and Paul from Rome proudly allude to the connection of the two leading apostles with the city and its powerful bishops. In this example, they are depicted as Roman gentlemen of high social status, as the purple stripe of their togas attests.

PETRVS   PAVLVS

581–1279
China

After the barbarian invasions of the 4th and 5th centuries (page 38) the Sui dynasty (581-617) reunified China. They consolidated their empire through standardized institutions, a state-supported broadbased Buddhism, and the construction of a canal system linking the Yangtze with the Yellow River and the Lo-yang region. The T'ang dynasty (618-907) continued the process, creating a uniform administrative organization of prefectures, in which officials recruited through an examination system replaced the traditional aristocracy. The T'ang also extended their control to the Tarim basin and northern Korea: in the 660s, the Chinese empire reached its greatest extent and 88 Asiatic peoples recognised Chinese overlordship, adopting its culture, its written language and its political institutions (map 1).

In 751, however, at the Talas River, an Arab army defeated the Chinese, while a major rebellion rocked T'ang power in 755-62, causing many of the new conquests to be abandoned. Within the empire, power began to pass to the provinces until in 907, following a wave of peasant uprisings, China split into ten separate regional states. Although the Sung dynasty reunified the country between 960 and 979, they failed to regain the new territories. Nevertheless, Chinese economic growth continued. A massive movement of population into the fertile Yangtze valley and southern China produced large agricultural surpluses which stimulated trade and economic development. Between 750 and 1100, the population of the empire doubled; trade reached new heights; and a great concentration of industries arose around the capital, K'ai-feng, centre of the canal system and of the eastern road network.

Turkish people, converted to Judaism. Their nomad empire destroyed by Russia at end of the 10th century

Talas River 751 Arabs defeat T'ang armies

Arabs invade Khurasan 667, settle from 670; settle Transoxiana 705-15. Final Arab dominance from 739 in central Asia as far as Ferghana

Arabs invade Sind 711

2 Sung China, 960–1279
- • provincial capitals
- — canals
- — principal roads
- boundary between Southern Sung and Chin after 1127

A foreign merchant. Most of the trade along the Silk Road – the trade routes linking China and West Asia – was handled by the Chinese and the nomadic peoples of central and western Asia. The T'ang generally regarded them with interested amusement, as is evident in this glazed pottery figure of a camel groom or trader with his exaggeratedly large nose.

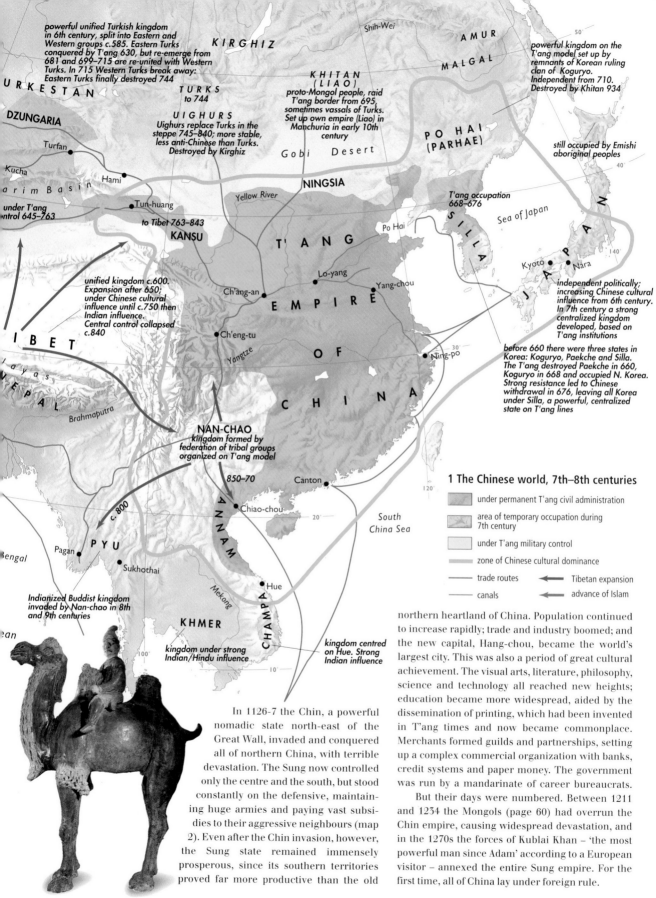

powerful unified Turkish kingdom in 6th century, split into Eastern and Western groups c.585. Eastern Turks conquered by T'ang 630, but re-emerge from 681 and 699–715 are re-united with Western Turks. In 715 Western Turks break away: Eastern Turks finally destroyed 744

KIRGHIZ

Shih-Wei

AMUR

MALGAL

powerful kingdom on the T'ang model set up by remnants of Korean ruling clan of Koguryo. Independent from 710. Destroyed by Khitan 934

URKESTAN

DZUNGARIA

TURKS to 744

UIGHURS
Uighurs replace Turks in the steppe 745–840; more stable, less anti-Chinese than Turks. Destroyed by Kirghiz

KHITAN (LIAO)
proto-Mongol people, raid T'ang border from 695, sometimes vassals of Turks. Set up own empire (Liao) in Manchuria in early 10th century

PO HAI (PARHAE)

still occupied by Emishi aboriginal peoples

Turfan

Kucha

Hami

arim Basin

Gobi Desert

NINGSIA

under T'ang
ntrol 645–763

Tun-huang

Yellow River

T'ang occupation 668–676

Po Hai

SILLA

Sea of Japan

to Tibet 763–843

KANSU

T'ANG

J
A
P
A
N

Kyoto

Nara

unified kingdom c.600. Expansion after 650; under Chinese cultural influence until c.750 then Indian influence. Central control collapsed c.840

Ch'ang-an

Lo-yang

EMPIRE

Yang-chou

independent politically; increasing Chinese cultural influence from 6th century. In 7th century a strong centralized kingdom developed, based on T'ang institutions

T I B E T

Ch'eng-tu

OF

Yangtze

Ning-po

layas

NEPAL

Brahmaputra

CHINA

NAN-CHAO
kingdom formed by federation of tribal groups organized on T'ang model

before 660 there were three states in Korea: Koguryo, Paekche and Silla. The T'ang destroyed Paekche in 660, Koguryo in 668 and occupied N. Korea. Strong resistance led to Chinese withdrawal in 676, leaving all Korea under Silla, a powerful, centralized state on T'ang lines

850–70

Canton

c.800

A
N
N
A
M

Chiao-chou

South China Sea

1 The Chinese world, 7th–8th centuries

under permanent T'ang civil administration

area of temporary occupation during 7th century

under T'ang military control

zone of Chinese cultural dominance

trade routes
canals

Tibetan expansion
advance of Islam

Bengal

Pagan

PYU

Sukhothai

Mekong

Hue

Indianized Buddist kingdom invaded by Nan-chao in 8th and 9th centuries

KHMER

C
H
A
M
P
A

kingdom under strong Indian/Hindu influence

kingdom centred on Hue. Strong Indian influence

In 1126-7 the Chin, a powerful nomadic state north-east of the Great Wall, invaded and conquered all of northern China, with terrible devastation. The Sung now controlled only the centre and the south, but stood constantly on the defensive, maintaining huge armies and paying vast subsidies to their aggressive neighbours (map 2). Even after the Chin invasion, however, the Sung state remained immensely prosperous, since its southern territories proved far more productive than the old

northern heartland of China. Population continued to increase rapidly; trade and industry boomed; and the new capital, Hang-chou, became the world's largest city. This was also a period of great cultural achievement. The visual arts, literature, philosophy, science and technology all reached new heights; education became more widespread, aided by the dissemination of printing, which had been invented in T'ang times and now became commonplace. Merchants formed guilds and partnerships, setting up a complex commercial organization with banks, credit systems and paper money. The government was run by a mandarinate of career bureaucrats.

But their days were numbered. Between 1211 and 1234 the Mongols (page 60) had overrun the Chin empire, causing widespread devastation, and in the 1270s the forces of Kublai Khan – 'the most powerful man since Adam' according to a European visitor – annexed the entire Sung empire. For the first time, all of China lay under foreign rule.

610–1453
The Byzantine world

Almost from its inception, the Roman empire's centre of gravity moved to the east, first pulled by the lure of economic wealth in Egypt and western Asia; then pushed by the loss of the western provinces to Germanic invaders (page 36) and by the pressure of Sassanid Persia on its eastern frontier. Except during the reign of Justinian (page 37), the west was neglected and the Roman empire became an eastern, Greek-speaking state – normally known, from the reign of Heraclius (610-641), as Byzantium.

Heraclius ended the long contest with Persia victoriously, capturing Nineveh in 628, but almost at once Byzantium faced two even more redoubtable foes: Islam (page 50) and the Slavs. However, after the failure of two long Arab sieges of Byzantium (674-8 and 717-18), the empire launched a succession of vigorous counter-offensives. Basil II (976-1025) even managed to advance the imperial frontiers close to their earlier limits: the Arabs retreated into Palestine; the Russians met defeat at Silistra on the Danube; the Bulgars, who had advanced to within 60 miles of Constantinople, became imperial subjects; plans were laid to recover the former Byzantine territories in Italy. However, the constant campaigns imposed heavy financial strains, as well as profound and debilitating social change, and in spite of further phases of recovery, the frontiers steadily shrank (map 1).

The crucial development was the emergence, in the 11th century, of the Seljuk Turks (page 50), whose crushing victory over Byzantine forces at Manzikert in 1071 induced Emperor Alexius I (1081-1118) to call on the west for help, thus initiating the sequence of events that led to the First Crusade (1096-9). It proved a disastrous move since the Franks were less concerned to aid Byzantium than to set up their own principalities in Palestine and Asia Minor; the Normans, already in control of Sicily and Byzantine Italy, coveted lands in Greece; and the Italian cities, led by Venice, strove to increase their share of Mediterranean trade. After a century of mounting tension, the soldiers of the Fourth Crusade in 1204 conquered and pillaged Constantinople, partitioned the Byzantine empire, and established Latin states all over the Balkans (map 2).

The Latin Empire proved short-lived – its Greek-speaking subjects resented it and a new dynasty, the Palaeologi, restored the Greek empire in 1261 – but the new Byzantine state was only a shadow of its former self and when, shortly afterwards, the Ottoman Turks established themselves first in Asia Minor and then advanced into Byzantium's European territories, its fate was sealed. The capital of the east Roman empire fell in 1453 (page 70).

Nevertheless, the history of Byzantium includes both greatness and lasting achievements. For centuries it transmitted Roman culture back to areas from which earlier invasions had largely effaced it. It also passed on its culture and its religion to the Balkan peoples and to Russia. 'Two Romes have fallen', a Russian monk wrote shortly after 1453, 'but the third is still standing and a fourth shall never be.' He referred to Moscow (page 56), now emerged as the heir to the Byzantine inheritance.

The emperor Constantine IV Pogonatus and his brothers hand privileges to the Ravenna church of Sant'Apollinare in Classe and to archbishop Mauro. During his reign Constantinople withstood a four year siege by Arab armies (674–8), although much of the Balkans was overrun by Slav tribes and the Bulgars.

1 Byzantine greatness and decline

Imperial frontiers
— c. 628
— c. 1030
— c. 1143
— 1328

special areas:
— Exarchate of Ravenna to Lombards, 751
— Exarchate of Africa to Arabs from 670
— Catapanate of Italy to Normans from 1071

temporary reconquests:
▦ Africa, 685–710
▨ Syria, 975–6
▨ Sicily, 1038–43
▦ Ani, 1054
▨ Edessa, 1052
▨ Rum, c. 1118

general territorial losses:
▩ to Arabs, 636–641
▢ to Arabs after 641
— to Seljuk Turks from 1065
┄ Sultanate of Rum from 1071

(Map labels: Ve, Bor, Genoa, Flor, Corsica, Sardinia, Caralis, Valentia, Balearic Islands, Carthago Nova, Carthage, AFRICA)

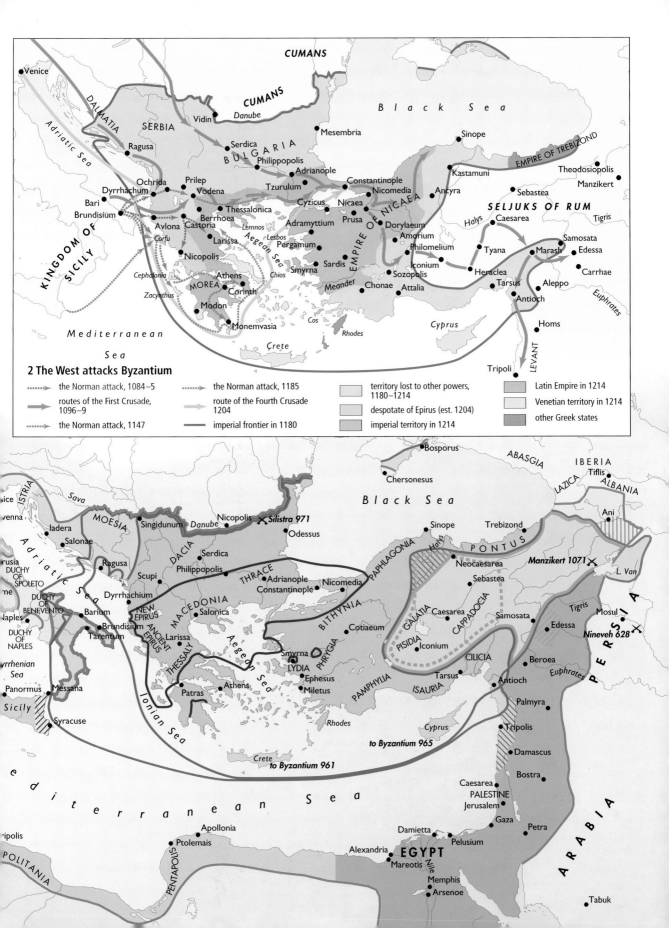

CUMANS

CUMANS

Black Sea

Venice

Adriatic Sea

DALMATIA

SERBIA

Ragusa

Vidin

Danube

Serdica

BULGARIA

Philippopolis

Mesembria

Sinope

EMPIRE OF TREBIZOND

Theodosiopolis

Manzikert

Kastamuni

Ochrida

Prilep

Vodena

Adrianople

Tzurulum

Constantinople

Nicomedia

Ancyra

Sebastea

SELJUKS OF RUM

Dyrrhachium

Bari

Brundisium

Cyzicus

Nicaea

Halys

Caesarea

Tigris

Avlona

Castoria

Berrhoea

Adramyttium

Prusa

EMPIRE OF NICAEA

Dorylaeum

Tyana

Samosata

Marash

Edessa

KINGDOM OF SICILY

Corfu

Larissa

Pergamum

Lemnos

Lesbos

Aegean Sea

Amorium

Philomelium

Carrhae

Nicopolis

Smyrna

Sardis

Iconium

Heraclea

Tarsus

Antioch

Aleppo

Euphrates

Cephalonia

Athens

Chios

Chonae

Sozopolis

Attalia

Zacynthus

MOREA

Corinth

Meander

Homs

Modon

Cos

Cyprus

Mediterranean

Monemvasia

Rhodes

LEVANT

Tripoli

Sea

Crete

2 The West attacks Byzantium

- ┈┈► the Norman attack, 1084–5
- ━━► routes of the First Crusade, 1096–9
- ┈┈► the Norman attack, 1147
- ┈┈► the Norman attack, 1185
- ━━► route of the Fourth Crusade 1204
- ━━ imperial frontier in 1180

territory lost to other powers, 1180–1214

despotate of Epirus (est. 1204)

imperial territory in 1214

Latin Empire in 1214

Venetian territory in 1214

other Greek states

Bosporus

ABASGIA

IBERIA

Chersonesus

Black Sea

Tiflis

LAZICA

ALBANIA

ice

ISTRIA

Sava

MOESIA

Singidunum

Danube

Nicopolis

✕ Silistra 971

Ani

venna

Iadera

Salonae

DACIA

Serdica

Odessus

Sinope

Trebizond

PONTUS

Manzikert 1071 ✕

L. Van

rusia

DUCHY OF SPOLETO

me

Ragusa

Scupi

Philippopolis

THRACE

Adrianople

Nicomedia

PAPHLAGONIA

Halys

Neocaesarea

PERSIA

DUCHY OF BENEVENTO

Naples

Dyrrhachium

NEW EPIRUS

Barium

Constantinople

MACEDONIA

Salonica

BITHYNIA

Sebastea

Caesarea

GALATIA

CAPPADOCIA

Samosata

Tigris

Mosul

Edessa

Nineveh 628 ✕

DUCHY OF NAPLES

Brundisium

Tarentum

ANCIENT EPIRUS

Larissa

THESSALY

Aegean Sea

Cotiaeum

PHRYGIA

PISIDIA

Iconium

CILICIA

Beroea

Antioch

Euphrates

rrhenian Sea

Panormus

Messana

Smyrna

LYDIA

Ephesus

Miletus

PAMPHYLIA

ISAURIA

Tarsus

Palmyra

Sicily

Syracuse

Ionian Sea

Patras

Athens

Rhodes

Cyprus

to Byzantium 965

Tripolis

Damascus

to Byzantium 961

Crete

Bostra

Caesarea

e

d i t e r r a n e a n   S e a

PALESTINE

Jerusalem

Gaza

Petra

ARABIA

ripolis

POLITANIA

Apollonia

Ptolemais

PENTAPOLIS

Damietta

Alexandria

Mareotis

Pelusium

EGYPT

Nile

Memphis

Arsenoe

Tabuk

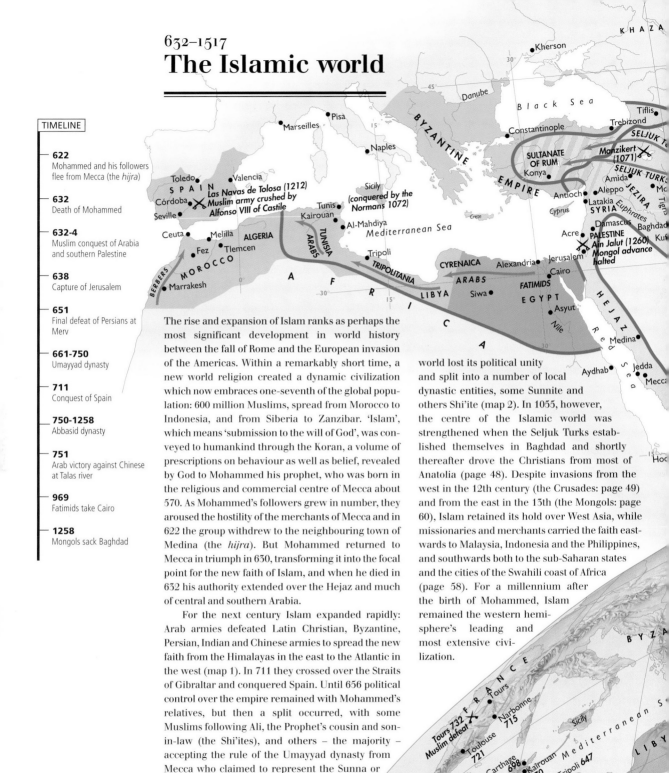

632–1517
The Islamic world

TIMELINE

622
Mohammed and his followers flee from Mecca (the *hijra*)

632
Death of Mohammed

632-4
Muslim conquest of Arabia and southern Palestine

638
Capture of Jerusalem

651
Final defeat of Persians at Merv

661-750
Umayyad dynasty

711
Conquest of Spain

750-1258
Abbasid dynasty

751
Arab victory against Chinese at Talas river

969
Fatimids take Cairo

1258
Mongols sack Baghdad

The rise and expansion of Islam ranks as perhaps the most significant development in world history between the fall of Rome and the European invasion of the Americas. Within a remarkably short time, a new world religion created a dynamic civilization which now embraces one-seventh of the global population: 600 million Muslims, spread from Morocco to Indonesia, and from Siberia to Zanzibar. 'Islam', which means 'submission to the will of God', was conveyed to humankind through the Koran, a volume of prescriptions on behaviour as well as belief, revealed by God to Mohammed his prophet, who was born in the religious and commercial centre of Mecca about 570. As Mohammed's followers grew in number, they aroused the hostility of the merchants of Mecca and in 622 the group withdrew to the neighbouring town of Medina (the *hijra*). But Mohammed returned to Mecca in triumph in 630, transforming it into the focal point for the new faith of Islam, and when he died in 632 his authority extended over the Hejaz and much of central and southern Arabia.

For the next century Islam expanded rapidly: Arab armies defeated Latin Christian, Byzantine, Persian, Indian and Chinese armies to spread the new faith from the Himalayas in the east to the Atlantic in the west (map 1). In 711 they crossed over the Straits of Gibraltar and conquered Spain. Until 656 political control over the empire remained with Mohammed's relatives, but then a split occurred, with some Muslims following Ali, the Prophet's cousin and son-in-law (the Shi'ites), and others – the majority – accepting the rule of the Umayyad dynasty from Mecca who claimed to represent the Sunna or traditions of the Prophet. The Umayyads ruled from Damascus in Syria between 661 and 750, followed by the rival Abbasid dynasty, who created a new capital at Baghdad in Mesopotamia and opened government to non-Arab Muslims (known as *mawali*).

Gradually, the Muslim world lost its political unity and split into a number of local dynastic entities, some Sunnite and others Shi'ite (map 2). In 1055, however, the centre of the Islamic world was strengthened when the Seljuk Turks established themselves in Baghdad and shortly thereafter drove the Christians from most of Anatolia (page 48). Despite invasions from the west in the 12th century (the Crusades: page 49) and from the east in the 13th (the Mongols: page 60), Islam retained its hold over West Asia, while missionaries and merchants carried the faith eastwards to Malaysia, Indonesia and the Philippines, and southwards both to the sub-Saharan states and the cities of the Swahili coast of Africa (page 58). For a millennium after the birth of Mohammed, Islam remained the western hemisphere's leading and most extensive civilization.

50

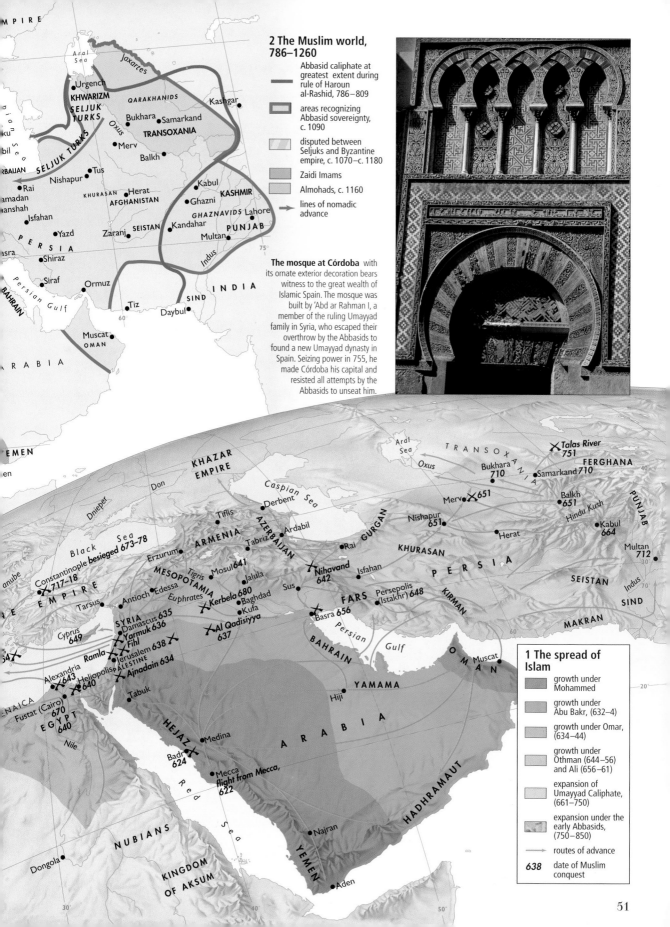

2 The Muslim world, 786–1260

— Abbasid caliphate at greatest extent during rule of Haroun al-Rashid, 786–809

areas recognizing Abbasid sovereignty, c. 1090

disputed between Seljuks and Byzantine empire, c. 1070–c. 1180

Zaidi Imams

Almohads, c. 1160

→ lines of nomadic advance

The mosque at Córdoba with its ornate exterior decoration bears witness to the great wealth of Islamic Spain. The mosque was built by 'Abd ar Rahman I, a member of the ruling Umayyad family in Syria, who escaped their overthrow by the Abbasids to found a new Umayyad dynasty in Spain. Seizing power in 755, he made Córdoba his capital and resisted all attempts by the Abbasids to unseat him.

1 The spread of Islam

growth under Mohammed

growth under Abu Bakr, (632–4)

growth under Omar, (634–44)

growth under Othman (644–56) and Ali (656–61)

expansion of Umayyad Caliphate, (661–750)

expansion under the early Abbasids, (750–850)

→ routes of advance

638 date of Muslim conquest

Franks and Anglo-Saxons

Within a century of the Germanic invasions, settled kingdoms had grown up in western Europe, but not in Britain, where invaders from the continent met with resistance. During the 7th century, however, seven separate important kingdoms – which are traditionally known as the Heptarchy – emerged in England. Geographical obstacles seem to have prevented the states in the south-east (Sussex, Kent, Essex, East Anglia) from expanding, and leadership at first passed to Northumbria, whose progress benefitted from its early conversion to Christianity. Mercia led the opposition, sometimes in alliance with the 'Britons' on the periphery, and by the time of Offa (757-96) its pre-eminence was unquestionable: it controlled the four southeastern kingdoms, and even Wessex recognized Mercian overlordship.

On the continent, the Franks (whose original power base lay in what is now northern France, the Low Countries and the Rhineland) converted to Christianity under Clovis (481-511) and began to expand south and east. From their new capital at Paris, Clovis and his sons and grandsons defeated the Visigoths, conquered Burgundy and Provence, and extended their overlordship in Germany as far as the middle Danube.

Most of the new lands served to maintain the loyalty of the Frankish warriors, however, and when the conquests ceased in the mid-7th century the kings had to reward their followers and endow the Church by granting away their own estates and revenues. In doing so they diminished their resources and, in time, power passed to the families which had benefitted from royal favour. Eventually Pippin of Herstal, from a leading Austrasian family, achieved prominence, and at Tertry (687) defeated his chief rivals.

Pippin and his son Charles Martel (from whom the dynasty took the name 'Carolingian') restored Frankish fortunes and inaugurated a second surge of territorial expansion (map 2). Charles Martel (714-41) defeated the Arabs at Tours in 732, halting their rapid incursion into western Europe, while his son Pippin the Short (d. 768) expelled them from southern France. In 751, with the sanction and support of the pope, Pippin made himself king of the Franks. His son Charles the Great or Charlemagne (768-814) conquered Lombardy (774) and established Frankish rule in much of Italy. He won great victories over the Frisians (784-5), Bavarians (788) and Saxons (finally subdued in 804); and created a march, or boundary province, across the Pyrenees

An image of Charlemagne from his tomb at Aachen. The tomb was endowed by Frederick Barbarossa in the 12th century. The masterpiece of gold enamels and gems shows that, for the later emperor, Charlemagne was a saint and a personal patron, able to confer political legitimacy.

between 795 and 812. In 800 the pope in Rome crowned him emperor of the west.

However, Frankish custom called for the royal domain to be partitioned. Charlemagne's father had divided it between his two sons – Charlemagne only inherited the whole when his brother died in 771 – and the new emperor likewise planned in 806 to partition his possessions among his three sons, a scheme frustrated only by the early death of two of them. This made it possible for the survivor, Louis the Pious (814-40), to inherit the whole empire. After his death, however, the treaty of Verdun (843) created three kingdoms: one in the east, one in the west, and a 'middle kingdom' which ran from the North Sea to Italy.

The Carolingians ruled through direct agents, rather than through Gallo-Roman bishops and counts as their predecessors had done; and throughout the 8th century these men generally remained loyal. After Charlemagne's death, however, their descendants tended to identify with the particular interests of their own localities, at the expense of the whole. Frankish hegemony in western Europe was thus disrupted by fragmentation just as it came under attack from the Vikings and Magyars.

1 Anglo-Saxon England, c. AD 800

Mercia and subordinate kingdoms under Offa (757–96)

allied with Mercia

British kingdoms

2 The empire of Charlemagne

Frankish realm 714

added to Frankish empire by 814

Frankish dependencies (with date of formation)

⛪ Frankish royal residences

✝ archbishoprics

✛ important monasteries

GASCONY 769 province with date of acquisition

A carved wooden head from the Oseberg cart (c. 800) depicts a fearsome Viking warrior. Viking success was in large part achieved not through superior organization or tactical skill, but depended on their greater mobility. They were able to launch lightning attacks on undefended coastal settlements and penetrate far inland in shallow boats or on horseback.

Three separate groups of invaders in the 9th century shattered the relative stability achieved by Charlemagne in western Europe and by Offa of Mercia in England (page 52). The Saracens occupied the islands of the western Mediterranean and raided Italy and France; the Magyars of Hungary devastated northern Italy and Germany; the Vikings from Scandinavia not only plundered settlements around the European coast as far as the Mediterranean, but also created trade routes through Russia to Byzantium (page 56) and settled substantial parts of Britain, Ireland, northern France, Iceland and even Greenland.

The invasions disrupted royal authority and caused political fragmentation. In the Carolingian empire, the Frankish kings virtually capitulated to the Vikings, leaving defence to the local magnates who swiftly created their own power bases. In England, although determined resistance by Alfred the Great of Wessex (871-99) held the Danes at bay,

a second wave of Scandinavian invasions a century later proved irresistible. However in the eastern half of the Frankish empire, Otto I's defeat of the Magyars at the Lechfeld (955) proved a turning point, and Germany became the first country in Europe to recover from the invasions. This achievement assured its predominance in Europe for almost three centuries.

German rulers rarely sought to assert control over the west Frankish lands but, as heirs to the Carolingians, they claimed the imperial title and the right to rule over Italy and the lands of the former "middle kingdom" (page 53). In 962 Otto's coronation as emperor sealed the connection between Germany and Italy, and in 1034 his successors annexed Burgundy. However the emperors became increasingly dependent upon the wealth of Italy, and this embroiled Frederick I of Hohenstaufen (1152-90) with both the papacy and the populous fortified cities of the Lombard plain,

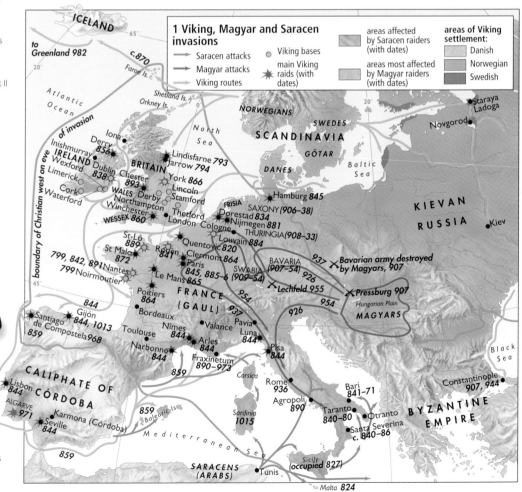

which all saw Imperial power in Italy as a threat to their independence. The conquest of Sicily by Frederick's son Henry VI in 1194 made the Hohenstaufen the richest rulers in Europe; but the prospect of total encirclement once more alarmed the papacy and the Lombard towns, leading to a long and costly struggle with Henry's son Frederick II (1212-50). After his death, the Imperial position in Italy steadily deteriorated, and the last Hohenstaufen prince met defeat and death at the battle of Tagliacozzo in 1268.

Meanwhile, in Germany, the princes took advantage of their rulers' preoccupation with Italy both to consolidate their power and, on the eastern frontier, to direct a major expansion. The Slavs were driven out or enslaved, in favour of German settlers who, by 1250, had increased the German kingdom by about one-third and shifted its centre of gravity from the Rhine to the Elbe. The empire might no longer have been the strongest or richest polity in Europe, but it remained the largest.

2 The German empire to 1250

- eastward spread of German peasant settlement, 12th century
- German settlement, 1200–1250
- city with over 10,000 inhabitants
- member of Lombard Leagues of 1167 and 1226
- member of 1167 League only
- member of 1226 League only
- main royal routes
- German invasions, 1190–94
- Henry VI's Genoese and Pisan fleet, 1194
- main Hohenstaufen palaces and castles
- monasteries

The first Russian state: Kievan Russia

862
Vikings seize Novgorod

882
Oleg unites Novgorod and Kiev

941
Rus attack on Constantinople

964-71
Campaigns of Grand Prince Svyatoslav

c.987
Conversion of Vladimir of Kiev to Christianity

1093
Polovtsy sack Kiev

1237-8
Mongols attack Vladimir-Suzdal

1240
Mongols sack Kiev

1240
Alexander of Novgorod defeats Swedes at the River Neva

Three factors shaped the early history of Russia: the eastward movement of Slav settlers; the impact of the Vikings (who were known to the Slavs as Varyagi or Varangians) from the north; and, most important of all, the division of the region into forests (in the north and centre) and treeless steppe (in the south). Before the arrival of the Vikings in the 9th century, the Slavs had begun to settle the central river basins, clearing the forests and living by agriculture, hunting, trapping and the fur trade, while nomadic tribes from Asia, such as the Pechenegs, occupied the grasslands of the south. At first the Slavs resisted the Varangians, but in 862 they called in 'Rurik the Viking' to protect them from Pecheneg raiders.

Since most of the rivers of Russia follow a north-south axis, great potential existed for trade between the Baltic and the Black Sea, and the Vikings sought to dominate and exploit these waterways and the territories adjoining them (map 2). Rurik therefore occupied Novgorod, and his followers soon pushed south to Smolensk and then down the Dnieper to Kiev (882). The principal trade route established by the Vikings ran from the Gulf of Finland up the river Neva, through Lake Ladoga to the river Volkhov, thence by portages to the Dnieper and on across the Black Sea to Byzantium.

Grand Prince Svyatoslav (962-72) campaigned to the south and east, greatly extending the frontiers of the Kievan state, which forged strong links with Byzantium, its chief trading partner; and from Byzantium it received the Christian faith during the reign of Vladimir Svyatoslav (980-1015). At the same time Kiev retained numerous connections with the West: one of Vladimir's granddaughters married the king of France, another the king of Hungary and a

A scene from Novgorod's victory over Suzdal in 1169. Novgorod was the capital of the Rus until Oleg moved his capital to Kiev in 882. In 1019 Iaroslav I granted Novgorod a charter of self-government, and thereafter the town elected its own prince. Grown rich on the trade in furs, Novgorod became pre-eminent in northern Russia. During the 12th century it came into conflict with the growing power of Vladimir-Suzdal to the south. However Novgorod defeated Vladimir-Suzdal in 1169 and 1216. It avoided the Mongol destruction and defeated the Germans and Swedes in 1240–2. A struggle for supremacy with Moscow in the 14th and 15th centuries saw the eclipse of Novgorod.

third the king of Norway. Half a century later, however, dynastic conflict and administrative inefficiency brought weakness and a new wave of Asiatic nomads, the Polovtsy, broke through the defences built by Svyatoslav and Vladimir. In 1093 they sacked Kiev itself.

A great northward exodus ensued to safer regions between the Oka and the Volga, where many new towns were founded (such as Vladimir, Suzdal, Rostov and Tver) and several new states developed – notably Vladimir-Suzdal, which included the fast growing commercial centre of Moscow (first mentioned in 1147), and Novgorod, which built up a fur-trading empire that reached to the Arctic and the Urals. Meanwhile, further south, Novgorod-Seversk, Vladimir-Volynsk and Galich broke away from Kievan rule (map 1).

Mongol invaders struck the final blow to the old order (page 60). In 1237-8, moving along the frozen rivers, they struck north and sacked the wealthy towns of Vladimir-Suzdal; in 1239-40 they advanced through southern Russia, systematically destroying settlements, including Kiev. Meanwhile Novgorod, although it escaped the Mongol onslaught as the onset of spring thawed the frozen rivers, faced repeated attacks by both Swedes and Germans in the Baltic region until Prince Alexander decisively defeated the former in 1240 on the river Neva (thus earning the title 'Nevsky') and the latter in 1242 on the ice of Lake Peipus. Despite these successes, however, even Novgorod had to recognize Mongol overlordship, exercised by the Golden Horde on the lower Volga, while the Lithuanian state expanded into the old Kievan heartland.

The Mongol invasion had other lasting economic, social and political effects. The destruction of so many towns decimated both trade and industry, while the elimination of the urban middle class smoothed the path of an autocracy which imitated its overlords in ruthless terror and extortion. The fall of Kiev destroyed the cultural centre of medieval Russia, with its rich Byzantine-based literature and art, while the Mongol forces, controlling the grasslands around the Caspian and the Black Sea, prevented almost all contact with Byzantium. Russia therefore inevitably developed a distinctive culture, society and political system of its own.

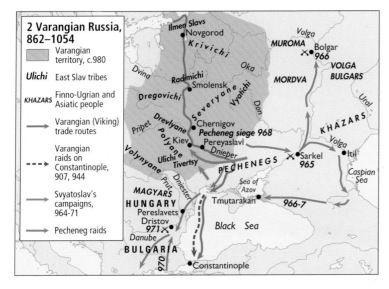

2 Varangian Russia, 862–1054

Varangian territory, c.980

Ulichi East Slav tribes

KHAZARS Finno-Ugrian and Asiatic people

→ Varangian (Viking) trade routes

- - - → Varangian raids on Constantinople, 907, 944

→ Svyatoslav's campaigns, 964-71

→ Pecheneg raids

Arctic
Ocean

1 Kievan Russia, 964–1242

— Kievan Russia, 1054   → campaigns of Svyatoslav, 964–71

Yatvagi tribes of the East Slavs   - - - waterway trade routes

MARI other peoples   ∿∿∿ defensive works built against nomads

→ movements of steppe nomads in the 11th century   ♔ Russian principalities, c.1200

White Sea

Pechora

Mezen

Pinega

SAMOYED

Northern Dvina

40°

Onega

NOVGOROD EMPIRE

CHUD

Vychegda

PERM

YUGRA

L. Onega

Beloozero

Sukhona

VYATKA TERRITORY

60°

Baltic Sea

20°

KARELA

L. Ladoga

Gulf of Finland

Storoyn Ladoga

Neva

Volkhov

Ves

Kama

MARI

ESTS

Vod

Ilmen

L. Peipus

Yuriev

Gulf of Riga

Riga

KURS

LIVONIAN ORDER

Izborsk

Pskov

Western Dvina

Slavs

Novgorod

L. Ilmen

Torzhok

Lovat

Tver

Toropets

VLADIMIR -SUZDAL

Pereyaslavl

Dmitrov

Rostov

Yaroslavl

Kostroma

Galich

Nizhniy Novgorod

ZHMUD

Kukeynoys

Gertsike

Polochanye

Polotsk

Vitebsk

K r i v i c h i

SMOLENSK

Smolensk

Golyad

Moscow

Moskva

Moskva

Kliazma

Suzdal

Vladimir

Murom

Muroma

Merya

Bolgar

966

Bilyar

TEUTONIC ORDER

LITVA

POLOTSK

Gorodno

Minsk

Orsha

Kopys

Oka

Koselsk

Vyatichi

Meshchera

MORDVA

VOLGA BULGARIA

Suvar

Yatvagi

Nesvizh

Klechesk

Rechitsa

Radimichi

1024✕

CHERNIGOV

Bryansk

Karachev

Novosil

MUROM -RYAZAN

Kolomna

Ryazan

Berestye

Drogochin

TUROV -PINSK

Pinsk

Turov

Listem

Lyubech

NOVGOROD -SEVERSK

Novgorod-Severskiy

Kursk

Ural

VLADIMIR-VOLYNSK

Volynyane

Kholm

Vladimir

Cherven

Belz

Drevlyane

Vruchy

Korosten

Desna

Chernigov

Rylsk

Gorodets

Severyane

Ros

1036✕

KIEV

Kiev

Polyane

Rodiya

Pereyaslavl

PEREYASLAV

Donets

Don

POLOVTSY (in 1054)

emyshl

Terebovl

Galich

Kamenets

Poltava

TORKI

966

Przemyshl

GALICH

Kolomyya

Tivertsy

965

Donets

Volga

SAKSINY

Khorvaty

Peresechen

Prut

Bug

PECHENEGS

P O L O V T S Y

965✕

Sarkel

ARIAN GDOM

Carpathian Mts

Dniester

Belgorod

Oleshe

Dnieper

KHAZARS

50°

Itil

Caspian Sea

Pereslavets

Dorostol

971✕

970

GARIA

Khersones (Korsun)

Sugdeya

Tmutarakan

Sea of Azov

Black Sea

30°

KASOGI

YASI

Tuban

966-7

Kuma

40°

50°

Trade and empire in Africa

By the end of the first millennium AD great changes had taken place in Africa. The rise of a culture based on iron-working (page 26) led to the appearance of extensive states and empires based on trade. In the south, Zimbabwe, with its monumental stone buildings, exported gold and copper via the port of Sofala; in the west, the Kongo state carried on an important trade. Further north, Arab traders developed the trans-Saharan trade routes and so assisted the growth of major sub-Saharan states. Although Ghana rose to prominence before the Islamic era, its successors, Mali and Songhay, owed much of their wealth and culture – described in glowing terms by Arab travellers – to the impact of Islam. So did the Kanem-Bornu empire around Lake Chad and the Hausa city-states. In the east Arab merchant colonies also spread down the Swahili coast as far as Kilwa and Sofala, bringing this part of Africa into an Indian Ocean trading complex. The staple exports in all cases were gold, ivory and slaves (map 1).

The arrival of the Portuguese in the 15th century at first made little impact on Africa. Their immediate object was to share directly in the gold trade, previously dominated by Muslim middlemen; the slave trade remained a secondary interest. However, with the development of labour-intensive sugar-plantations in the Americas (page 86), the slave trade attracted others. By the 18th century, nine European states maintained almost 50 fortified trading posts on the west coast, from Arguim to Lagos, to handle this burgeoning commerce, while the Portuguese continued to export slaves further south from Angola and Mozambique. Of some 15 million Africans shipped abroad by Europeans between 1450 and 1870, almost 90 per cent went to South America and the Caribbean, most of them during the 18th century. Muslim traders exported perhaps as many more again northward across the Sahara and from the Swahili coast. The effects on Africa of this appalling trade in human beings are impossible to quantify, not least because the loss of population was not evenly divided. Some states, such as Kongo and Lunda, suffered disproportionately, while others seem to have profited. Thus, after the destruction of the powerful Songhay empire by Moroccan troops in 1591, the forest states of Asante, Dahomey and Benin, having direct access to the Atlantic and thus to European slave-traders, increased in importance and political power (map 2).

1 The emergence of states, 1000–1500

- Islamic states or influence, 1000
- Christian states, 1000
- other states, 1000
- new states by 1300
- - - - - limit of Islamized areas, 1500
- ——— Christian Ethiopia, 1500
- new states by 1500
- IFAT states that disappeared by 1500
- major gold producing region
- ■ Muslim settlement
- ◪ gold
- M musk
- ◡ slaves
- ◣ bananas
- rice
- cattle
- C copper
- ▭ salt
- ∅ millet
- ♜ ivory

Apart from the Portuguese in Angola and Mozambique, and the fortified posts along the west coast, only the Dutch attempted to create a European colony in Africa before 1800: in the far south, around Cape Town. In the north-east, Islam continued to spread, but the Christian kingdom of Ethiopia still held its own. In the north, the Ottoman empire (page 70) maintained only nominal suzerainty over the states from Morocco to Egypt. In 1800, almost all of Africa thus remained independent of foreign control: a world unto itself, the 'dark continent'. However, precisely because of its autonomy, it would lack the ability to compete with the technological dynamism of the West in the 19th century (page 110).

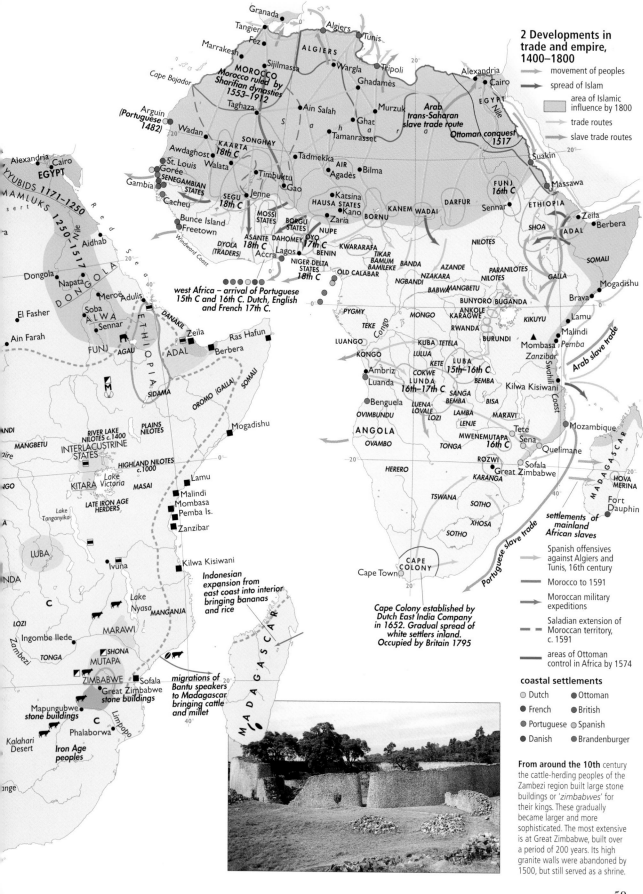

2 Developments in trade and empire, 1400–1800

→ movement of peoples
→ spread of Islam
area of Islamic influence by 1800
→ trade routes
→ slave trade routes

Granada · Tangier · Algiers · Tunis
Marrakesh · Fez · Sijilmassa
ALGIERS
MOROCCO
Morocco ruled by Sharifian dynasties 1553–1912
Cape Bojador
Arguin (Portuguese 1482)
Taghaza
Wadan · Ain Salah
Awdaghost · Tadmekka · Ghat · Murzuk
KAARTA 18th C · AIR · Agadès · Bilma
St. Louis · Walata · Timbuktu
Gorée · SONGHAY · Gao
SENEGAMBIAN STATES
Gambia · SEGU 18th C · Jenne
Cacheu · HAUSA STATES · Katsina · Kano
Bunce Island · MOSSI STATES · Zaria
Freetown · BORGU STATES · KANEM WADAI
ASANTE 18th C · DAHOMEY · OYO 17th C · NUPE · BORNU · DARFUR
DYOLA (TRADERS) · BENIN · KWARARAFA
Accra · Lagos · NIGER DELTA STATES 18th C
TIKAR · BAMUM · BAMILEKE · BANDA · AZANDE
OLD CALABAR · NGBANDI · NZAKARA · MANGBETU
Windward Coast
west Africa – arrival of Portuguese 15th C and 16th C. Dutch, English and French 17th C.

Ghadamès · Tripoli · Alexandria · Cairo
Wargla · EGYPT · Nile
Arab trans-Saharan slave trade route
Ottoman conquest 1517
Tamanrasset
Suakin · Massawa
FUNJ 16th C
Sennar · ETHIOPIA · Zeila · Berbera
SHOA · ADAL
NILOTES · SOMALI
Mogadishu · Brava · Lamu · Malindi · Pemba
BUNYORO BUGANDA · PARANILOTES NILOTES · GALLA
PYGMY · MONGO · ANKOLE KARAGWE · KIKUYU
TEKE · Congo · RWANDA · BURUNDI
LUANGO · KUBA TETELA · Mombasa · Zanzibar
KONGO · LULUA · KETE · LUBA 15th–16th C
Ambriz · COKWE · LUNDA 16th–17th C · SANGA BEMBA · BISA · Kilwa Kisiwani
Luanda · LUENA-LOVALE · LOZI · LAMBA · LENJE · MARAVI
Benguela · OVIMBUNDU · Swahili Coast
Arab slave trade
ANGOLA · OVAMBO · TONGA · MWENEMUTAPA 16th C · Tete · Sena · Mozambique
HERERO · ROZWI · Quelimane
KARANGA · Great Zimbabwe · Sofala
TSWANA · MADAGASCAR · HOVA MERINA · Fort Dauphin
SOTHO · XHOSA
CAPE COLONY · Cape Town

EGYPT
AYYUBIDS 1171–1250
MAMLUKS 1250–1517
Alexandria · Cairo
Aidhab · Dongola · Napata · Meroe
DONGOLA · Red Sea
El Fasher · Soba · ALWA · Adulis
Ain Farah · Sennar · Zeila · Ras Hafun
FUNJ · AGAU · ADAL · Berbera
DANAKIL · ETHIOPIA · SOMALI
SIDAMA · OROMO (GALLA)
Mogadishu
RIVER LAKE NILOTES c.1400
MANGBETU · INTERLACUSTRINE STATES · PLAINS NILOTES
HIGHLAND NILOTES c.1000 · Lamu
KITARA · Lake Victoria · MASAI · Malindi · Mombasa · Pemba Is.
LATE IRON AGE HERDERS · Zanzibar
Lake Tanganyika
LUBA · Ivuna · Kilwa Kisiwani
LOZI · Lake Nyasa · MANGANJA
Indonesian expansion from east coast into interior bringing bananas and rice
MARAWI · Ingombe Ilede
Zambezi · TONGA · SHONA · MUTAPA
ZIMBABWE · Sofala · **Great Zimbabwe stone buildings**
Mapungubwe **stone buildings**
Phalaborwa · Limpopo
Kalahari Desert · **Iron Age peoples**
migrations of Bantu speakers to Madagascar bringing cattle and millet
MADAGASCAR

Cape Colony established by Dutch East India Company in 1652. Gradual spread of white settlers inland. Occupied by Britain 1795

settlements of mainland African slaves

→ Spanish offensives against Algiers and Tunis, 16th century
— Morocco to 1591
→ Moroccan military expeditions
- - - Saladian extension of Moroccan territory, c. 1591
— areas of Ottoman control in Africa by 1574

Portuguese slave trade

coastal settlements
○ Dutch   ● Ottoman
● French   ● British
● Portuguese   ○ Spanish
● Danish   ● Brandenburger

From around the 10th century the cattle-herding peoples of the Zambezi region built large stone buildings or 'zimbabwes' for their kings. These gradually became larger and more sophisticated. The most extensive is at Great Zimbabwe, built over a period of 200 years. Its high granite walls were abandoned by 1500, but still served as a shrine.

59

The Mongol empire

The Mongols, a nomadic people from the grasslands of Central Asia, staged a sudden and devastating irruption into world history in the first half of the 13th century (map 1). Theirs was not the first empire of the steppe, however. In the 7th century AD, in the wake of the upheavals that destroyed the ancient world (page 40), a confederation of Turkish tribes had managed to dominate the plains of Asia from the Great Wall of China to the Black Sea; but by 750 their rule had collapsed and the area disintegrated into feud and faction. Thus it remained for four centuries, when a charismatic leader, Temujin (1167-1227), gained recognition as supreme ruler and in 1206 took the title Genghis Khan, 'prince of all that lies between the Oceans'. Under his leadership the Mongols first invaded the Chin empire in north China and then turned against the Islamic states to the west. By the time of Genghis's death, his empire stretched from the Pacific Ocean to the Caspian Sea. His successors continued the tide of destructive conquests: Kievan Russia (1237-40); the Abbasid Caliphate (1256-60); Sung China (1271-9). Europe and Japan were also threatened: one Mongol army reached the gates of Vienna while another defeated a German-Polish army at Liegnitz in 1241; two amphibious expeditions unsuccessfully attacked Japan in 1274 and 1281.

However the vast empire lacked coherence and stability, and the Mongols failed to develop appropriate institutions. On hearing of the death of Genghis's successor Ogedei in 1241, the victorious commander of the Mongol forces in Europe withdrew eastwards with his army, in order to take part in choosing a successor. They never returned. Likewise in 1260, on

Mongol brutality in war did not end with Genghis Khan. In this late-16th century Mughal miniature *(right)*, the troops of Tamerlane are shown demolishing the fort of Mikrit in the Hindu Kush, and using the defenders' heads to erect a tower of skulls.

2 The conquests of Tamerlane, c. 1360–1405

1 The Mongol empire

— the Mongol empire by 1259
→ campaigns under Genghis Khan
→ campaigns of his successors
▨ Mongol incursions and limited Mongol control
OIROTS Mongol tribes around 1220
— empire of Kublai Khan, 1260–94
CUMANS other peoples

unsuccessful expedition to Java 1292–3

hearing of the death of Ogedei's successor, the victorious commander of the Mongol forces in the Near East decided to return to the Mongol heartland, leaving only a skeleton force behind him. This soon became known in Cairo, and the Sultan of Egypt marched to the defence of Islam, still reeling from the sack of Baghdad, the capital of the Caliphs, two years before. At Ain Jalut on 3 September 1260 the Mongols suffered a defeat and withdrew to Persia.

The Mongol empire now fragmented. The title of Great Khan went to Kublai who, although never forgetting that he was the grandson of Genghis, spent most of his long reign (1260-94) seeking to reunify China and conquer Japan. The other Mongol states – the Golden Horde in the west; the Il-Khans in Persia; the Chagatai empire in the traditional Mongol heartland – went their own way.

Despite the widespread destruction of the Mongol onslaught, their temporary unification of Eurasia permitted the exchange of goods and ideas between the far east and the far west on an unprecedented scale.

For over a century the 'Silk Road' of ancient times revived: silver and gold from Europe and the Near East reached China while Chinese silks and porcelain circulated in Europe. But the Black Death (see page 66) and the rise of Timur, or Tamerlane, (1336-1405) changed all that, for he destroyed the Chagatai khanate, dislocated the Golden Horde, defeated the Ottoman empire at the battle of Ankara in 1402 (page 70), and initiated a policy of religious intolerance. However Timur died in 1405 before he had created the institutions and traditions required to ensure the survival of his vast empire (map 2). Instead, Mongol power in the west steadily lost ground to Russia (see page 84), and crumbled in China with the rise of the Ming dynasty (see page 94). Mongolia itself came under Chinese dominion in 1696.

The Muslim empires of India and Persia

Delhi, founded in the 8th century by a Rajput chief, remained the focus of north Indian politics and also the centre of Muslim culture from the 13th to the 19th century. It served as the capital of the six Muslim dynasties, all of Turkish or Afghan extraction, who sought (unsuccessfully) to extend their rule into the Deccan between 1206 and 1526; and, after the defeat of the last of the Sultans of Delhi at Panipat (1526) by Babur – a descendant of Timur (page 60) – it became the headquarters of his descendants, the Mughals.

Babur's grandson, Akbar (1556-1605), extended the frontiers of the empire to Bengal in the east, to Gujerat and the river Godavari in the south, and to Kashmir in the north. New territories were added under Akbar's grandson, Shahjahan (1627-56) and his son Aurangzeb (1656-1707), who annexed Bijapur and Golconda in the south, and Orissa in the east. However, these achievements depended absolutely upon the acquiescence of the 150 million or so Hindu peasant farmers and petty landlords who paid the taxes that supported the Mughals' 4 million warriors, and the court grandees who commanded them. It was a delicate balance, for if the peasants and landlords were overtaxed, they would revolt; and if the grandees were not rewarded with office and wealth they would desert the court. Around 1700 the Hindu Marathas began to ravage southern regions, while some Rajput states and the Sikhs rebelled. All this reduced tax yields, and after the death of Aurangzeb several frontier provinces split off from the empire (page 96).

Meanwhile, to the West, after 1500 the leader of a fanatical sect of Shi'a Muslims, Ismail Safavi, re-unified Persia – which had been in a state of chaos since Timur's invasions – and proclaimed himself Shah. However the Sunnite Ottomans under Selim I (page 70) invaded in 1514, defeated Ismail at the battle of Chaldiran and captured Tabriz, thus initiating a duel between the two powers that lasted for over a century. The conflict centred around the key cities of Mesopotamia, and Baghdad, Tiflis, Derbend and Basra changed hands repeatedly; but its intensity stemmed from the religious division within Islam between Sunnite and Shi'ite (page 50), which excited the same passions as the split between Protestant

and Catholic Christians at the same time. Eventually Shah Abbas (1587-1629), with assistance from both Russia and the Christian West, managed to regain most of the lost territories; but the Turks recaptured much of Mesopotamia in the 1630s.

Both empires boasted a rich civilization. Akbar and Abbas each built luxurious new capital cities – at Fatehpur Sikri and Isfahan respectively – and attracted to their courts local and foreign writers, artists and craftsmen. Shahjahan built the magnificent Taj Mahal outside Delhi. Nevertheless, two developments threatened these achievements. On the one hand, as in all autocracies, government authority could suddenly collapse under a weak ruler. Thus in 1739 Nadir Shah, who had usurped the Persian throne three years previously, invaded India and sacked Delhi, leaving the Mughal empire fatally weakened; but in 1747 Nadir was assassinated and Persia too suffered a period of anarchy. On the other

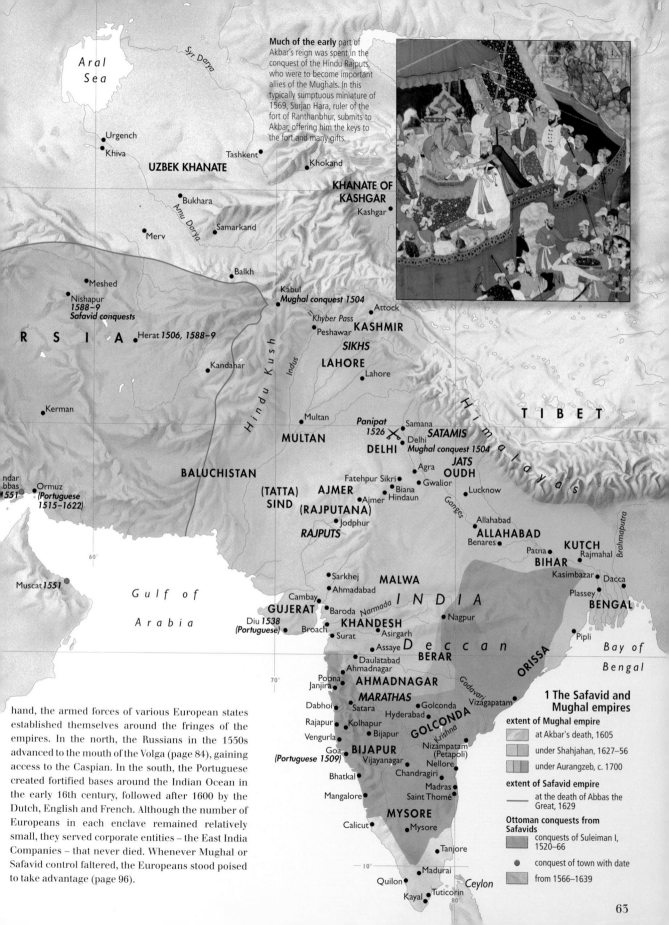

Aral
Sea

Syr Darya

Urgench
Khiva
Tashkent
Khokand

UZBEK KHANATE

**KHANATE OF
KASHGAR**

Amu Darya

Bukhara
Merv
Samarkand

Kashgar

Balkh

Much of the early part of
Akbar's reign was spent in the
conquest of the Hindu Rajputs,
who were to become important
allies of the Mughals. In this
typically sumptuous miniature of
1569, Surjan Hara, ruler of the
fort of Ranthanbhur, submits to
Akbar, offering him the keys to
the fort and many gifts.

Meshed
*Nishapur
1588–9
Safavid conquests*

Kabul
Mughal conquest 1504
Attock

Khyber Pass
Peshawar

KASHMIR

SIKHS

LAHORE

R   S   I   A   *Herat 1506, 1588–9*

Kandahar

Lahore

T I B E T

Kerman

Hindu Kush

Indus

Multan

MULTAN

*Panipat
1526*
Samana
Delhi
DELHI
Mughal conquest 1504

SATAMIS

Himalayas

BALUCHISTAN

**(TATTA)
SIND**

AJMER
(RAJPUTANA)

Fatehpur Sikri
Biana
Ajmer   Hindaun

Agra
Gwalior

**JATS
OUDH**

Lucknow

Ganges

ndar
bbas
551
Ormuz
*(Portuguese
1515–1622)*

Jodhpur

RAJPUTS

Allahabad
Benares
ALLAHABAD

Patna
BIHAR
Rajmahal

KUTCH

Brahmaputra

Muscat *1551*

G u l f   o f

A r a b i a

Sarkhej
Ahmadabad
Cambay
GUJERAT
Baroda   Narmada
Diu *1538*
(Portuguese)   Broach

MALWA

Kasimbazar   Dacca
Plassey
BENGAL

I N D I A

Nagpur

Pipli

KHANDESH
Asirgarh
Surat
Assaye

D e c c a n

*Bay of
Bengal*

BERAR

Daulatabad
Ahmadnagar
Poona
Janjira
AHMADNAGAR

MARATHAS

Dabhoi
Satara
Rajapur
Kolhapur
Vengurla   Bijapur
Goa
(Portuguese 1509)
BIJAPUR
Bhatkal
Vijayanagar

Golconda
Hyderabad
GOLCONDA
Krishna

Godavari
Vizagapatam

ORISSA

Nizampatam
(Petapoli)
Nellore
Chandragiri
Madras
Saint Thomé

Mangalore
MYSORE

Calicut   Mysore

Tanjore

Madurai
Quilon   Kayal   Tuticorin   *Ceylon*

hand, the armed forces of various European states
established themselves around the fringes of the
empires. In the north, the Russians in the 1550s
advanced to the mouth of the Volga (page 84), gaining
access to the Caspian. In the south, the Portuguese
created fortified bases around the Indian Ocean in
the early 16th century, followed after 1600 by the
Dutch, English and French. Although the number of
Europeans in each enclave remained relatively
small, they served corporate entities – the East India
Companies – that never died. Whenever Mughal or
Safavid control faltered, the Europeans stood poised
to take advantage (page 96).

**1 The Safavid and
Mughal empires**

extent of Mughal empire

at Akbar's death, 1605

under Shahjahan, 1627–56

under Aurangzeb, c. 1700

extent of Safavid empire

at the death of Abbas the
Great, 1629

**Ottoman conquests from
Safavids**

conquests of Suleiman I,
1520–66

conquest of town with date

from 1566–1639

South East Asia

Situated at one of the world's main cross-roads, civilization developed early in South-East Asia: traces of 'Java man' date from the middle Pleistocene and remains of *homo sapiens* from c. 40,000 BC; rice cultivation in South China began about 6000 BC and bronze working in Thailand and Vietnam in 1500 BC or earlier (pages 12 and 18). Early trade routes linked India with ports along the coasts of Burma, Thailand, Cambodia and Vietnam; Hindu-Buddhist influences from India reached the area around the 2nd or 3rd century AD; and by the 5th century Buddhist images and votive tablets appeared, along with Sanskrit inscriptions. These influences never obliterated the unique character of South-East Asian civilization; instead, the next thousand years saw their assimilation to produce distinctive societies in the area. The culture of Java and southern Sumatra likewise became Indianized, but these areas also developed commercial and political links with China, which welcomed tribute missions from a growing number of states. From the 8th century temple complexes, each combining Hindu and Buddhist influences, evolved in four main areas: central Java (notably at Borobudur and Prambanan, from the 8th to 10th centuries), Cambodia (especially at Angkor, from the 9th to 13th centuries), Burma (Pagan, from the 11th to 13th centuries) and, associated with the Hindu-Buddhist

kingdom of Champa, along the coast of central Vietnam. Meanwhile Palembang (a centre of Sanskrit culture from perhaps as early as the 7th century) emerged as the capital of the maritime empire of Srivijaya, which for centuries controlled international trade passing through the straits of Malacca and Sunda, and across the Isthmus of Kra (map 1).

The great temple-states fell into decline after the 12th century. In Java, the area of Prambanan was superseded in importance by eastern Java, where three states developed in succession: Kediri (12th century), Singhasari (13th century) and finally Majapahit (late 13th-early 16th century). On the mainland, first Mongols and then Shans sacked Pagan in the 13th century, while Angkor fell to Thai attacks after 1369. Sukothai, the first of the lowland Thai cities, was itself in decline by the late 14th century. New political centres replaced the old temple cities: in Burma, Toungoo (1347), Ava (1364), and Pegu (1369), capital of a new Mon kingdom in the south; in Thailand, Chieng Mai (1296) and Ayutthaya (1350); in Cambodia, Phnom Penh and other cities along the Mekong; in Laos, Luang Prabang (1353). All were Theravada Buddhist in the Sinhalese tradition, with stupas rather than temples. Meanwhile, in Vietnam, after the failure of Chinese attempts at reconquest (despite invasions in 1075-7 and 1285-8) a

2 Cultural divisions southeast Asia, 1500
distribution of major religions:

- Theravada Buddhism
- Mahayana Buddhism mixed with Confucianism and Taoism
- Hindu-Buddhism
- Islamic states
- places sending tribute to China between 1370 and 1440

KINGDOM OF PAGAN 11th–16th centuries

Halin
Ava
Pagan
eikthano
ri Ksetra

PYU KINGDOM

Toungoo
Pegu
Thaton

LAO KINGDOMS

Luang Prabang

Chieng Mai

VIETNAM from 1471

KINGDOM OF SUKHOTHAI

Sukhothai
Si Thep
Phimai

Mi Son
Dong Duong
Tra Kieu

Vijaya

MON KINGDOMS 8th–17th centuries

U-Thong
Nakhon Pathom
Ku Bua

Ayutthaya
Tonle Sap
(Great Lake)

Angkor
Preah Khan

CHAMPA PRINCIPALITIES 4th–15th centuries

Po Nagar (Nha Trang)

KINGDOM OF AYUTTHAYA

KHMER KINGDOM 7th–15th centuries

Phnom Penh

Po Klaung Gerai

Chaiya

Angkor Borei
Mekong
Oc Eo

Takuapa
Ko Kho Khao

Ligor

South China Sea

Manila

Philippines

Aceh

JOLO SULTANATE from 14th century

Celebes Sea

Straits of Malacca

Malacca

Sumatra

Borneo

Ternate
Tidore

SULTANATES OF TERNATE AND TIDORE from 14th century

SRI VIJAYA 7th–13th centuries

Sri Vijaya

Celebes

Java Sea

MAJAPAHIT EMPIRE 14th–16th centuries

Straits of Sunda

Dieng Plateau
Borobudur
Prambanan

Trowulan
Singhasari
Kediri

SALENDRA KINGDOM 8th–10th centuries

Java

1 Southeast Asia, AD 300–1511

● towns with inscriptions and monumental religious buildings

⚓ trading ports, no monumental buildings known

🏛 temples with inscriptions

new kingdom, called Dai Viet, emerged and gradually absorbed Champa (annexing its capital, Vijaya, in 1471). Further south, Srivijaya declined and a powerful new Muslim state developed after 1400 at Malacca, commanding the narrow straits through which most east-west trade passed. By that time the east Javanese empire of Majapahit was in decline, and the west Javanese kingdom of Pajajaran also collapsed before Muslim pressure from the north-ern coastal ports in the early 16th century.

Islam had began to influence northern Sumatra just before 1300; now it spread further, often under Malaccan influence, to the north Javanese trading ports, the Spice Islands, Borneo and, in the 16th century, the Philippines (map 2). When the Spaniards arrived, Mindanao had already been converted and the spread of Islam in Luzon was only halted by the Spaniards' capture of the Muslim fort at Manila in 1571 and their determined promotion of Christianity (page 80).

Meanwhile, in Vietnam, Confucian scholarship strengthened, despite the failure of another attempt at reconquest under the Ming; and all over South-East Asia the series of voyages made by the Muslim admi-ral Cheng Ho in the early 15th century revived and reinforced China's system of tributary relationships

(page 74). From the 1430s, however, China abandoned its interest in the wider world and South-East Asia began to assume its modern pattern of cultures and polities which even the arrival of the Europeans, starting with the Portuguese capture of Malacca in 1511 (page 80) influenced little until the 19th century.

Prambanan was built in the mid-9th century and was the largest and most ambitious temple complex ever constructed in central Java. There are three main temples dedicated to the gods of the Trimurti: Shiva in the centre; Vishnu on the north side; and Brahma on the south.

Europe

TIMELINE

1250
Death of Frederick II of Hohenstaufen leads to fragmentation of Italy and Germany

1315-17
Great Famine in northern Europe

1337-1453
Hundred Years' War between England and France

1346-51
The Black Death

1358
French peasant revolt (Jacquerie)

1378
Rebellion of Florentine clothworkers (ciompi)

1381
Peasants' Revolt, England

1386
Union of Poland and Lithuania

1397
Union of Kalmar brings together Scandinavian kingdoms

The 14th century brought to an end the rise and consolidation of national monarchies in western Europe (page 54). Though growth in population and productivity was steady until the later 13th century, both began to decline thereafter. Part of the problem lay in a sudden climatic deterioration which terminated the agricultural boom that had prevailed since 1150: crop yields fell and marginal areas brought into cultivation were abandoned. In 1315-17 Europe experienced the first of many famines; and the weakening of human powers of resistance through inadequate nourishment may have accelerated the spread of the 'Black Death', or bubonic plague, which killed perhaps 20 million Europeans between 1346 and 1353, wiping out in some areas as much as a third of the population within two years (map 1).

However, the impact of the plague was not even. Some areas escaped altogether, and Eastern Europe seems to have suffered relatively little: Bohemia under Charles IV (1333-78), Poland under Casimir III (1339-70) and Hungary under Louis the Great (1342-82) all made rapid strides – aided in part by skillful exploitation of their natural resources, such as the silver mines of Kutna Hora in Bohemia. Above all, in the wake of the Mongol invasions (page 60) Lithuania expanded into the former heartland of Kievan Russia and united in 1386 with Poland to form the largest state in Eastern Europe (map 2).

1 Famine, plague and popular unrest

—— main sea-trade routes

`wine` important commodities

extent of the spread of the Black Death

1346	end 1349
1347	1350
mid-1348	c. 1351
end 1348	c. 1353
mid-1349	little or no plague mortality

social unrest

areas of disturbance during Peasants' Revolt in England, 1381

● centre of urban revolt

rural uprisings

⊗ defeat of lower orders in battle

religious unrest

spread of Lollardy in England to death of Richard II, 1399

area of Hussite influence

■ Hussite centre

2 Eastern Europe, 1278–1389

growth of Lithuania, 1300-1377:

to 1300

under Gedymin, 1316–41

under Olgierd, 1345–77

under Jagiello and Witold from 1377

Poland-Lithuania after union of 1386

Habsburg lands

Bohemian lands

Map labels: SWEDEN, Baltic Sea, HOLSTEIN, Hamburg, Lübeck, POMERANIA, Danzig, Königsberg, POMERELIA, BRANDENBURG 1373, LUSATIA 1368, MEISSEN, Gniezno, Torún(Thorn), Poznań, POLAND, Breslau, SILESIA 1368, KINGDOM OF BOHEMIA, Prague, Kutna Hora, Lublin, MORAVIA, Brünn, UPPER PALATINATE 1359, AUSTRIA 1282, Vienna, STYRIA 1282, CARINTHIA 1335, Graz, Pest, CARNIOLA 1335, Trieste, Venice, REPUBLIC OF VENICE, Fiume, SLAVONIA, CROATIA, Pécs, Danube, KINGDOM OF HUNGARY, Belgrade, Smederevo, WALLACHIA, BOSNIA, Kosovo X 1389, Durazzo, Üsküb (Skoplje), SERBIAN EMPIRE under Stephen Dushan, BULGARIA, BYZANTINE EMPIRE, Hungarian Rule 1328; independent from 1353, TEUTONIC ORDER, LIVONIA, NOVGOROD, SAMOGITIA to Lithuania 1422, Polotsk, Vitebsk, SMOLENSK, Vyazma, Smolensk, Vilna, Minsk, Novogrudok, LITHUANIA, Bryansk, Kursk, Pripet, Chernigov, Kiev, Sandomierz, Lwów (Lvov), VOLHYNIA, Cracow, RUTHENIA Halicz, to Poland 1366, PODOLIA, Dnieper, KHANATE OF THE GOLDEN HORDE, MOLDAVIA, Hungarian suzerainty until 1365; independent until 1397; then under temporary Lithuanian control, under Hungary to 1369; Ottoman Tributary from 1389, Carpathian Mts.

Inset map labels: Santiago, Santander, iron, Léon, PORTUGAL, Lisbon, Tagus, wool, CASTILE, cattle, Córdoba, Seville, Cádiz, Granada, dried fruits, Ceuta, Toledo, 40

Shetlands

Orkneys

SCOTLAND

Edinburgh

Armagh

York
Chester Lincoln
Wexford

Newcastle

ENGLAND

wool

WALES

Bristol

London

Winchester

Bury St Edmunds

Roosebeke
1382
Bruges
Ypres
Ghent
FLANDERS
Crécy
Liège
Cologne

NORWAY

Bergen *cattle*

Oslo

Uppsala

Stockholm

SWEDEN

North
Sea

fish

DENMARK

Copenhagen

Visby

Riga
amber
ORDER

furs

Baltic Sea

Lübeck
Hamburg
Bremen
HOLLAND *cattle*
FRIESLAND
Amsterdam
SAXONY
BRANDENBURG
POMERANIA

Danzig
Königsberg
TEUTONIC

LITHUANIA

rye

Warsaw

POLAND

Kiev

Cracow

UKRAINE

wheat

Lynn
Norwich

Rhine

Brunswick

HOLY

Elbe
SILESIA
Oder

Mello 1358
Meaux 1358
Rouen
Amiens
Rheims
Paris
Troyes
Orléans
Mainz
FRANCONIA
Frankfurt
Trier
ROMAN

Prague
BOHEMIA
Tabor
MORAVIA
Regensburg

salt
wine

FRANCE

Loire

Poitiers

LORRAINE
SWABIA
Basle
Augsburg
BAVARIA
Salzburg
AUSTRIA
Passau
Vienna

metals

Buda Pest

HUNGARY

wheat

wheat
Caffa

BRITTANY

Crécy

BURGUNDY

SWISS
CONFED.
Geneva
Lyons
SAVOY
ALPS
DAUPHINÉ

EMPIRE

metals

CARINTHIA
Trieste

Venice

Danube

Turin
Milan

Belgrade
WALLACHIA
Bucharest
wheat
Danube

Black Sea

Bordeaux
ENGLISH
GASCONY
AQUITAINE
wine
Cahors
Toulouse
wool

PROVENCE
wheat
Marseilles

Genoa

Ravenna
Pisa
Florence
Siena
Ancona
saffron
PAPAL
STATES
Rome

REPUBLIC OF VENICE

BOSNIA
silver
SERBIAN
PRINCES
Ragusa
PRINCIPALITY OF ALBANIA

Adrianople

Constantinople

BULGARIA

Saragossa
CATALONIA
ARAGON
Barcelona

Corsica

Valencia

salt

Majorca City

Sardinia
Cagliari
salt

Alghero
wheat

KINGDOM
wool
OF
NAPLES
Naples
Amalfi
Bari

Salonica

OTTOMAN TURKS

alum

Algiers
Bougie

Mediterranean

Palermo
Messina
wheat
KINGDOM
OF
SICILY

*dried
fruits*
DUCHY
OF
ATHENS
Athens

Tunis

Sea

ACHAEA

Crete

Rhodes

Cyprus

Unlike famine, plague affected every social class, and the psychological impact was profound. Until the mid-17th century, scarcely a decade passed without a recurrent outbreak. The disease, spread by infected fleas carried by rats, was particularly virulent, and few who caught it ever recovered. This illustration *(left)* from the Stiny Codex shows death strangling a plague victim.

But elsewhere the setback proved more serious. All the western states had overextended themselves financially, and the economic and demographic crisis exacerbated by the Black Death – combined with the tensions caused by the fragmentation of Italy and Germany after the end of Hohenstaufen rule in 1250 (page 55) or the Hundred Years' War between England and France – produced a series of popular uprisings in both cities and the countryside: the Jacquerie (1358) in France; the Peasants' Revolt (1381) in England; urban insurrections in Spain, Italy and the Low Countries. Few rebellions achieved their aims, but they all weakened state power even further.

China and Japan

The Mongol invasion of China caused immense destruction. During the conquest of the north (1211-34: page 60) much of the land went out of cultivation, many cities and industries perished, and countless people died or became slaves. The conquest of the south (1271-9) brought similar hardships, and Mongol rule proved harsh. Popular resentment erupted in a wave of popular uprisings after 1335, exacerbated by disastrous floods in coastal regions in the 1350s. One of the rebel leaders, Chu Yüan-chang, gradually overcame his rivals and in 1368 established a new dynasty, the Ming.

The Ming rebuilt irrigation and drainage works in great numbers, reforested on a grand scale, and moved vast numbers of people to repopulate the devastated north. New crops were introduced and the canal system extended to transport produce: by 1421 the 'Grand Canal' stretched from Hang-chou to just south of Peking and carried some 200,000 tons of grain northwards every year. Thanks to these measures, the Chinese population rose from some 60 million in 1393 (40 per cent fewer than a century before) to about 130 million by 1580. The great cities of the Yangtze delta became major industrial centres, particularly for textiles, while the southern ports fitted out the enormous fleets sent by Chu's son, the Yung-lo emperor (1402-24), to the South China Sea and the Indian Ocean (page 74).

The Ming entrusted control over the vast population to a gentry class of degree-holders, who had passed through the examination system and shared the values of the bureaucracy without actually holding office. But the system discouraged innovation and was overcentralized, with all major decisions dependent upon the emperor; and few of Yung-lo's successors possessed the dedication necessary for such heavy responsibilities. Nevertheless, the early Ming engaged in an aggressive foreign policy. They restored Korea to vassal status in 1392, occupied Annam from 1407 to 1427, and invaded Mongolia (map 1). However, after a northern campaign in 1449 resulted in the capture of the emperor, the Ming reverted to a defensive strategy, strengthening the Great Wall until it ran for almost 2,500 miles, and increasing the garrisons in the north and north-west. China remained relatively stable for another century, but in the 1430s the government banned all overseas trade by sea, except under close supervision. Not surprisingly, by 1500 smuggling had become commonplace in the southeastern provinces and by 1550 heavily-armed bands of smugglers and pirates infested the seas around China and terrorized the coastal regions from their bases in Japan.

Central authority in Japan had collapsed in the 1330s and the country became plagued by local and provincial wars – almost continuously in the century after 1467. By about 1560, some nine leading families had formed alliances that covered most of the country, and competed openly for supreme power (map 2). In 1568 Nobunaga, leader of the Oda clan, captured Kyoto, the imperial capital, and by the time he was assassinated in 1582 by a jealous rival he had forced almost all the other lords to accept his orders. Within a decade, his ablest general Toyotomi Hideyoshi had completely reunified Japan, reorganizing the tax system and redistributing land to provide sufficient funds for his ambitious policies – including the invasion of Korea in the 1590s. After his death in 1598 another of Nobunaga's generals, Tokugawa Ieyasu, assumed power and in 1603 established the dynasty of shoguns who ruled Japan until the 19th century (page 88).

The Tokugawa put an end to the pirate problem, thus easing the pressure on the Chinese coast; but at just this time a new threat arose in the north-east, where the Manchu gradually expanded their power into the areas immediately to the north of the Great Wall and (in 1637) into Korea. Ming authority now

2 Civil War in Japan, 1467–1590

spheres of influence of the most powerful Daimyo clans

boundaries of Daimyo domains

Uesugi

Takeda

Hojo

Oda

Imagawa

Kyoto

Nara

Sea of Japan

Mori

Sogabe

Otomo

Shimazu

Pacific Ocean

1 Ming China

- ▬▬ major post roads
- — minor roads
- ⊓⊔⊓ Great Wall
- ═══ Grand Canal
- ⊡ national capital
- ⊙ provincial capitals
- ☐ the nine frontier defence areas
- ○ prefectures and regional military commissioners

- ◼ guard units
- ➡ attacks by pirates based in Japan before 1600
- ➡ Japanese invasions of Korea in 1590s

expeditions of Yung-lo against the Mongols:
- ⟶ 1st 1410
- – – ⟶ 2nd 1414
- –·–⟶ 3rd 1422
- ······⟶ 4th 1424

MONGOLIA

Onon Gol
1410
Tuul Gol
✕ *1414*
Kerulen
Dalai Nor
✕ *1422*
Buyr Nuur
✕ *1424*
✕ *1410*
✕ *1422*

Gobi Desert

KHALKHA

TUMET

MANCHUS

Shara Muren

The 'Willow Palisade' surrounding area of Chinese settlement in Liao-tung.

-chou

Kan-chou

CH'INGHAI

Liang-chou

Koko Nor

Hsi-ning

T'ao-chou

Lan-chou

P'ing-liang

Ku-yüan

Yen-an

Ning-hsia

Ling

Yü-lin

Sui-te

SHENSI

Yellow (Huang Ho)

Kuei-hua-ch'eng

Hsüan-fu

Ta-t'ung

Yü

Pao-an

PEI CHIH-LI

Chi-chou

Shen-yang

Chien-chou

Liao-tung

Chin-chou

KOREA

Ming counter-attacks to defend Korea, 1592, 1597–8

Sea of Japan

T'ai-yüan

I-chou

Peking ung-chou (Shun-t'ien-fu)

Pao-ting

Ho-chien

Ts'ang

Po Hai

Chin-chou

SHANSI

Lu-an

Chiang

Shun-te

Chao

Chen-ting

T'ai-an

Chi-nan

Lai-chou

Teng-chou

Ching-chou

Hai-ning

Feng-hsiang

Hsi-an

Fu

P'ing-yang

P'u

Ho-nan

K'ai-feng

Ju

Pu-chou

Yen-chou

Ts'ao

Ts'ao

SHANTUNG

Tung

Han-chung

Hsing-an

HONAN

Nan-yang

Kuei-te

Hsu

P'ei

NAN CHIH-LI

Japanese invasions of Korea under Toyotomi Hideyoshi, 1592, 1597–8

T'ung-ch'uan

Ch'eng-tu

ZECHWAN

Yangtze

Ch'ung-ch'ing

Ts'un-i

Kuei-yang

An-shun

KWEICHOW

Hsiang-yang

I-ling

Shih-chou

HUPEH

Ching-chou

Ch'ang-te

Chen-chou

Ch'ang-sha

HUKUANG

Wu-ch'ang

Yüeh-chou

Sui

Lu-chou

Feng-yang

Huai-an

Ch'u

Yang-chou

ANHWEI

Nanking (Ying-t'ien-fu)

Wu-hsi

Su-chou

Shang-hai

Sung-chiang

Hirado

Hakata

JAPAN

Botsu

An-ch'ing

Hsin-an

Hui-chou

Hang-chou

Shao-hsing

Ning-po

Chiu-chiang

Ching-te-chen

Jao-chou

Yen-chou

Chin-hua

Chü-chou

T'ai-chou

Nan-ch'ang

HUNAN

Lin-chiang

KIANGSI

Chi-angsi

Shao-wu

Chien-ning

Fu-ning

Wen-chou

Heng-chou

Ch'uan

Yung-ning

Yung-chou

Liu-chou

Kuei-lin

KWANGSI

Kuei-yang

Chao-ch'ing

Yung-an-chou

Wu-chou

Shao-chou

Lien

FUKIEN

Fu-chou

Ch'üan-chou

Chang-chou

Hsia-men

Ch'ao-chou

Nan-ning

Chiao-tu

Lien-chou

Lo ting-chou

Kuang-chou

KWANGTUNG

Macao (Ao-men)

Lei-chou

Ch'ing-hua

Hainan

Ryukyu Islands

T'ai-nan

M)

M)

Chu Yüan-chang (1328–98), founder of the Ming dynasty. In 1368 he proclaimed himself the founder of a new imperial dynasty, taking the title Hung-wu, meaning 'mightily martial'.

collapsed. After 1627 a wave of rebellions broke out in the wake of repeated crop failures in the north-west, and much of central and northern China soon came under rebel sway. In 1644, one of the rebel leaders captured Peking and the last Ming emperor committed suicide. Almost immediately the Manchus intervened, seized Peking, and began the conquest of China (page 94).

The Ottoman empire

The overthrow of the Abbasid Caliphate by the Mongols in 1256-60 (page 60) left the Muslim world in disarray for half a century. One of the centres of recovery lay in north-west Anatolia where, around 1300, a Turkish leader named Osman founded a state which became the core of the future Ottoman empire (map 1). The damage to the structure of the Byzantine empire caused by the Fourth Crusade in 1204 (page 48) facilitated the Ottomans' rapid advance in the 14th century. By 1354 the Turks had crossed the Dardanelles to Gallipoli, and their victories at Kosovo (1389) and Nicopolis (1396) left them masters of the Balkans. The invasion of Timur (page 61) and his destruction of the Turkish army at Ankara (1402) gave the hard-pressed Byzantine empire some respite, but the renewal of expansion under Murad II (1413-51) and Mohammed II (1451-81) sealed its fate. In 1453 Constantinople fell, and Mohammed went on to extend control over Moldavia, the Crimea and Trebizond, thereby turning the Black Sea into an Ottoman lake.

Selim I (1512-20) defeated the new Safavid rulers of Persia (page 62) and conquered the Mamlukes, and his son Suleiman the Magnificent (1520-66) annexed much of Hungary and besieged Vienna (1529), making the Ottoman empire one of the world's largest powers. It now extended over one million square miles, with some 14 million inhabitants; and its capital, Istanbul, had become the largest city in Europe with 500,000 inhabitants. Suleiman's son, Selim II managed to add Cyprus (1570-1) and Tunis (1574), although his fleet of galleys met with defeat at the hands of a Christian coalition at Lepanto (1571). However the wars of his successors against Persia (1578-90 and 1607-39) and against the Austrian Habsburgs (1593-1606) resulted in the loss of the Caucasus to the former and of annual tribute for Hungary from the latter.

The end of expansion, coupled with rapid price inflation (from 1584), a rising population and a static economy provoked a spate of popular and military uprisings between 1596 and 1610 in the Anatolian heartland of the empire (map 2). Nevertheless, Mesopotamia was regained from Persia in the 1630s and Crete conquered from the Venetians in the 1660s; and in 1683 a great army laid siege once more to Vienna. But it failed, and a Christian counter-attack drove the Turks out of Hungary by 1699 – although the Turks still remained a formidable power, controlling the entire Arab world east of Libya and most of the Balkans until the 19th century.

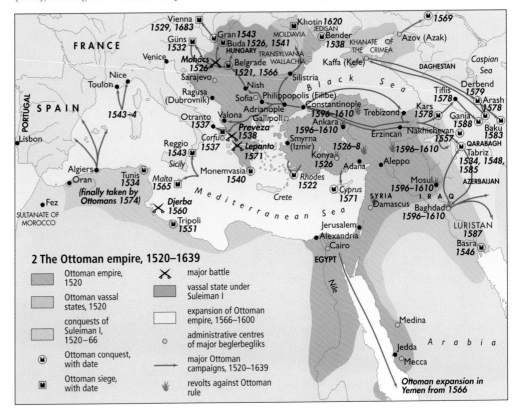

2 The Ottoman empire, 1520–1639

- Ottoman empire, 1520
- Ottoman vassal states, 1520
- conquests of Suleiman I, 1520–66
- ⦿ Ottoman conquest, with date
- ⦿ Ottoman siege, with date
- ✕ major battle
- vassal state under Suleiman I
- expansion of Ottoman empire, 1566–1600
- ○ administrative centres of major beglerbegliks
- → major Ottoman campaigns, 1520–1639
- ↡ revolts against Ottoman rule

Ottoman expansion in Yemen from 1566

TEUTONIC ORDER

LITHUANIA

HOLY ROMAN EMPIRE

POLAND

RUSSIA

Moscow

Danube

Cracow

Kiev

Dnieper

Vienna (Beç)

Buda

Suceava

Dniester

Cossack settlements

H U N G A R Y

Carpathian Mountains

Yaş (Jassy)

BOĞDAN (MOLDAVIA) 1455

Akkerman (1484)

KHANATE OF THE CRIMEA (vassal 1475)

Don

Sava

Zagreb

Danube

TRANSYLVANIA

BUJAK

Kilia

Sea of Azov

Azov

BOSNIA

Jajce 1463 1528

Bosna Saray (Sarajevo)

Belgrade

Semendire 1444

EFLĀK (WALLACHIA) 1396

Bükres (Bucharest)

Bakhchesaray (Bahçesaray)

Kerç

VENETIAN REPUBLIC

Vidin

Yergögü (Giurgiu)

Kefe (Caffa)

SERBIA 1389

Danube

ÇERKES (CIRCASSIA)

HERZEGOVINA (1463–83)

Kosovo 1389

Nish

DOBRUJA

Caucasus Mountains

Sea

Dubrovnik

REPUBLIC OF DUBROVNIK Ottoman vassal 1430–1804

Sofia

B U L G A R I A

Filibe (Philippopolis) 1393

Varna

Black Sea

Elbasan

Manastir (Bitolj)

Gelibolu (Gallipoli) 1354

Edirne (Adrianople) 1361

Kastamonu

Sinop

Samsun

Trabzon (Trebizond)

Tiflis

Otranto temporary Ottoman occupation 1480

Corfu

R O M

Selanik (Salonica) 1430

Constantinople 1453

CANDAR (KASTAMONU) 1393 1461

Amasya

1461 EMPIRE OF TREBIZOND

Yenisehir (Larissa)

A N

Bursa 1326

Ankara 1402

Cephalonia

Zante

Aegean Sea

KARASI 1345

Söğüt 1265

Eskişehir 1289

A N A T O L I A

SIVAS 1398

Otluk-Beli 1473

Negroponte (Euboea) 1470

Izmir (Smyrna)

SARUHAN 1390 1405

E M

Amasya

Erzurum

to Genoa

MOREA 1460

Athens

AYDIN 1390 1426

GERMIYAN 1380 1428

Kayseri

P I R E

Sivas

Modon (Ottoman 1500)

Naxos

HAMID 1381–90

MENTESE 1390 1426

KARAMAN 1390 1468

Konya

KARAKOYUNLU

KNIGHTS OF ST JOHN

Rhodes

TEKE 1391 1427

DHU'L-QADR 1398 1515

AKKOYUNLU

Lake Van

Crete

Adana

Çaldiran 1514

Diyarbakir

Cyprus (Venetian 1489, Ottoman tributary 1517)

Marj Dabiq 1516

Aleppo 1516

Raqqa

Tigris

Tabriz 1514

Lake Urmia

M A M L U K   E M P I R E

Tripoli

Beirut

Damascus 1516

Euphrates

Mosul

SAFAVID EMPIRE (from 1501)

Jerusalem

1 The rise of the Ottoman empire, 1301–1520

probable extent of Ottoman state, c. 1300

conquests of Osman, c. 1300–26

conquests of Orkhan, 1326–62

conquests of Murad I, 1362–89

TEKE 1390 — absorbed Emirates with date of first absorption

conquests of Bayezid, 1389–1402

✕ major battles

1398 dates of Ottoman control

Venetian territories, 1510

◉ successive centres of Ottoman state, with dates of conquest

reduced frontiers of Ottoman state after Tamerlane's invasion and civil war of 1403–13

Emirates restored by Tamerlane, 1402

1427 final reincorporation into Ottoman empire

boundary of Ottoman state at the accession of Mehmed II, 1451

vassal states, 1512

Ottoman empire, 1512

western frontiers of Safavid state, c. 1512 including tributary states

Ottoman sphere of influence, c. 1520

The fall of Constantinople, in 1453, came as no surprise to observers in the east. Sultan Mehmet II had managed to close the Bosphorus by building castles at its narrowest point; the city was now cut off from western naval assistance and from its traditional sources of food and supply. When the final siege began, on 6 April, there were only some 7000 Christian defenders facing and Ottoman army of more than 80,000. On 29 May a final assault took the city within a few hours.

71

Precolumbian America

Two major civilizations confronted the Spaniards when they arrived on the American mainland in the early 16th century: the Aztec Empire in Mexico, with a subject population of perhaps 12 million, and the Inca empire in Peru, ruling some 6 million. The rest of the continent remained sparsely inhabited – perhaps 1 million people lived north of the Rio Grande with another million in the rest of South America – divided among more than a thousand small tribal societies with distinct languages. Few regions, particularly in the north, had reached the stage of settled agriculture, despite some contacts in the north-east with Europeans around the year 1000 (map 1).

The Aztec and Inca Empires differed markedly in character, and no evidence exists of any contact between them. Like the Toltecs, who between 968 and about 1170 controlled much of the valley of Mexico from their capital at Tula, the Aztecs came from the north. In 1325 they arrived in the valley and settled on a group of islands in the swampy margins of Lake Texcoco, where they built their capital,

Tenochtitlán (site of Mexico City). Serving at first as mercenary warriors for neighbouring towns, by 1428 they had overthrown them all and, led by a priest-king and an hereditary warrior aristocracy, embarked upon an ambitious programme of conquest. When the Spaniards arrived in 1519, the Aztecs controlled the greater part of Mexico and had entered Maya territory in Yucatán (map 2).

The Inca formed one of the numerous tribes of Quechua stock inhabiting the central Andes, but until the accession of Pachacuti Inca in 1438 they played only a minor role. Within 45 years, however, Pachacuti's conquests extended Inca control from Lake Titicaca to Huánaco in the north, while his son Topa pushed north into Ecuador and south to Chile, and from the Pacific coast to the Upper Amazon. This created an empire 200 miles wide and 2500 miles long, held together by an impressive system of highways, post-stations and relay runners (map 3).

The Incas created a genuine imperial system, with an hereditary dynasty of absolute, 'divine' Incas, a Quechua aristocracy, and a highly trained bureaucracy. All land was state-owned, with a complex system of irrigation. The ordinary Inca subject spent 9 months working for the state, but in return received protection from

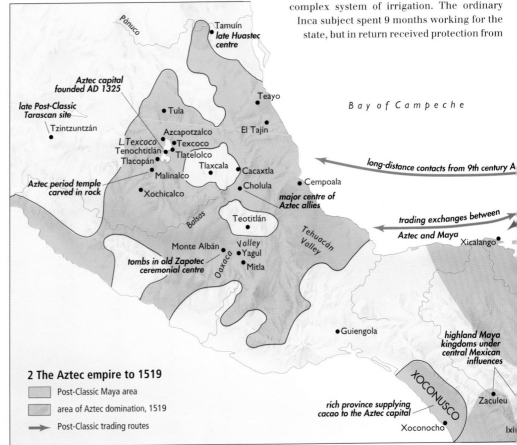

2 The Aztec empire to 1519

▫ Post-Classic Maya area

▫ area of Aztec domination, 1519

→ Post-Classic trading routes

famine (through state-owned food stores) and support during sickness and old age. The Aztec Empire, on the other hand, exercised harsh military dominion over vassal peoples who enjoyed political autonomy provided they paid heavy tribute to Tenochtitlán in food, textiles and other goods – increasingly in humans for ritual sacrifice to the Aztec gods (up to 50,000 a year by 1510). These demands help to explain why so many people in the valley of Mexico welcomed the Spaniards, just as a recent succession dispute provided allies for the European invaders in Peru. Although both the Aztec and Inca polities expanded faster than any 15th-century state in Latin Christendom, neither empire proved as stable as it seemed. Mexico fell to a force spearheaded by under 2,000 Europeans in 1519-22, Peru to a band of less than 200 in 1531-3 (see page 86).

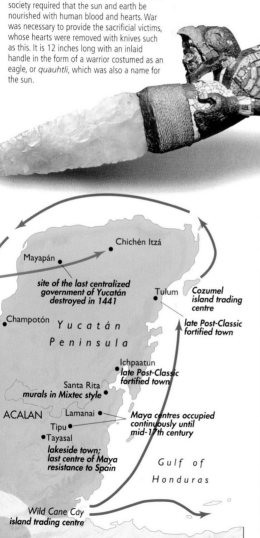

An Aztec or Mixtec sacrificial knife. The Aztecs believed that the continuation of human society required that the sun and earth be nourished with human blood and hearts. War was necessary to provide the sacrificial victims, whose hearts were removed with knives such as this. It is 12 inches long with an inlaid handle in the form of a warrior costumed as an eagle, or *quauhtli*, which was also a name for the sun.

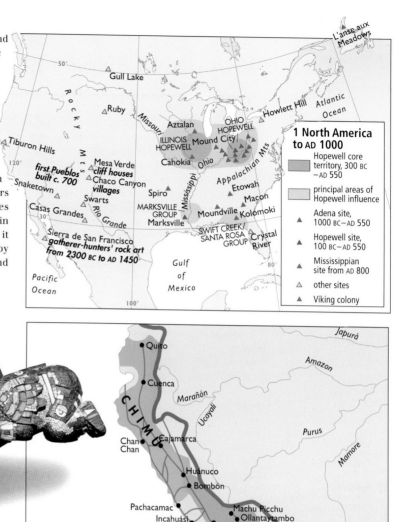

1 North America to AD 1000

- Hopewell core territory, 300 BC –AD 550
- principal areas of Hopewell influence
- ▲ Adena site, 1000 BC–AD 550
- ▲ Hopewell site, 100 BC–AD 550
- ▲ Mississippian site from AD 800
- △ other sites
- ▲ Viking colony

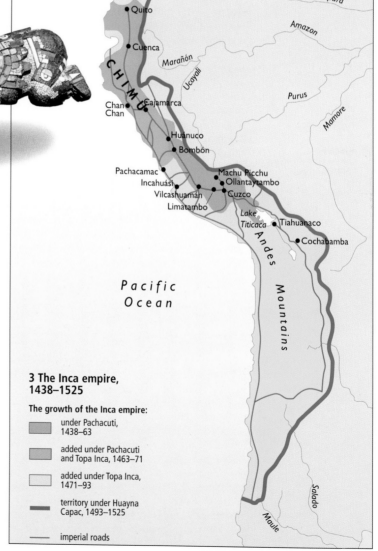

3 The Inca empire, 1438–1525

The growth of the Inca empire:

- under Pachacuti, 1438–63
- added under Pachacuti and Topa Inca, 1463–71
- added under Topa Inca, 1471–93
- territory under Huayna Capac, 1493–1525
- imperial roads

The world circa 1492

The central feature of world history since the 1490s has been the expansion of Europe and the spread of European civilization throughout the globe. Until then, the world had, on the whole, pressed in on Europe; thereafter the roles became reversed. In the 16th century, however, Europe continued to stand on the periphery of the civilized world, eclipsed by Ming China (the most powerful and advanced state of the period, with over 100 million inhabitants – equal to the whole of Europe) and by the rising Ottoman, Safavid and Mughal empires of the Middle East. Meanwhile Islam won converts in central and South-East Asia, and among the peoples of sub-Saharan Africa.

The total area occupied by the major civilizations, roughly co-terminous with the area of plough cultivation, nevertheless remained relatively small. Almost 80 per cent of the world's surface was inhabited either by food gatherers or herdsmen (as in Australia and most of Siberia, North America and much of Africa) or by hand cultivators (especially in South-East Asia, West Africa and Central and South America). But plough cultivators proved far more productive, and the relatively small area that had been brought under the plough probably supported between two-thirds and three-quarters of the global population (map 1).

Until the 1490s, worldwide racial segregation prevailed. Although Christians and Muslims from all over Eurasia made pilgrimages to their Holy Places in the Middle East, they seldom settled; and although merchants travelled widely across and around Asia, their numbers remained few. In the early 15th century a succession of Chinese voyages, commanded by the Muslim admiral Cheng Ho, secured tribute and extended recognition of the new Ming dynasty; but they led to no lasting interchange of population.

Until the 1490s, therefore, the Negroids remained concentrated in sub-Saharan Africa and a few Pacific islands; the Mongoloids in Asia and the Americas; the Caucasoids in Europe, North Africa, the Middle East and India; and the Australoids in Australia (map 2). By 1800, however, the pattern had fundamentally altered as the result of six inter-continental migrations: from Europe and Africa to the Americas; from northern Europe to Africa and (later) Australasia; from Russia into Siberia; from China to South-East Asia; and from India to Africa, South-East Asia and the Caribbean. By far the greatest change occurred in the Americas, where the native population declined dramatically in the

1 The economies of the world, c. AD 1500

non-agricultural economies

- generalized gathering, hunting and fishing
- specialized hunting

agricultural economies

- root crops dominant
- grain crops dominant
- nomadic pastoralism
  - △ dromedary   ◻ horse/reindeer   ◦ cattle

— limit of plough cultivation

— Cheng-ho's voyages, 1405–33

century following the first contact with the Europeans – in some cases by 90 per cent – to be replaced by Europeans, Africans, and in some parts of Latin America by a mixed race of mestizos (map 2).

Nevertheless, the tempo of change must not be exaggerated. Although in America the Aztec and Inca empires collapsed suddenly in 1521 and 1533 respectively (page 72), elsewhere the political impact of Europe remained limited until the 18th century. China and Japan survived intact, and India kept the Europeans at arm's length for 250 years following the arrival of Vasco da Gama in 1498. There, as in Africa and South-East Asia, the European presence long remained confined largely to trading stations and fortresses along the coast.

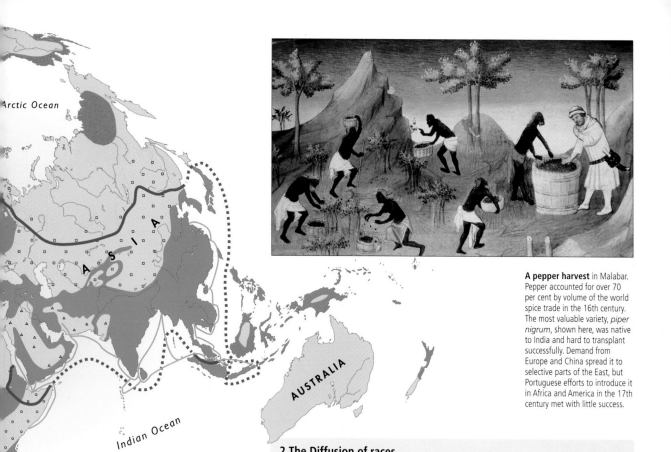

A pepper harvest in Malabar. Pepper accounted for over 70 per cent by volume of the world spice trade in the 16th century. The most valuable variety, *piper nigrum*, shown here, was native to India and hard to transplant successfully. Demand from Europe and China spread it to selective parts of the East, but Portuguese efforts to introduce it in Africa and America in the 17th century met with little success.

The cultural influence of Europe was even more negligible: Christianity made little headway, except when imposed by the conquerors (as in the Americas and the Philippines), until it received the backing of western technology in the 19th century.

The comparative fragility of the Aztec and Inca civilizations in the Americas, and of the African kingdoms immediately south of the Sahara, despite their outstanding achievements, may be partially explained, first, by their geographical isolation and relative lack of external stimulus and, second, by their dependence on hand cultivation. After 1492, when all the continents came into direct contact with each other for the first time, many of these non-Eurasian civilizations proved unable to offer more than a feeble resistance to outside aggression. To be sure not until the 19th century, with the opening of the Suez Canal and the construction of the transcontinental railways in North America, Siberia and Africa, did areas that had previously been separate finally blend into a single world economy; but the first stages of global integration were completed in the three centuries following 1492.

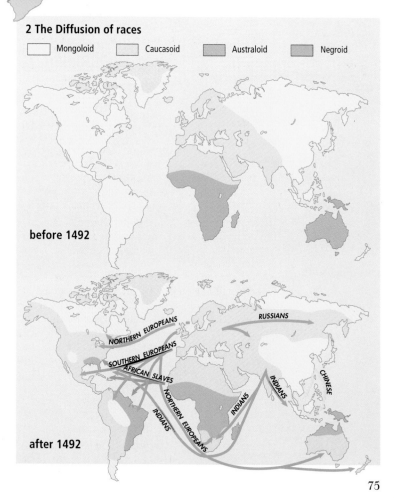

2 The Diffusion of races

Mongoloid | Caucasoid | Australoid | Negroid

before 1492

after 1492

NORTHERN EUROPEANS
SOUTHERN EUROPEANS
AFRICAN SLAVES
RUSSIANS
NORTHERN EUROPEANS
INDIANS
INDIANS
INDIANS
CHINESE

THREE

The Rise of
the West

Before 1500, civilization had been essentially land-centred, and contacts by sea relatively unimportant; thereafter direct sea contact linked the continents. This resulted not only in the growth of a global system of regions which hitherto had developed in isolation, but in a challenge to the traditional land-centred balance between the civilizations of Eurasia.

Nonetheless, the impact of European expansion should not be exaggerated. To many Europeans, the Ottoman, Mughal and Chinese empires exemplified civilized living. Industrialization put Europe ahead; but the fruits of that process – some of them poisonous – were only garnered in the 19th century. Until then, for all its thrusting novelty, Europe remained closer to its agrarian past than to its industrial future.

Between 1815 and 1914 Europe expanded and inaugurated the process of transformation throughout the world which dethroned agricultural society as it had existed for thousands of years, replacing it with an urban, industrialized, technocratic society.

Marble bust of Louis XIV
by Bernini, 1665

European exploration

In 1480 European shipping remained largely confined to the North Atlantic, the Baltic and the
Mediterranean, while the West African coast had
been explored cursorily, and only very recently by
Europeans; Indian, Persian, and Arab vessels plied the
northern Indian Ocean; Chinese and Indonesian junks
sailed in the western Pacific, but rarely went beyond
Japan, the Philippines and the Indonesian archipelago; and local craft navigated the Caribbean and the
coasts of Peru and Ecuador. No shipping used the
southern Indian Ocean, the South Atlantic, or the main
basin of the Pacific. In the course of the next 150 years,
however, European navigators opened all the seas,
except in the regions of circumpolar ice and the South
Pacific, to European ships. Initially, in the 15th century, two series of voyages sought a sea passage to southern Asia in the hope of initiating direct trade in spices.
One series, mounted from Portugal, sailing by a
south-eastern route and employing local navigators in the East, eventually reached their
declared destinations: the entrance to
the Indian Ocean (1488), Malabar
(1498), Malacca (1509), and the
Moluccas (1512-13). The
other series, mounted from
Spain and sailing west
or south-west, proved
less successful in its
immediate pur-
pose but more
fruitful in incid-
ental discovery:
the Spaniards
hit upon the
West Indies
(1492) and the
Spanish Main
(1498).
Eventually
they too reached
South-East Asia
(1521), but by a
route too long and
arduous for commer-
cial use – for to reach
the Pacific they had to
circumnavigate an immense
land-mass which, although it was
initially thought to be a peninsula of
Asia, by the 1520s had been recognized
as a new world. They immediately began to
settle the area (page 72). Taken together, the
Spanish and Portuguese discoveries proved that all
the oceans of the world, at least in the southern
hemisphere, were connected.

For most of the 16th century, by the use and
threat of force, the Iberian powers managed to prevent other Europeans from using the connecting
passages, except for occasional raids. The third
great series of voyages, therefore, mostly by
English, French and Dutch navigators, searched for
alternative routes to Asia in the northern hemisphere, in the west, northwest, and northeast.
Although unsuccessful in their primary purpose,
they revealed another continental land-mass with a
continuous coast extending from the Caribbean to
the Arctic, and opened the way for the European
exploration and settlement of eastern North
America (page 86).

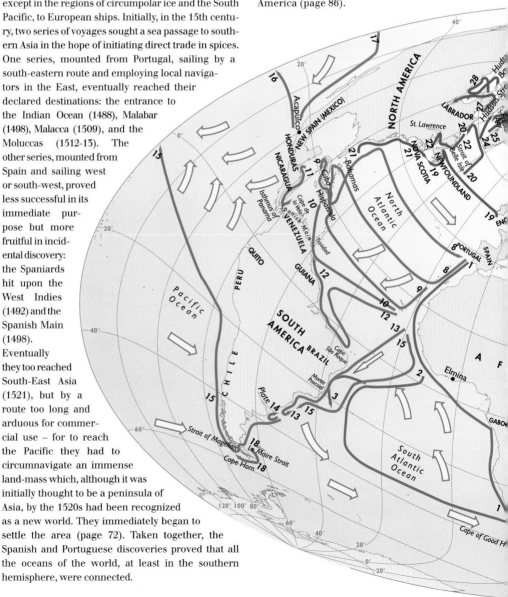

VOYAGES INTENDED FOR SOUTH ASIA BY SOUTH-EAST ROUTE:

1/Dias 1487–8 (outward) discovered open waters of Cape Agulhas; entered Indian Ocean; reached Great Fish River.

2/Vasco da Gama 1497–8 (outward) made best use of Atlantic winds on way to Cape of Good Hope; reached India, guided by local pilot.

3/Cabral 1500 (outward) second Portuguese voyage to India; landed in Brazil, probably accidentally.

4/First Portuguese voyage to Malacca, 1509.

5/Abreu 1512–3 visited Moluccas.

6/First Portuguese visits to Macao, 1516.

VOYAGES INTENDED FOR CHINA AND SOUTH ASIA BY WEST OR SOUTHWEST ROUTE:

7/Da Mota, Zeimoto and Peixoto 1542–3 Portuguese reach Japan.

8/Columbus 1492–3 (outward and homeward) visited Bahama group, explored north coasts of Cuba and Hispaniola; found best return route.

9/Columbus 1493–4 (outward) explored south coast of Cuba; reported it as peninsula of mainland China.

10/Columbus 1498 (outward) explored Trinidad and Venezuela; recognized coast as mainland.

11/Columbus 1502–4 explored coast of Honduras, Nicaragua and the Isthmus.

12/Ojeda and Vespucci 1499–1500 (outward) reached Guiana coast, failed to round Cape São Roque, followed coast west to Cape de la Vela.

13/Coelho and Vespucci 1501 (outward) followed coast south from Cape São Agostinho to 35°S.

14/Solís 1515 entered River Plate estuary and investigated north bank.

15/Magellan and Elcano 1519-22 discovered Strait of Magellan, crossed Pacific, reached Moluccas via Philippines; first circumnavigation.

16/Saavedra 1527 discovered route from Mexico across Pacific to Moluccas.

17/Urdaneta 1565 found feasible return route Philippines to Mexico in 42°N. using west winds.

18/Schouten and Le Maire 1616 discovered route into Pacific via Le Maire Strait and Cape Horn.

VOYAGES INTENDED FOR ASIA BY NORTHWEST AND NORTHEAST ROUTE:

19/Cabot 1497 (outward) encountered Newfoundland, first sighted by Norsemen 11th C.

20/Corte-Real 1500 visited Greenland.

21/Verazzano 1524 traced east coast of North America from (probably) 34°N. to 47°N.; revealed continental character of North America.

22/Cartier 1534 and 1535 explored Strait of Belle Isle and St Lawrence as far as Montreal.

23/Willoughby and Chancellor 1553 rounded North Cape and reached Archangel.

24/Frobisher 1576 reached Frobisher Bay in Baffin Island, which he took for a 'strait'.

25/Davis 1587 explored west coast of Greenland to the edge of the ice in 72° N.

26/Barents 1596–7 discovered Bear Island and Spitsbergen; wintered in Novaya Zemlya.

27/Hudson 1610 sailed through Hudson Strait to the south extremity of Hudson Bay.

28/Button 1612 explored west coast of Hudson Bay, concluded Bay landlocked on the west.

29/Baffin and Bylot 1616 explored whole coast of Baffin Bay; concluded no navigable northwest. passage existed in that area.

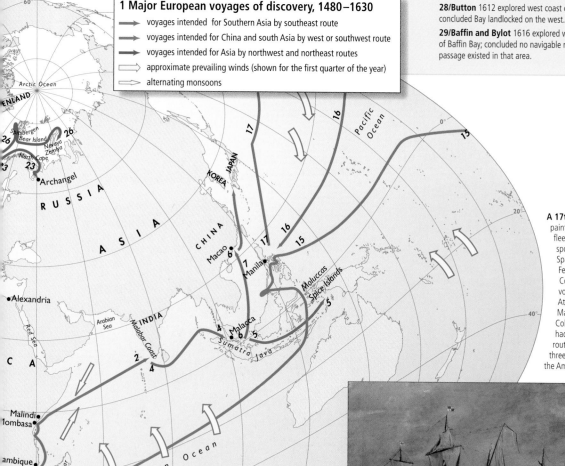

1 Major European voyages of discovery, 1480–1630

→ voyages intended for Southern Asia by southeast route

→ voyages intended for China and south Asia by west or southwest route

→ voyages intended for Asia by northwest and northeast routes

⇨ approximate prevailing winds (shown for the first quarter of the year)

⇨ alternating monsoons

A 17th-century Spanish painting of Columbus's fleet *(below)*. Under the sponsorship of the Spanish monarchs Ferdinand and Isabella, Columbus made his first voyage across the Atlantic in 1492. Making landfall on Haiti, Columbus believed he had found a westward route to Asia. He made three further voyages to the Americas.

1492–1713
European overseas expansion

By 1492, Portugal already possessed several archipelagos in the Atlantic and the Gulf of Guinea, some fortresses in Morocco, and a few trading stations in West Africa (above all the castle at Elmina). In the next half century she established some 50 forts and trading posts around the shores of the Indian Ocean, as well as coastal enclaves in Angola and Brazil. Strategically, the most important bases were Mozambique (1507), a port of call for fleets sailing to India; Goa (1510), headquarters of Portuguese Asia; Malacca (1511), a major market on the strait connecting the Indian Ocean with the South China Sea; and Ormuz (1515), a key entrepôt of the international spice trade. East of Malacca the position of the Portuguese was far more precarious and their activities remained purely commercial. A few bases, some fortified, grew up in the Moluccas; a clandestine settlement developed at Macao on the Chinese mainland after 1557; and from 1580 Jesuit missionaries held a lease on the Japanese port-city of Nagasaki (map 1).

In Africa and Asia the Portuguese generally sought to control trade rather than production; and though they could not eliminate the commerce of others in the Indian Ocean, they forced many ships to use harbours under their control, and extorted tolls or duties from the rest. The Spaniards in the Americas, by contrast, embarked on a deliberate policy of conquest and colonization: from the 1490s in the Caribbean islands; from the 1520s in Mexico; from the 1530s in Peru; and from the 1570s in the Philippines.

Few dared to challenge the Iberian monopoly – apparently enhanced by the union of Portugal and Spain in 1580 – before the 17th century. However, the

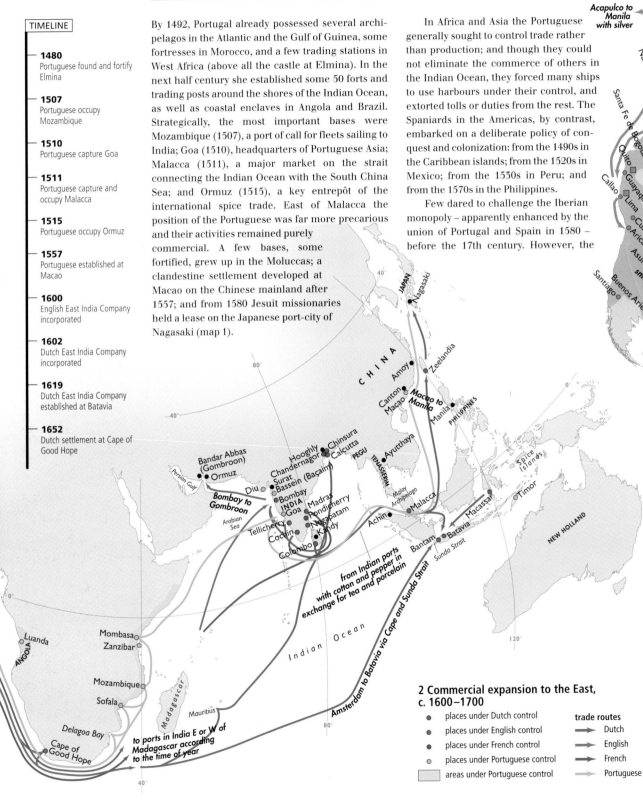

2 Commercial expansion to the East, c. 1600–1700

- places under Dutch control
- places under English control
- places under French control
- places under Portuguese control
- areas under Portuguese control

trade routes
→ Dutch
→ English
→ French
→ Portuguese

1 Spanish and Portuguese trade and settlement by c. 1600

→ principal Portuguese trade routes
→ principal Spanish trade routes

■ areas under effective Portuguese control
■ areas under effective Spanish control

○ Portuguese-controlled towns
○ Spanish-controlled towns

■ seat of Audiencia (Spanish admintraive division)

Manila to Acapulco with silk

MEXICO

Charcas
San Agostin
Havana
Santo Domingo
Havana to Seville via Azores
North Atlantic Ocean
Seville to Veracruz via Canary Is
Seville to Nombre de Dios via Canary Is.

Azores

roximate position of Tordesillas marcation line
Elmina to W. Indies with slaves

Olinda
mbuco
Recife
ahia
Elmina to Bahia with slaves
Luanda to Bahia with slaves
Bahia to Luanda with tobacco and sugar

South Atlantic Ocean

Lisbon
Seville
Cape Verde Islands
Canary Islands

A F R I C A

Alexandria
Cairo
Red Sea
Elmina
Gulf of Guinea
São Tomé
Guato
Bab el Mandeb
Aden
Luanda
ANGOLA
Malindi
Pemba
Zanzibar
Mombasa
Kilwa
Mozambique
Sofala
Madagascar
Réunion

A S I A

Ormuz
Arabian Sea
Diu
Goa
INDIA
Calicut
Cochin
Ceylon
Colombo
Laccadive Islands
Maldives
Hooghly

Indian Ocean

Sea of Japan
JAPAN
Nagasaki
CHINA
Canton
Macao
Luzon
Philippines
South China Sea
Cebu
Manila
Malacca
Maly Archipelago
Sumatra
Java
Borneo
Celebes
Moluccas
Ambonia
Ternate
Spice Islands
Timor

Manila galleons with silk
Manila galleons with silver

Lisbon to Goa (alternative route, second half of year)

CONQVISTA
CORTALE·LA·CAVESA·A
ATAGVALPA·INGA·VMATACVCHV

foundation of East India Companies by the Dutch, the English and (later) the French brought the Portuguese under increasing attack. Dutch forces first established independent bases in the East (above all at Batavia, the heavily fortified headquarters of the Dutch East India Company) and then between 1640 and 1660 wrested Malacca, Ceylon, most South Indian ports and the lucrative Japan trade from the Portuguese. In 1652 they also created a useful south African base on the route to the East at Cape Town. The English and French also established modest settlements in India, and developed a promising trade with China. Even the Spaniards undermined the Portuguese, exporting Chinese goods after 1572 through their colony in the Philippines (map 2). Elsewhere in Asia, however, Europeans during this period traded in competition with local merchants on terms laid down by local rulers, and their efforts constituted but a fraction of Asia's total commerce.

The murder of Atahuallpa (right) in November 1532 set the seal on Spain's conquest of the Inca empire. Although there were perhaps only 180 Europeans in Peru, most of them young men in their twenties, their brutal murder of the 'divine Inca' broke the resistance of the Peruvian peoples. This vigorous illustration of the deed comes from the *Royal Commentaries* published between 1609 and 1616 by Garcilaso de la Vega, the son of a conquistador and an Inca princess

81

The expansion of France

In 1415 English troops invaded France and by 1429 had established suzerainty over almost half the kingdom. In the 1440s, however, with the aid of a powerful artillery train, Charles VII (1422-61) began a rapid reconquest which by 1453 had expelled the English from all but the port-city of Calais, and doubled the size of the royal domain. His successors annexed Burgundy (1477), Brittany (1491) and Bourbon (1527) by force, and inherited Anjou and Provence (1481). Several other semi-independent fiefs came to the crown at the accession of Louis XII (1498), Francis I (1515) and Henry IV (1589) (map 1).

After Henry's death in 1610, continuing religious division, costly foreign wars and aristocratic faction, culminating in the Fronde revolt (1648-53), brought France to the brink of dissolution again. However Henry's grandson Louis XIV (1643-1715) restored order and made France the dominant state of Europe. During the relatively peaceful years between 1659 and 1672 the king and his ministers struggled to develop the French economy (agriculture, manufacture and trade), to extend overseas possessions, and to expand the army and navy. They also developed commercial harbours and sponsored public works, such as the Languedoc Canal connecting the Atlantic and the Mediterranean. The richness of resources available to the French, including a population of perhaps 20 million (the largest of any 17th-century European state), undoubtedly played a part in these achievements; but so did the ceaseless efforts, directives, and resources emanating from the Court (map 2).

Despite France's gains at the peaces of Westphalia (1648) and the Pyrenees (1659), Louis still feared Habsburg encirclement (page 92). He sought both to secure territories that might plug the gaps in his frontier (in wars fought in 1667-8 and 1672-8 which brought the acquisition of territory from the Spanish Netherlands and of Franche-Comté), and to erect an 'iron frontier' of state-of-the-art fortresses, thickest on the ground in the north and east, to create a defence in depth that would prevent any enemy forces from penetrating to the heart of the realm as the English and the Habsburgs had done in the past. Perhaps his success in this endeavour made him too bold, for in 1700 he accepted the will of the childless Spanish Habsburg Carlos II which bequeathed to Louis's grandson Philip the entire Spanish empire – Spain, Spanish America, the South Netherlands and half of Italy – even though he knew this sudden concentration of territory in the hands of the Bourbon dynasty would provoke a general European war. After some initial French victories (1702-3), followed by a string of searing defeats (1704-9), the 'iron frontier' showed its worth and forced France's exhausted enemies to conclude the compromise peaces of Utrecht (1713) and Rastatt (1714), by which Philip retained Spain and Spanish

1 The reunification of France 1440–1589

- lands recognizing English suzerainty, 1429
- frontier of France, 1492
- Royal domain, c. 1475
- lands annexed from Burgundy, 1477
- lands of René of Anjou, annexed 1481
- lands of Duke of Brittany, annexed 1491
- lands brought to the crown by Louis XII, 1498
- lands brought to the crown by Francis I, 1515
- lands of Duke of Bourbon, annexed 1527
- lands brought to the crown by Henry IV, 1589
- other fiefs annexed, with date
- fiefs still independent at the end of the 16th century

Calais **1558**
ARTOIS **(lost 1493)**
ST POL **1477**
PICARDY
NORMANDY
BRITTANY
ALENÇON **1525**
PERCHE **1483**
VALOIS
RETHEL
Verdun
CHAMPAGNE **1552** Metz
BAR **1552**
Toul **1552**
MAINE
ORLÉANAIS
VENDÔME
NEMOURS **1503**
ANJOU
BLOIS
TOURAINE
POITOU
BERRY
NEVERS
BURGUNDY
LA MARCHE
BOURBON
CHAROLAIS
Habsburg possession from 1493
ANGOULÊME
FOREZ
LIMOGES
PÉRIGORD
AUVERGNE
GUYENNE
DAUPHINÉ
ALBRET
ROUERGUE
GASCONY
ARMAGNAC
COMTAT VENAISSIN *papal state*
BÉARN BIGORRE
ASTARAC
COMMINGES
LANGUEDOC
PROVENCE

In the vast palace of Versailles, seen in the background behind Jean-Baptiste Tuby's bronze sculpture of Apollo rising from the waters *(right)*, Louis XIV directed the fortunes of France. The complex served as the king's court, the centre of his government and a source of inspiration – and envy – to monarchs throughout Europe.

America, while Savoy, Britain and the Austrian Habsburgs partitioned the rest (map 3).

Louis had thus secured the integrity of France's frontiers, and ended for ever the threat of Habsburg encirclement; but the ruinous cost of his wars created a legacy of financial disorder and internal discontent which served to hamstring his successors. Although Louis XV (1715–74) managed to incorporate Lorraine in 1766, and his successor Louis XVI (1774–93) assisted the successful rebellion of the American colonies against Great Britain (page 104), both monarchs sacrificed (as Louis XIV had done) France's overseas possessions and accumulated such monstrous public debts that, in 1789, the government summoned a representative assembly, the States-General, to solve the financial crisis. In doing so, it unleashed revolution (page 116).

2 Administrative units and defensive fortifications

— frontier of France 1713–14

— administrative units of Louis XIV's reign, the *généralités* (generalities)

⊙ seat of *intendants*, Louis XIV's royal commissioners

⊕ *parlement* (law courts)

<u>ALSACE</u> *pays d'état*

defence:

▉ fortifications (the so-called *barrière* or *frontière de fer*)

▣ fortifications built by Vauban but ceded during the reign of Louis XIV

◣ galley port

⊞ naval port

economic:

‡ commercial harbours

major manufactures:

⊟ brandy		◗ pottery	
◇ cloth		◡ printing	
☐ glass		▤ salt	
⊟ iron		◇ silk	
◒ madder dye		◇ soap	
⬡ paper		⊠ tapestry and carpets	
		▼ wine	

3 The War of the Spanish Succession, 1701–14

✗ Allied victory

✕ Bourbon (French) victory

✕ inconclusive

principal territorial changes

to Spanish House of Bourbon

to Great Britain

to Austria

to Savoy

to France

to Prussia

1462-1815
Russian expansion in Europe and Asia

After the Mongol invasion of the 13th century (page 60), the lands which had formed part of Kievan Russia fragmented. Lithuania expanded in the west, while the east and south became subject to Mongol overlords, in whose service the principality of Muscovy rose to prominence. Ivan III (1462-1505) opened another phase of expansion: in 1478 he annexed the city republic of Novgorod and in 1480 proclaimed independence from the Mongols. In 1510 his son Vassily (1505-33) overran the republic of Pskov, bringing Muscovite control close to the Baltic; and his grandson Ivan IV (1533-84) conquered the Tatar states of Kazan (1552) and Astrakhan (1556), gaining control of the Volga down to the Caspian Sea (map 1). In addition, from the 1580s, the lucrative fur trade lured enterprising Russians deep into Siberia. Crossing the Urals, they followed the River Ob until they came within portage of the Yenisey, where they built and fortified Turukhansk (1607); thence they reached the Lena river system, where they built Yakutsk (1632), and finally the Pacific, where they built Okhotsk (1649) – some 6,000 miles (9,700km) east of Moscow (map 2).

However Ivan IV failed to realise his principal territorial ambition, the acquisition of Livonia and direct access to the Baltic, while his attempt to break the power of the traditional nobility by creating a 'private domain' (the *oprichnina*) around Moscow resulted in massive depopulation. Muscovy was also still not entirely safe from the Crimean Tatars, who sacked Moscow in 1571. Then succession disputes following the extinction of the old Muscovite ruling house (the 'Time of Troubles', 1598-1613) caused the loss of much territory to Poland and Sweden.

Recovery came only in the mid-17th century, when a successful war with Poland (1654-67) brought substantial gains, including Smolensk and the Ukraine. Meanwhile the settlement of Siberia continued: 23,000 Russians lived there by 1622, 105,000 by 1662 and 230,000 by 1709. However the Amur Basin, acquired in the 1650s, had to be ceded to China in 1689 (albeit in return for useful trading concessions: map 2) and attempts to force access to the Black Sea failed. Instead, Peter I ('the Great', 1682-1725) concentrated on achieving a 'window on the west', wresting Estonia and Livonia from Sweden in 1721, acquiring the ancient port of Riga and founding the new one of St Petersburg (1703). Peter's successors reverted to his policy of expansion on the Black Sea. Catherine II ('the Great', 1762-96) annexed the Tatar khanate of the Crimea. She also acquired large parts of Poland – although the cost of her campaigns, on top of the oppressive social system which required serfs to spend almost all their time labouring on their lords' lands, provoked a major peasant uprising under Emelyan Pugachev (1773-5). The period 1772 to 1815 saw the Russian land frontier expand 600 miles (970 km) at the expense of Poland. Finally, despite a French invasion which reached Moscow in 1812, the Congress of Vienna in 1815 confirmed Russia's acquisition of Finland, Poland, Bessarabia and Transcaucasia (page 116).

The population ruled from Moscow had grown, both by territorial acquisition and by natural increase, from some 10 million in 1600, to over 15 million in 1725 and to almost 43 million in 1812, and the empire – the largest in the world – now stretched over 11 of the world's 24 time-zones.

2 Russian expansion in Siberia, 1581–1800

- Russian territory in 1581
- territory added 1581–98
- territory added 1598–1618
- territory added 1618–89
- territory added in 1650s; returned to China 1689
- territory added 1689–1725
- territory added 1725–62
- territory added 1762–1800
- Bratsk forts and trading posts 1630 (with date of foundation)

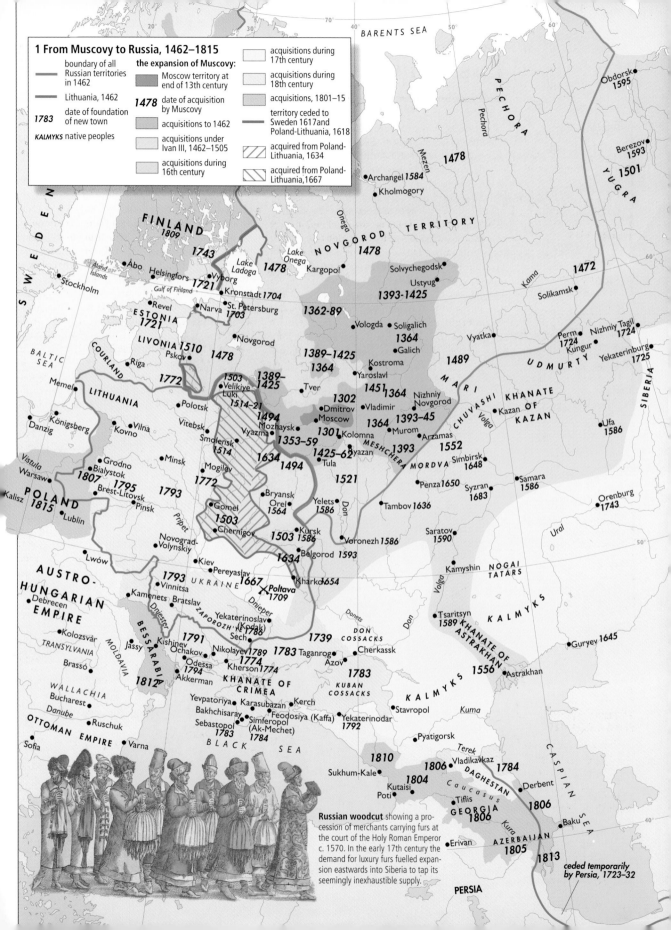

1 From Muscovy to Russia, 1462–1815

- boundary of all Russian territories in 1462
- Lithuania, 1462
- *1783* date of foundation of new town
- *KALMYKS* native peoples

the expansion of Muscovy:
- Moscow territory at end of 13th century
- *1478* date of acquisition by Muscovy
- acquisitions to 1462
- acquisitions under Ivan III, 1462–1505
- acquisitions during 16th century
- acquisitions during 17th century
- acquisitions during 18th century
- acquisitions, 1801–15
- territory ceded to Sweden 1617 and Poland-Lithuania, 1618
- acquired from Poland-Lithuania, 1634
- acquired from Poland-Lithuania, 1667

Russian woodcut showing a procession of merchants carrying furs at the court of the Holy Roman Emperor c. 1570. In the early 17th century the demand for luxury furs fuelled expansion eastwards into Siberia to tap its seemingly inexhaustible supply.

ceded temporarily by Persia, 1723–32

1500–1783
The Americas

(page 73)

The daring conquest of Mexico by Hernán Cortés in 1519-21 and of Peru by Francisco Pizarro in 1531-3 (page 73) laid the foundations of a huge Spanish colonial empire in the Americas. By 1535, when the crown established viceregal government in Mexico and Lima became the capital of Peru, all the major centres of indigenous population in the former Aztec and Inca empires lay in Spanish hands: an area four times the size, and containing eight times the population, of the country from which the conquerors had come. Although the frontiers of colonial settlement continued to advance – with new viceroyalties in New Granada (1739) and Rio de la Plata (1776) and new military governments in Texas (1718) and California (1767) – none of these later, sparsely inhabited conquests compared with Mexico and Peru in wealth and importance. Potosí in Peru and Zacatecas in Mexico became the largest producers of silver in the world, and by 1560 silver formed America's principal export to Europe.

Elsewhere on the continent colonization proved slower. The Portuguese only settled the Atlantic coast of south America after 1549 for fear that the French might do so. By 1600, although coastal Brazil had become studded with profitable sugar plantations and mills, worked by slaves from Africa, the Brazilian interior remained the domain of native Indian tribes until the 1690s, when the discovery of enormous gold deposits in the interior provoked a new wave of colonization. In the north-west, Russian explorers and traders pressed on; but by 1819 only 19 settlements existed between the Aleutian islands and California (map 1).

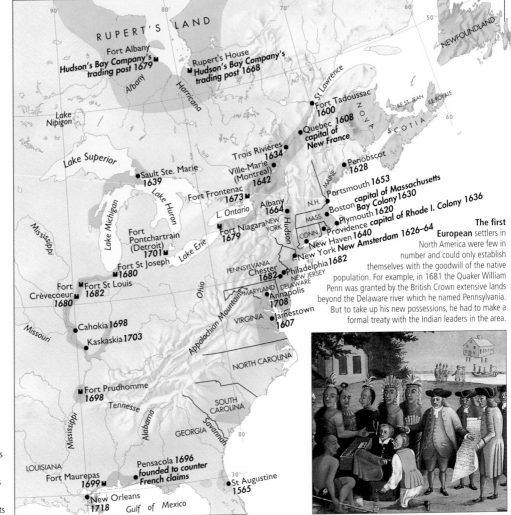

The first **European** settlers in North America were few in number and could only establish themselves with the goodwill of the native population. For example, in 1681 the Quaker William Penn was granted by the British Crown extensive lands beyond the Delaware river which he named Pennsylvania. But to take up his new possessions, he had to make a formal treaty with the Indian leaders in the area.

2 European settlement in North America

- early English settlements and claims
- early French settlements and claims
- early Spanish settlements

The Atlantic seaboard of north America, with its harsher climate and poor soil, also at first attracted few Europeans (who came mostly for fish and furs). Settlement only began with the foundation of Acadia (Nova Scotia) by the French in 1604, of Virginia (1607) and Massachusetts Bay (1620) by the English, and of New Amsterdam (later New York) by the Dutch (1624). Gradually, however, the Europeans pressed inland: the French advanced down the St Lawrence and (after 1682) the Mississippi, creating a chain of fortified posts all the way to the Gulf of Mexico and founding New Orleans in 1718; the English spread out around the rich fur-hunting grounds of Hudson Bay. Wars between the European states now regularly involved the Americas, with England gaining first the Dutch colonies along the Hudson (1664) and then French Canada (1763). By 1700, perhaps 250,000 Europeans lived in North America, but by 1820 that number had soared to 9 million (compared with just over 3 million in Spanish America).

The Spaniards in America relied from the first on Indian labour, both in ranching and mining, and readily intermarried; hence an extensive mestizo population developed, especially in Mexico and Peru. The British, however, who wanted land for farms and plantations, expelled or exterminated the native population: by 1820, only 600,000 lived in the English speaking areas (compared with 7.5 million in Spanish America). Instead, in Virginia, and then later in the Carolinas, where tobacco was introduced as a cash-crop, African slaves were imported to work on the plantations (like those of the sugar producers of Brazil and the Caribbean islands). By 1820, almost 2 million Africans lived in north America (compared with 800,000 in Spanish America).

Throughout the period, each mother country maintained a tight grip on its colonies. The colonists tolerated this as long as they felt insecure – whether from the threat of native uprisings or through the series of wars between the mother countries. Britain's resounding victory over France in 1763, however, brought total security to her American colonies, whose elites soon came to resent the continuing tax demands of the government in London. In 1776 they demanded their independence (page 98) and the colonies of Latin America followed suit after 1808. (page 112).

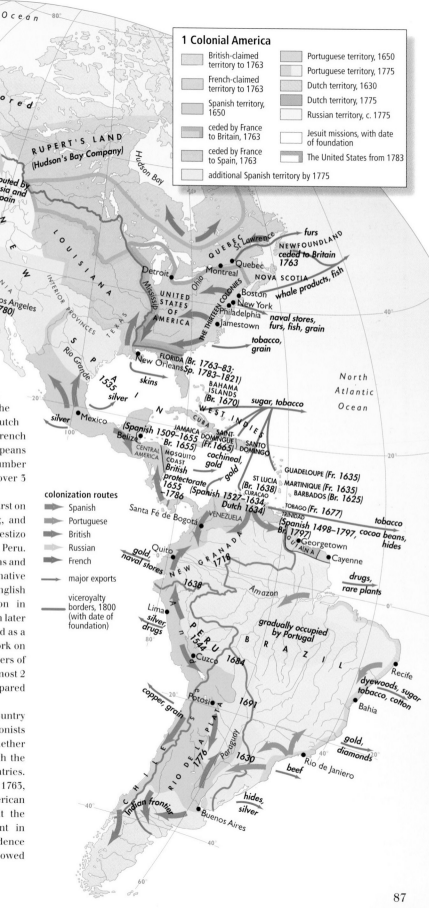

1 Colonial America

- British-claimed territory to 1763
- French-claimed territory to 1763
- Spanish territory, 1650
- ceded by France to Britain, 1763
- ceded by France to Spain, 1763
- additional Spanish territory by 1775
- Portuguese territory, 1650
- Portuguese territory, 1775
- Dutch territory, 1630
- Dutch territory, 1775
- Russian territory, c. 1775
- Jesuit missions, with date of foundation
- The United States from 1783

colonization routes
- Spanish
- Portuguese
- British
- Russian
- French
- major exports
- viceroyalty borders, 1800 (with date of foundation)

South-east Asia and Japan

In 1603 the Japanese emperor conferred the title of Shogun (military leader) on Tokugawa Ieyasu, who had established control over the state re-unified in the 1590s (page 68). The Tokugawa dynasty exercised power until 1868, giving Japan a prolonged period of political stability. A complex system of government emerged in which the shoguns in Edo (modern Tokyo) dominated or regulated the 250 or so fiefs of the feudal lords, organized society in a hierarchy of classes, and enacted a comprehensive legal code. From 1612 they banned the Christian missionaries (active in many areas since the mid-16th century) and persecuted their adherents. They also forbade all Japanese to travel abroad; limited foreign contacts to the Dutch (who maintained a trading post at Nagasaki), the Chinese and the Koreans; and until 1853 successfully repulsed various attempts by the Russians, British, French and Americans to open trade (map 1). Yet despite this isolation, Tokugawa Japan prospered: trade and cities grew rapidly; the population rose from 20 to 30 million; high literacy rates prevailed; industry and credit spread widely. By the mid-19th century, Japan was far better prepared than any other part of Asia to meet the challenge of Western expansion (page 122).

Initially, however, Western traders showed far more interest in the spices of South-East Asia. The disintegration of the empires of Srivijaya and Majapahit (page 64) left behind scores of petty states with little cohesion, opening the way to Portuguese acquisition of Malacca (1511) and footholds in the Moluccas (page 80). Their presence at first changed little: in Asia they aimed to dominate the spice trade

through a chain of fortified stations, linked by naval power, not to acquire territory. The arrival of the Dutch and then the English after 1595 (page 80) did not initially change this, for they too sought primarily to monopolize the spice trade, and even after the establishment of a fortress at Batavia (1619) the Dutch directed most of their territorial ambitions towards acquiring Portuguese and English bases, rather than to conquering native states. The only substantial European colony in the area remained the Philippines, where the Spanish authorities began to foster the cultivation of tobacco, sugar, hemp and other commercial products from the later 18th century (map 2).

The mainland monarchies of Southeast Asia – Arakan, Burma, Siam, Cambodia, Luang Prabang and Annam – had little direct involvement in European trade, and concentrated instead on extending their power at the expense of their neighbours. Over the period as a whole, Annam (Vietnam) and Siam expanded at the expense of Luang Prabang (Laos) and Cambodia. Burma almost disintegrated after the Mons rebelled in 1740, set up a king of their own at Pegu, and in 1752 captured the Burmese capital of Ava. However a charismatic leader, Alaungpaya (1735-60), defeated the Mons and established Rangoon as the southern port of a reunited Burma (1755), while his successors invaded Siam (1767) and conquered Arakan (1785).

Two factors complicated state-building in the area: the constant pressure of the hill peoples of the interior (like the Mons), always eager to assert their independence, and the steadily increasing interference of the Europeans. A group of Iberian adventurers temporarily seized power

Daimyo **and their retinues** enter Edo castle to participate in one of the many courtly ceremonials *(right)*. Edo, now Tokyo, was originally a fishing village, near which a castle was built in 1456. It rapidly became a powerful centre and in 1590 Tokugawa Ieyasu selected Edo for his residence, building an elaborate castle which remained the seat of the shogunate for 260 years, although it became the capital only in the 19th century.

1 Japan in isolation

— provincial borders
═ Five Highways
━ extensions to the Five Highways
— secondary roads
— sea routes
● important castle towns

feudal territories:
▨ major Tokugawa domains

⇒ American, Russian, British and other naval visits

HOKKAIDO

EZO Hakodate

Sea of Japan

HONSHU

Kubota
Morioka
Miyako
Niigata
Aizu Sendai

CHOSHU (NAGATO)
Shimonoseki Hagi
Fukuoka Yamaguchi
HIZEN Mitajiri Tottori
Nagasaki Saga Kurume Hiroshima Kanazawa KAGA
SAGA Okayama Fukui
Kumamoto
KYUSHU SHIKOKU Nishinomiya Kyoto Nakasendo Koshu-kaido Nikko-kaido Oshu-kaido
Tokushima Hyogo Fushimi MITO
SATSUMA TOSA Kochi Sakai Osaka OWARI
Kagoshima Wakayama Gojo Tsu Nagoya Mito
Tokaido Yokohama Mito
KII (KISHUI) Yokosuka Edo (Tokyo)
Uraga

SAM

Naga Hills
Mogaung • Myitkyina
Imphal
ANIPUR
Tagaung
YUN-NAN
BURMA
Bhamo
Shwebo
Ava • Mandalay SHAN
in Hills Amarapura STATES
af Myohaung 1785
RAK AN 1767 1564
KARENNI
STATE
Magwe An Pass
Thayetmyo
Chiengmai
Taungup Lamphun
Pass Pegu Lampang
Bassein Thaton Sawankhalok
Rangoon Martaban Sukhothai
from 1755 Moulmein
Syriam SIAM
to 1755
MONS
Tavoy Thon Buri
Mergui Chanthaburi
Mergui
Archipelago
daman Is. Isthmus of Kra

CHINA

Canton
Macao

TONGKING
Hanoi • Bac Ninh
Haiphong

Chiang Saen
Luang Thanh Hoa
Prabang
Chiang Rai
Ha Tinh
Vientiane Porte d'Annam
Hue
Tourane French from 1787
Lopi Buri Champassak
Korat Binh Dinh
Bangkok Ayutthaya Stung Treng Qui Nhon
Sisophon Angkor
Battambang CAMBODIA Kratie Nha Trang
Kompong Cham
Phnom Penh COCHIN
Kampot CHINA
Ha Tien Chau Bien Hoa
Doc Saigon
Cho Lon

Hainan

to Japan

to Japan

from
Canton
to all
major
S.E. Asian
ports

FORMOSA
Spanish colonies in
north Taiwan, 1626-37;
Dutch in southwest
Taiwan, 1624-61

to Acapulco

Pacific
Ocean

20

Luzon

PHILIPPINES
Manila

from Acapulco

South China
Sea

Mindanao

Nakhon Si Thammarat
Phuket
Trang
Songkhla
Pattant
Penang
British from 1786
MALAYA

Madras
Calcutta

Malacca
Portuguese 1511-1641
Dutch 1641-1826
Singapore
British from 1819

Tiku
Fort de Kock
(Bukit Tinggi)
Padang
Painan

2 The Europeans
in southeast Asia
European possessions, 1826
British Spanish
Dutch Portuguese
trade routes:
developed by Dutch and
English East India Companies
developed by Arab and Gujerati traders
developed by the Dutch in the 17th cen
used by English shipping from 1786
used by the 'Manila Galleon'
local trade routes
principal trading centre

Vietnamese expansion
Vietnamese border, 1500
expansion to 1611
acquisitions from
Cambodia in early
18th century
Vietnamese expansion
in 19th century
kingdom of Luang
Prabang, 1707
area which broke away
under Vientiane in 1707
Burmese conquests
Siamese conquests

Brunei

SARAWAK

Borneo

Pontianak

Djambi
Bangka
Palembang
Billiton

Benkulen

Sukadana
Bantam
Batavia
(Jakarta)
MATARAM
Jogjakarta
Surabaya

Indian
Ocean

Balambangan

Sulu
Sea

Sulu Archipelago

Manado

Tidore

Halmahera

Moluccas
(Spice Islands)

Buru

Ceram
Amboina

Banda Is.

Celebes

Strait of Macassar

Karimata Strait

Java Sea

Macassar

Bandjarmasin

Bali
Lombok

Sumbawa
Flores
Sumba

Banda Sea

Timor

in Cambodia in the 1590s; the French briefly
garrisoned some Siamese strongholds in the 1680s;
both the French and English East India Companies
intervened in Burma in the 1750s. Meanwhile, the
Dutch began to extend their control over Java and the
Spice Islands, and at the same time the British established their base at Penang (1786) and a free trade
port at Singapore (1819) on the Malayan peninsula.

These acquisitions led to tension between the
two colonial powers, which only abated after a treaty
in 1824 obliged the British to withdraw from Sumatra

and the Dutch from Malacca. Secure in the east, the
British now turned on Burma and, after a short war
(1824-6), annexed Arakan, Assam and Tenasserim.
The future Dutch and British colonial empires in
Southeast Asia were taking shape, but their control
remained loose and indirect. Only after the industrial
revolution, and the expanding demand for raw
materials at home, did the Europeans seriously
impinge upon the lives and fortunes of the peoples of
the region.

The Reformation and Catholic Reformation

Of the 250,000 or so works printed in Europe between 1447 and 1600, about 75 per cent concerned religion. The Reformation and the Catholic response would have been impossible without printing presses like this one *(below)*, from the cover of a book printed in Frankfurt in the early 17th century.

The shattering of the unity of Latin Christendom altered the course of European history. The fall of Constantinople (page 48) allowed the Roman church to ignore the Orthodox areas; and, except in Bohemia and Moravia, heresy scarcely existed in the West. Complacent, the Papacy failed to deploy its immense wealth adequately, producing widespread pluralism and absenteeism; this, coupled with the materialism of the hierarchy, discredited the Western church in the eyes of many Christians. Some, like Erasmus of Rotterdam (1466-1536) and Thomas More (1478-1535), hoped for spiritual renewal within the church; but in Saxony Martin Luther (1483-1546) criticized clerical abuse and in 1520 called upon the German nobility to reform the church. Meanwhile, inspired by Huldreych Zwingli (1484-1531), the magistrates of the Swiss canton of Zürich renounced allegiance to Rome.

These successful protests sparked others. By 1560, seven out of every ten inhabitants of the Holy Roman Empire no longer accepted papal authority, and Protestantism (as the dissident creeds became known) also prevailed in Scandinavia, the Baltic lands, and England. Further defections from Rome came through the teaching of John Calvin (1509-64) in Geneva. Calvinism made rapid progress in France, Poland, Hungary and Scotland (where it became the official creed after 1560).

In addition, a number of more radical sects sprang up, called 'Anabaptists' by their enemies because of their belief that only adult baptism was valid. They rejected ritual, spiritual and temporal authority, and many social conventions in favour of Biblical simplicity. Many combined evangelism with social protest, and participated both in the major rising of the German peasantry in 1524-5 and in the radical government of the city of Münster in 1534-5. Both movements were brutally repressed and Anabaptism, where it survived, became a secret, separate creed.

Eventually the Catholic church reformed itself. The Council of Trent (three sessions 1545-63) condemned abuses, defined doctrine, and created a more effective and educated clergy; at the same time new religious orders (most notably the Jesuits, incorporated in 1540) targeted key areas for reconversion. By 1650 the Protestants had been expelled from Bavaria (1579), Austria (1597) and Bohemia (1628), and the number of Protestant churches in Poland had declined from 560 in 1572 to 240 in 1650. Spain eradicated its small Protestant minorities, and in 1609 expelled its substantial Moorish population. In the Holy Roman Empire, however, the Protestants fought back, provoking the savage religious conflict known as the Thirty Years' War (page 92).

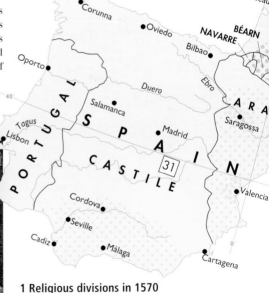

1 Religious divisions in 1570

- Roman Catholic
- Orthodox
- Greek Catholic (Uniate)
- Lutheran
- Calvinist
- Anabaptist
- Islam
- Anglican
- Hussite

NORWAY
(Danish)

● Bergen

SWEDEN

● Åbo ■ 1528

● Helsingfors

ICELAND
■ 1552

60

● Christiania
■ 1539

■ 1527

● Stockholm

● Reval
■ 1524

ESTONIA

RUSSIA

● Pskov

LIVONIA

■ 1561 ● Riga
COURLAND
■ 1524

SCOTLAND
1560
ow ● Edinburgh

North
Sea

● Aarhus

Baltic Sea

● Königsberg
■ 1523

● Vilna

LITHUANIA

● Minsk

0

● York

● Copenhagen ● Malmö

■ 1525
PRUSSIA

● Danzig

Chester

ENGLAND ▲ 1534

● Oxford
ol ● London

DENMARK

SLESVIG ■ 1542 ■ 1536
HOLSTEIN ■ 1542 ■ 1529 ● Lübeck
● Emden ■ 1526 ■ 1531
▲ 1542 ● Hamburg POMERANIA ■ 1534
■ 1548 1549 ● Stettin

● Amsterdam

● Bremen ■ 1525

NETHERLANDS

● Münster

● Hannover

● Poznán

● Warsaw

BRUNSWICK ■ 1545
LÜNEBURG
■ 1539

BRANDENBURG

2

Rhine ● Cologne

● Brussels
● Mons

HESSE
■ 1524

NASSAU
■ 1528

● Magdeburg
● Wittenberg ■ 1525
■ 1522
● Leipzig

● Berlin ■ 1525

ELEC. OF
SAXONY ● Dresden
■ 1525

Vistula

POLAND

2

● Frankfurt
■ 1530

DUCHY OF
SAXONY
■ 1539

● Prague
BOHEMIA ■ 1524

Elbe

● Breslau
■ 1524

SILESIA

Oder

● Cracow

● Lwów

PALATINATE
● Metz ▲ 1546
▲ 1559
● Nuremberg

MORAVIA

Dniester

FRANCE

● Rouen
● Rheims
Seine
● Paris

● Orléans
Loire
● Tours

● Limoges

26

WÜRTTEMBERG
● Strassburg ▲ 1534
■ 1524 ● Ulm ■ 1530

■ 1528

Danube

● Brünn

● Vienna
● Pozsony

AUSTRIA

● Munich
● Salzburg

2

H
U
N
G
A
R
Y

● Kassa

● Eger

● Buda

MOLDAVIA

● Jassy

BASLE ▲ 1523
NEUCHÂTEL ■ 1529 ▲ 1524 THURGAU
● Dijon ■ 1530 ● Zurich ▲ 1524 APPENZELL
FRANCHE- ● Berne ▲ 1524
COMTÉ VAUD ● Geneva ▲ 1524 SANKT GALLEN
▲ 1536 ▲ 1536 SWISS ▲ 1525 GLARUS
● Lyons CONFEDERATION GRAUBÜNDEN

2

● Graz

● Debrecen

● Zágráb

● Pécs

● Kolozsvár

● Szeged

TRANSYLVANIA

● Brassó

● Temesvár

● Toulouse

SAVOY

VENAISSIN
ORANGE
● Avignon

● Marseille

● Turin

MONTFERRAT

MILAN
● Milan

● Mantua

PARMA

MONACO

● Nizza

REP. OF GENOA

● Genoa

MASSA
LUCCA

● Trieste

● Venice
● Verona

VENETIAN

● Belgrade

WALLACHIA

● Bucharest

● Ruschuk

Danube

● Nish

● Sofia

NDORRA

Barcelona

SARDINIA

● Cagliari

10

● Florence

TUSCANY

STATO
DEI
PRESIDI

PAPAL
● Perugia

STATES

187 ● Rome

DUCHY
OF
CASTRO

DUCHY OF
URBINO

SAN MARINO

REP
UB
LI
C

● Zara

● Spalato

R
E
P
U
B
L
I
C

1

REPUBLIC OF
RAGUSA

PONTECORVO

● Bari

○ BENEVENTO

● Naples

NAPLES

● Taranto

MONTENEGRO

● Bosna
Saray

● Mostar

● Üsküb

OTTOMAN

● Salonica

● Philippopolis

● Adrianople

EMPIRE

● Janina

SICILY

● Palermo

● Messina

20

● Athens

3 delegates sent to last session
of Council of Trent, (1562–3)

■ date of change from
Catholicism to Lutheranism

▲ date of change to Calvinism,
Zwinglianism or Anglicanism

The Habsburg ascendancy in Europe

Charles V's election as Holy Roman Emperor in 1519 created a Habsburg hegemony in Europe. He already ruled lands in Austria, South Germany and the Netherlands, and the realms bequeathed by his maternal grandparents in Spain, Italy and North Africa. Each of these inheritances soon increased. In 1526 his brother Ferdinand succeeded to the crowns of Bohemia (which included Moravia, Silesia and Lusatia) and Hungary. In 1535 Charles himself acquired both Lombardy and Tunisia, and throughout his reign he added to his holdings in the Netherlands (map 1). Moreover, in America, his Castilian subjects toppled first the Aztec and then the Inca states (see page 80). Although the central European lands (and the Imperial title) passed to Ferdinand and his successors, Charles's son Philip II also ruled a formidable inheritance. He, too, managed to extend it – adding the Philippines by conquest after 1571, and Portugal with her overseas possessions by inheritance after 1580.

Such centralization did not prove popular, however. Apart from provoking the enmity of France, which felt encircled, Charles V faced rebellions from his subjects in Spain (1520-2) and Germany (1552-5), the former provoked by taxation,

the latter arising from religious dissent provoked by the Reformation (page 90). Philip II (1556-98) contended, in the Netherlands, with the longest-lasting revolt in modern European history (map 2). The various provinces inherited or acquired by Charles V became part of a single state only in 1548. Local customs, often guaranteed by charter against central government interference, nevertheless survived and Philip II's attempts to override them – both to raise taxes and to persecute heretics – provoked insurrection. A timely display of force stifled an uprising in 1566; but in 1572 the provinces of Holland and Zeeland sustained rebellion, helped by the threat of a French invasion which made difficult a concentration of Spanish forces, until the cost of opposing them compelled Philip to withdraw his troops in 1576-7. Although forces loyal to (and maintained by) Spain reconquered many areas in the 1580s, fighting went on with the northern rebels for more than 20 years. Only in 1609 did Spain finally conclude a 12-year truce with the largely Calvinist Dutch Republic.

The Netherlands' struggle resumed during Emperor Ferdinand II's war against his rebellious subjects in Bohemia and Austria (map 3). He routed them at the battle of White Mountain in 1620.

Spain's attempts to suppress the Dutch Revolt provoked much hostile propaganda. Here *(below)* the devil crowns the duke of Alba, who led Spain's efforts 1567-1573, while a Cardinal wields bellows to fill his head with Catholic zeal. Alba holds allegorical figures of the Dutch provinces on a chain, while his agents execute Counts Egmont and Hornes, defenders of Dutch liberties. (The execution itself took place in Brussels on 5 June 1568).

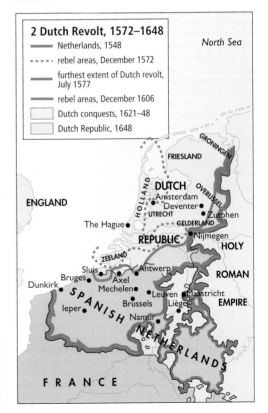

2 Dutch Revolt, 1572–1648
— Netherlands, 1548
- - - - rebel areas, December 1572
═══ furthest extent of Dutch revolt, July 1577
— rebel areas, December 1606
▨ Dutch conquests, 1621–48
▢ Dutch Republic, 1648

North Sea

GRONINGEN
FRIESLAND
ENGLAND
DUTCH
OVERIJSSEL
Amsterdam
Deventer
UTRECHT
Zutphen
The Hague
GELDERLAND
REPUBLIC
Nijmegen
HOLY
ZEELAND
Sluis
Axel
Antwerp
ROMAN
Bruges
Dunkirk
Mechelen
Leuven
Maastricht
S P A I N
Brussels
Liège
EMPIRE
Ieper
Namur
N E T H E R L A N D S

F R A N C E

Encouraged by this success, with Spanish and Papal support Ferdinand turned in 1621 against the German Protestant states, especially the Calvinists. Despite aid from Britain, Denmark and the Dutch, they lost and in 1629 Ferdinand issued an 'Edict of Restitution' by which he reclaimed Church lands acquired by Protestant rulers. Swedish military aid turned the tables against the emperor, and saved the German Protestants from collapse: an army led by King Gustavus Adolphus routed the Imperialists at Breitenfeld (1631) and drove them from much of Germany. Spain intervened to restore Habsburg fortunes but its victory at Nördlingen (1634) provoked France to declare war first on Spain (1635) and then on the emperor (1636). The war spread to almost the whole continent.

After many more years of largely unsuccessful campaigning, at the peace of Westphalia (1648) the emperor was abandoned virtually all his powers in Germany, agreed to toleration for Protestants and Catholics, and promised not to assist his Spanish cousins in their war against the Dutch rebels; by the peace of Münster (1648) Spain formally recognized the independence of the Dutch Republic (and their possession of all territories conquered since 1621); and by the peace of the Pyrenees (1659), Spain ceded all areas gained by France on the frontiers of both Spain and the Netherlands. The religious and political frontiers of central Europe which were agreed by these treaties lasted unchanged for 100 years. The Habsburg bid for European hegemony had failed.

3 The Thirty Years' War, 1618–48

- → route of Gustavus Adolphus, 1630–2
- → route of the Spanish army, 1634
- ✕ Imperial (Catholic) victory
- ✕ Imperial (Catholic) defeat
- — Holy Roman Empire
- — affected by Edict of Restitution, 1629
- ■ date region became Lutheran
- ▲ date region became Calvinist

the religious position in 1640:
- Lutheran
- Calvinist
- Catholic
- regained by Roman Catholics

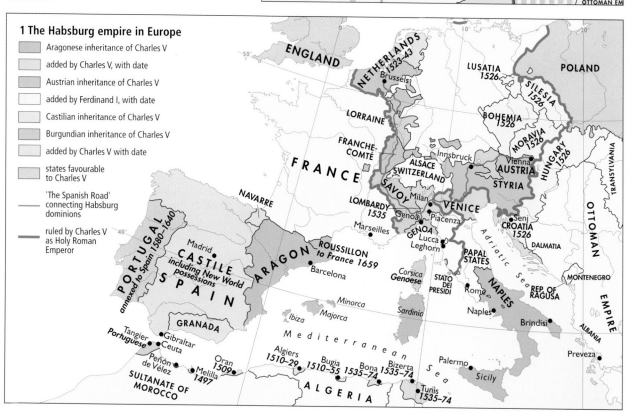

1 The Habsburg empire in Europe

- Aragonese inheritance of Charles V
- added by Charles V, with date
- Austrian inheritance of Charles V
- added by Ferdinand I, with date
- Castilian inheritance of Charles V
- Burgundian inheritance of Charles V
- added by Charles V with date
- states favourable to Charles V
- 'The Spanish Road' connecting Habsburg dominions
- ruled by Charles V as Holy Roman Emperor

1644–1911
China under the Ch'ing Dynasty

A new era in Chinese history opened in 1644 when the Ming dynasty, beset for a century by pirate raids, civil wars, and northern invaders (see page 68), fell to the forces of a Manchurian dynasty which ruled the country until 1911. The Manchu, or Ch'ing, rulers met with resistance in southern China for half a century, but quickly established a working relationship with the gentry who staffed the Chinese bureaucracy and, with its support, began a successful policy of territorial expansion which continued until the mid-18th century (map 1).

At the same time population trebled from about 100 million in 1650 to 300 million in 1800 and reached 420 million by 1850, while vast quantities of tea, silk, cotton, lacquer and porcelain were exported (mostly to Europe). But the financial strain of the wars of expansion and the pressure of the growing population on land and food caused hardships that led to recurrent unrest and revolt, not only among the ethnic minorities who were harshly exploited by Chinese and Manchus alike, but also in the heartland itself, beginning with the 'White Lotus' rebellion, 1796-1805. China remained the world's largest and most populous state, but its economic difficulties and inadequate bureaucracy prevented effective resistance to the pressures of the Western powers who sought to open the Chinese market for the goods produced by their empires.

China's defeat in the Opium War (1839-42) resulted in the cession of Hong Kong to Britain and the opening of the first five Treaty Ports (their number steadily increased)

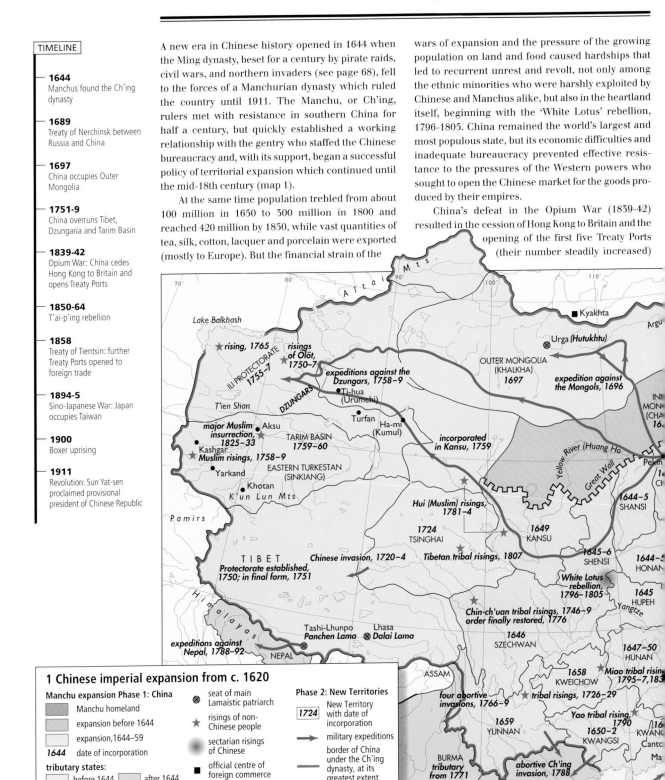

1 Chinese imperial expansion from c. 1620

Manchu expansion Phase 1: China

- Manchu homeland
- expansion before 1644
- expansion, 1644–59
- *1644* date of incorporation

tributary states:
- before 1644
- after 1644

- ⊗ seat of main Lamaistic patriarch
- ★ risings of non-Chinese people
- ● sectarian risings of Chinese
- ■ official centre of foreign commerce

Phase 2: New Territories
- New Territory with date of incorporation *1724*
- → military expeditions
- — border of China under the Ch'ing dynasty, at its greatest extent

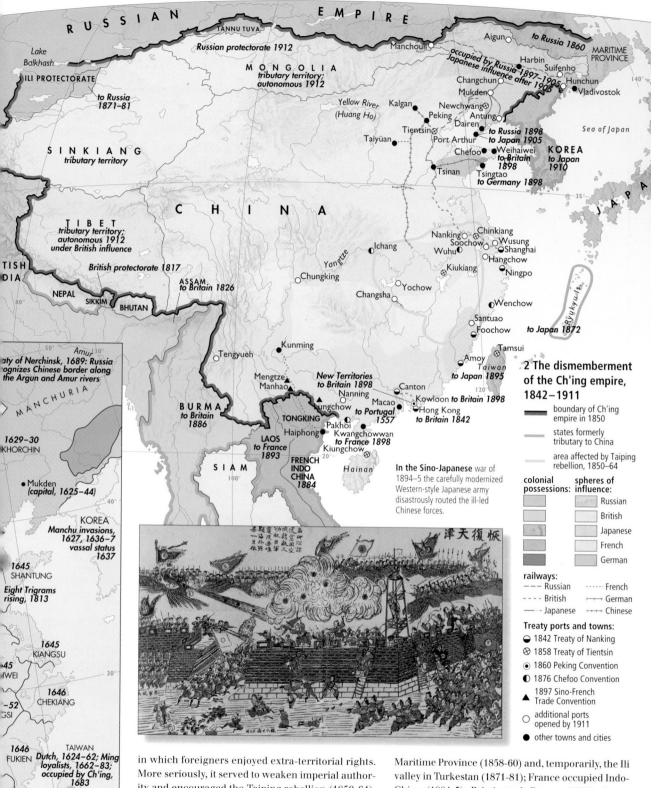

R U S S I A N   E M P I R E

Lake Balkhash

TANNU TUVA

Russian protectorate 1912

Manchouli

Aigun

to Russia 1860

MARITIME PROVINCE

ILI PROTECTORATE

M O N G O L I A
tributary territory;
autonomous 1912

occupied by Russia 1897–1905
Japanese influence after 1905

Harbin
Suifenho
Hunchun
Vladivostok

to Russia 1871–81

Changchun
Mukden
Newchwang
Antung

Sea of Japan

Yellow River (Huang Ho)
Kalgan
Peking
Tientsin
Taiyüan

Dairen
to Russia 1898
to Japan 1905
Port Arthur

KOREA
to Japan 1910

Chefoo
Weihaiwei
to Britain 1898
Tsingtao
to Germany 1898

S I N K I A N G
tributary territory

Tsinan

J A P A N

C H I N A

T I B E T
tributary territory;
autonomous 1912
under British influence

British protectorate 1817

TISH DIA

NEPAL
SIKKIM
BHUTAN

ASSAM
to Britain 1826

Nanking
Chinkiang
Soochow
Wusung
Wuhu
Shanghai
Hangchow
Kiukiang
Ningpo

Ichang

Yangtze

Chungking

Changsha
Yochow

Wenchow

Santuao
Foochow

to Japan 1872

Ryukyu Is.

Treaty of Nerchinsk, 1689: Russia recognizes Chinese border along the Argun and Amur rivers

Amur

M A N C H U R I A

Tengyueh

Kunming

Mengtze
Manhao

New Territories to Britain 1898
Nanning
Lungchow

Canton

Kowloon to Britain 1898
Macao to Portugal 1557
Hong Kong to Britain 1842

Tamsui

Amoy

Taiwan
to Japan 1895

120

1629–30
KHORCHIN

Mukden
(capital, 1625–44)

B U R M A
to Britain 1886

TONGKING
Pakhoi
Haiphong

Kwangchowwan to France 1898
Kiungchow

LAOS
to France 1893

SIAM

FRENCH INDO CHINA 1884

Hainan

KOREA
Manchu invasions,
1627, 1636–7
vassal status
1637

1645
SHANTUNG

Eight Trigrams rising, 1813

1645
KIANGSU
WEI

1646
CHEKIANG
GSI

1646
FUKIEN

TAIWAN
Dutch, 1624–62; Ming loyalists, 1662–83; occupied by Ch'ing, 1683

rising of Heaven and Earth Society, 1787–8

Vietnamese pirate raids, 1800–9

In the Sino-Japanese war of 1894–5 the carefully modernized Western-style Japanese army disastrously routed the ill-led Chinese forces.

2 The dismemberment of the Ch'ing empire, 1842–1911

▬▬ boundary of Ch'ing empire in 1850

▬▬ states formerly tributary to China

area affected by Taiping rebellion, 1850–64

colonial possessions:

spheres of influence:

Russian
British
Japanese
French
German

railways:
--- Russian   ····· French
--- British   ++++ German
-·- Japanese   —— Chinese

Treaty ports and towns:
◒ 1842 Treaty of Nanking
⊗ 1858 Treaty of Tientsin
◉ 1860 Peking Convention
◐ 1876 Chefoo Convention
▲ 1897 Sino-French Trade Convention
○ additional ports opened by 1911
● other towns and cities

in which foreigners enjoyed extra-territorial rights. More seriously, it served to weaken imperial authority and encouraged the Taiping rebellion (1850–64), the most serious of the many revolts that shook Manchu power. The Taiping and Nien uprisings alone left 25 million dead. These grave disorders also convinced the Western powers that Ch'ing China stood on the verge of collapse and encouraged them to secure a share: Russia gained the Amur basin, the

Maritime Province (1858–60) and, temporarily, the Ili valley in Turkestan (1871–81); France occupied Indo-China (1884–5); Britain took Burma (1886); Japan annexed Taiwan (1895) and Korea (1910) (map 2). These losses convinced many Chinese that radical changes were inevitable, and when in 1911 a small mutiny broke out among the Manchu army, disaffection spread rapidly throughout the whole country and the imperial government collapsed (page 130).

India

George V was crowned King Emperor of India at a durbar, or assembly of notables, in Delhi in 1911. In an effort to placate nationalist emotions, the annulment of the unpopular partition of Bengal was announced at the durbar .

2 India in 1857

- territory under British rule in 1805
- territory under British rule at close of Lord Dalhousie's administration, 1856
- main area affected by Indian Mutiny, 1857
- main centres of rebellion

Shortly after Aurangzeb's death in 1707 (page 62), Mughal power declined. In the north, Oudh and Bengal became effectively independent, owing only nominal allegiance to Delhi; in the centre, the power of the Maratha confederacy increased; in the south the Muslim state of Mysore expanded rapidly. Meanwhile European influence in India continued to increase, with both the French and English East India Companies acquiring new territory in the southeast. Robert Clive's victory at Plassey in 1757 gave the English control over the lands and resources of Bengal, Orissa and Bihar, allowing the Company to maintain an army of over 100,000 men – most of them Indian soldiers (sepoys) trained to fight in European fashion – with which they not only destroyed France's Indian ambitions but also extended their control over the entire eastern coast of the subcontinent (map 1). Mysore went down to defeat in 1799, the Marathas in 1805, both delivering extensive new territories to British control, and most other major Indian rulers soon recognized British suzerainty.

Over the next half-century the conquest of Sind (1843) and the Punjab (1849), brought the dominions of the Company up to the country's natural frontier in the northwest, while a war with Nepal (1814-16) extended them to the Himalayas. To the east the British clashed with the Burmese empire and in 1824-6 annexed Assam and Arakan (page 89). Within India, the 'Doctrine of Lapse' introduced by Governor-General Dalhousie (1847-56) resulted in the absorption of autonomous but dependent states, such as Oudh and several Maratha kingdoms, into the directly administered territories (map 2). Not surprisingly, this policy provoked disaffection which found violent outlet in 1857. Beginning as a mutiny of the Company's native soldiers, the revolt soon involved princes, landlords and peasants throughout northern India; but the loyalty of the Sikhs and the passivity of southern India enabled the British to restore control after 14 months of bitter fighting.

The mutiny proved a watershed in the history of British India. It thoroughly discredited the Company and in 1858 the London government assumed direct control. The subcontinent now acquired a pivotal position in Britain's Imperial system, leading to intervention in Afghanistan to block Russian expansion into central Asia (page 114), and in Burma to counter French influence in Southeast Asia. From East Africa to China, the Indian army regularly acted to advance British interests. Within India, the autonomy of the princes was henceforth respected and active steps were taken to develop the economy: the construction of first-class roads and a major rail network, together with the opening of the Suez Canal in 1869, made possible the exploitation of raw materials and the introduction of export crops, such as tea. Between 1869 and 1929 India's foreign trade increased sevenfold. However, although some modern industries developed under Indian entrepreneurs, most of the trade involved importing British manufactures and exporting raw materials; and in most areas neither the character of the economy nor traditional agriculture experienced any basic change (map 3). The

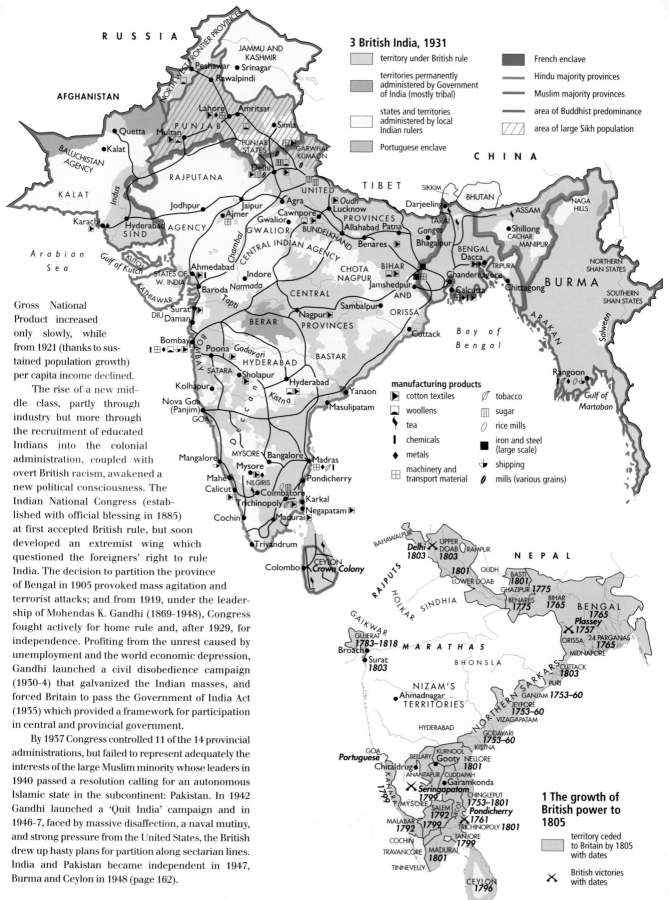

3 British India, 1931

- territory under British rule
- territories permanently administered by Government of India (mostly tribal)
- states and territories administered by local Indian rulers
- Portuguese enclave
- French enclave
- Hindu majority provinces
- Muslim majority provinces
- area of Buddhist predominance
- area of large Sikh population

manufacturing products

- ▶ cotton textiles
- ▭ woollens
- ⟋ tea
- I chemicals
- ◆ metals
- ⊞ machinery and transport material
- ∥ tobacco
- ⫼ sugar
- ◖ rice mills
- ■ iron and steel (large scale)
- ⏥ shipping
- ⫽ mills (various grains)

Gross National Product increased only slowly, while from 1921 (thanks to sustained population growth) per capita income declined.

The rise of a new middle class, partly through industry but more through the recruitment of educated Indians into the colonial administration, coupled with overt British racism, awakened a new political consciousness. The Indian National Congress (established with official blessing in 1885) at first accepted British rule, but soon developed an extremist wing which questioned the foreigners' right to rule India. The decision to partition the province of Bengal in 1905 provoked mass agitation and terrorist attacks; and from 1919, under the leadership of Mohendas K. Gandhi (1869-1948), Congress fought actively for home rule and, after 1929, for independence. Profiting from the unrest caused by unemployment and the world economic depression, Gandhi launched a civil disobedience campaign (1930-4) that galvanized the Indian masses, and forced Britain to pass the Government of India Act (1935) which provided a framework for participation in central and provincial government.

By 1937 Congress controlled 11 of the 14 provincial administrations, but failed to represent adequately the interests of the large Muslim minority whose leaders in 1940 passed a resolution calling for an autonomous Islamic state in the subcontinent: Pakistan. In 1942 Gandhi launched a 'Quit India' campaign and in 1946-7, faced by massive disaffection, a naval mutiny, and strong pressure from the United States, the British drew up hasty plans for partition along sectarian lines. India and Pakistan became independent in 1947, Burma and Ceylon in 1948 (page 162).

1 The growth of British power to 1805

- territory ceded to Britain by 1805 with dates
- ✕ British victories with dates

The age of revolution

The later 18th century saw an unprecedented wave of uprisings throughout the western hemisphere (map 1). Many reflected a long-standing desire for independence, as in Corsica (1755, 1793), Haiti (1791), Sardinia (1793), Ireland (1798), Serbia (1804) and Spain (1808). Most, however, owed something to the Enlightenment, a European intellectual movement which emphasized certain fundamental rights of human beings and rejected traditional authority. Paradoxically, this could lead to rebellions by conservative elements against reforming rulers – such as the Austrian Netherlands (1787) and Hungary (1790) against the 'Enlightened' policies of Emperor Joseph II – or the resistance of colonial societies to the centralizing policies of the home government – as in North America after 1775 (page 104) and in South America after 1808 (page 112). More commonly opposition came from the middle classes: against a closed patriarchate in the Dutch Republic (1785-7); against the absolute monarchy and its aristocratic supporters in France.

In France, between 1789 and 1791 a representative assembly, summoned to solve a financial crisis, abolished feudalism, and created a constitutional monarchy and equality before the law. The king, however, refused to cooperate and was deposed in 1792, provoking Austrian, Prussian and (from 1793) British attempts to overthrow the Republic by force. They failed: instead, the revolutionary government in Paris purged its opponents at home and, by mobilizing unprecedented numbers of its citizens, conquered the Low Countries, Switzerland and Italy, imposing satellite republics.

In 1799 a successful general, Napoleon Bonaparte, took power as military dictator. He secured peace abroad (1802), and reorganized French local government, laws and education. But Britain declared war again in 1803 and, although her command of the seas (confirmed at Trafalgar, 1805) provided immunity from invasion, Napoleon defeated her continental allies – Austria, Prussia and Russia – in a brilliant series of battles (1805-7). Next, in order to create a continental blockade against British trade, Napoleon overran Spain (1808) and extended France's frontiers to Catalonia, the Baltic and Rome (1809-10). However Britain supported his opponents in the Iberian peninsula, expelling French forces by 1814. Meanwhile Russia's refusal to cooperate in the continental blockade led to a French invasion in 1812 which, although it reached Moscow, exhausted Napoleon's resources and led to his defeat and abdication in 1814 and again in 1815 (the 'Hundred Days').

Nevertheless, despite his failure, Napoleon's achievements inspired even his enemies: throughout the 19th century, Spanish, German and Italian reformers envisaged the state in essentially Napoleonic mode (page 116), while his administrative, legal and educational reforms in France survived the restoration of royal power.

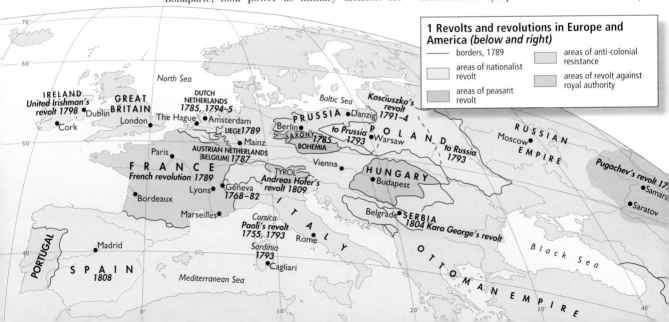

1 Revolts and revolutions in Europe and America (*below and right*)

— borders, 1789

areas of nationalist revolt

areas of peasant revolt

areas of anti-colonial resistance

areas of revolt against royal authority

North Sea

IRELAND
United Irishman's revolt 1798 • Dublin

GREAT BRITAIN
• London

DUTCH NETHERLANDS 1785, 1794-5
The Hague • Amsterdam
LIEGE 1789

Baltic Sea

Kosciuszko's revolt 1791-4

PRUSSIA • Danzig

• Berlin
SAXONY 1785
BOHEMIA

POLAND
• Warsaw
to Prussia 1793

RUSSIAN EMPIRE
Moscow •

• Cork

• Paris
• Mainz

AUSTRIAN NETHERLANDS (BELGIUM) 1787

Vienna •

to Russia 1793

Pugachev's revolt 17..
• Samara

FRANCE
French revolution 1789

TYROL
Andreas Hofer's revolt 1809

HUNGARY
• Budapest

• Lyons • Geneva
1768-82

• Saratov

• Bordeaux

• Marseilles

Corsica
Paoli's revolt 1755, 1793
Rome •

ITALY

Belgrade • SERBIA 1804 Kara George's revolt

Black Sea

PORTUGAL

• Madrid

SPAIN 1808

Sardinia 1793
• Cagliari

Mediterranean Sea

OTTOMAN EMPIRE

Corunna 1809

Oporto

Vimeiro 1808

Salamanca
(captured)
Madrid 1808

Lisbon 1809

Badajoz (captured) 1812
Cordova

Talavera

Vit..
18..

Cadiz

Seville

Bailén 18..

Trafalgar 1805

Gibraltar (British)
Ceuta (Spanish)

MOROCCO

Melilla (Spanish)

2 Napoleon and the reshaping of Europe

- French territories ruled from Paris, c. 1812
- states ruled by members of Napoleon's family, c. 1812
- other dependent states, c. 1812
- ☒ French victory
- ☒ French defeat
- ☒ battles of the Italian campaign
- ☒ battles of the War of the Second Coalition
- ☒ battles of the War of the Third Coalition
- ☒ battles in the Austrian War, 1809
- ☒ battles in the Peninsular War
- ☒ battles of the Russian campaign
- ☒ battles of the War of Liberation from French rule
- ☒ battles in the defence of France
- ☒ battles in the War of the 100 Days

On 14th July 1789 a crowd of Parisians stormed the Bastille fort to release a handful of political prisoners housed there *(below)*. The incident sparked off a more widespread revolt against the authority of Louis XVI, which led, four years later, to his imprisonment and execution. Bastille Day became the symbol for liberation struggles worldwide.

FINLAND
Helsinki
St Petersburg
NORWAY (Danish)
SWEDEN
Stockholm
Revel
RUSSIAN EMPIRE
Pskov
Riga
Dvinsk
Moscow (captured) 1812
Borodino 1812
Smolensk (captured) 1812
Maloyaroslavets 1812
Vitebsk
Berezina (crossed) 1812
Krasnoi 1812
Minsk
Kursk
Gothenburg
North Sea
Edinburgh
UNITED KINGDOM
Dublin
Liverpool
Bristol
London
Amsterdam
Aarhus
Copenhagen
Malmö
DENMARK
Baltic Sea
Königsberg
REPUBLIC OF DANZIG
to Sweden
Nieman
Tilsit
Vilna
Berezina
Lübeck
Hamburg
Hannover
Rhine
Berlin
PRUSSIA
GRAND DUCHY OF WARSAW
Poznań
Warsaw
Brest-Litovsk
Friedland 1807
Eylau 1807
CONFEDERATION OF THE RHINE
WESTPHALIA
Waterloo 1815
Brussels
Laon 1814
Château Thierry 1814
Ligny 1815
Rheims 1814
Paris 1814
Champaubert 1814
Montereau 1814
Tours
Montmirail/ Vauchamps 1814
La Fère Champenoise 1814
NEUCHÂTEL
Hanau 1813
Jena/ Auerstädt 1806
Ratisbon 1809
Ulm 1805
Zurich 1799
HELVETIC REPUBLIC
Geneva
Lyons
Lützen 1813
Dresden 1813
Bautzen 1813
Leipzig (Battle of the Nations) 1813
Prague 1813
Eckmühl/ Ebersberg 1809
Hohenlinden 1800
Vienna
Austerlitz 1805
Wagram 1809
Aspern/Essling 1809
Buda Pest
AUSTRIAN EMPIRE
HUNGARY
Cracow
FRENCH EMPIRE
Bordeaux
Toulouse
Saragossa (captured) 1809
Marseilles
Toulon
CATALONIA
Barcelona 1808
Valencia 1808
Castiglione 1796
Lonato 1796
Rivoli 1797
Lodi 1796
Marengo 1800
Mondovi 1796
Dego 1796
Montenotte 1796
Bassano 1796
Arcole 1796
KINGDOM OF ITALY
LUCCA
SAN MARINO
PIOMBINO
Florence
Zara
Spalato
Ragusa
MONTENEGRO
ILLYRIAN PROVINCES
Adriatic Sea
Corsica
Ajaccio
Rome
PONTECORVO
BENEVENTO
KINGDOM OF NAPLES
Naples
Bari
Taranto
Corfu
KINGDOM OF SARDINIA
Cagliari
Mediterranean Sea
ALGIERS
TUNIS
Palermo
KINGDOM OF SICILY
Messina
Malta (British)
Danube
Zágráb
Belgrade
OTTOMAN EMPIRE
Nish
Sofia
Ruschuk
Varna
Danube

VICE-ROYALTY OF NEW SPAIN
THIRTEEN COLONIES
Boston
New York
War of Independence, 1775
Gabriel's slave revolt, 1800
Mexico City
Port-au-Prince
HAITI Toussaint l'Ouverture's revolt 1791
Santo Domingo
Panama
Caracas
Santa Fé de Bogotá
VICE-ROYALTY OF NEW GRANADA
Quito
Lima
VICE-ROYALTY OF PERU
La Paz
VICE-ROYALTY OF BRAZIL
Bahia
Santiago
VICE-ROYALTY OF RIO DE LA PLATA
Buenos Aires
Pacific Ocean
SPANISH AMERICA
Mississippi

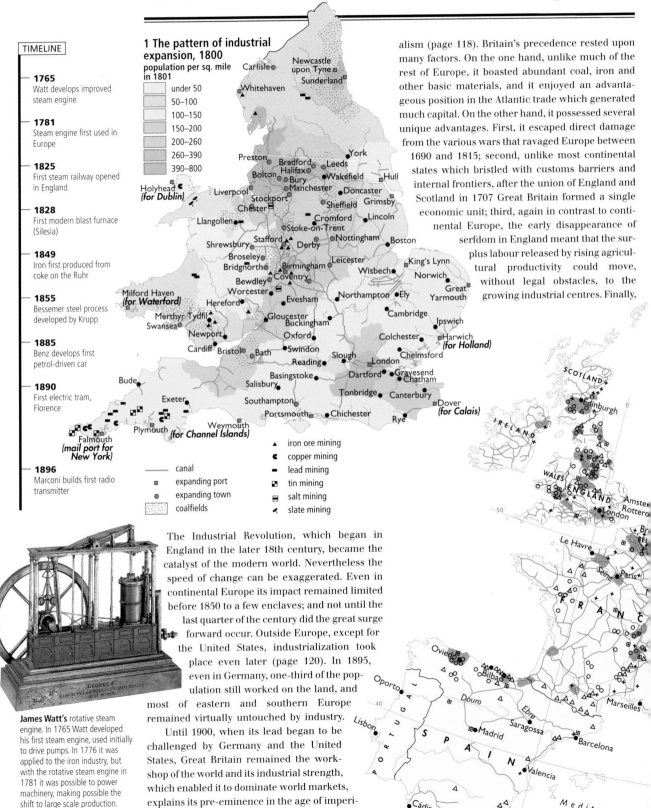

C. 1750–1914
The industrial revolution in Europe

1 The pattern of industrial expansion, 1800
population per sq. mile in 1801

- under 50
- 50–100
- 100–150
- 150–200
- 200–260
- 260–390
- 390–800

iron ore mining
copper mining
lead mining
tin mining
salt mining
slate mining

canal
expanding port
expanding town
coalfields

James Watt's rotative steam engine. In 1765 Watt developed his first steam engine, used initially to drive pumps. In 1776 it was applied to the iron industry, but with the rotative steam engine in 1781 it was possible to power machinery, making possible the shift to large scale production.

alism (page 118). Britain's precedence rested upon many factors. On the one hand, unlike much of the rest of Europe, it boasted abundant coal, iron and other basic materials, and it enjoyed an advantageous position in the Atlantic trade which generated much capital. On the other hand, it possessed several unique advantages. First, it escaped direct damage from the various wars that ravaged Europe between 1690 and 1815; second, unlike most continental states which bristled with customs barriers and internal frontiers, after the union of England and Scotland in 1707 Great Britain formed a single economic unit; third, again in contrast to continental Europe, the early disappearance of serfdom in England meant that the surplus labour released by rising agricultural productivity could move, without legal obstacles, to the growing industrial centres. Finally,

The Industrial Revolution, which began in England in the later 18th century, became the catalyst of the modern world. Nevertheless the speed of change can be exaggerated. Even in continental Europe its impact remained limited before 1850 to a few enclaves; and not until the last quarter of the century did the great surge forward occur. Outside Europe, except for the United States, industrialization took place even later (page 120). In 1895, even in Germany, one-third of the population still worked on the land, and most of eastern and southern Europe remained virtually untouched by industry.

Until 1900, when its lead began to be challenged by Germany and the United States, Great Britain remained the workshop of the world and its industrial strength, which enabled it to dominate world markets, explains its pre-eminence in the age of imperi-

England possessed a unique network of navigable rivers and canals (map 1), which proved of immense importance before the railway age for moving both raw materials and finished goods.

In its earliest phase, English manufacturers had also relied on water as a source of energy; but in the century to 1870 industrial power depended on steam, generated by the combustion of coal. At first, except in Britain and (from 1820) Belgium, steam power came only slowly, held back by political fragmentation, lack of capital and, above all, poor communications which severely limited markets. The steel firm of Krupp, founded in 1811 and later to be a giant of German industry, still employed only 7 men in 1826 and 122 in 1846. The pace of industrialization only accelerated with railway development. Between 1830 and 1870 the rail networks of Britain, Belgium and Germany became virtually complete, and construction began elsewhere. At much the same time, barriers to trade came down: France demolished her internal tariffs in 1790, Prussia followed suit in 1818 and in 1834 joined the German Customs Union, which included 17 states and some 26 million people.

A new period, sometimes called the Second Industrial Revolution, opened in the 1870s (see map 2). The new German empire (page 116) led the way, increasing its coal output from 38 million tons in 1871 to 279 million tons in 1913, and its iron output from 1.5 million tons to 15 million tons. But it also led in new areas of industrial enterprise, especially chemicals, electricity and steel. By 1910, Krupp employed 70,000 men. At a time of growing international tension (page 124), such rapid economic growth was bound to produce a reaction among Germany's neighbours and Russia began a campaign of rapid industrialization in 1890 (page 114), France in 1895 and Italy in 1905. In all these states, much heavy industry was keyed to armaments. Although the bulk of the population of Europe remained largely untouched, industrialization had both changed the face of the continent and rendered its future uncertain.

2 The industrialization of Europe, 1870–1914

- ▨ areas of industrial concentration 1870–1914
- + centres of textile industry
- ○ coalfields
- ⊞ centres of engineering, armaments and metal industries
- △ iron ore fields
- ◑ lignite fields
- ◓ potash fields
- ╿ centres of petroleum industry
- —— railway network, 1870

The emerging global economy

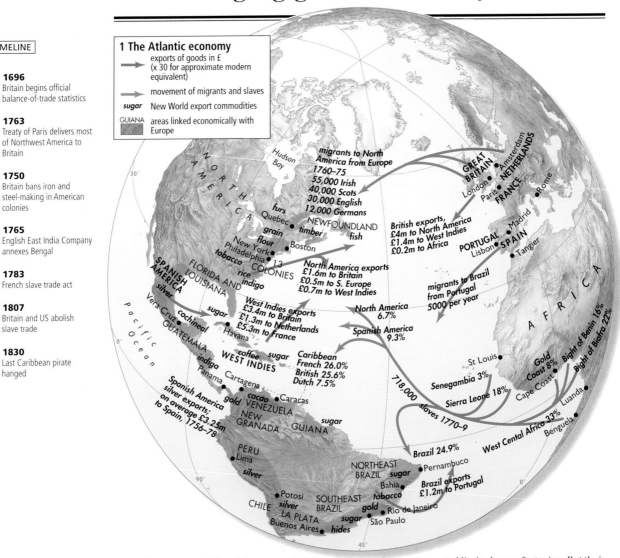

1 The Atlantic economy

→ exports of goods in £ (x 30 for approximate modern equivalent)

→ movement of migrants and slaves

sugar New World export commodities

GUIANA areas linked economically with Europe

Hudson Bay

migrants to North America from Europe 1760–75
55,000 Irish
40,000 Scots
30,000 English
12,000 Germans

furs
Quebec • timber
grain
New York • Boston
flour
Philadelphia • 13
tobacco COLONIES
rice
indigo

NEWFOUNDLAND
fish

NORTH AMERICA

GREAT BRITAIN • Amsterdam
London • NETHERLANDS
Paris • FRANCE
Rome •

British exports,
£4m to North America
£1.4m to West Indies
£0.2m to Africa

PORTUGAL SPAIN
Lisbon • Madrid •
• Tangier

SPANISH AMERICA
FLORIDA AND LOUISIANA

silver
Vera Cruz • cochineal
GUATEMALA
Havana
sugar
coffee sugar
WEST INDIES
indigo
Panama Cartagena
gold
cacao • Caracas
VENEZUELA
NEW GRANADA
GUIANA sugar

North America exports
£1.6m to Britain
£0.5m to S. Europe
£0.7m to West Indies

West Indies exports
£3.4m to Britain
£1.3m to Netherlands
£5.3m to France

North America 6.7%

Spanish America 9.3%

Caribbean
French 26.0%
British 25.6%
Dutch 7.5%

migrants to Brazil from Portugal 5000 per year

AFRICA

St Louis •
Senegambia 3%
Sierra Leone 18%
718,000 slaves 1770–9

Gold Coast 8%
Cape Coast
Bight of Benin 16%
Bight of Biafra 22%
Luanda •
West Central Africa 33%
Benguela •

Pacific Ocean

Spanish America silver exports on average £3.25m to Spain, 1756–78

Spanish America silver exports: on average £3.25m to Spain, 1756–78

PERU
Lima •
silver

Potosi •
silver
CHILE
LA PLATA
Buenos Aires •
hides

SOUTHEAST BRAZIL
sugar
Rio de Janeiro •
gold
São Paulo •

NORTHEAST BRAZIL sugar
Bahia •
tobacco
Pernambuco •
Brazil 24.9%

Brazil exports £1.2m to Portugal

30°
0°
90°
45°

In 1775, the areas of Spanish conquest and settlement in central and south America still ranked as the most valuable European overseas possession, thanks to the silver production of Mexico and Peru and the gold exports of Brazil, most of which went to Europe in return for manufactured goods. Along the Atlantic coast from Brazil to the Chesapeake, but above all in the Caribbean islands, plantation societies had developed to meet the rising demand both in Europe and in British North America (where over 2 million whites now dwelt) for tropical agricultural produce: cacao, tobacco, cotton and (especially) sugar. Since most plantations depended on the labour of African slaves, increased consumption in Europe meant increased shipments of slaves from Africa.

A closely integrated Atlantic economy had thus emerged. By 1775 the mainland colonies throughout the Americas were generally self-sufficient in food

and some supported limited manufacturing. But their white populations consumed prodigious quantities of imported European manufactured goods, and prosperity almost everywhere depended on the ability to export to Europe. Transatlantic commerce, in turn, contributed substantially to the economic development of Spain, France and Britain (almost 40 per cent of whose total exports in 1775 went to America).

In Asia, although the volume of European trade also greatly increased in the 18th century, it remained largely confined to ports or small coastal enclaves to which Asian merchants delivered goods. The Dutch and English East India Companies, founded in 1600-2 (page 80), still dominated trade with maritime Asia, but the shipment of spices to Europe had by the 18th century been overtaken by a boom in textiles (above all silks and cottons) and new drinks (tea and coffee). Since, however, in contrast to the Americas, few European manufactures proved competitive in Asia (except in the Mediterranean ports of the Ottoman empire), increased imports of Asian goods generally depended on shipments of American silver, either re-exported from Europe or carried across the Pacific to the Philippines and thence to China.

European trade also stimulated the demand for export commodities from, and injected large quantities of silver into, India and China; but most of Asia's economic life remained relatively unaffected by contact with the West, and much of its long-distance trade continued to be conducted by Asian merchants using their own pack-animals or ships. However, conditions were changing rapidly in two areas of great economic importance: the British had gained control of Bengal, a major centre of textile

manufacture, in the 1760s and now used its huge tax revenues to maintain a substantial army ready to annex other areas of the subcontinent; and the Dutch in Java could impose commercial controls and receive commodities (above all coffee) as tribute.

Only Africa remained almost totally resistant to European penetration. Although the slave trade reached its apogee in the 18th century, with some 2.3 million slaves shipped out between 1770 and 1800, the prices paid by the Europeans for each slave steadily rose – suggesting that the African rulers who dealt in slaves more than held their own, despite the disruption arising from wars and slave-raiding, and the sustained loss of population.

In short, Europe's rapid commercial expansion overseas (for better or worse) hastened the economic integration of the world. The Americas outside the plantations enjoyed a degree of self-sufficiency, but Europe still determined the economic development of much of the continent. Although, except in Bengal, Java and the Philippines, the West could not yet shape the economies of Asia and Africa, with Britain now poised to conquer India (page 96) and with the Industrial Revolution underway in Europe (page 100), the stage was set for the creation of an integrated global economy.

The loading plan of a slave ship *(below)* shows how many slaves could be crammed below decks. The crowding marked a callous compromise between the slavers' desire to ferry as many slaves as possible and the need to ensure as many as possible of those embarked survived the voyage. By the late 18th century most ships lost less then 10 per cent of their human cargo. In earlier times, however, losses had sometimes exceeded 30 per cent, leading the Portuguese to refer to their slave ships as *tumbeiros* – coffins.

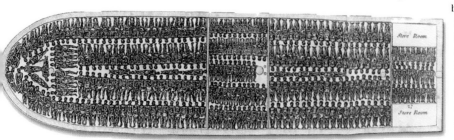

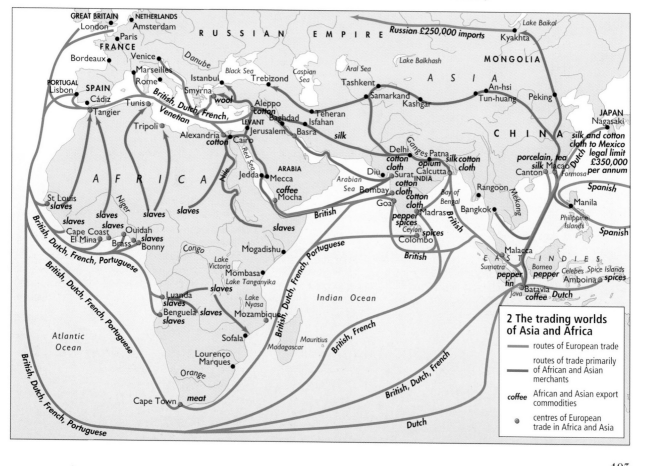

2 The trading worlds of Asia and Africa

— routes of European trade

— routes of trade primarily of African and Asian merchants

coffee African and Asian export commodities

• centres of European trade in Africa and Asia

The disputes and difficulties leading to the American War of Independence and the foundation of the United States began almost immediately after the English victory over France in the Seven Years' War (page 86). Britain began to reorganize her vastly expanded North American possessions, establishing a huge Indian reserve west of the Alleghenies (1763) and extending the boundaries of Quebec (formerly French Canada) to the Mississippi and Ohio rivers (1774). The 'thirteen colonies' bitterly resented both this check to their westward expansion and the simultaneous insistence by Britain that its colonies should henceforth bear a greater share of the costs of their defence. Armed opposition began at Lexington and Concord in Massachusetts in 1775 (map 1). The colonies' representatives declared Independence in 1776, compelled the main British field army to surrender at Yorktown (1781), and fought on until the Treaty of Versailles (1783) recognized their sovereignty and extended the frontiers of the 'United States of America' to the Great Lakes and the Mississippi.

Expansion now proceeded rapidly. In 1783 the new republic comprised some 800,000 square miles (2,072,000 km^2) of territory, but the purchase of Louisiana from France (1803) more than doubled its size. West Florida was taken by force in 1812 and East Florida (60,000 square miles, 155,400 km^2) during the presidency of James Monroe. Thereafter extensive territories in the south and west were added, largely at the expense of Mexico (map 2), and in 1846 a compromise with Britain was reached over Oregon, increasing the number of states from 13 to 34. The population expanded from 3 million in 1783 to 31 million in 1860, fuelled by the arrival of a new wave of European immigrants, predominantly German and Irish.

These developments had important political consequences. The ruling elites of the southern states, with their plantation economy and large black slave population, felt increasingly threatened by the industrializing north and the growing Midwest. This, rather than the issue of slavery, underlay the American Civil War (1861-5); but the issues in fact proved inseparable because, with over 90 percent of

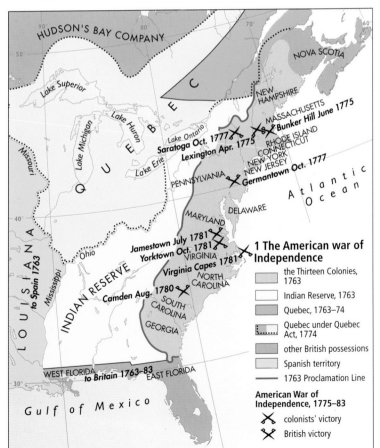

1 The American war of Independence

- the Thirteen Colonies, 1763
- Indian Reserve, 1763
- Quebec, 1763–74
- Quebec under Quebec Act, 1774
- other British possessions
- Spanish territory
- 1763 Proclamation Line

American War of Independence, 1775–83

- ✗ colonists' victory
- ✗ British victory

Dead soldiers at Gettysburg *(below).* The small market town of Gettysburg, Pennsylvania, was the scene of the greatest battles of the war. Lee, advancing into the North to force Lincoln to negotiate peace on the basis of Southern independence, attacked General Meade's Union army, but in the course of a three-day battle was comprehensively beaten. The Union lost 23,000 men, the Confederacy 28,000.

the black population living in the South, the moral question was also a regional question. Abraham Lincoln, elected President in 1860 by the votes of the Northern states, was right to claim that the nation could not permanently remain 'half slave and half free'.

Soon after Lincoln's election, South Carolina seceded from the Union and was quickly joined by ten other states which came together as the Confederate States of America with their capital at Richmond, Virginia (map 4). For Lincoln the fundamental issue was whether a constitutional republic could preserve its territorial integrity; he recognized no constitutional right of secession. By 1863, however, pressure from radical Republicans added the aim of freeing the slaves in the rebel states to the commitment to restore the Union. Thanks to the superior military skill of their commanders, and to their shorter lines of communications, the confederacy fought on for four years (1861-5). The Northern strategy was to deny the South vital resources by a naval blockade, to gain control of key river routes and forts in the west and to capture Richmond. Eventually the superior demographic and economic resources of the North prevailed – albeit at the cost of 635,000 Union and 383,000 Confederate military casualties – and created the 'second American Revolution' which, by crippling the southern ruling class and liberating its labour force, determined that the thrusting, urban, industrialized North, with its creed of competitive capitalism, would stamp its pattern (for good or ill) on the entire United States.

4 Comparative resources: Union and Confederate states, 1861

- Union States
- Confederate States

Total pop.: 2.5 to 1 | Naval ship ton.: 25 to 1 | Farm acreage: 3 to 1

Male adult pop.: 4.4 to 1 | Factory prod.: 10 to 1 | Draft animals: 1.8 to 1

Free men 18–60 yrs in military service: 1864 **44%** **90%** | Textile prod.: 17 to 1 | Livestock: 1.5 to 1

Wealth produced: 3 to 1 | Iron production: 20 to 1 | Wheat prod.: 4.2 to 1

Railroad mileage: 2.4 to 1 | Coal production: 38 to 1 | Corn production: 2 to 1

Merchant ship ton.: 9 to 1 | Firearms prod.: 32 to 1 | Cotton prod.: 1 to 24

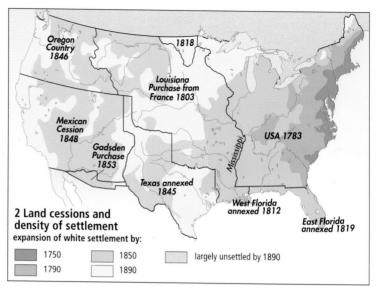

2 Land cessions and density of settlement

expansion of white settlement by:

- 1750
- 1790
- 1850
- 1890
- largely unsettled by 1890

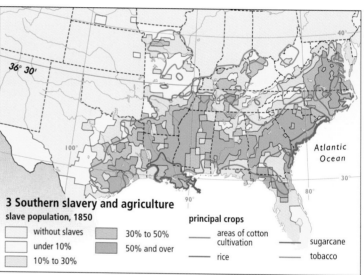

3 Southern slavery and agriculture

slave population, 1850

- without slaves
- under 10%
- 10% to 30%
- 30% to 50%
- 50% and over

principal crops

- areas of cotton cultivation
- rice
- sugarcane
- tobacco

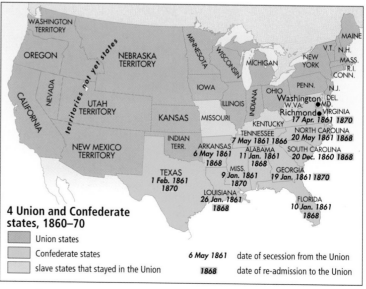

4 Union and Confederate states, 1860–70

- Union states
- Confederate states
- slave states that stayed in the Union

6 May 1861 — date of secession from the Union
1868 — date of re-admission to the Union

Australia and New Zealand

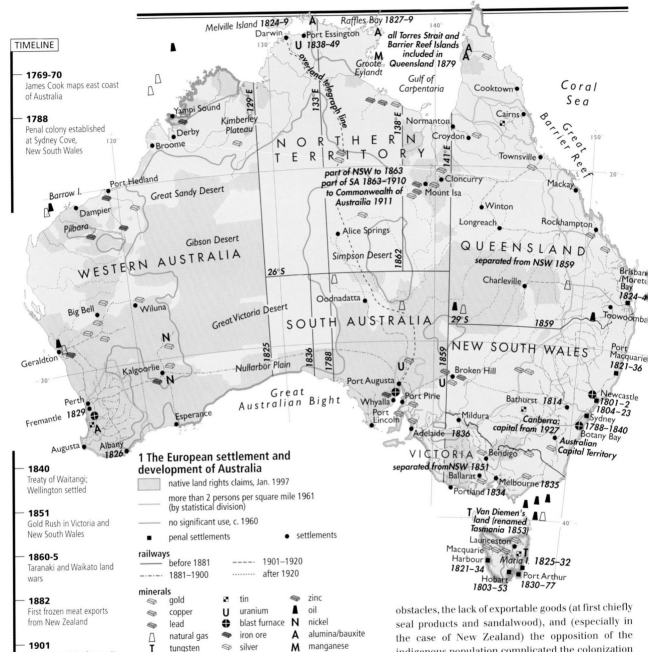

TIMELINE

1769-70
James Cook maps east coast
of Australia

1788
Penal colony established
at Sydney Cove,
New South Wales

1840
Treaty of Waitangi;
Wellington settled

1851
Gold Rush in Victoria and
New South Wales

1860-5
Taranaki and Waikato land
wars

1882
First frozen meat exports
from New Zealand

1901
Commonwealth of Australia
created

1975
Waitangi Tribunal
established

1992
Mabo judgement on native
title in Australia

Melville Island 1824–9
Raffles Bay 1827–9
Darwin
Port Essington
1838–49
all Torres Strait and
Barrier Reef Islands
included in
Queensland 1879
Groote
Eylandt
Gulf of
Carpentaria
Cooktown
Coral
Sea
Yampi Sound
Kimberley
Plateau
Normanton
Cairns
Great
Barrier Reef
Derby
Croydon
Broome
NORTHERN
TERRITORY
part of NSW to 1863
part of SA 1863–1910
to Commonwealth of
Austrailia 1911
Cloncurry
Mount Isa
Townsville
Mackay
Port Hedland
Barrow I.
Dampier
Pilbara
Great Sandy Desert
Winton
Longreach
Rockhampton
Gibson Desert
Alice Springs
Simpson Desert
QUEENSLAND
separated from NSW 1859
Brisbane
/Moreton
Bay
1824–4
WESTERN AUSTRALIA
Charleville
Big Bell
Wiluna
Oodnadatta
SOUTH AUSTRALIA
Toowoomba
Great Victoria Desert
NEW SOUTH WALES
Port
Macquarie
1821–36
Geraldton
Kalgoorlie
Nullarbor Plain
Broken Hill
Bathurst 1814
Newcastle
1801–2
1804–23
Perth
Port Augusta
Mildura
Canberra:
capital from 1927
Sydney
1788–1840
Botany Bay
Australian
Capital Territory
Fremantle 1829
Esperance
Whyalla
Port Pirie
Great
Australian Bight
Port
Lincoln
Augusta
Albany
1826
Adelaide 1836
VICTORIA
separated from NSW 1851
Ballarat
Bendigo
Portland 1834
Melbourne 1835
Van Diemen's
land (renamed
Tasmania 1853)
Launceston
Macquarie
Harbour
1821–34
Maria I. 1825–32
Hobart
1803–53
Port Arthur
1830–77

1 The European settlement and development of Australia

native land rights claims, Jan. 1997

more than 2 persons per square mile 1961
(by statistical division)

no significant use, c. 1960

■ penal settlements   ● settlements

railways
— before 1881   ---- 1901–1920
-·-·- 1881–1900   ········ after 1920

minerals
gold   ▣ tin   zinc
copper   U uranium   ▲ oil
lead   ⊕ blast furnace   N nickel
▱ natural gas   iron ore   A alumina/bauxite
T tungsten   silver   M manganese

Although Australia and New Zealand were recon-
noitred by the Dutch explorer Abel Tasman in 1642,
colonization only began in 1770 when James Cook
raised the British flag at Botany Bay. New South Wales
served as a penal colony from 1788 to 1839, as did van
Diemen's land (later Tasmania) from 1804 to 1853,
but in 1829 the British government, in order to
forestall the French, claimed the whole Australian
continent. Fear of France also led to the annexation of
New Zealand in 1840. However, the geographical
obstacles, the lack of exportable goods (at first chiefly
seal products and sandalwood), and (especially in
the case of New Zealand) the opposition of the
indigenous population complicated the colonization
process in both territories. In 1850, the total white
population of Australia still numbered only 350,000,
and that of New Zealand was less than 100,000.

The discovery of gold in New South Wales and
Victoria in 1851 initiated a new phase, and encouraged the growth of the inland population. Even more
important was the rapid growth of sheep-farming:
in 1850 Australia sent 17,000 tons of wool to
Great Britain, but 134,000 tons in 1879. Nevertheless,
as centralizing systems of communications and

transportation developed, the dominance of the coastal cities – especially Sydney and Melbourne – increased. By the 1890s, two-thirds of Australia's population lived in urban areas along the coast (a pattern that steadily intensified throughout the 20th century.) In New Zealand, where wool remained largely a South Island product, exports rose in value from £67,000 in 1853 to £2.7 million twenty years later. The development of the North Island, which was held back by the bitter Maori Wars (1860-71), only came after the introduction of refrigeration, which made possible the export of frozen lamb, butter and cheese. Dairy farming developed rapidly, and the North Island now drew ahead of the South in population.

Political development kept pace with economic growth. In 1855 New South Wales, Victoria, South Australia and Tasmania became self-governing colonies, followed by Queensland in 1859; in 1901 they joined together to form the Commonwealth of Australia. New Zealand, which had been divided in 1852 into six provinces, each with an elected council, became a united Dominion (after measures had been taken to safeguard the rights of the Maori population) in 1876. Both countries achieved sovereign status under the Statute of Westminster in 1931. The economy of both dominions remained heavily dependent on primary exports – wool, meat, grain and dairy products – which enjoyed preferential treatment in the British market. Even the spectacular discoveries of minerals, coal, oil and gas in and about Australia after 1950 went largely into exports. However Britain's decision to join the European Economic Community and dismantle 'imperial preference' in 1973 (page 166), coupled with the conviction that the countries of the Pacific Rim would become the economic hub of the world in the 21st century, drove both Australia and New Zealand to develop new economic activities and to foster trade with countries outside the British Commonwealth.

This romanticized picture of an attack on a Maori *pa* (fort) during the first New Zealand War suggests the storming of a castle. In fact, recent research has revealed that the *pa* evolved rapidly into sophisticated trench and bunker systems which anticipated those of the Western Front by over 50 years. By the end of the conflict large tracts of Maori land had been confiscated by the colonial government.

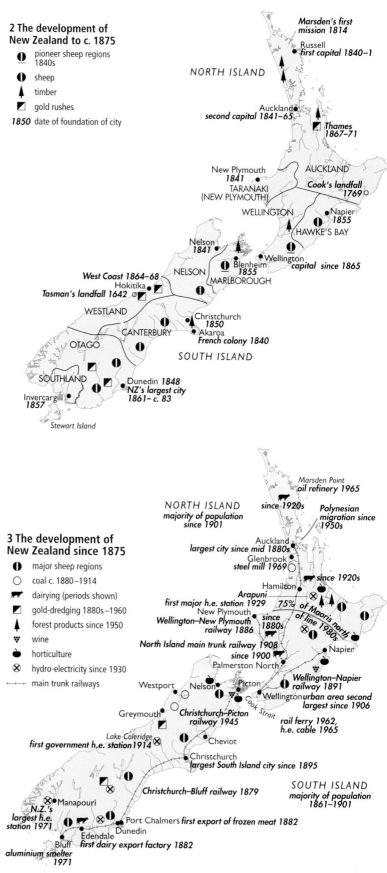

2 The development of New Zealand to c. 1875

- pioneer sheep regions 1840s
- sheep
- timber
- gold rushes

1850 date of foundation of city

NORTH ISLAND

Marsden's first mission 1814
Russell first capital 1840-1
Auckland second capital 1841-65
Thames 1867-71
Cook's landfall 1769
AUCKLAND
New Plymouth 1841
TARANAKI (NEW PLYMOUTH)
Napier 1855
WELLINGTON
HAWKE'S BAY
Nelson 1841
Wellington capital since 1865
Blenheim 1855
NELSON
MARLBOROUGH
West Coast 1864-68
Hokitika
Tasman's landfall 1642
WESTLAND
Christchurch 1850
CANTERBURY
Akaroa French colony 1840
OTAGO
SOUTH ISLAND
SOUTHLAND
Dunedin 1848 NZ's largest city 1861- c. 83
Invercargill 1857
Stewart Island

3 The development of New Zealand since 1875

- major sheep regions
- coal c. 1880–1914
- dairying (periods shown)
- gold-dredging 1880s–1960
- forest products since 1950
- wine
- horticulture
- hydro-electricity since 1930
- main trunk railways

NORTH ISLAND majority of population since 1901
Marsden Point oil refinery 1965
since 1920s
Polynesian migration since 1950s
Auckland largest city since mid 1880s
Glenbrook steel mill 1969
since 1920s
Hamilton
Arapuni first major h.e. station 1929
New Plymouth
75% of Maoris north of line 1980s
Wellington–New Plymouth railway 1886
since 1880s
North Island main trunk railway 1908
Napier
since 1900
Palmerston North
Wellington–Napier railway 1891
Westport
Nelson
Picton
Wellington urban area second largest since 1906
Greymouth
Christchurch–Picton railway 1945
Cook Strait
rail ferry 1962, h.e. cable 1965
Lake Coleridge
first government h.e. station 1914
Cheviot
Christchurch largest South Island city since 1895
Christchurch–Bluff railway 1879
SOUTH ISLAND majority of population 1861–1901
N.Z.'s largest h.e. station 1971
Manapouri
Port Chalmers first export of frozen meat 1882
Edendale
Dunedin
Bluff aluminium smelter 1971
Edendale first dairy export factory 1882

The decline of the Ottoman empire

The period between 1798 and 1923 saw the disintegration and final collapse of the Ottoman Empire, the major power in West Asia since the 16th century (see page 70). Plagued by foreign invasions, wars, and the revolts of subject peoples demanding national independence, the empire steadily lost territory.

In 1798 a French army led by Napoleon Bonaparte invaded Egypt and Syria, only to be defeated by the British. Peace was arranged in 1802 and three years later the sultan appointed Mohammed Ali governor of Egypt. Under his rule, however, the province gained de facto independence and in 1841 Mohammed was recognized as hereditary viceroy. Meanwhile, between 1830 and 1847 the French conquered Algeria, and in 1881 they annexed Tunis; the following year the British occupied Egypt. There were also wars with Russia, rebellions in the Arab provinces and almost constant revolts in the Balkans – starting with the Greek War of Independence in 1821, which resulted (following the pressure of foreign powers) in the recognition of a sovereign Greek state in 1830. Foreign intervention also

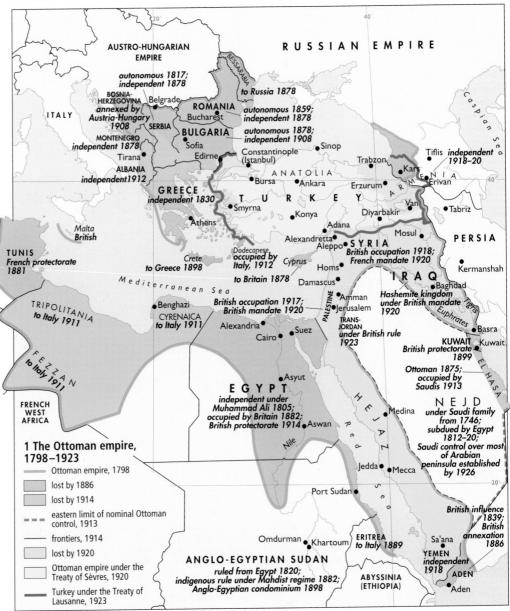

1 The Ottoman empire, 1798–1923

- Ottoman empire, 1798
- lost by 1886
- lost by 1914
- --- eastern limit of nominal Ottoman control, 1913
- — frontiers, 1914
- lost by 1920
- Ottoman empire under the Treaty of Sèvres, 1920
- — Turkey under the Treaty of Lausanne, 1923

precipitated the Crimean War (1853-6) and the Lebanese crisis of 1860-1, while Russian and Austrian demands helped secure the independence of Montenegro, Serbia and Romania by 1878. By 1882, the Ottomans had lost 40 per cent of their empire.

Their finances also deteriorated rapidly until in 1875 the state became virtually bankrupt and the Sultan suspended payment of the interest due on the Ottoman debt. In 1881, he agreed to supervision of his treasury by European bankers: the empire's survival became dependent on foreign governments which preferred the preservation of a weakened Ottoman state to the dangerous power vacuum that would follow Turkish collapse. Nevertheless, further territorial losses followed: Italy annexed Libya in 1911 and, at the end of the Balkan wars in 1913 (page 124), the Ottomans surrendered Crete, most of the Aegean islands, Thrace, Macedonia and Albania. In all, between 1908 and 1911, the Turks lost 30 per cent of their remaining possessions.

Throughout the 19th century the sultans made various attempts to modernize their empire, but not always successfully: Selim III, who aimed to create a modern army, was deposed in 1807 when his troops mutinied against the proposed reforms. The Janissaries rebelled in 1826 against reforms decreed by Mahmud II, but this provoked their abolition.

After a decade of agitation, in 1876 Sultan Abdul Hamid II introduced a constitution, and a Parliament met the following year; but it was dissolved almost immediately and only pressure by the Ottoman Society for Union and Progress (the 'Young Turks') forced its restoration in 1908. The following year Abdul Hamid abdicated, and the Young Turks came to dominate the administration. However, their nationalist policies and opposition to any further surrender of territory contributed substantially to the Arabs' willingness to seek accommodation with the Turks' enemies, once the Ottoman empire entered World War I on the side of Germany and Austro-Hungary (page 132).

Despite tenacious resistance, the Turks were eventually defeated and West Asia (despite earlier promises to the Arabs) came under the control of the victorious French and British governments. The Sultan collaborated with Great Britain after his defeat, and in 1920 agreed to the treaty of Sèvres which would dismember the empire. However, the arrival of Greek troops at Izmir provoked a nationalist uprising which crystallized around the Turks' only undefeated general, Mustafa Kemal. The sultanate was abolished and, after some reverses, Turkish forces drove back the Greeks and their allies and secured recognition of the sovereignty of the Turkish Republic at the treaty of Lausanne in 1923.

Mustafa Kemal, or Atatürk *(above),* – 'father of the Turks', as he styled himself – was an Ottoman commander in the First World War. His effective leadership of Turkish forces in 1922 led to his becoming president of the new Turkish republic that year. He was determined to turn Turkey into a modern, industrialized, Western-style secular state.

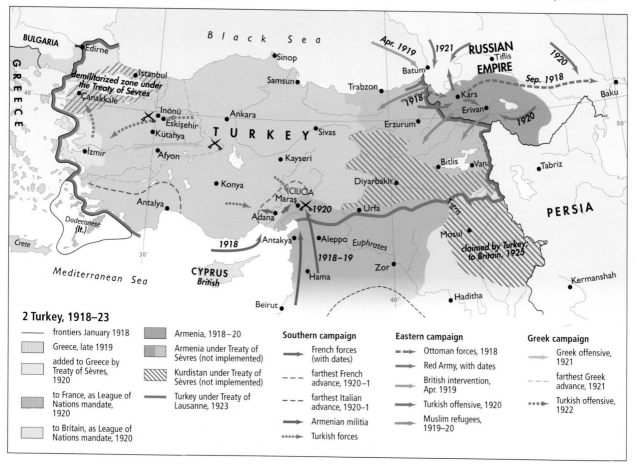

2 Turkey, 1918–23

——	frontiers January 1918
▨	Greece, late 1919
▨	added to Greece by Treaty of Sèvres, 1920
▨	to France, as League of Nations mandate, 1920
▨	to Britain, as League of Nations mandate, 1920
▨	Armenia, 1918–20
▨	Armenia under Treaty of Sèvres (not implemented)
▨	Kurdistan under Treaty of Sèvres (not implemented)
——	Turkey under Treaty of Lausanne, 1923

Southern campaign
- → French forces (with dates)
- – – – farthest French advance, 1920–1
- – – – farthest Italian advance, 1920–1
- → Armenian militia
- ••••• Turkish forces

Eastern campaign
- ⇢ ⇢ Ottoman forces, 1918
- → Red Army, with dates
- → British intervention, Apr. 1919
- → Turkish offensive, 1920
- → Muslim refugees, 1919–20

Greek campaign
- → Greek offensive, 1921
- – – – farthest Greek advance, 1921
- ••••• Turkish offensive, 1922

Africa in the 19th century

By 1870 the Western powers had finally ended the slave trade, responsible for the forced migration of at least 10 million Africans to the Americas since 1500. Otherwise, however, Europe's impact on the African interior remained limited to two areas: Algeria, conquered by France between 1830 and 1847, and Cape Colony, where Dutch settlers (subjected to British rule after 1806) moved north-east in the Great Trek (1835) in search of land and freedom, and founded settlements which eventually became the Orange Free State and Transvaal. In West Africa, the followers of a Muslim religious leader from Hausaland, Usuman dan Fodio, conquered much of Upper Nigeria after 1804, and his son became sultan of Sokoto. Somewhat later, two other charismatic Islamic leaders also carved out new states: al-Hajj Umar north of the Niger in the 1850s, and Samory south of it in the 1870s and '80s. In the north-east, Mohammed Ali of Egypt conquered northern Sudan in 1820, and his grandson Ismail consolidated

2 Alien rule in Africa, 1913

French		Anglo-Egyptian condominium
British		independent
German	1882–95	date of determination of colonial boundary
Portuguese		
Belgian	—	frontiers, 1914
Spanish		
Italian		

Egyptian control over much of the littoral of the Red Sea. Finally, in the south, the formation of the Zulu kingdom by Shaka in 1818 led to widespread disruption as neighbouring peoples moved away from the aggressive new state.

Meanwhile, the progress of industrialization in Europe (page 100) created a demand for new sources of raw materials and new markets, while the mass-production of quinine (which offered protection against the malaria endemic in Africa) and machine-guns gave the Europeans the ability to satisfy these demands by force. In the 1870s the French advanced inland from Senegal while the British began the conquest of Nigeria. In 1882 the British invaded and occupied Egypt, and the Belgians advanced up the Congo river. Next, Germany laid claim to Togoland, the Cameroons, Southwest Africa and

The Battle of Isandhlwana on 22 January 1879 was the first major engagement of the Zulu war (right). A British force of 1700 white and African troops under Lord Chelmsford was routed by 20,000 Zulu, the consequence rather of British arrogance and carelessness than of overwhelming numbers. It demonstrated the continuing possibility that African tactics and weaponry could triumph over well-armed European forces.

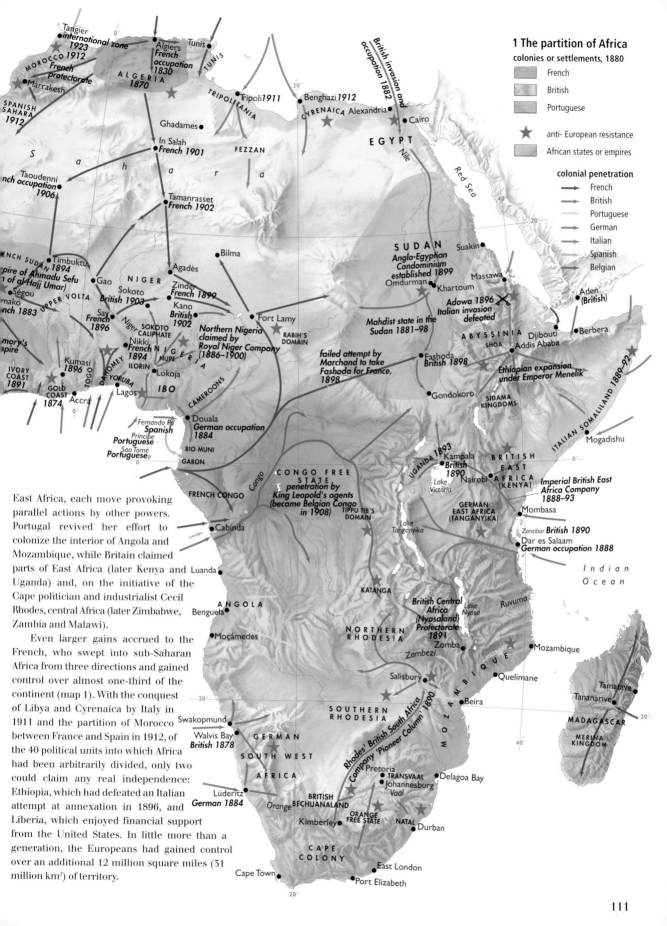

1 The partition of Africa

colonies or settlements, 1880

French

British

Portuguese

★ anti- European resistance

African states or empires

colonial penetration

→ French

→ British

→ Portuguese

→ German

→ Italian

Spanish

Belgian

Tangier
international zone
1923

MOROCCO 1912
French protectorate

Marrakesh

SPANISH SAHARA
1912

Algiers *French occupation 1830*

Tunis

ALGERIA 1870

TUNIS

TRIPOLITANIA

Tripoli 1911

Ghadames

FEZZAN

Benghazi 1912

CYRENAICA

Alexandria

Cairo

British invasion and occupation 1882

EGYPT

Nile

Red Sea

S a h a r a

ench occupation 1906

Taoudenni

In Salah *French 1901*

Tamanrasset *French 1902*

Bilma

FRENCH SUDAN 1894
pire of Ahmadu Sefu n of al-Hajj Umar

Timbuktu

Gao

Agadès

NIGER

Zinder *French 1899*

SUDAN
Anglo-Egyptian Condominium established 1899

Omdurman

Khartoum

Suakin

Massawa

Aden (British)

Berbera

Segou

UPPER VOLTA

Sokoto *British 1903*

Kano *British 1902*

Fort Lamy

RABIH'S DOMAIN

Mahdist state in the Sudan 1881–98

Adowa 1896 *Italian invasion defeated*

ABYSSINIA

SHOA

Djibouti

Addis Ababa

mory's pire

IVORY COAST 1891

Kumasi 1896

GOLD COAST 1874

Accra

Say *French 1896*

Niger

Nikki *French 1894*

NUPE

SOKOTO CALIPHATE

ILORIN

Lokoja

NIGERIA

IBO

YORUBA

DAHOMEY

TOGO

Lagos

CAMEROONS

Northern Nigeria claimed by Royal Niger Company (1886–1900)

failed attempt by Marchand to take Fashoda for France, 1898

Fashoda *British 1898*

Gondokoro

Ethiopian expansion under Emperor Menelik

SIDAMA KINGDOMS

ITALIAN SOMALILAND 1889–92

Mogadishu

Fernando Po
Spanish

Principe *Portuguese*

Sao Tomé *Portuguese*

Douala *German occupation 1884*

RIO MUNI

GABON

FRENCH CONGO

Congo

CONGO FREE STATE
penetration by King Leopold's agents (became Belgian Congo in 1908)

TIPPU TIB'S DOMAIN

UGANDA 1893 *British 1890*

Kampala

Lake Victoria

Nairobi

BRITISH EAST AFRICA (KENYA)

Imperial British East Africa Company 1888–93

GERMAN EAST AFRICA (TANGANYIKA)

Mombasa

Zanzibar *British 1890*

Dar es Salaam *German occupation 1888*

I n d i a n   O c e a n

East Africa, each move provoking parallel actions by other powers. Portugal revived her effort to colonize the interior of Angola and Mozambique, while Britain claimed parts of East Africa (later Kenya and Uganda) and, on the initiative of the Cape politician and industrialist Cecil Rhodes, central Africa (later Zimbabwe, Zambia and Malawi).

Even larger gains accrued to the French, who swept into sub-Saharan Africa from three directions and gained control over almost one-third of the continent (map 1). With the conquest of Libya and Cyrenaica by Italy in 1911 and the partition of Morocco between France and Spain in 1912, of the 40 political units into which Africa had been arbitrarily divided, only two could claim any real independence: Ethiopia, which had defeated an Italian attempt at annexation in 1896, and Liberia, which enjoyed financial support from the United States. In little more than a generation, the Europeans had gained control over an additional 12 million square miles (31 million km²) of territory.

Cabinda

Luanda

ANGOLA

Benguela

Moçâmedes

KATANGA

NORTHERN RHODESIA

British Central Africa (Nyasaland) Protectorate 1891

Lake Nyasa

Zomba

Ruvuma

Mozambique

Quelimane

Zambezi

Salisbury

SOUTHERN RHODESIA

Beira

MOZAMBIQUE

Tamatave

Tananarive

MADAGASCAR

MERINA KINGDOM

Swakopmund

Walvis Bay *British 1878*

GERMAN SOUTH WEST AFRICA

Lüderitz *German 1884*

Orange

Rhodes' British South Africa Company 'Pioneer Column' 1890

BRITISH BECHUANALAND

Kimberley

Pretoria

TRANSVAAL

Johannesburg

Vaal

Delagoa Bay

ORANGE FREE STATE

NATAL

Durban

CAPE COLONY

Cape Town

Port Elizabeth

East London

111

1808–1929
Latin America

TIMELINE

- **1808**
  Napoleonic invasion of Portugal and Spain stimulates independence movements in Latin America

- **1819**
  Battle of Boyacá leads to independence of Colombia

- **1821**
  Battle of Carabobo finally secures Venezuelan independence

- **1822**
  Brazil declares independence

- **1823**
  Mexican Republic declared

- **1879**
  War of the Pacific (Chile, Bolivia, Peru)

- **1910**
  Start of Mexican revolution

Napoleon's invasion of Spain and Portugal in 1808 (page 98) enabled these countries' American colonies to gain independence. The revolt began in Argentina in 1810 and in Venezuela in 1811, helped by the decision of Great Britain and the United States to oppose intervention by the Iberian powers. The fall of Lima (1821) and Simón Bolívar's victory at Ayacucho (1824), deprived Spain of control over South America. In the North, early rebellions in Mexico were suppressed, but in 1823 a republic was proclaimed, and a last Spanish attempt at reconquest in 1829 met with defeat. Only Brazil made the transition to independence peacefully, as Portugal agreed to provide a constitution and in 1822 the Portuguese king's eldest son became Emperor Pedro I of Brazil. Only in 1889 when, following the abolition of slavery (1888), disgruntled plantation owners rose in revolt, did a federal republic replace the empire.

Independence remained in essence a political movement confined to the colonial aristocracy, who desired a transfer of authority without social change. The next half-century was dominated by military dictators who ruled in the interests of the privileged classes and squandered their assets on repeated territorial disputes. Mexico lost most, forfeiting vast territories to the United States (see page 104); but it was also the first state to introduce limited social reforms after the election of the Indian Benito Juarez as President in 1861.

A subsistence economy still prevailed in most areas. Although Brazil with its slave-operated coffee plantations offered an exception, elsewhere the great rural estates showed little interest in producing for the market. After 1880, overseas investment increased rapidly, but selectively, concentrated mainly in Argentina, Brazil, Mexico and Chile. Moreover, even there, the foreign stimulus shifted those economies sharply towards the export of primary products: grain and meat from Argentina, nitrate from Chile, coffee and rubber from Brazil, oil from Mexico, and fruit from the so-called 'Banana Republics' of the central isthmus.

Most of these countries modernized and commercialized their production, and built docks and railways to expedite the export of food and raw materials. This attracted a new wave of immigrants and created a new urban and industrial proletariat as well as a middle class prospering from the export trade; but it left the majority of the rural population in abject poverty. Mexico under the repressive regime of Porfirio Díaz (1876-1911) exemplified these trends until in 1910 the country erupted in revolution: eventually, in 1917, a constitution incorporating major social and political reforms was adopted. Elsewhere, as long as prosperity continued – that is, until the Great Crash of 1929 (see page 138) – political and social pressures remained under control (albeit sometimes only thanks to armed intervention by the United States); but rapid and unbalanced economic expansion steadily undermined the regimes that promoted it.

abbreviations to map below

A	AGUASCALIENTES	N	NUEVO LEÓN
C	CAMPECHE	P	PUEBLA
G	GUANAJUATO	Q	QUERÉTARO
H	HIDALGO	S	SAN LUIS POTOSÍ
ME	MÉXICO	T	TLAXCALA
M	MORELOS	V	VERACRUZ

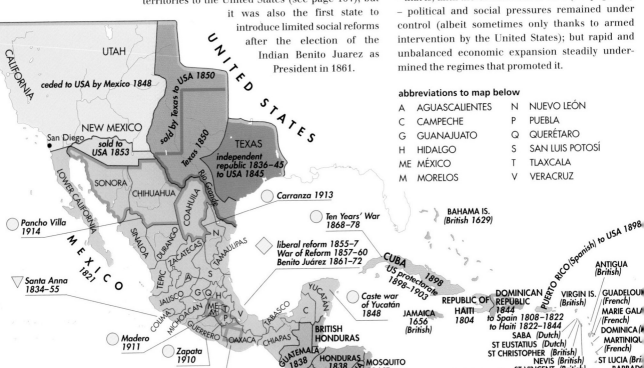

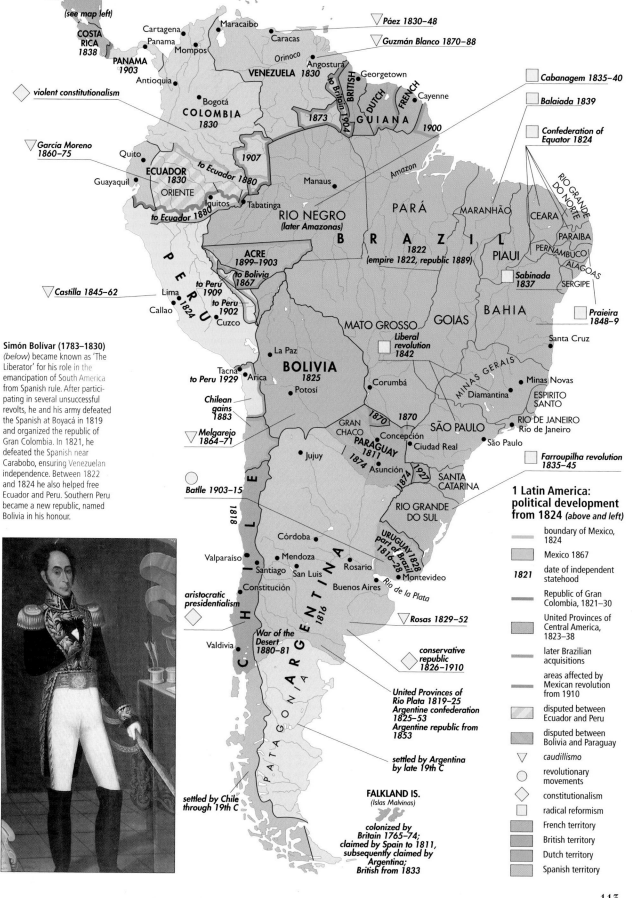

Páez 1830–48

Guzmán Blanco 1870–88

Cabanagem 1835–40

Balaiada 1839

Confederation of Equator 1824

◇ violent constitutionalism

▽ García Moreno 1860–75

▽ Castilla 1845–62

Simón Bolívar (1783–1830)
(below) became known as 'The Liberator' for his role in the emancipation of South America from Spanish rule. After participating in several unsuccessful revolts, he and his army defeated the Spanish at Boyacá in 1819 and organized the republic of Gran Colombia. In 1821, he defeated the Spanish near Carabobo, ensuring Venezuelan independence. Between 1822 and 1824 he also helped free Ecuador and Peru. Southern Peru became a new republic, named Bolivia in his honour.

(see map left)

Cartagena
Maracaibo
Panama
Mompos
Caracas
Orinoco
Angostura
Georgetown

COSTA RICA 1838

PANAMA 1903

Antioquia

Bogotá

COLOMBIA 1830

VENEZUELA 1830

BRITISH GB Britain 1904
DUTCH
FRENCH
GUIANA
Cayenne

1873

1900

Quito

ECUADOR 1830
ORIENTE

to Ecuador 1880

Guayaquil

Iquitos
Tabatinga

to Ecuador 1880

1907

Manaus

Amazon

RIO NEGRO (later Amazonas)

PARÁ

MARANHÃO

RIO GRANDE DO NORTE

CEARA

PARAIBA

PERNAMBUCO

ALAGOAS

SERGIPE

B R A Z I L
1822
(empire 1822, republic 1889)

PIAUI

Sabinada 1837

ACRE 1899–1903

to Bolivia 1867

Lima
Callao

P E R U

1824

to Peru 1909
to Peru 1902

Cuzco

Praieira 1848–9

BAHIA

Santa Cruz

La Paz

MATO GROSSO

Liberal revolution 1842

GOIAS

Minas Novas

MINAS GERAIS

Diamantina

ESPIRITO SANTO

▽ Castilla 1845–62

Tacna
Arica

to Peru 1929

Chilean gains 1883

▽ Melgarejo 1864–71

BOLIVIA 1825

Potosí

Corumbá

1870   1870

GRAN CHACO

Concepción

PARAGUAY 1811

Ciudad Real

SÃO PAULO

São Paulo

Rio de Janeiro

RIO DE JANEIRO

○ Batlle 1903–15

Jujuy

1874

Asunción

1874

1927

SANTA CATARINA

RIO GRANDE DO SUL

Farroupilha revolution 1835–45

◇ aristocratic presidentialism

1818

Córdoba

Valparaíso

Mendoza

San Luis

Rosario

Santiago

Constitución

Buenos Aires

Montevideo

Rio de la Plata

URUGUAY 1828 part of Brazil 1816–28

C H I L E

A R G E N T I N A

1816

▽ Rosas 1829–52

Valdivia

War of the Desert 1880–81

◇ conservative republic 1826–1910

United Provinces of Rio Plata 1819–25
Argentine confederation 1825–53
Argentine republic from 1853

P A T A G O N I A

settled by Argentina by late 19th C

settled by Chile through 19th C

FALKLAND IS.
(Islas Malvinas)

colonized by Britain 1765–74; claimed by Spain to 1811, subsequently claimed by Argentina; British from 1833

1 Latin America: political development from 1824 (above and left)

    boundary of Mexico, 1824

    Mexico 1867

1821   date of independent statehood

    Republic of Gran Colombia, 1821–30

    United Provinces of Central America, 1823–38

    later Brazilian acquisitions

    areas affected by Mexican revolution from 1910

    disputed between Ecuador and Peru

    disputed between Bolivia and Paraguay

▽   caudillismo

○   revolutionary movements

◇   constitutionalism

    radical reformism

    French territory

    British territory

    Dutch territory

    Spanish territory

113

The expansion of the Russian empire

For 40 years after the Congress of Vienna (1815) Russia remained the strongest military power in Europe, focusing her interests on the Balkans and on the straits leading from the Black Sea. Since most Balkan subjects of the Ottoman empire were Orthodox Slavs, Russia considered herself their natural protector; and because Turkey lay in the way of Russia's access to the Mediterranean, it desired Constantinople to remain amenable to Russian influence alone. However, France and Austria also had imperial ambitions in these areas, while Britain opposed any further Russian expansion. In 1854, therefore, following Russia's invasion of Turkey's Danubian provinces and destruction of the Ottoman fleet, France and Britain (supported by Austria) declared war and invaded the Crimea, eventually forcing Russia to evacuate the Balkans and to dismantle its Black Sea fleet. A further Russian attempt to liberate the Balkan Slavs from Turkish rule in 1877-8 also failed (page 108).

Russia proved far more successful in Asia (map 1). Her forces subdued the Kazakhs (1816-54), completed Russian control of the Caucasus (1857-64) and annexed the khanates of central Asia (1865-76). The imperial frontier now reached – and sometimes penetrated – the great mountain chains that separated it from Persia, Afghanistan, India and China. The colonization of North America also continued into the early 19th century, and forts were built as far

south as California; but most were soon abandoned and Alaska was sold to the United States in 1867. On the other hand, China ceded to the Tsar the Amur basin and parts of the Pacific coast (where Vladivostok was founded in 1860), and leased Port Arthur (1898). This warm-water harbour, unimpeded by winter ice, was soon linked to the main Trans-Siberian railway (completed in 1903). But Russian expansion conflicted with Japanese designs. The two powers had already clashed over their interests in Korea and south Manchuria, following Japan's victory over China in 1894-5 (page 130), and in 1904-5 Japan attacked Russia, forcing her to abandon most of her gains in the Far East and to cede south Sakhalin.

This humiliating defeat fanned the flames of domestic unrest. Shaken by the backwardness exposed in the Crimean War, Tsar Alexander II (1855-81) had initiated a number of reforms in the 1860s: new local government organizations; educational improvements; and radical changes to the legal system. The emancipation of the serfs in 1861 was the cornerstone of the reforms (map 2). However, still confined to their villages, many peasants felt aggrieved that they often had to acquire by purchase less land than they had previously worked. From 1890 the government embarked on an industrialization programme with railways at its centre. Many of the lines aimed to facilitate the movement of troops to frontier areas in case of war, but they allowed not

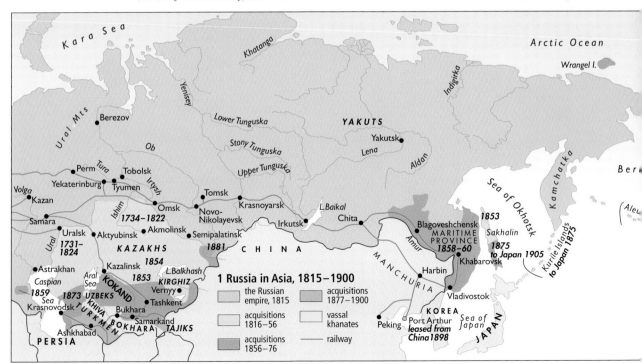

1 Russia in Asia, 1815–1900

- the Russian empire, 1815
- acquisitions 1816–56
- acquisitions 1856–76
- acquisitions 1877–1900
- vassal khanates
- railway

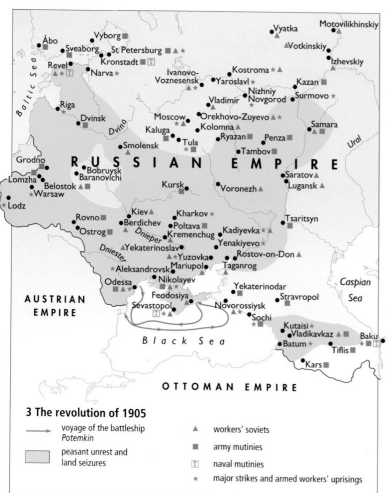

3 The revolution of 1905

→ voyage of the battleship *Potemkin*

▨ peasant unrest and land seizures

▲ workers' soviets

■ army mutinies

⊡ naval mutinies

★ major strikes and armed workers' uprisings

2 Serfdom in Russia, 1860

serfs as a percentage of the population

▨ over 50

▨ 30–50

▨ 10–30

☐ under 10

— boundary of Russia, 1871

serfs' obligations

◆ *obrok*: dues in kind or cash

◇ *barshchina*: labour service to landlord

⬦ both *obrok* and *barshchina* dues

ALASKA
sold to USA 1867

Port Alexander

Pacific Ocean

only migration from overcrowded central Russia to western Siberia, but also the movement of peasants to urban areas to man a growing number of factories. Between 1863 and 1914 Russia's urban population increased from 6 to 18.6 million.

In 1905, in the wake of Japan's victory, revolutionary parties proved quick to exploit the low incomes and general hardships created by these rapid changes, while the new professional classes pressed for political reform (map 3). Unrest in the towns spread to the countryside, to the army and even to the Black Sea fleet, led by the battleship Potemkin, forcing Tsar Nicholas II (1894-1917) to grant a constitution, including a duma, or parliament; but by 1907 the government had regained full control. Nevertheless the 1905 revolution irreparably weakened the old order, and after 1912 another wave of social unrest swept the empire. Internally, Russia was in no position to meet the challenge of the First World War in 1914.

Although mobilization took place with a rapidity that took the Germans by surprise (page 132), the tsar's government proved incapable of supplying its millions of troops with equipment, munitions or (eventually) with food.

'It is better to abolish serfdom from above than wait for it to abolish itself from below,' declared Alexander II *(left)* in 1857. Four years later Alexander did indeed free the serfs. He soon found that it was one thing to emancipate them, another to feed, clothe and educate them. Radical though they were in Russian terms, Alexander's reforms failed to address the core problems facing his country.

Nationalism in Europe

Nationalism flourished in Europe in the wake of the French Revolution (page 98), but it remained confined largely to the middle classes and proved relatively short-lived. The Great Powers at the Congress of Vienna in 1815 aimed to restore Europe (as far as possible) to its pre-war condition by combating both liberalism and nationalism and by creating a barrier around France. To that end Holland received the Austrian Netherlands (later Belgium); Prussia took over Westphalia and much of the Rhineland; Sardinia-Piedmont annexed Genoa; Russia retained Finland and most of Poland; and Austria gained Venetia and Lombardy.

By 1830, however, when a new wave of liberal and national agitation arose, the Great Powers no longer worked in unison, enabling Greece (page 108) and Belgium to obtain independence. In 1848-9, when an outburst of nationalism erupted into full-scale revolution, the solidarity of the conservative powers – coupled with divisions among the nationalists themselves – still sufficed to maintain the status quo. Shortly afterwards, a new generation of statesmen began to use nationalism for their own ends. Cavour

Known as the 'Iron Chancellor', Otto von Bismarck *(above)* became minister-president of Prussia in 1862. After wars against Denmark (1864) and Austria (1866), he formed the North German confederation (1867) and after the Franco-Prussian war (1870-1) inaugurated the German empire. As German chancellor (1871-90) he played a leading role in the European alliance systems of the 1870s and 1880s.

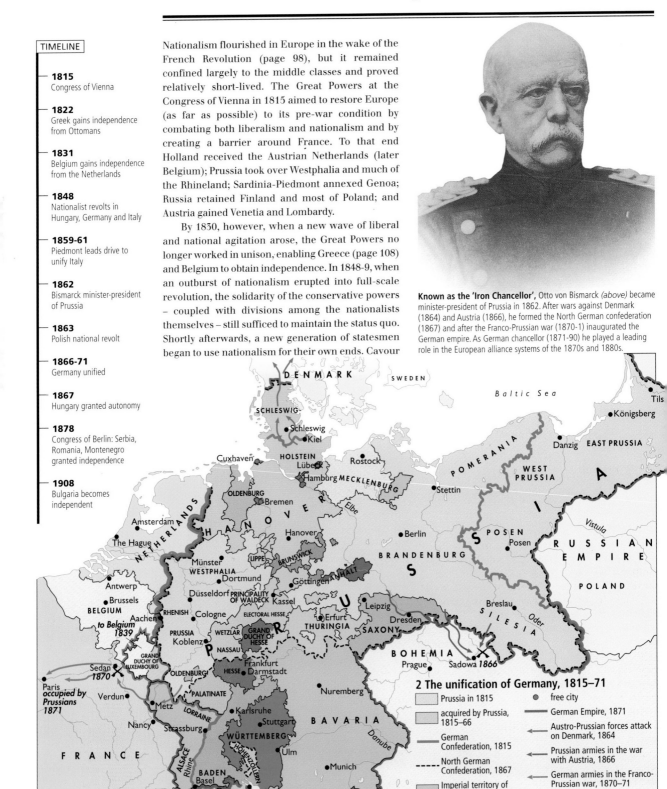

2 The unification of Germany, 1815–71

- Prussia in 1815
- acquired by Prussia, 1815–66
- German Confederation, 1815
- North German Confederation, 1867
- Imperial territory of Alsace-Lorraine, 1871
- free city
- German Empire, 1871
- Austro-Prussian forces attack on Denmark, 1864
- Prussian armies in the war with Austria, 1866
- German armies in the Franco-Prussian war, 1870–71

1 The unification of Italy, 1859–70

SWITZERLAND

AUSTRO-HUNGARIAN EMPIRE

French from 1768, formerly Genoese

Kingdom of Sardinia in 1815

territory annexed 1859

territory annexed March 1860

territory annexed November 1860

territory lost to France 1860

territory annexed 1866

territory annexed 1870

Austrian empire, 1815

Italian border, 1914

TYROL

Bergamo

Trent (Trento)

Udine

Görz
(Gorizia)

VENETIA

Trieste

Aosta

Como

Brescia

SAVOY

PIEDMONT

Monza

Custoza 1848, 1866

Fiume

Magenta 1859

LOMBARDY

Milan

Verona

Venice

Susa

Novara 1849

Solferino 1859

Mantua

Padua

Pola

Turin

KINGDOM
OF
SARDINIA

Alessandria

Parma

Guastalla

Ferrara

PARMA

ROMAGNA

SAN
MARINO

Zara

Genoa

Pontremoli

MODENA

Modena

Bologna

LIGURIA

La Spezia

Rimini

D
a
l
m
a
t
i
a

NICE

Lucca

Pesaro

OTTOMAN
EMPIRE

Monaco

Pisa

Arno

Florence

Urbino

Nice

Livorno
(Leghorn)

Arezzo

Ancona

Castelfidardo

*Lissa
1866*

F
R
A
N
C
E

Elba

Siena

MARCHES

TUSCANY

UMBRIA

PAPAL
STATES

Adriatic Sea

Spoleto

Civitavecchia

Mentana

T
i
b
e
r

Rieti

CORSICA

Rome

Pontecorvo

K I N G D O M

Terracina

Gaeta

Benevento

Bari

Sassari

*Volturno
1860*

N A P L E S

Naples

Castellammare

Potenza

Salerno

KINGDOM

OF

*Mediterranean
Sea*

SARDINIA

O F

Tyrrhenian Sea

Taranto

Cagliari

T H E

Cosenza

T W O

Lipari Is.

*Aspromonte
1862*

Messina

S I C I L I E S

Reggio

Palermo

Marsala

Catania

Syracuse

sought a unification of Italy along conservative lines, in the interests of Piedmont-Sardinia, and was hostile to the more revolutionary nationalism of Garibaldi and Mazzini. Bismarck in Prussia wanted unification to achieve his aim of a conservative, Prussian-dominated German state. Both used diplomacy and war to achieve their objectives: Cavour allied with France before attacking Austria in 1859, securing the unification of Italy (except for Venetia and the Papal States) by 1861 (see map 1). Bismarck allied with Austria in order to defeat Denmark (1864), then in concert with Italy attacked Austria (1866), and finally defeated France (1870-1), achieving in the process the unification of Germany (map 2).

Liberal nationalists later endorsed both achievements, but neither satisfied the nationalism they had aroused. Italy still laid claim to the Alto Adige and Istria; Bismarck's 'Small German' solution, which excluded Austria, disappointed those who hankered after a Greater Germany.

Nevertheless, the four short wars fought between 1859 and 1871 solved the Italian and German questions, and re-drew the map of Central Europe. Moreover, the Great Powers now remained at peace for over four decades and although nationalist grievances continued to fester, territorial disputes within Europe ceased to divide most governments.

Imperialism

Until 1830, the search for oriental luxuries remained the driving force behind European imperialism, and (with the important exception of India: page 96) the European stake in Asia and Africa remained confined to trading stations and the strategic outposts necessary to protect trade. Thereafter two new factors transformed the situation. First came the enforced 'opening' of key markets – Turkey and Egypt (1838), Persia (1841), China (1842), Japan (1858) – to European, particularly British, commerce. Then, from the 1870s, a new phase of the Industrial Revolution (page 100) provoked a search for raw materials to feed the new industries. In the scramble for these resources between 1880 and 1914, Europe added almost 9 million square miles (23.4 million km^2) – one-fifth of the land area of the globe – to its overseas colonial possessions.

France and Britain took the lead. The former conquered Algeria after 1830, annexed Tahiti and the Marquesas in the 1840s, expanded its colony in Senegal in the 1850s and began the conquest of Indo-China in 1859. Britain, both to forestall the French and to safeguard its position in India, claimed sovereignty over Australia and New Zealand (page 106), and acquired Singapore (1819), Malacca (1824), Hong Kong (1842), Burma (1852), and Lagos (1861) (map 1).

1 Colonial penetration, 1815–70
see key right

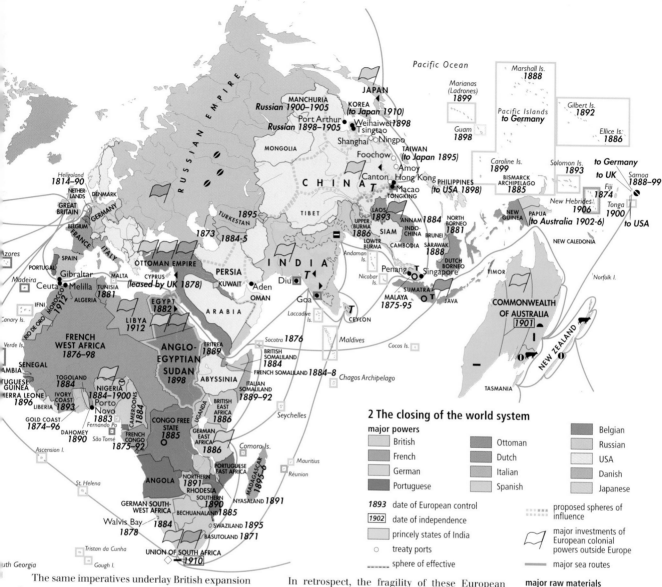

2 The closing of the world system

major powers

- British
- French
- German
- Portuguese
- Ottoman
- Dutch
- Italian
- Spanish
- Belgian
- Russian
- USA
- Danish
- Japanese

1893 date of European control

1902 date of independence

princely states of India

○ treaty ports

- - - - - sphere of effective

· · · · · proposed spheres of influence

major investments of European colonial powers outside Europe

major sea routes

major raw materials exported to Europe

- grain
- meat
- tea
- cane sugar
- dairy produce
- cotton
- jute
- silk
- rubber
- veg oil
- copra
- wool

The same imperatives underlay British expansion after 1880, except that the number of competitors to forestall increased. Thus the French empire grew between 1871 and 1914 by nearly 4 million square miles (10.4 million km²) and 47 million people (mainly in north and west Africa and Indo-China, where Laos and Tongking were added to Cambodia and Cochin-China, but it also secured Madagascar and some Pacific islands); Germany also acquired an empire of 1 million square miles (2.6 million km²) and 14 million colonial subjects (in South-West Africa, Togoland, the Cameroons, Tanganyika and the Pacific islands); Italy obtained several outposts in Africa; the United States annexed the Philippines, Guam, Hawaii and some Caribbean islands; and Russia began to expand in central Asia. Britain too managed to acquire extensive new territories in Africa which almost linked Cape Town with Cairo, more Pacific islands (including Fiji), and parts of the Indonesian archipelago (map 2). It added 88 million subjects to her empire and, by 1914, exercized authority over a fifth of the world's landmass and a quarter of its peoples.

In retrospect, the fragility of these European empires, so hastily assembled, is obvious. None of the imperial powers possessed the resources to govern them effectively and European imperialism proved more ephemeral than anyone at the time imagined; yet it left an indelible mark on the peoples of Africa and Asia, propelling them willingly or unwillingly into the 20th century.

Advertisements often unconsciously reflect the assumptions on which societies operate. The Victorian tobacco advert (left) shows the wealthy European manufacturers receiving the raw material from crudely parodied native growers, to whom the finished product will eventually be resold.

Although the United States made a remarkably rapid recovery after the Civil War (page 104), development remained very uneven. In the defeated South, the period of Reconstruction (1865-77) proved a bitter experience. South Carolina, which in 1860 had ranked third in the nation in per capita wealth, ranked 40th ten years later; and other once-prosperous states did scarcely better. The 4 million liberated black slaves fared worst, being left (as Frederick Douglass wrote) without money, property or friends. Although the population of the Union surged from 31 million in 1861 to 92 million in 1910, most of the increase by-passed the South and concentrated wealth and power in the north-east and the upper Mid-West. Only around 1920 did cheap labour attract textile industry to the South (map 1).

The settlement of the Great Plains, made possible by the railway boom after 1870, constituted perhaps the most striking achievement of the post-war period. The track in operation increased from 30,000 miles (48,000 km) in 1860 to 163,000 (262,000 km) in 1890 (at which point it exceeded the size of the entire European rail system); the number of farms rose from 2 million in 1860 to 6 million in 1910; and the population living west of the Mississippi grew from 6 million to 26 million. Yet the bulk of the population remained concentrated in the north-east (map 3), and most of the 25 million immigrants arriving between 1870 and 1914 stayed there, providing cheap labour for American industry.

Railways played an even more prominent role in the development of Canada. The United States made no secret of its hope to absorb the provinces and thus create a continent-wide empire. After the acquisition

Pittsburgh, Pennsylvania, surrounded by huge coal-fields and beds of iron and at the confluence of two important rivers, became the leading centre of iron and steel production in the United States. So vast and dramatic was the sight of its blast furnaces and coke ovens at work that early 20th-century artists and commentators began to refer to it as 'Hell with the lid off.'

2 Canada, 1867–1929

land occupied;
- prior to 1851
- 1851–1871
- 1871–1901
- 1901–1921

population of towns, 1871;
- ☐ 25,000-100,000 people
- ■ over 100,000 people

population of towns, 1911;
- ○ 25,000-100,000 people
- ● over 100,000 people

railways 1916:
- —— Canadian Pacific Railway
- --- Canadian Northern (Main Line)
- .... National Trans-continental Railway
- —— main industrial regions

ALBERTA date of accession to
1905 Dominion of Canada

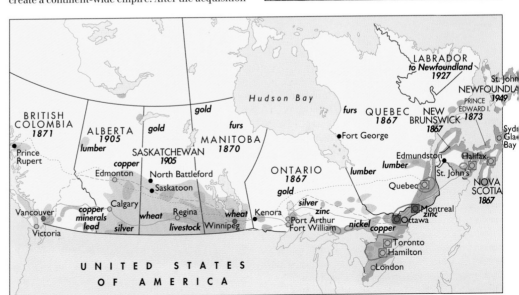

1 Urban and industrial growth in the United States, 1860–1929

main industrial areas:
- 1860
- 1900
- 1920

urban population 1920:
- ● 100,000–500,000
- ● 500,000–1,000,000
- ● over 1 million

industry:
- ▷ textiles
- ■ iron and steel
- 🚗 motor manufacturing
- ★ strikes and industrial unrest

1 Haymarket Square demonstration, 1886
2 Pullman railway workers' strike, 1894
3 railroad strikes, 1877
4 anthracite strikes, 1877–8; 1902
5 Homestead steelworkers' strike, 1892
6 Patterson textile workers' strikes, 1877–9

3 Population density in the United States, 1900

inhabitants per square mile:
- 0-2
- 2-6
- 6-18
- 18-45
- 45-90
- 90 and over

of Alaska by the United States (1867), this pressure grew, but the Canadians frustrated their neighbours' intentions by forming the Canadian Federation in 1867, completed by the purchase of Rupert's Land from the Hudson's Bay Company (1869) and the adhesion of Manitoba (1870) and British Columbia (1871). The great transcontinental railways – the Canadian Pacific (completed 1885) followed by the Canadian Northern and the National Trans-continental – became the lifeblood of the new Dominion, opening Manitoba and Saskatchewan, and turning Canada into one of the world's leading wheat producers. It also facilitated the exploitation of rich mineral deposits, particularly copper and nickel (map 2). Overall, Canada's industrial output increased from $190 million in 1890 to over $500 million in 1914.

This achievement was dwarfed, however, by the economic and territorial growth of the United States. Output of iron and steel increased 20-fold between 1870 and 1913, by which time steel production exceeded that of Britain and Germany combined, and the United States remained the world's leading agricultural producer. Meanwhile, in 1898 (following a successful war with Spain), the Philippines, Guam, Puerto Rico and Hawaii were annexed, the latter after many years of American encroachment in the islands' affairs; and in 1903 Cuba and the Panama Canal Zone became protectorates. The United States now possessed the political and economic might to intervene almost anywhere on the world stage: in Mexico in 1914 and again in 1916, and – on a far greater scale – in Europe in 1917-18 (page 132).

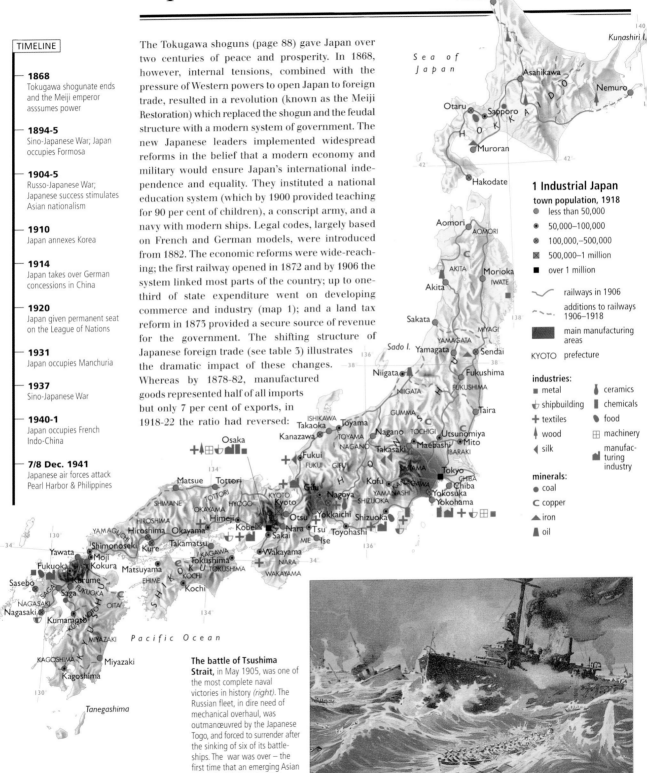

Japan

The Tokugawa shoguns (page 88) gave Japan over
two centuries of peace and prosperity. In 1868,
however, internal tensions, combined with the
pressure of Western powers to open Japan to foreign
trade, resulted in a revolution (known as the Meiji
Restoration) which replaced the shogun and the feudal
structure with a modern system of government. The
new Japanese leaders implemented widespread
reforms in the belief that a modern economy and
military would ensure Japan's international independence and equality. They instituted a national
education system (which by 1900 provided teaching
for 90 per cent of children), a conscript army, and a
navy with modern ships. Legal codes, largely based
on French and German models, were introduced
from 1882. The economic reforms were wide-reach-
ing; the first railway opened in 1872 and by 1906 the
system linked most parts of the country; up to one-
third of state expenditure went on developing
commerce and industry (map 1); and a land tax
reform in 1873 provided a secure source of revenue
for the government. The shifting structure of
Japanese foreign trade (see table 3) illustrates
the dramatic impact of these changes.
Whereas by 1878-82, manufactured
goods represented half of all imports
but only 7 per cent of exports, in
1918-22 the ratio had reversed:

TIMELINE

1868
Tokugawa shogunate ends
and the Meiji emperor
asssumes power

1894-5
Sino-Japanese War; Japan
occupies Formosa

1904-5
Russo-Japanese War;
Japanese success stimulates
Asian nationalism

1910
Japan annexes Korea

1914
Japan takes over German
concessions in China

1920
Japan given permanent seat
on the League of Nations

1931
Japan occupies Manchuria

1937
Sino-Japanese War

1940-1
Japan occupies French
Indo-China

7/8 Dec. 1941
Japanese air forces attack
Pearl Harbor & Philippines

1 Industrial Japan

town population, 1918
- less than 50,000
- 50,000–100,000
- 100,000,–500,000
- 500,000–1 million
- over 1 million

- railways in 1906
- additions to railways 1906–1918
- main manufacturing areas

KYOTO   prefecture

industries:
- metal
- shipbuilding
- textiles
- wood
- silk
- ceramics
- chemicals
- food
- machinery
- manufac-turing industry

minerals:
- coal
- copper
- iron
- oil

The battle of Tsushima Strait, in May 1905, was one of the most complete naval victories in history *(right)*. The Russian fleet, in dire need of mechanical overhaul, was outmanœuvred by the Japanese Togo, and forced to surrender after the sinking of six of its battle-ships. The war was over – the first time that an emerging Asian power had defeated a Western one; the news resounded throughout the colonial world.

finished manufactures now accounted for over 40 per cent of sales and only 15 per cent of purchases. Moreover the total value of Japan's exports rose in this period from 30 million to 1.8 billion yen.

International recognition of Japan's new status was nevertheless slow in coming: consular jurisdiction survived until 1894, and the unequal treaties negotiated in the 1850s with the Western powers remained in force until 1911. As Japan's strength and confidence grew, however, so did nationalist and imperialist ambitions. In 1894-5 a victorious war against China, arising from disputes in Korea, ended in a treaty granting Taiwan to Japan. Russo-Japanese rivalry over Manchuria culminated in Japanese victory in the war of 1904-5. The Treaty of Portsmouth (1905) gave Japan a lease of territory in China and extensive rights in South Manchuria. In 1910 she acquired Korea. Japanese support for the victorious Western powers in World War I brought few further rewards, however, and the country's military leaders became frustrated. After 1931, under the impact of the Great Depression (page 138), Japan overran first Manchuria and then – despite strong opposition from the United States – northern China in an attempt to achieve economic self-sufficiency (map 2). Germany's victory over France and the Netherlands in 1940 offered an opportunity to expand southwards – thereby gaining control over valuable oil fields in Borneo and Burma – precipitating full-scale war with the Western powers (page 142). Paradoxically, Japan's total defeat and the ensuing American occupation propelled her even more decisively into the modern world than the Meiji restoration had done.

2 Japanese expansion from 1914

- Japanese territory by 1914, with dates of acquisition
- spheres of Japanese influence, 1918
- expansion to 1933
- expansion to Nov. 1941
- ✳ Japanese conflict with USSR
- → Japanese attacks
- ■ Chinese capitals
- ■ Allied bases
- — railways

3 Structure of Japanese trade

food, drink | raw materials | semi-manufactured goods | finished goods | other

1878-82 export / import
1918-22 export / import

0%   25%   50%   75%   100%

European rivalries and alliances

The unification of Germany and Italy (page 116) seemed for a time to have resolved the major questions which had disturbed the peace of Europe since 1848. Bismarck, the architect of German unification, concentrated after 1871 on building a system of alliances that would ensure the future of the new empire, mainly by isolating France, which proved unable to reconcile itself to the rise of the new German empire, and for almost 20 years he succeeded in convincing the rest of Europe of Germany's conservative and pacific intentions. In time, however, the alliances that had seemed defensive became aggressive and destabilizing.

Meanwhile, although the achievements of Bismarck and Cavour reduced nationalist fervour in central Europe, they stirred up a hornet's nest in the Balkans, where the struggles of various national groups for independence from the Turks inevitably involved the neighbouring powers, Russia and Austria (which, after its exclusion from Germany in 1866 became far more interested in the Balkans).

Revolts in the Balkans between 1875 and 1878, culminating in Russian intervention and war with the Turks, resulted in the treaty of Berlin (brokered by Bismarck) which either confirmed or established the independence of Serbia, Montenegro, Romania and Bulgaria and granted Austria a mandate to govern Bosnia and Herzegovina. In 1879 Germany and Austria signed a defensive alliance, expanded to include Italy in 1882 (map 1). Russia, satisfied that Slav interest had been met in the Balkans, turned increasingly to Central Asia and the Far East. The main European rivalries were now between Britain and Russia in Asia, and Britain and France in Africa. Britain remained isolated in Europe, while France and Russia signed an alliance in 1894 as a counterweight to the strength of the alliance bloc based around Germany.

The situation changed after 1897, however, when Germany began to seek a 'place in the sun'. This was not unreasonable; but by then most places in the sun had been occupied by others, and German policy – which involved building a High Seas Fleet to rival that of Britain – therefore seemed to constitute a threat to the established imperial powers. As a result, Britain resolved its differences with France in 1904,

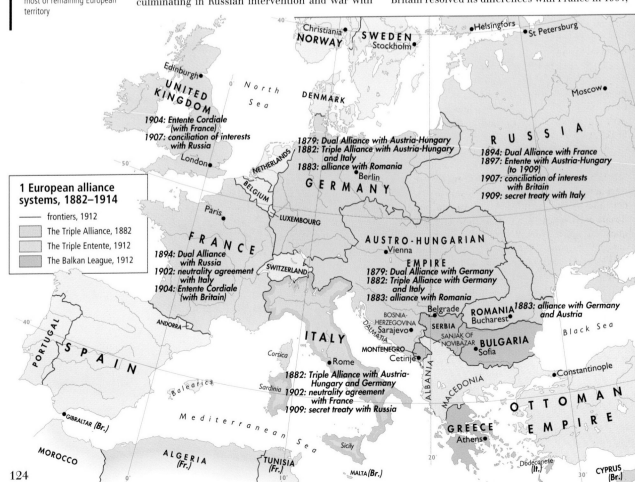

**1 European alliance
systems, 1882–1914**

— frontiers, 1912

The Triple Alliance, 1882
The Triple Entente, 1912
The Balkan League, 1912

Lake Balaton
Budapest

AUSTRO-HUNGARIAN EMPIRE

Sava

Banja Luka
BOSNIA-HERZEGOVINA
administered by Austria-
Hungary 1878; annexed 1908
Sarajevo

Belgrade
principality 1817;
independent 1878

S E R B I A
Nish

Jassy

MOLDAVIA
semi-independent
1829

Galatz

R O M A N I A
united 1859; independent 1878;
kingdom 1881

WALLACHIA
semi-independent
1829
Vidin
Bucharest

Danube

Kotor
(Cattaro)
MONTENEGRO
Cetinje
Scutari
Tirana
to Serbia
1913

Adriatic Sea

ALBANIA
principality
1913
Koritsa

Uskūb
(Skoplje)
Monastir

Sofia
B U L G A R I A
principality 1878
independent 1908

EASTERN RUMELIA
to Bulgaria 1885
Maritsa

Balchik
Varna
Burgas

Black Sea

to Bulgaria 1913

M a c e d o n i a
to Greece 1913
Kavalla
to Bulgaria 1913

Adrianople

T h r a c e

Constantinople

EPIRUS
Yannina
to Greece 1913

Salonica
Thasos

Lemnos

Corfu
to Greece 1864
Preveza
Arta

THESSALY
to Greece 1881
Larissa

to Greece 1913
Mytilene

**O T T O M A N
E M P I R E**

Ionian Islands

to Greece
1864

K I N G D O M   O F   G R E E C E
independent 1830
Patras
Athens
Piraeus
Tripolis

Aegean Sea
Chios

Nikaria

Smyrna

Ionian Sea

to Greece 1864

CRETE
independent 1898
to Greece 1913
Candia

Dodecanese
Rhodes
occupied by Italy
1912

40°
22°
36°
24°
28°

Carpathian Mts

**2 The Balkans,
1878–1913**

- - - frontier of Ottoman
empire, 1800
——— frontier of Ottoman
empire, 1885
——— national frontiers
after the Balkan
wars 1912–13

and with Russia in 1907, and France settled its long-standing dispute with Italy in 1902. Thereafter, the Triple Entente with France and Russia became the lynch-pin of British foreign policy, the only firm assurance against the German 'threat'. Germany, on the other became concerned with the danger of 'encirclement' by a hostile ring constructed by Great Britain (map 1).

As a result, a dangerous simplification of alignments occurred into a bi-polar system: the Triple Alliance and the Triple Entente drew tighter, and Germany in particular grew closer to its only dependable ally, Austria. When Austria annexed Bosnia and Herzegovina in 1908, Germany gave her qualified support, though it rekindled Austro-Russian antagonism in the Balkans. During the Balkan wars (1912-13), in which a Russian-sponsored Balkan League consisting of Serbia, Greece and Bulgaria attempted to drive the Turks out of Europe, the two diplomatic systems still cooperated; but Austria stood aghast at the consequent enlargement of Serbia – which almost doubled its size – and feared Serb agitation for an independent south Slav state (map 2).

The assassination of the heir to the Austrian throne in Sarajevo (Bosnia) in June 1914 provided what seemed to the Austrian government like its last chance to deal with Serbia before it grew too powerful, and Germany threw its entire weight behind its ally. Russia, however, could not afford to leave Serbia

in the lurch and began to mobilize against Austria. Germany regarded this as a direct threat, and also began to mobilize. However, to forestall an attack from Russia's allies in the West, German Grand Strategy called for an immediate attack on France – in the hope that it could be knocked out of the war before Russia advanced in force. On 28 July, Austria declared war on Serbia; on 1 August 1914 Germany declared war on Russia, and two days later on France. The diplomatic system created by Bismarck, coupled with the volatile situation in the Balkans, had produced a world war (page 132).

HMS Temeraire, depicted on a pre-war postcard. Britain responded to Germany's increased warship building after 1900 with a rival programme based on the most modern Dreadnought battleships. The Royal Navy was fully mobilized for exercises at the outbreak of war.

The formation of a world economy

The integration of the global economy into a single interdependent whole formed one of the principal developments of the period 1870-1914. Europe (and to a lesser extent the United States) stood at the heart of this process, emitting the impulses that opened up the remaining areas of the globe to Western exploration and exploitation.

Three interrelated aspects deserve special attention. First came the development of better means of communication. In 1870, railways remained largely confined to Europe (60,400 miles, 97,250 km of track) and North America (56,300 miles, 90,600 km): the rest of the world could boast only 9100 miles (14,650 km). By 1911, however, the total network of tracks had increased to 657,000 miles (1.06 million km) – 175,000 miles (280,000 km) of them outside Europe and North America – and included some spectacular transcontinental links: across the United States (four between 1869 and 1893), Canada (1885), Russia (1904) and the Andes (1910). The expansion of world shipping was equally striking, with not only a spectacular rise in the total tonnage, but a shift from sail to steam which increased the speed and regularity of shipments. However, the main shipping traffic, both passenger and freight, took place among the advanced countries and the white dominions, or between them and the producers of the raw materials they required. Canal construction also continued apace – above all the Suez Canal, completed in 1869, which carried 437,000 tons in 1870 and over 20 million in 1913; and the Panama Canal, completed in 1914, which carried 5 million tons of cargo in its first year. These spectacular totals reflected the enormous savings in distance – 41 per cent for vessels sailing from Liverpool to Bombay, 60 per cent for vessels sailing from New York to San Francisco.

Finally, messages travelled around the world with increasing speed. Cables laid beneath the oceans linked the continents – between Britain and North America (1866); from Vancouver to Brisbane (1902) – followed by telephones (with international lines from 1887) and wireless stations (from 1897).

These developments paralleled a boom in commerce. Foreign trade tripled in volume between 1870 and 1914, although (again) most of the activity occurred among the industrialized countries, or between them and their suppliers of primary goods or their new markets. In 1913, only 11 per cent of the

1 The development of the world economy

foreign investment, 1914
(in $ million)

- 535 United Kingdom
- 420 United States
- 3180 France
- 1050 Germany

—— busiest shipping routes
—— other major shipping routes, c. 1900
—— international telegragh cables

Colonial empires in 1900

Belgian		Japanese	
British		Ottoman	
Danish		Portuguese	
Dutch		Russian	
French		Spanish	
German		USA	
Italian		other countries	

500
400
850 MEXICO

Gulf of Mexico

Panama canal, 1914

4250
400
950

UNITED STATES OF AMERICA

DOMINION OF CANADA
2800
200
880

Caribbean Sea

340

COLOMBIA
VENEZUELA

PERU

CHILE
BOLIVIA
300

ARGENTINA
400
1550
200 200
PARAGUAY
URUGUAY

BRAZIL
700
500
700

North Atlantic Ocean

3 The share of world trade

1860 total $8 billion

Others
United Kingdom
USA
France

Russia
Spain
Austria-Hungary
Italy

Germany
Holland and Belgium
Switzerland
Scandinavia

1913 total $39 billion

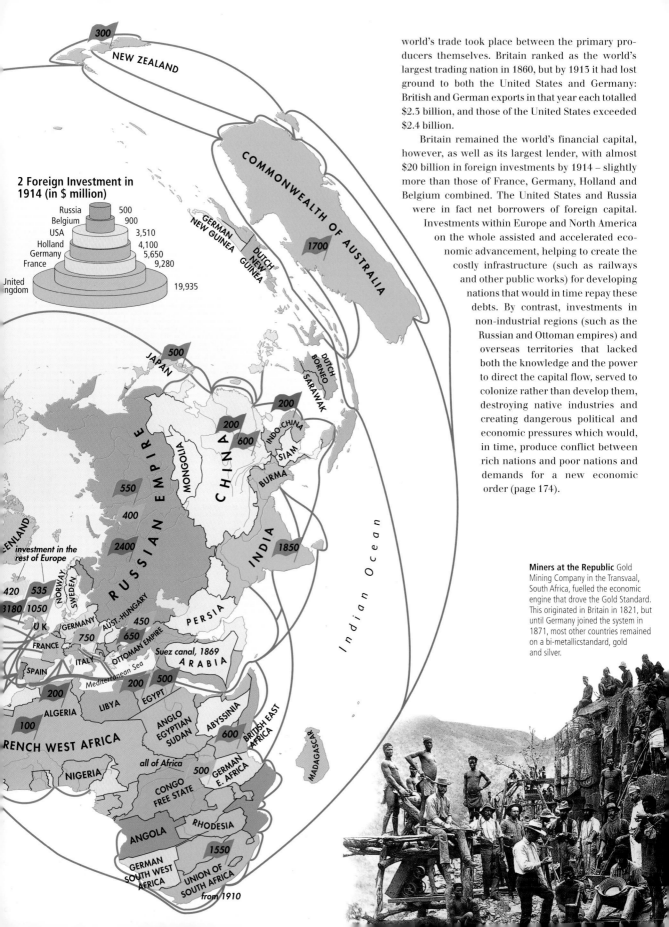

world's trade took place between the primary producers themselves. Britain ranked as the world's largest trading nation in 1860, but by 1913 it had lost ground to both the United States and Germany: British and German exports in that year each totalled $2.3 billion, and those of the United States exceeded $2.4 billion.

Britain remained the world's financial capital, however, as well as its largest lender, with almost $20 billion in foreign investments by 1914 – slightly more than those of France, Germany, Holland and Belgium combined. The United States and Russia were in fact net borrowers of foreign capital. Investments within Europe and North America on the whole assisted and accelerated economic advancement, helping to create the costly infrastructure (such as railways and other public works) for developing nations that would in time repay these debts. By contrast, investments in non-industrial regions (such as the Russian and Ottoman empires) and overseas territories that lacked both the knowledge and the power to direct the capital flow, served to colonize rather than develop them, destroying native industries and creating dangerous political and economic pressures which would, in time, produce conflict between rich nations and poor nations and demands for a new economic order (page 174).

Miners at the Republic Gold Mining Company in the Transvaal, South Africa, fuelled the economic engine that drove the Gold Standard. This originated in Britain in 1821, but until Germany joined the system in 1871, most other countries remained on a bi-metallic standard, gold and silver.

2 Foreign Investment in 1914 (in $ million)

Russia	500
Belgium	900
USA	3,510
Holland	4,100
Germany	5,650
France	9,280
United Kingdom	19,935

NEW ZEALAND 300

COMMONWEALTH OF AUSTRALIA 1700

GERMAN NEW GUINEA

DUTCH NEW GUINEA

JAPAN 500

DUTCH BORNEO

SARAWAK

INDO-CHINA 200

200 600

SIAM

BURMA

CHINA

MONGOLIA

RUSSIAN EMPIRE

550

400

2400

INDIA 1850

Indian Ocean

GREENLAND

investment in the rest of Europe

NORWAY 420

SWEDEN 535

3180

1050

UK

GERMANY 750

AUST-HUNGARY 450

PERSIA

ARABIA

FRANCE

ITALY 650

OTTOMAN EMPIRE

Suez canal, 1869

SPAIN

Mediterranean Sea

200

200

500

EGYPT

ALGERIA

LIBYA

100

FRENCH WEST AFRICA

ANGLO EGYPTIAN SUDAN

ABYSSINIA 600

BRITISH EAST AFRICA

MADAGASCAR

NIGERIA

all of Africa

CONGO FREE STATE

500

GERMAN E. AFRICA

ANGOLA

RHODESIA

GERMAN SOUTH WEST AFRICA

UNION OF SOUTH AFRICA from 1910

1550

FOUR

The Modern World

By making the world one, the European powers stirred up forces that eventually caused their own eclipse. The world wars between 1914 and 1945 whittled away their resources and Europe's exhaustion benefited the Soviet Union and the United States, the two superpowers on the eastern and western flanks, whose rivalry produced an age of bipolarity. But bipolarity, too, proved to be temporary. The recovery of Europe, the emancipation of Asia and Africa, the rise of Japan and finally the collapse of the Soviet empire brought a new constellation into being, and with it the threat of confrontation between rich and poor nations and of the exhaustion of global resources through overpopulation. No one can foretell the shape of things to come. All this section can do is show, in historical perspective, how the world of the 20th century changed and chart the emergence of significant new factors.

Devastation inflicted by the first atomic bomb
Hiroshima, 1945

The Chinese Republic

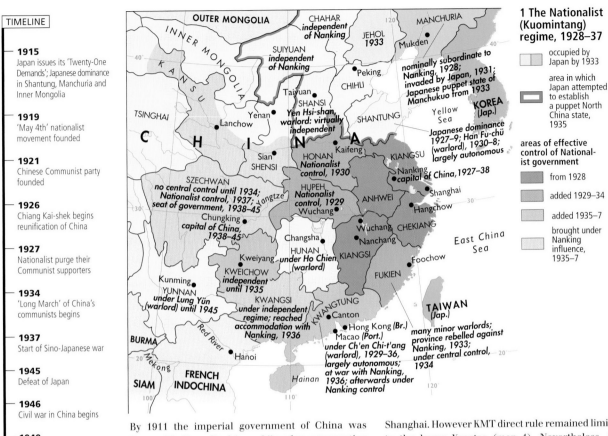

1 The Nationalist (Kuomintang) regime, 1928–37

- occupied by Japan by 1933
- area in which Japan attempted to establish a puppet North China state, 1935

areas of effective control of Nationalist government
- from 1928
- added 1929–34
- added 1935–7
- brought under Nanking influence, 1935–7

Map labels: OUTER MONGOLIA, INNER MONGOLIA, CHAHAR *independent of Nanking*, JEHOL 1933, MANCHURIA, Mukden, SUIYUAN *independent of Nanking*, KANSU, Peking, CHIHLI, *nominally subordinate to Nanking, 1928; invaded by Japan, 1931; Japanese puppet state of Manchukuo from 1933*, TSINGHAI, Taiyuan, SHANSI, *Yen Hsi-shan, warlord: virtually independent*, Yenan, Lanchow, SHANTUNG, KOREA (Jap.), Yellow Sea, *Japanese dominance 1927–9; Han Fu-chü (warlord), 1930–8; largely autonomous*, C H I N A, Sian, SHENSI, HONAN *Nationalist control, 1930*, Kaifeng, KIANGSU, Nanking *capital of China, 1927–38*, SZECHWAN *no central control until 1934; Nationalist control, 1937; seat of government, 1938–45*, HUPEH *Nationalist control, 1929*, Wuchang, ANHWEI, Shanghai, Chungking *capital of China, 1938–45*, Yangtze, Hangchow, Wuchang, CHEKIANG, Changsha, Nanchang, East China Sea, HUNAN *under Ho Chien (warlord)*, KIANGSI, Foochow, KWEICHOW *independent until 1935*, Kweiyang, FUKIEN, Kunming, YUNNAN *under Lung Yün (warlord) until 1945*, KWANGSI *under independent regime; reached independent accommodation with Nanking, 1936*, KWANGTUNG, Canton, TAIWAN (Jap.), BURMA, Red River, Hong Kong (Br.), Macao (Port.) *under Ch'en Chi-t'ang (warlord), 1929–36, largely autonomous; at war with Nanking, 1936; afterwards under Nanking control*, *many minor warlords; province rebelled against Nanking, 1933; under central control, 1934*, Mekong, SIAM, FRENCH INDOCHINA, Hanoi, Hainan

By 1911 the imperial government of China was thoroughly discredited (page 94) and an army mutiny led to the emperor's abdication. But the Republic proclaimed in 1912, with Sun Yat-sen as its first president, was overwhelmed by its inherited problems, and Sun was soon deposed by Yuan Shih-k'ai, the most powerful general of the old regime. After Yuan's death in 1916 power passed to provincial warlords, whose armies caused untold damage and millions of casualties. Compounding this misery were the expansionist policies of Japan and the foreign powers, based in the Treaty Ports (page 88), which interfered in the Chinese economy and in Chinese politics.

In 1919, the refusal of the Paris Peace Conference to abrogate foreign privileges provoked spontaneous urban uprisings (the 'May 4th' movement). These provided a new opportunity for Sun Yat-sen, who in 1923 reorganized his Nationalist (Kuomintang; KMT) Party, allied with the Chinese Communist Party (founded 1921), and prepared to reunite the country. But Sun died in 1925 and it was Chiang Kai-shek, the Moscow-trained general of the KMT army, who in 1926 marched northwards to eliminate the warlords. Helped by peasant and workers' uprisings along his route, Chiang proved remarkably successful, but in 1927 he turned on his allies, massacring the Communists in

Shanghai. However KMT direct rule remained limited to the lower Yangtze (map 1). Nevertheless, the Japanese, fearing the potential challenge from a reunited China, decided to reinforce their hold in the north and overran Manchuria (1931) and Jehol (1933).

Although KMT purges had virtually eliminated Communism from the cities, peasant disaffection – arising from the absence of land reform – offered an alternative constituency. From his base at Chingkang Shan, Mao Tse-Tung and others created a new centre of revitalized communism, developing a peasant-based party rather than an urban, proletarian party on the Russian model. In 1929 KMT pressure

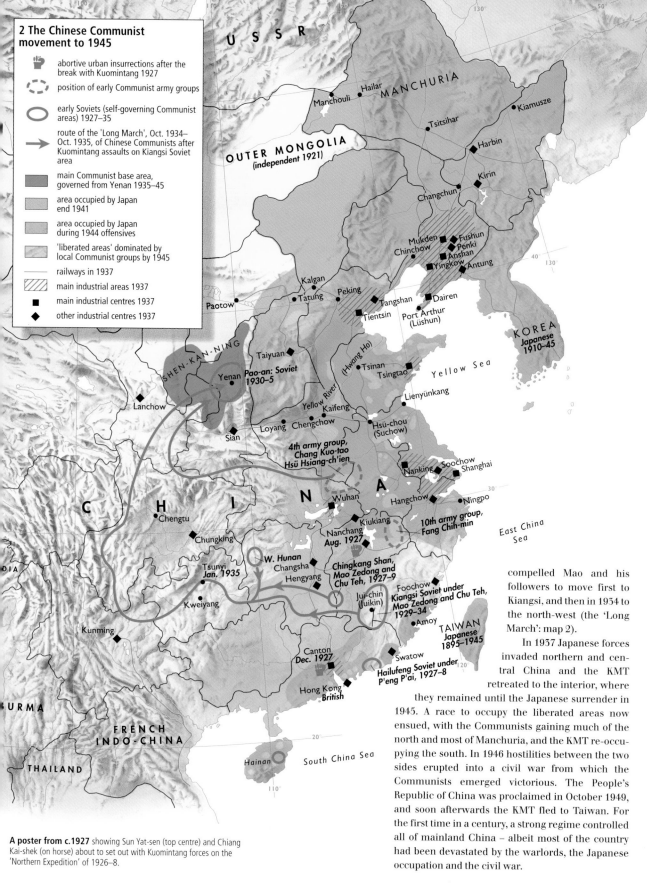

2 The Chinese Communist movement to 1945

- ✊ abortive urban insurrections after the break with Kuomintang 1927
- ⭕ position of early Communist army groups
- ⬭ early Soviets (self-governing Communist areas) 1927–35
- → route of the 'Long March', Oct. 1934–Oct. 1935, of Chinese Communists after Kuomintang assaults on Kiangsi Soviet area
- main Communist base area, governed from Yenan 1935–45
- area occupied by Japan end 1941
- area occupied by Japan during 1944 offensives
- 'liberated areas' dominated by local Communist groups by 1945
- railways in 1937
- main industrial areas 1937
- ■ main industrial centres 1937
- ◆ other industrial centres 1937

U S S R

MANCHURIA

Manchouli   Hailar   Tsitsihar   Kiamusze

OUTER MONGOLIA
(independent 1921)

Harbin

Kirin

Changchun

Mukden   Fushun
Chinchow   Penki
Anshan
Yingkow   Antung

KOREA
Japanese
1910–45

Kalgan
Peking
Paotow   Tatung   Tangshan   Dairen
Tientsin   Port Arthur
(Lüshun)

SHEN-KAN-NING
Taiyuan
Yenan Pao-an: Soviet
1930–5
Lanchow   (Hwang Ho)   Tsinan
Tsingtao   Yellow Sea

Yellow River
Sian   Kaifeng   Lienyünkang
Loyang   Chengchow
Hsü-chou
(Suchow)

4th army group,
Chang Kuo-tao
Hsü Hsiang-ch'ien   Nanking   Soochow
Shanghai

C   H   I   N   A
Chengtu   Wuhan   Hangchow   Ningpo

10th army group,
Fang Chih-min   East China
Sea

Chungking   Kiukiang
Nanchang
Aug. 1927

Tsunyi   W. Hunan   Chingkang Shan,
Jan. 1935   Changsha   Mao Zedong and
Hengyang   Chu Teh, 1927–9
Jui-chin   Kiangsi Soviet under
(Juikin)   Mao Zedong and Chu Teh,
1929–34

Kweiyang   Foochow
TAIWAN
Japanese
1895–1945
Kunming   Amoy

Canton
Dec. 1927   Swatow
Hailufeng Soviet under
P'eng P'ai, 1927–8

Hong Kong
British

FRENCH
INDO-CHINA
Hainan   South China Sea

THAILAND

BURMA

DIA

compelled Mao and his followers to move first to Kiangsi, and then in 1934 to the north-west (the 'Long March': map 2).

In 1937 Japanese forces invaded northern and central China and the KMT retreated to the interior, where they remained until the Japanese surrender in 1945. A race to occupy the liberated areas now ensued, with the Communists gaining much of the north and most of Manchuria, and the KMT re-occupying the south. In 1946 hostilities between the two sides erupted into a civil war from which the Communists emerged victorious. The People's Republic of China was proclaimed in October 1949, and soon afterwards the KMT fled to Taiwan. For the first time in a century, a strong regime controlled all of mainland China – albeit most of the country had been devastated by the warlords, the Japanese occupation and the civil war.

A poster from c.1927 showing Sun Yat-sen (top centre) and Chiang Kai-shek (on horse) about to set out with Kuomintang forces on the 'Northern Expedition' of 1926–8.

1914–1918
The First World War

All the war-plans of the Great Powers in 1914 envisaged a short war. The German Schlieffen Plan called for an attack on northern France through Belgium, leading to the rapid collapse of the French government before Russia had time to mobilize (page 125). It almost succeeded: the Germans came within 40 miles of Paris, but not before Russian armies had invaded East Prussia. Although their advance was halted at Tannenberg (August), important German reserves were diverted from the Western front just as a spirited counter-attack by French and British troops began at the Marne (September). The two sides now spread their forces out and dug in, until their trenches stretched from the Channel coast to Switzerland.

The war in the west (map 2) turned into a war of attrition. Each side launched repeated offensives, with appalling casualties but little gain, for railways were able to bring up reinforcements before the slow-moving front-line troops could make good any advantage. In 1916 the British, under Sir Douglas Haig, made a major frontal assault on German lines at the river Somme. On the first day of the battle 60,000 British casualties were mowed down as they advanced through the barbed wire. Haig threw his forces into an unwinnable conflict for another four months. Both sides experienced terrible losses and achieved little. Neither side could break the trench

stalemate by pursuing alternative strategies. The British and French attempted a series of attacks from the rear: in the Dardanelles and Mesopotamia against the Ottoman empire, which entered the war in November 1914 on the side of the Central Powers (Germany and Austria); on Austria's southern frontier after Italy declared war in May 1915; at Salonika in Greece in support of Serbia. All failed. The Germans countered by building a fleet of submarines with the express intention of bringing Britain to its knees by attacking vulnerable food imports on which Britain relied. In 1917 unrestricted submarine warfare failed to halt Britain's food supply, but provoked the United States into war with Germany.

On the eastern front, which stretched for twice the distance of that in the west, warfare remained more mobile and both Germany and Austria scored major successes. In 1915 the former overran a huge area of Poland, whose resources it ruthlessly exploited, while the latter occupied most of Serbia. In 1917 the combination of huge losses and economic chaos broke the fighting spirit of the Russian forces and provoked revolution and military collapse (page 134). At the peace of Brest-Litovsk in March 1918 Germany gained the Ukraine, Poland, Finland and the Baltic provinces.

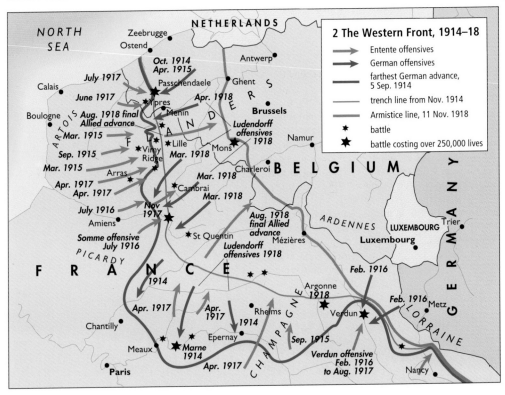

2 The Western Front, 1914–18

→ Entente offensives
→ German offensives
— farthest German advance, 5 Sep. 1914
— trench line from Nov. 1914
— Armistice line, 11 Nov. 1918
★ battle
★ battle costing over 250,000 lives

1 The Great War in Europe, 1914–18

- Entente Powers
- Central Powers
- major Entente Power offensives
- major Central Power offensives
- farthest advance by Entente Powers: (east 1914, west 1918)
- farthest advance by Central Powers: (west 1914, east 1918)
- ★ battle
- ★ battle costing over 250,000 lives
- ⚓ naval base

Map labels:

naval blockade of Germany effective end 1916
1916: Battle of Jutland
1914: Russian offensive in East Prussia
1917: Riga offensive
1918
1914: Tannenberg counter-offensive
1914
1916: Brusilov offensive
1917
1918: Central Powers advance through Ukraine
1915: Gorlice campaign
1916: Asiago offensive
1917
1918
1915: conquest of Serbia
1916: Central Powers conquest of Romania
1918: Allied advance into Serbia
1916
1915: British land at Salonica to support Serbia
1915: Gallipoli offensive

Instead of moving its forces across to the West, however, Germany sent its troops to occupy these new territories – even Finland – and at the same time launched a final, all-out offensive in the West, in an attempt to break the deadlock. Once again it came close to success but the Allied line held and in July, aided by tanks and reinforced by American forces and money, a counter-attack began that pushed the German army back towards the German frontier. Morale collapsed: by October 1918, with Austria close to disintegration and with Germany facing a grave political crisis at home, the Berlin government sued for an unconditional armistice, granted on 11 November 1918.

At the peace conferences held in and around Paris in 1919, the victors imposed upon Germany, Austria, Hungary, and Bulgaria notable losses of territory, huge reparations and stringent reductions in their armed forces. The draconian nature of the settlement made it inevitable that, although over 9 million men had perished in the fighting, and the financial cost of the war totalled over $186 billion worldwide, it would not be (as so many had hoped) 'the war to end all wars'.

The Menin Road (left), vividly recalled by the British painter Paul Nash, saw some of the Western Front's worst fighting. In the second half of 1917, a British campaign to re-capture seven miles of Flanders towards Menin and Passchendaele floundered in heavy rain and mud. The British lost 265,000 men and Menin remained in German hands

133

The USSR from Lenin to Stalin

2 Collectivization, 1923–39

2-10% of all farms collectivized by 1928	70-85% of all farms collectivized by 1933
25-50% of all farms collectivized by 1933	famine areas, 1932
50-70% of all farms collectivized by 1933	*Kraslag* labour camp admin. zone
	corrective labour camps, 1932

By 1917 the strain of war had fatally weakened the Tsarist government: liberals, businessmen, generals and aristocrats all plotted its overthrow. In the end sheer hunger turned a general strike and bread queues into a revolutionary movement which in February forced the Tsar to abdicate, and power passed to a provisional government of prominent *duma* (parliament) politicians. The revolutionary committees (soviets) did not disband, however, and gradually the 'peace, bread and land' programme of the Bolshevik group, led by V. I. Lenin, gained support. In October, the Bolsheviks seized control of strategic points in Petrograd (formerly St Petersburg), arrested the Provisional Government, and assumed power in the name of the soviets. The same soon happened in other cities (map 1).

No one thought they would retain power for long. The overriding need was for peace, and Lenin accepted the onerous terms imposed by Germany in the treaty of Brest-Litovsk (March 1918: page 133); but almost immediately the Bolsheviks (who now took the name 'Communists') faced massive invasions by forces loyal to the Tsar and assisted by troops from

Britain, France, Czechoslovakia, Poland and other anti-Bolshevik powers. Nevertheless, by 1920 the civil war had been won, albeit at the cost of 13 million lives and immense damage to property. Lenin now introduced his 'New Economic Policy', which by 1925 allowed the Russian economy to regain its pre-war industrial level. In 1928 Lenin's successor, Joseph Stalin, introduced a Five Year Plan of industrialization, and the following year embarked on the forced collectivization of agriculture, which transformed small, individual peasant holdings into huge state collective farms. The results of the policy proved disastrous, however. It was implemented without adequate machinery, and poorly organized. Crop yields fell, and a great famine in 1932-3 claimed millions of victims. This rural catastrophe caused some 40 million people to move into the cities, where their fresh labour was used mainly for construction, making the industrial growth rates of the Soviet economy under the first and second Five Year Plans (1928-37) look both startling and unique amid the Great Depression that prevailed elsewhere.

This industrialization took place against a background of state-directed terror as Stalin consolidated the Communist dictatorship. The security forces (the NKVD) executed perhaps 12 million people, while a further 10 million suffered imprisonment in forced labour camps (see map 2). Russia survived the German invasion in 1941 (page 140), partly because over 1500 factories were moved to safety further east, but the setback remained undeniable. A further 20 million Soviet citizens died in the conflict and, although the USSR mobilized more fully than any other state in World War II, its industrial output in 1946 stood at only 70 per cent of the 1940 level.

A poster of Stakhanov, a model mine-worker who exceeded his norm through exceptional efforts. He became a hero of the Soviet State and a propaganda tool in Communist efforts to increase worker participation.

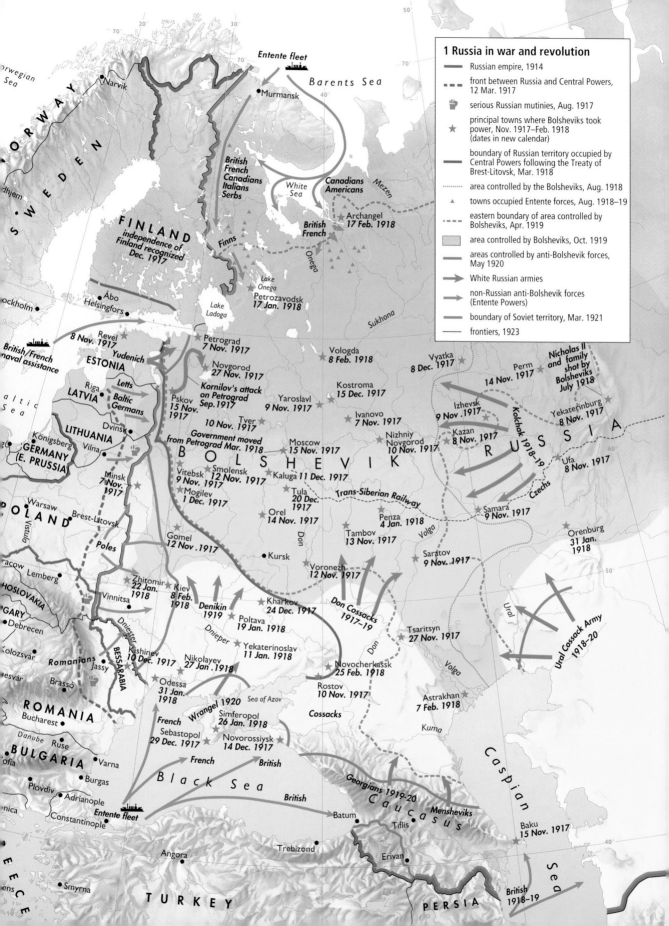

1 Russia in war and revolution

— Russian empire, 1914

--- front between Russia and Central Powers, 12 Mar. 1917

✊ serious Russian mutinies, Aug. 1917

★ principal towns where Bolsheviks took power, Nov. 1917–Feb. 1918 (dates in new calendar)

— boundary of Russian territory occupied by Central Powers following the Treaty of Brest-Litovsk, Mar. 1918

········ area controlled by the Bolsheviks, Aug. 1918

▲ towns occupied Entente forces, Aug. 1918–19

--- eastern boundary of area controlled by Bolsheviks, Apr. 1919

▦ area controlled by Bolsheviks, Oct. 1919

— areas controlled by anti-Bolshevik forces, May 1920

➜ White Russian armies

➜ non-Russian anti-Bolshevik forces (Entente Powers)

— boundary of Soviet territory, Mar. 1921

— frontiers, 1923

Norwegian Sea

Narvik

NORWAY

SWEDEN

dhjem

ockholm

Åbo
Helsingfors

Baltic Sea

British/French naval assistance

Revel 8 Nov. 1917

Yudenich

ESTONIA

Riga Letts
LATVIA

Baltic Germans

Dvinsk

Königsberg

GERMANY (E. PRUSSIA)

Vilna

LITHUANIA

POLAND

Warsaw

Vistula

Brest-Litovsk

Poles

racow Lemberg

HOSLOVAKIA

GARY

Debrecen

Kolozsvár

esvár

Brassó

ROMANIA

Bucharest

Danube Ruse

BULGARIA

ofia

Plovdiv

Adrianople

nica

Constantinople

Varna

Burgas

Smyrna

TURKEY

Angora

Entente fleet

Barents Sea

Murmansk

White Sea

British French Canadians Italians Serbs

Canadians Americans

British French

Archangel 17 Feb. 1918

Finns

FINLAND
independence of Finland recognized Dec. 1917

Lake Onega

Petrozavodsk 17 Jan. 1918

Lake Ladoga

Mezen

Onega

Sukhona

Petrograd 7 Nov. 1917

Novgorod 27 Nov. 1917

Kornilov's attack on Petrograd Sep. 1917

Pskov 15 Nov. 1917

Tver 10 Nov. 1917

Government moved from Petrograd Mar. 1918

Vologda 8 Feb. 1918

Vyatka 8 Dec. 1917

Nicholas II and family shot by Bolsheviks July 1918

Perm 14 Nov. 1917

Izhevsk 9 Nov. 1917

Yekaterinburg 8 Nov. 1917

Kolchak 1918–19

RUSSIA

Ufa 8 Nov. 1917

Kostroma 15 Dec. 1917

Yaroslavl 9 Nov. 1917

Ivanovo 7 Nov. 1917

Kazan 8 Nov. 1917

B O L S H E V I K

Vitebsk 9 Nov. 1917

Smolensk 12 Nov. 1917

Moscow 15 Nov. 1917

Kaluga 11 Dec. 1917

Nizhniy Novgorod 10 Nov. 1917

Mogilev 1 Dec. 1917

Minsk 7 Nov. 1917

Tula 20 Dec. 1917

Trans-Siberian Railway

Czechs

Samara 9 Nov. 1917

Orel 14 Nov. 1917

Penza 4 Jan. 1918

Volga

Orenburg 31 Jan. 1918

Kursk

Gomel 12 Nov. 1917

Don

Tambov 13 Nov. 1917

Voronezh 12 Nov. 1917

Saratov 9 Nov. 1917

Ural

Zhitomir 22 Jan. 1918

Kiev 8 Feb. 1918

Denikin 1919

Kharkov 24 Dec. 1917

Don Cossacks 1917–19

Ural Cossack Army 1918–20

Vinnitsa

Poltava 19 Jan. 1918

Dnieper

Yekaterinoslav 11 Jan. 1918

Tsaritsyn 27 Nov. 1917

Dniester

Kishinev 10 Dec. 1917

Nikolayev 27 Jan. 1918

Don

Novocherkassk 25 Feb. 1918

Astrakhan 7 Feb. 1918

Romanians

Jassy

BESSARABIA

Odessa 31 Jan. 1918

Sea of Azov

Rostov 10 Nov. 1917

Cossacks

Kuma

Caspian Sea

Wrangel 1920

Simferopol 26 Jan. 1918

French

French Sebastopol 29 Dec. 1917

Novorossiysk 14 Dec. 1917

French

British

Black Sea

British

Georgians 1919–20

Mensheviks

Batum

Tiflis

Baku 15 Nov. 1917

Trebizond

C a u c a s u s

Erivan

PERSIA

British 1918–19

GREECE

European political problems

The collapse of the Central Powers in the autumn of 1918, and the subsequent peace treaties (page 133), brought about major frontier changes, the emergence of several new states, and the enlargement of others on the winning side (see map 1). The dismemberment of the Austro-Hungarian empire, the disarmament and the imposition of reparation payments on Germany and her allies, and the effects of the Russian Revolution and civil war (page 134) completely altered the balance of political power in Europe. In terms of population and industrial strength, however, Germany, although weakened, still had no rival in central Europe. The only hope of those who stood behind the peace treaties was the maintenance of overwhelming collective military strength against any revival of German strength. France tried to restrain Germany by signing alliances with the new states of Poland and Czechoslovakia, but Britain proved reluctant to enter into new continental commitments, and the United States withdrew into isolationism. However, Germany's formal recognition of the post-war frontier settlements with France and Belgium by the Locarno treaties (1925) inaugurated a new spirit of cooperation and it was welcomed back into the community of nations. After 1928 many nations signed the 'Kellogg-Briand Pact', which outlawed aggressive war.

But indications of stability proved illusory. Many

PLEBISCITES AND TERRITORIAL DISPUTES

1 plebiscite Feb. 1920: divided between Denmark and Germany
2 occupied by France 1923–5
3 to Belgium 1919
4 to Belgium 1919
5 evacuated 1930, remilitarized, 1936
6 League of Nations Mandate by plebiscite to Germany 1935
7 to France 1919
8 divided between Germany and Poland by plebiscite Mar. 1921
9 Allied occupation 1920–3, annexed by Lithuania 1923, autonomous 1924, to Germany 1939
10 to Germany July 1920
11 to Poland Dec. 1918
12 partitioned between Czechoslovakia and Poland 1920
13 to Hungary 1921
14 to Austria 1920
15 occupied by Poland 1920, annexed by Poland following elections 1922
16 to Greece from Bulgaria 1919
17 demilitarized 1924, remilitarized 1936
18 Greek-Bulgarian conflict, 1925

states, especially in eastern Europe, displayed alarming political instability; and all European participants emerged economically weakened from the World War. Italy – which had run up huge debts and lost 600,000 men in the war, but gained only 9000 square miles (14,400 km²) of new territory at the peace – soon became ungovernable, with civil war between left- and right-wing extremists prevailing in many cities until in 1922 the Fascist party, led by Benito Mussolini, took power. In other parts of Europe, the cost of the war and the defects of the peace settlements, coupled with the strains of economic readjustment and disastrous inflation, strengthened anti-parliamentary and revolutionary movements of both left and right. And with the onset of the Great Depression in 1929 (page 138), financial and economic chaos returned to the entire continent. Unemployment rose drastically, especially in Germany where after 1930 the anti-parliamentary movements of both right and left, the Nazis (National Socialists)

and the Communists, increased their strength enormously until in 1933 the Nazi leader, Adolf Hitler, became Chancellor and proceeded to absorb or abolish all the other parties.

Hitler's victory, combined with the economic weakness of Britain and the political instability of France, irretrievably damaged the precarious balance of peace in Europe. The League of Nations, created in 1920 to regulate international disputes and protect member states from aggression, remained only as strong as its members. Its failure to prevent Italy's annexation of Ethiopia in 1935-6, and Germany's remilitarization of the Rhineland in 1936 encouraged further aggression (map 2 and inset). Hitler, who rapidly increased and modernized Germany's armed forces, annexed Austria and parts of Czechoslovakia in 1938, then Bohemia and Memel in spring 1939, while Italy invaded and occupied Albania (1939). Whether an early alliance between the western democracies and the Soviet Union would have halted the aggressors is a matter of dispute. However, fearing that he might be next in line, and already engaged in hostilities with Hitler's ally, Japan, in August 1939 Stalin signed a non-aggression pact with Germany. The collapse of the unstable system created after World War I was now unavoidable.

Adolf Hitler (1889-1945) is greeted by a crowd in the Sudetenland, shortly after its occupation by Germany in 1938. Born in a small Austrian town, Hitler fought in the German army in the First World War. In 1919 he joined a small radical nationalist party in Munich. During a two-year jail sentence for his part in an unsuccessful coup in Munich in 1923, he wrote his major work *Mein Kampf*. In it he called for revenge for Germany's defeat in 1918 by building a racially strong Germany and overturning the Versailles settlement. His message proved attractive to the conservative masses in the Depression after 1929 an in January 1933 he assumed the chancellorship.

1 National conflicts and frontier disputes, 1919-36

— German empire, 1914

— Austro-Hungarian empire, 1914

— Russian empire, 1914

— post-settlement frontiers

▲ plebiscites held

new states

areas of dispute

areas temporarily autonomous or independent

areas under armed occupation

areas under League of Nations High Commissioners

2 Axis expansion, 1935-9

Germany, 1935

— frontiers, 1937

German annexations:

Mar. 1938

Oct. 1938

Mar. 1939

→ Italian campaigns 1935-6

remilitarized by Germany, 1936

incorporated by plebiscite, 1935

to Poland, 1938

client state of Germany, nominally independent from Mar. 1939

to Hungary, 1938-9

ALBANIA annexed by Italy 1939

conquered by Italy, 1935-6

The New York Stock Market crash in October 1929 reflected deep weaknesses in the world economy. Commodity prices world-wide had been falling since 1926, reducing the capacity of exporters such as Australia and Latin America to buy products from Europe and the United States. Within the latter, wages lagged behind profits, impairing the development of domestic markets and limiting the potential of new industries, such as automobiles, to replace old ones, such as textiles. International finance never recovered from the strains of World War I, which caused a dramatic increase in productive capacity, particularly outside Europe, without a corresponding increase in sustained demand. Fixed exchange rates and free convertibility gave way to a compromise – the Gold Exchange Standard – that lacked the stability necessary to rebuild world trade.

In the scramble for liquidity that followed the Great Crash, funds flowed back from Europe to America and Europe's fragile prosperity crumbled. In many industrial countries one-quarter of the labour force was thrown out of work. Prices and wages plummeted, industrial production fell to 53 per cent of its 1929 level in Germany and world trade sank to 35 per cent of its 1929 value (see map 1). Early attempts to solve the problem did more harm than good. In 1930 the United States imposed the highest tariff in its history; in 1932 Britain responded with the Ottawa agreements, a series of preferential tariffs for the Commonwealth. Britain also left the Gold Standard in 1931, followed by other countries, dividing virtually the entire world into closed currency blocs which inhibited trade still further. Only Soviet Russia, largely isolated from the world economy, continued to increase its industrial production (page 134).

Economic nationalism fostered political nationalism, just as mass unemployment and the erosion of middle-class living standards fostered political extremism. In Japan, the fall of the Hamaguchi government in 1931 marked the end of constitutional democracy and the beginning of aggression in

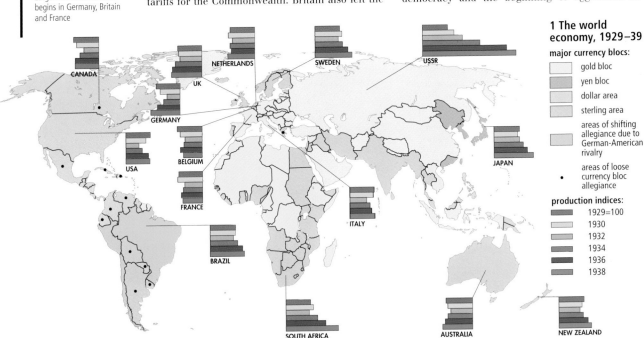

1 The world economy, 1929–39

major currency blocs:
- gold bloc
- yen bloc
- dollar area
- sterling area
- areas of shifting allegiance due to German-American rivalry
- areas of loose currency bloc allegiance

production indices:
- 1929=100
- 1930
- 1932
- 1934
- 1936
- 1938

CANADA · NETHERLANDS · SWEDEN · USSR · UK · GERMANY · BELGIUM · USA · FRANCE · JAPAN · ITALY · BRAZIL · SOUTH AFRICA · AUSTRALIA · NEW ZEALAND

[Map detail, western United States:]
Seattle · WASHINGTON · Columbia · OREGON · IDAHO · farm workers begin organizing, 1933 · NEVADA · San Francisco general strike, May–July 1934 · CALIFORNIA · Los Angeles · Salt La... · UTA... · ARIZO... · Phoenix

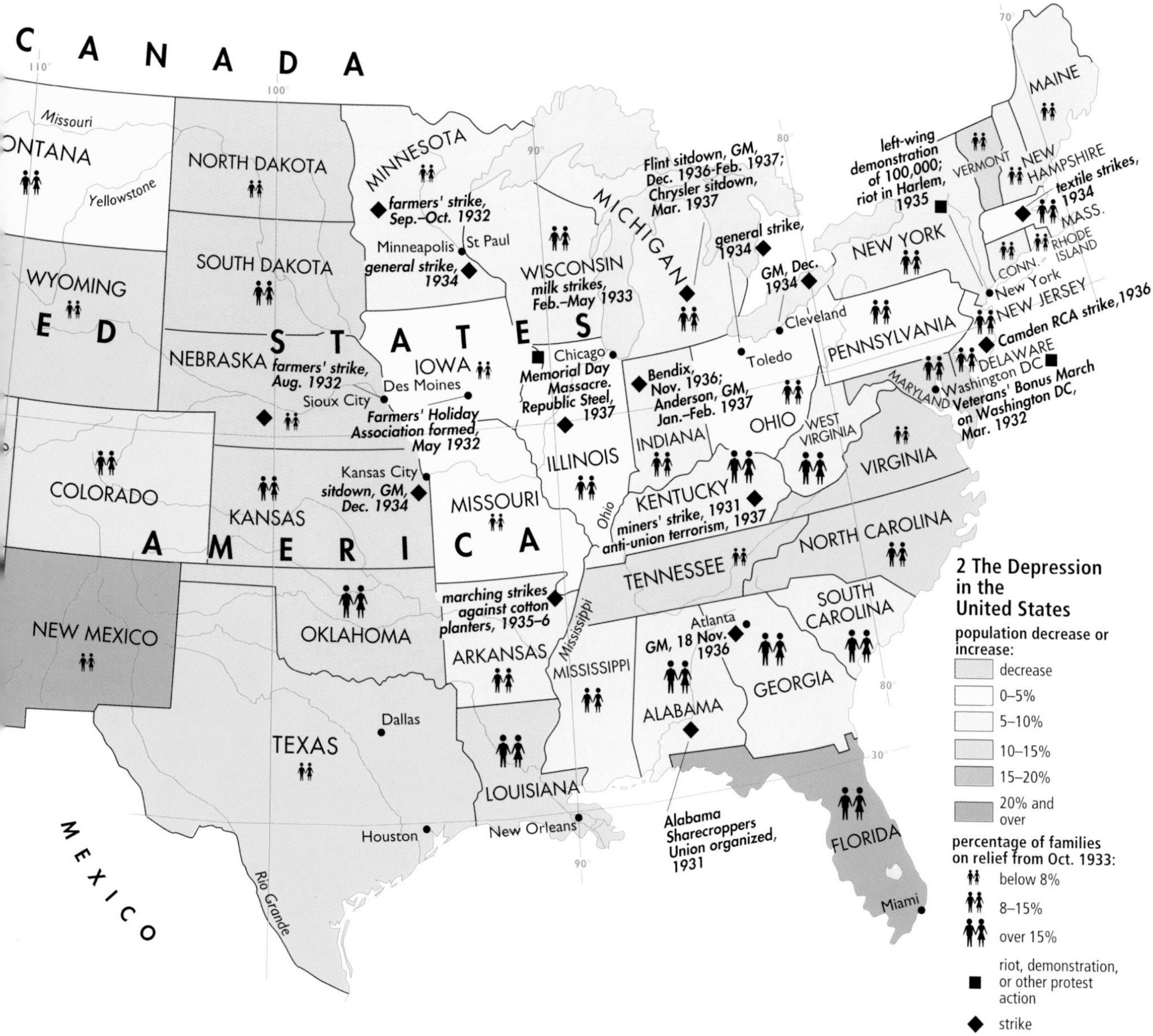

CANADA
UNITED STATES OF AMERICA
MEXICO
MONTANA
NORTH DAKOTA
MINNESOTA
farmers' strike, Sep.–Oct. 1932
Minneapolis
St Paul
general strike, 1934
SOUTH DAKOTA
WYOMING
NEBRASKA
farmers' strike, Aug. 1932
Sioux City
Des Moines
IOWA
Farmers' Holiday Association formed, May 1932
WISCONSIN
milk strikes, Feb.–May 1933
MICHIGAN
Flint sitdown, GM, Dec. 1936-Feb. 1937; Chrysler sitdown, Mar. 1937
general strike, 1934
GM, Dec. 1934
Chicago
Memorial Day Massacre, Republic Steel, 1937
Toledo
Cleveland
left-wing demonstration of 100,000; riot in Harlem, 1935
NEW YORK
New York
VERMONT
NEW HAMPSHIRE
MAINE
textile strikes, 1934
MASS.
RHODE ISLAND
CONN.
NEW JERSEY
Camden RCA strike, 1936
PENNSYLVANIA
DELAWARE
MARYLAND
Washington DC
Veterans' Bonus March on Washington DC, Mar. 1932
Bendix, Nov. 1936; Anderson, GM, Jan.–Feb. 1937
INDIANA
OHIO
WEST VIRGINIA
VIRGINIA
ILLINOIS
COLORADO
KANSAS
Kansas City
sitdown, GM, Dec. 1934
MISSOURI
KENTUCKY
miners' strike, 1931 anti-union terrorism, 1937
Ohio
TENNESSEE
NORTH CAROLINA
SOUTH CAROLINA
NEW MEXICO
OKLAHOMA
marching strikes against cotton planters, 1935–6
ARKANSAS
Mississippi
MISSISSIPPI
Atlanta
GM, 18 Nov. 1936
ALABAMA
GEORGIA
Dallas
TEXAS
LOUISIANA
New Orleans
Houston
Rio Grande
Alabama Sharecroppers Union organized, 1931
FLORIDA
Miami
Missouri
Yellowstone
population decrease or increase:
decrease
0–5%
5–10%
10–15%
15–20%
20% and over
percentage of families on relief from Oct. 1933:
below 8%
8–15%
over 15%
riot, demonstration, or other protest action
strike

2 The Depression in the United States

Manchuria (page 123). In Europe, Hitler rose to power in 1933 partly in response to the deflationary policies of his predecessors that raised unemployment from 3 million in 1930 to 6 million in 1932 (page 137). Even in Britain and the United States, fascist movements exercised considerable pressure. In the former, a right-wing National Government, formed in 1931, preserved democratic rule; in the latter, President Franklin Roosevelt, elected in 1932, implemented a 'New Deal' that laid the foundations for recovery. Nevertheless in 1934 some 20 billion days were lost in the US through industrial action and in 1938 over 10 million Americans remained out of work (map 2). Only World War II, and the boost it gave to production, pulled the United States out of the Depression.

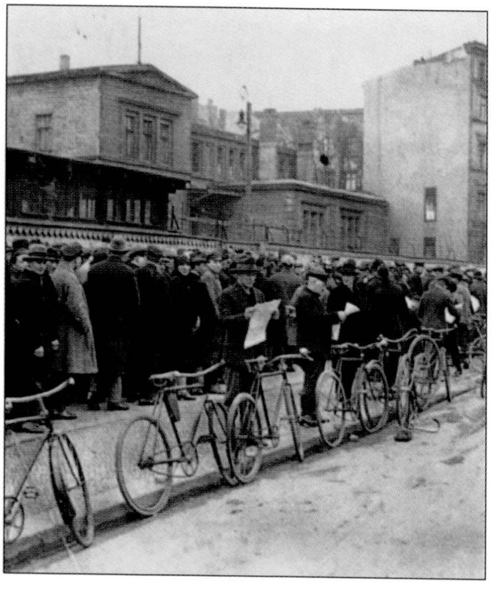

By 1932 two out of every five Germans were out of work, and many of the rest were on short time. Here (*right*) the unemployed queue for newspapers carrying lists of jobs. Official efforts were made to limit the employment of women and to give preference to unemployed men.

3 World commodity production, 1926–38

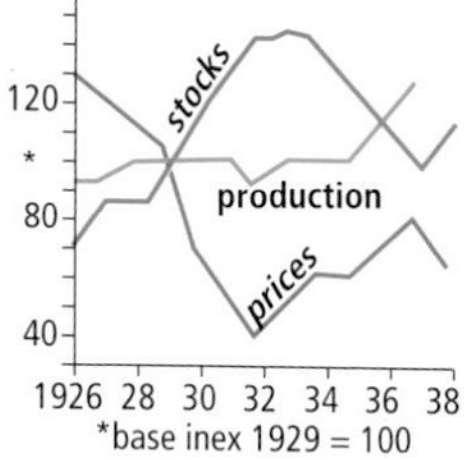

160
120
*
80
40
stocks
production
prices
1926 28 30 32 34 36 38
*base inex 1929 = 100

4 World unemployment in the 1930's

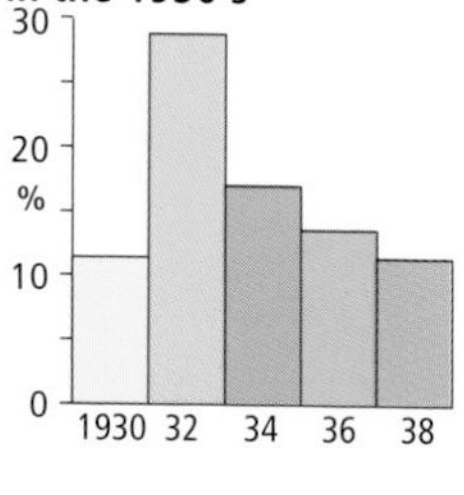

30
20
%
10
0
1930 32 34 36 38

The Second World War: the West

Hitler's accession to power in 1933 added a new dimension to international politics. At first his expansionist designs had to await economic recovery, but his virtually unopposed annexation of Austria and Czechoslovakia (1938-9) and the Nazi-Soviet Pact of August 1939 (page 137) led him to expect similar acquiescence when, the following month, he invaded Poland. This time he miscalculated: the western democracies declared war (though this did nothing to aid the Poles).

Over the next two years, Germany rapidly secured first Denmark and Norway, then France and the Low Countries, and finally Yugoslavia and Greece, while Italy annexed Albania and invaded Egypt (map 1). Despite the Nazi-Soviet pact, however, Hitler's ultimate goal was the conquest of Russia: his operations in the West, like the Schlieffen Plan in 1914 (page 132),

merely aimed to eliminate Germany's western enemies before the main struggle began in the east. In this Hitler failed because Britain – though defeated on the continent and subjected to sustained aerial bombing – refused to concede defeat. Nevertheless, in June 1941 Hitler launched his forces on Russia and, thanks to the

1 The Axis advance, 1939–41

- Axis territory, 1 Sep. 1939
- Axis co-belligerents
- occupied by Axis after Sep. 1939
- Vichy France and territories
- Soviet annexed territory, 1939–41
- neutral powers
- frontiers, 1 Sep. 1939
- Axis advances, 1939
- Axis advances, 1940
- Axis advances, 1941
- Axis airborne landings
- Allied forces
- Soviet advances, 1939–40
- Allied retreat and withdrawal
- major cities severely damaged by bombing

combination of strategic surprise and tactical superiority, made rapid progress, taking over 3 million Russian prisoners-of-war. But the winter killed many Germans, who had far outrun their logistical support and lay stranded outside Moscow, Leningrad and Rostov. At precisely this point, on 7 December 1941, Japan attacked the United States (page 142), and Hitler – in an act of egregious folly – also declared war.

Although Germany launched another major thrust in Russia in 1942, reaching the Volga at Stalingrad, that too failed, with the loss of a major army, and its troops fell back in the face of superior Soviet forces, supplied both by the industrial complex built up beyond the Urals (page 134) and by the United States. Meanwhile, Anglo-American troops cleared Axis forces first from Africa and then from Sicily in 1942-3, leading Italy to make peace (though German forces there fought on); partisans gradually took over Yugoslavia; and from June 1944 allied armies liberated France and Belgium before moving into Germany. They met the Soviets on the Elbe in May 1945.

The costs of the war were appalling: 15 million military personnel and 35 million civilians perished, 20 million of them Soviet citizens. The Germans murdered prisoners of war

(Canadians, Americans and Britons in the West as well as Russians in the east); they murdered all captured partisans and members of the communist party; and they murdered all Jews they could find, many in mass shootings and at least 6 million in special extermination camps. However, they also lost heavily: the Anglo-American strategic bombing offensive reduced most of their major cities to rubble, and the Soviet troops carried out a systematic campaign of destruction as they advanced in 1944-5. By war's end, almost all Europe lay in ruins, yet already the differences between the victors had appeared which would darken the post-war years (page 164).

German troops fighting on the Eastern Front in June 1943. From early in 1943 the Soviet army experienced an almost uninterrupted run of successes against the Germans. In 1944 the Red Army pushed as far west as Warsaw, and in 1945 into Germany itself. Nearly 3 million German soldiers died during the war.

2 The defeat of Germany, 1942–5

- ☐ Grossdeutches Reich, 1942
- ← Axis attacks
- ◄-- Axis withdrawals
- ← Allied attacks
- ● major cities under heavy air attack
- ✹ major battle with date
- ✊ partisan/resistance movements
- ● commando raids
- ↘ V1 launching sites
- ◣ V2 launching sites
- — frontiers 1942

The Second World War: Asia and the Pacific

Japanese expansion in Asia after 1931 (page 123) stemmed from a desire for economic self-sufficiency, military security and a self-imposed leadership of East Asia. By 1940, however, with no end in sight to the Chinese war, Japan widened its ambitions to include the empires of the colonial powers – those of France and the Netherlands, recently defeated by her ally Germany, and those of Britain, at war with Germany (page 140) – as an alternative source of raw materials and markets that would free Japan from economic dependence on an increasingly unfriendly United States.

In September 1940 Japan occupied French Indo-China and the United States promptly placed an embargo on sending all iron and steel scrap to Japan. Next, following a sharp defeat in summer 1939 at Nomonhan (Kalkhin Gol), Japan

concluded a neutrality pact with Russia – which had been seen as the empire's principal potential enemy since the Russo-Japanese war (page 122) – and prepared to occupy the rest of the European colonies in South-East Asia. But first she felt it necessary to forestall a counterstrike by the United States: at dawn on 7 December 1941 her aircraft attacked and partially destroyed the US Pacific fleet at Pearl Harbor, Hawaii.

Japan hoped to fight the world's greatest industrialised power to a stalemate that would result in a negotiated peace recognizing Japanese hegemony in east Asia. Within six months, her forces had conquered the American outposts of Guam and the Philippines, and occupied the British and Dutch colonies throughout South-East Asia. Their forces also overran the Bismarck archipelago and much of New Guinea, and captured most of the island redoubts necessary to create a defensive perimeter in the mid-Pacific (map

On 2 September 1945 Japanese representatives finally signed the act of surrender (*below*) on board the battleship *USS Missouri* in Tokyo Bay.

1 The Japanese advance, 1941–2

- – – – Japanese empire, 1941
- → Japanese advance or strike
- ● Japanese base
- ■ Allied base
- ✕ battle

1). In June 1942, however, at Midway Island, aggressive tactics shaped by superb intelligence allowed the aircraft carriers of the US Pacific fleet (which had not been in Pearl the previous December) to destroy a major Japanese carrier force. The United States, although following a 'Europe first' policy in the world war, still possessed abundant resources to advance on two distinct axes against Japan: in the south Pacific, an island-hopping strategy (by-passing the major centres of Japanese resistance and executed by amphibious forces) aimed for the Philippines; in the central Pacific, carrier-borne forces advanced towards the Marianas, from whose airbases bombing raids could be launched on Japan itself. At the same time, Allied forces moved from India into Burma; and in August 1945 Russia finally broke her neutrality pact and invaded Manchuria (map 2).

But Japan, though utterly exhausted, succumbed to none of these conventional threats: rather two atomic bombs, dropped on Hiroshima and Nagasaki in August 1945, precipitated the unconditional surrender of the millions of her troops still in arms. The brief Japanese colonial adventure had caused almost as much destruction as Hitler's war in Europe; but it also unleashed forces of revolutionary nationalism that would shape events throughout Asia over the next five decades (page 162).

U S S R

Soviet army attacks 9 Aug. 1945

Bering Sea 60

Sea of Okhotsk

Kamchatka 17 Aug. 1945

Komandorski Is.

Attu Aleutian Is. Kiska Amchitka

May–Aug. 1943

Kurile Is.

10 Oct. 1943

Japanese perimeter Mar. 1944

Khabarovsk

MANCHURIA (MANCHUKUO)

INNER MONGOLIA

Peking

Hokkaido

Japanese perimeter Oct. 1944

Tientsin Dairen Seoul

KOREA

Sea of Japan

40

JAPAN Tokyo

Fusan

Hiroshima 6 Aug. 1945

fighters sweep over Japan from May 1945

...nese advance into ...ma after Oct. 1943 ...nese offensive into ...India Feb.–June 1944 ...sh offensive into ...na after Nov. 1944 ...goon retaken May 1945

C H I N A

Nanking

Nagasaki 9 Aug. 1945

Shikoku

Shanghai

bombing raids from June 1944

Kyushu

Chinese counter-offensive Apr.– June 1945

1944 Japanese Ichi-Go Offensive

Amoy

Okinawa

direct air attack on Japan from Okinawa from May 1945

Iwo Jima Feb.–Mar. 1945

Bonin Is.

Volcano Is.

20th Air Force begins direct air attack on Japan from 24 Nov. 1944–14 Aug. 1945

Pacific Ocean

Midway

Kunming

Formosa

Canton

Laokai

Hong Kong

Hanoi

Gulf of Tongking

Hainan

Luzon landings Jan. 1945

Battle of Philippine Sea. Japanese carrier aviation annihilated June 1944

Wake I.

Hawaiin Is.

Oahu Pearl Harbor

20

BURMA

Mandalay

SIAM

Philippine Is.

Manila

25 Oct. 1944 Battle of Leyte Gulf. Heavy Japanese naval losses

Saipan June 1944

Tinian

Leyte landing 20 Oct. 1944

Guam July 1944

Marianas

Eniwetok Feb. 1944

Pacific Ocean area forces

...ngoon Bangkok

FRENCH INDO-CHINA

Leyte

Ulithi Sep. 1944

Caroline Is.

Marshall Is.

...hnom Penh Saigon

Gulf of Siam

Sulu Sea

Mindanao May 1945

Palau Sep. 1944

Truk

Kwajalein Feb. 1944

Majuro Jan. 1944

MALAY STATES

Kuala Lumpur

Singapore

SARAWAK

BRUNEI June 1945

Tarakan May 1945

Borneo July 1945

Morotai Sep. 1944

Halmahera Sansapor

Noemfoor July 1944

Sorong

Manus Feb. 1944

Bismarck Arch.

Admiralty Is.

New Ireland

Makin

Christmas I.

Gilbert Is. Tarawa Nov. 1943

0

D U T C H   E A S T   I N D I E S

Sumatra

Celebes Amboina Ceram

May 1944

Hollandia

New Guinea

Rabaul

Bougainville Nov. 1943

Abemama

Ellice Is.

Palembang

Bandjarmasin

Macassar

Banda Sea

Aru Is.

Tanimbar Is.

Saidor Jan. 1944

Solomon Is.

Battle of Santa Cruz Oct. 1942

Eastern Solomons Aug. 1942 Japanese forces repulsed

Batavia

Java Surabaya

Lombok

Flores

Timor

Sumba

Buna

Port Moresby

Tulagi

South Pacific area forces

Japanese perimeter Aug. 1945

Timor Sea

Darwin

Cape York

17–25 Sep. 1942 Japanese ground forces repulsed

Guadalcanal 7 Aug. 1942– 9 Feb. 1943

Espiritu Santo

New Hebrides

Fiji Is.

20

Coral Sea

New Caledonia

2 The Allied counter-offensive

→ Allied advance	● Japanese base	**Japanese perimeters**
⊣ Allied air attack	■ Japanese base bypassed or neutralized	···· March 1944
■ Allied base		–·–· October 1944
✱ atomic bomb target	✕ battle	– – – August 1945

A U S T R A L I A

Sydney

Melbourne

The United States since 1945

The requirements of wartime production solved the unemployment problem (page 138) of the United States at last, and the gigantic output achieved and allies demonstrated the economic potential which, when realized, would create an era of unprecedented prosperity for the United States. Gross National Product almost trebled in real terms between 1950 and 1990, while real income per head nearly doubled.

A number of factors brought about the economic surge: rapid population increase (from 132 million in 1940 to 281 million in 2000); technological advances coupled with the emergence of new consumer goods; the sudden spending of wartime savings; and the rearmament programmes connected with the Cold War and the Korean War (page 164 and 154). Affluence came to seem entirely normal and business confidence was seldom less than buoyant: on this basis of wealth and hope most American people began to transform their entire way of life. The expansion of the suburbs constituted perhaps the most obvious change. Easy credit, cheap fuel (both for homes and cars), mass production of housing and automobiles, and giant road-building programmes (40,000 miles of interstate highways by 1980), all helped encourage Americans in their millions to move off the farms and out of the cities into endless miles of suburbs. So although the population of the central cities grew from 48 million to 79 million between 1950 and 1990, that of their urban fringes also rose from 21 million also to 79 million (map 1).

By 1990, less than one-third of the US population lived in non-metropolitan areas, but the flight from the farms did not reduce productivity: on the contrary, the number of people fed by one farm worker doubled from 15 in 1950 to 30 in 1970. Thanks to mechanization, improved seeds and fertilisers and government subsidies, the United States provided a significant proportion of the world's staple foods, such as wheat, maize and soya beans. The economy at large grew steadily, with the service sector (as in western Europe: page 166) expanding far more rapidly than manufacturing.

But beneath the prosperity lurked tensions. American capitalists tended to spend their profits rather than re-invest them, and industrial workers claimed higher wages and easier conditions of work without regard to the effect such claims (if successful) might have on prices and on the international competitiveness of American industry. The Vietnam War (1965-73: page 162) created high inflation and bitter internal divisions. Explicit discrimination against Blacks and Asians exploded in urban riots during the 1960s and gave rise to a widespread movement for civil rights led by Dr Martin Luther King (map 2). Then came the policies of Presidents Ronald Reagan (1981-9) and George Bush (1989-93), who cut taxes by a third (releasing a flood of spending power on the markets), slashed welfare programmes (turning the inner cities into ghettoes), increased expenditure on armaments (so creating the biggest deficit in history), and failed to remedy the structural defects of American industry (so that the new purchasing power went overwhelmingly into imports, creating an equally unprecedented trade deficit).

Under the presidency of Bill Clinton (1993-2001), Americans rediscovered their national self-confidence. The United States played a decisive role in the conflicts in the Middle East and the Balkans and its economy boomed. Much of this prosperity depended on sales of computers and satellite communications, however, and when demand for these slackened in 2000, recession threatened. The terrorist attacks of September 2001, by shaking public confidence and precipitating a decline in consumer spending, turned the threat into reality.

On 11 September 2001, two planes hijacked by Islamic extremists were deliberately crashed into the World Trade Centre in New York, killing thousands of people. A third plane crashed into the Pentagon in Washington. The shock to a nation which had never suffered a peace-time atrocity on this scale was profound. Defence and the need to secure the nation against similar attacks immediately rose to the top of the political agenda. The blame for the assault was squarely laid on the Islamic al-Qaeda network led by Osama bin Laden and based in Taleban-ruled Afghanistan. An American-led bombing campaign which began in October led, by December, to the collapse of the Taleban regime and the destruction of much of al-Qaeda's infrastructure in Afghanistan.

3 Growth of consumer durables, 1950–98

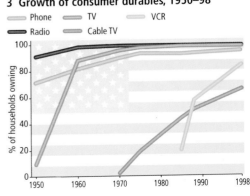

- Phone
- Radio
- TV
- Cable TV
- VCR

(y-axis: % of households owning, 0 to 100; x-axis: 1950, 1960, 1970, 1980, 1990, 1998)

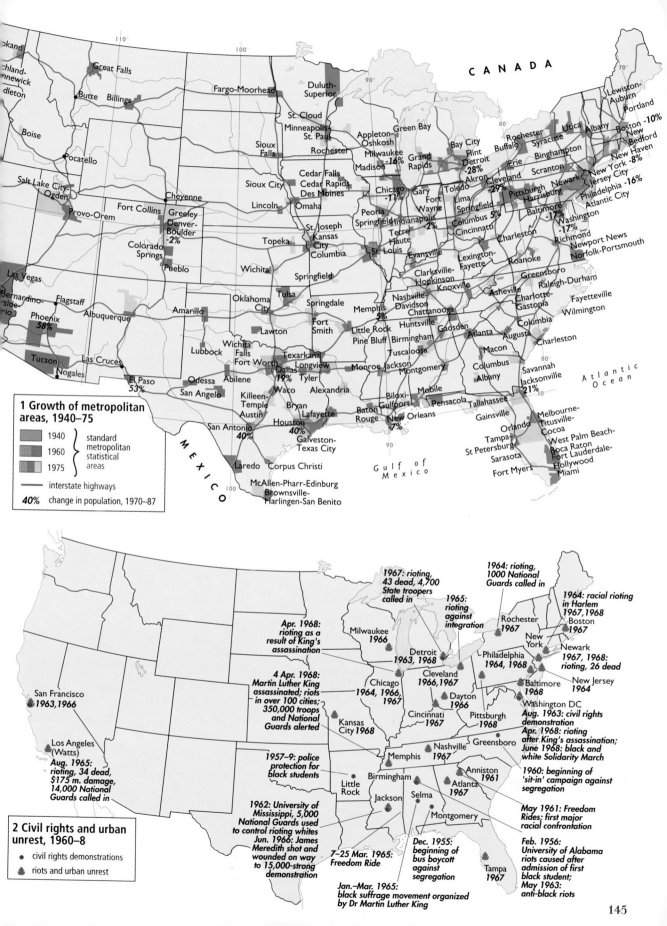

1 Growth of metropolitan areas, 1940–75

1940	standard metropolitan statistical areas
1960	
1975	

— interstate highways

40% change in population, 1970–87

Great Falls
Butte Billings
Boise
Pocatello
Salt Lake City-Ogden
Provo-Orem
Fort Collins
Greeley
Denver-Boulder -2%
Colorado Springs
Pueblo
Las Vegas
Bernardino-side-rio
Flagstaff
Phoenix 58%
Albuquerque
Tucson
Nogales Las Cruces
El Paso 53%
San Angelo
Odessa Abilene
Lubbock
Wichita Falls
Amarillo
Oklahoma City
Lawton
Fort Smith
Laredo Corpus Christi
McAllen-Pharr-Edinburg
Brownsville-Harlingen-San Benito
San Antonio
Houston 40%
Galveston-Texas City
Austin
Bryan
Lafayette
Killeen-Temple
Waco
Dallas 19%
Fort Worth
Texarkana
Longview Tyler
Monroe Jackson
Alexandria
Baton Rouge
New Orleans 7%
Biloxi-Gulfport
Mobile
Pensacola
Tallahassee
Gainsville
Melbourne-Titusville-Cocoa
Orlando
West Palm Beach-Boca Raton
Fort Lauderdale-Hollywood
Miami
Sarasota
Fort Myers
Tampa-St Petersburg

Fargo-Moorhead
Duluth-Superior
St. Cloud
Minneapolis-St. Paul
Sioux Falls
Rochester
Sioux City
Cedar Falls
Cedar Rapids
Des Moines
Lincoln
Omaha
St. Joseph
Kansas City
Topeka
Columbia
Wichita
Springfield
St. Louis
Springfield
Peoria
Chicago -11%
Madison
Milwaukee -16%
Appleton-Oshkosh
Green Bay
Grand Rapids
Bay City Flint
Detroit -28%
Gary
Fort Wayne
Toledo
Akron
Lima
Springfield
Indianapolis -2%
Terre Haute
Columbus 5%
Cincinnatti
Evansville
Clarksville-Hopkinson
Lexington-Fayette
Nashville-Davidson 5%
Memphis 5%
Chattanooga
Knoxville
Asheville
Huntsville
Birmingham
Gadsden
Tuscaloosa
Atlanta 21%
Macon
Columbus
Albany
Montgomery
Jackson
Little Rock
Pine Bluff
Springdale
Tulsa
Columbia
Charleston
Augusta
Charleston
Savannah
Jacksonville
Roanoke
Greensboro
Raleigh-Durham
Charlotte-Gastonia
Fayetteville
Wilmington
Richmond
Newport News
Norfolk-Portsmouth
Washington -17%
Baltimore -17%
Harrisburg
Pittsburgh
Cleveland -29%
Akron
Erie
Buffalo
Rochester
Syracuse
Utica
Binghampton
Scranton
Albany
Lewiston-Auburn
Portland
Boston -10%
New Bedford
New Haven
New York -8%
Jersey City
Newark
Philadelphia -16%
Atlantic City

CANADA
MEXICO
Gulf of Mexico
Atlantic Ocean

2 Civil rights and urban unrest, 1960–8

- • civil rights demonstrations
- 🔥 riots and urban unrest

San Francisco 1963, 1966

Los Angeles (Watts)
Aug. 1965: rioting, 34 dead, $175 m. damage, 14,000 National Guards called in

1957–9: police protection for black students

1962: University of Mississippi, 5,000 National Guards used to control rioting whites
Jun. 1966: James Meredith shot and wounded on way to 15,000-strong demonstration

7–25 Mar. 1965: Freedom Ride

Jan.–Mar. 1965: black suffrage movement organized by Dr Martin Luther King

Dec. 1955: beginning of bus boycott against segregation

Feb. 1956: University of Alabama riots caused after admission of first black student; May 1963: anti-black riots

Apr. 1968: rioting as a result of King's assassination

4 Apr. 1968: Martin Luther King assassinated; riots in over 100 cities; 350,000 troops and National Guards alerted

Milwaukee 1966

1967: rioting, 43 dead, 4,700 State troopers called in

1965: rioting against integration

1964: rioting, 1000 National Guards called in

1964: racial rioting in Harlem 1967, 1968

Rochester 1967

Boston 1967

New York

Newark
1967, 1968: rioting, 26 dead

New Jersey 1964

Detroit 1963, 1968

Chicago 1964, 1966, 1967

Cleveland 1966, 1967

Dayton 1966

Philadelphia 1964, 1968

Baltimore 1968

Washington DC
Aug. 1963: civil rights demonstration
Apr. 1968: rioting after King's assassination; June 1968: black and white Solidarity March

Cincinnati 1967

Pittsburgh 1968

Kansas City 1968

Nashville 1967

Greensboro

1960: beginning of 'sit-in' campaign against segregation

Memphis

Little Rock

Birmingham

Jackson

Selma

Montgomery

Anniston 1961

Atlanta 1967

May 1961: Freedom Rides; first major racial confrontation

Tampa 1967

145

World War II left Europe politically disorganized and economically prostrate, a situation greatly exacerbated by large-scale population movements. The German collapse released millions of incarcerated prisoners-of-war and slave-workers, and a further 5 million Russian prisoners, refugees and servicemen were repatriated. Two more lasting shifts of population also occurred: some 12 million Germans abandoned (voluntarily or forcibly) their pre-war homes in the east, especially in lands annexed by the Nazis after 1938; and over 2 million Russians moved into the territories annexed by the Soviet Union during its westward advance (map 1).

The political frontiers of the new Europe were established at conferences between the victors (USA, USSR, Britain and France) held at Yalta and Potsdam in February and July 1945: the union of Germany and Austria decreed by Hitler in 1938 was dissolved and Germany lost territory to Poland and the Soviet Union; both countries were divided into occupation zones under four power control. In Austria the system worked relatively smoothly, and in 1955 the country achieved independence, albeit as a permanently neutralized state; but co-operation between the USSR and her allies in Germany broke down in 1948. Britain and the United States had already amalgamated their

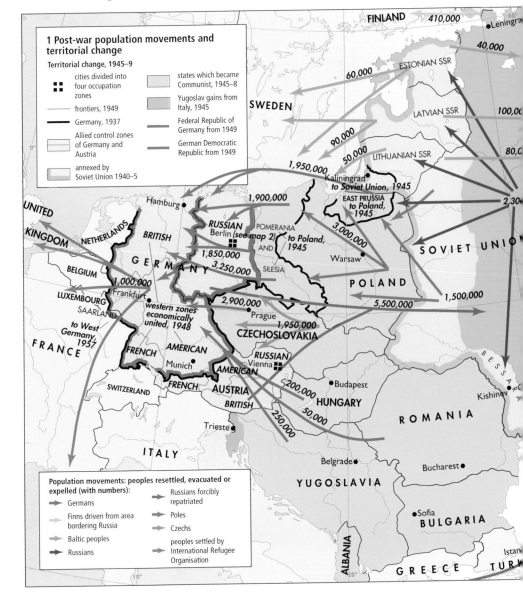

1 Post-war population movements and territorial change

Territorial change, 1945–9

cities divided into four occupation zones

frontiers, 1949

Germany, 1937

Allied control zones of Germany and Austria

annexed by Soviet Union 1940–5

states which became Communist, 1945–8

Yugoslav gains from Italy, 1945

Federal Republic of Germany from 1949

German Democratic Republic from 1949

Population movements: peoples resettled, evacuated or expelled (with numbers):

Germans

Finns driven from area bordering Russia

Baltic peoples

Russians

Russians forcibly repatriated

Poles

Czechs

peoples settled by International Refugee Organisation

zones in 1947 and, in conjunction with France, they now prepared for the formation of a West German government (the Federal Republic: BRD). After an attempt to prevent this by means of a blockade on Berlin, the Soviets prepared their zone for quasi-independence as the German Democratic Republic (DDR): the two states came into existence in 1949 (map 1).

They immediately took their place in the two political blocs into which Europe had become divided. The eastern republics had all come under communist rule by 1948 and economic growth, though continuous, remained slow thanks to Stalinist methods of production. In the western democracies, thanks largely to lavish American aid (the Marshall Plan from 1947; map 3), an economic miracle took place, with smooth and rapid growth year after year. The two blocs had their own military groups – NATO in the west (1949) and the Warsaw Pact in the east (1955) – and their own economic organizations – in the east Comecon (1949) and in the west the European Community (six members 1957; 9 by 1973) and the less successful European Free Trade Association (map 4). However the growth surge suffered a serious check in 1973 when the Arab-led Organization of Petroleum Exporting Countries (OPEC) increased the price of oil by 250 per cent.

On 23 June 1948, the Soviet Union set up a blockade of the Western sectors of Berlin. The Western states mounted an airlift *(left)* until May 1949, which brought in 2.3 million tons of supplies.

2 Berlin, 1945–90

- American sector
- British sector
- French sector
- Soviet sector
- city borders
- the Berlin Wall, 1961–89
- Autobahn
- international railway
- ⊕ airport
- ■ headquarters
- ▫ allied HQ
- → air corridor

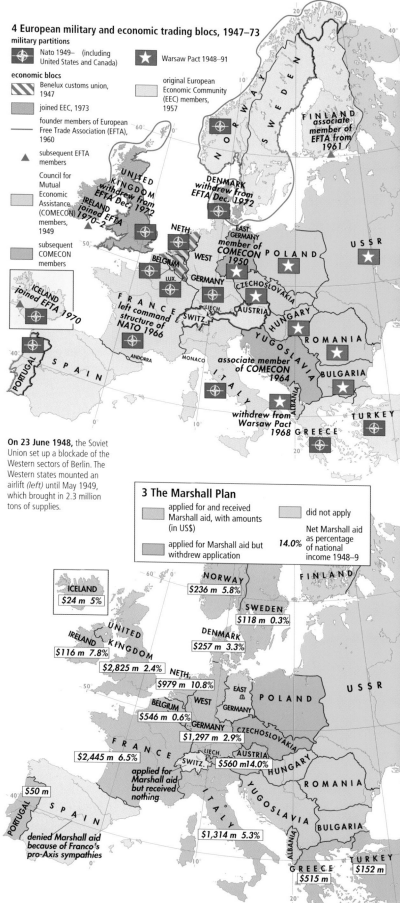

4 European military and economic trading blocs, 1947–73

military partitions

- Nato 1949– (including United States and Canada)
- ★ Warsaw Pact 1948–91

economic blocs

- Benelux customs union, 1947
- joined EEC, 1973
- founder members of European Free Trade Association (EFTA), 1960
- ▲ subsequent EFTA members
- Council for Mutual Economic Assistance (COMECON) members, 1949
- subsequent COMECON members
- original European Economic Community (EEC) members, 1957

UNITED KINGDOM withdrew from EFTA Dec. 1972
IRELAND joined EFTA 1970–2
ICELAND joined EFTA 1970
DENMARK withdrew from EFTA Dec. 1972
EAST GERMANY member of COMECON 1950
FINLAND associate member of EFTA from 1961
FRANCE left command structure of NATO 1966
AUSTRIA associate member of COMECON 1964
ALBANIA withdrew from Warsaw Pact 1968

3 The Marshall Plan

- applied for and received Marshall aid, with amounts (in US$)
- applied for Marshall aid but withdrew application
- did not apply
- 14.0% Net Marshall aid as percentage of national income 1948–9

ICELAND $24 m 5%
NORWAY $236 m 5.8%
SWEDEN $118 m 0.3%
DENMARK $257 m 3.3%
IRELAND $116 m 7.8%
UNITED KINGDOM $2,825 m 2.4%
NETH. $979 m 10.8%
BELGIUM $546 m 0.6%
WEST GERMANY $1,297 m 2.9%
FRANCE $2,445 m 6.5%
AUSTRIA $560 m 14.0%
EAST GERMANY applied for Marshall aid but received nothing
PORTUGAL $50 m
SPAIN denied Marshall aid because of Franco's pro-Axis sympathies
ITALY $1,314 m 5.3%
GREECE $515 m
TURKEY $152 m

The Soviet Union

ALASKA

CANADA

UNITED STATES OF AMERICA

North Atlantic Ocean

MEXICO

CUBA *1962*

NICARAGUA

PERU

BOLIVIA

BRAZIL

CHILE

ARGENTINA

Despite the extensive loss of life and property inflicted on Russia during World War II (page 141 above), remarkable economic recovery began after 1945. The output of heavy industry rose steadily and light industry, neglected under Stalin (who died in 1953), also progressed under his successors. The agricultural problems created by collectivization (page 134) remained – grain production only increased in the late 1950s, and even then the USSR continued to depend on imports – but vast reserves of oil, gas and mineral ores were discovered and exploited in Siberia. Russia's east European satellites were obliged to supply high-quality engineering products and expert personnel (as well as more basic items), which immensely assisted the USSR's economic progress. The development of the atom bomb (1949), of the first satellite (the sputnik: 1957), and of the first manned space flight (1961) all indicated the ability of Russian science to innovate.

After 1945 the Soviet military became a central feature of the state. One-fifth of the budget was devoted to military spending while between 1952 and 1976 101 military leaders became full members of the Central Committee of the Communist Party. The Soviet Union, along with the United States, had become a 'superpower', with a comparable degree of military strength. Although its gross national product fell well short of its rival's, the USSR overtook the USA in the production of iron ore, cement, steel and oil. Nevertheless the Soviet economy entered a period of crisis in the 1970s. Increasingly, the USSR found the arms-race more costly than did the USA (not least because the latter enjoyed far better credit and so could finance much of its expenditure

1 The USSR and the world, 1945–85

☐ USSR and client states, 1938

☐ annexed 1944–5

☐ territorial ambitions thwarted, 1945–6

☐ unsuccessful attempt to gain or maintain control by 1949

☐ control or influence secured by 1954

— Warsaw pact, 1955

— turned antagonistic to USSR from the early 1960s

▨ acknowledgement demanded from China that 19th-century Russian annexations were by unequal treaties

— ties from USSR loosened from mid 1960s

☐ brought into or kept in Soviet sphere in 1970s by military intervention

☐ other allies in 1985

c,v pro-Soviet regime maintained or installed by Cuban or Vietnamese forces, with date

☐ Soviet influence aborted or sought unsuccessfully, 1960–85

✳ Soviet forces in action or deployed in confrontation, with date

⊕ foreign aircraft downed, with detail

— frontiers, 1985

through loans: page 144), and the position became critical when the USA threatened to extend its defence system into outer space (the 'Strategic Defense Initiative'). In 1985 a new Soviet leader, Mikhail Gorbachev, came to power with a programme of reform designed to achieve a 'revolution within the revolution'.

From 1985 to 1990 Gorbachev successfully improved relations with both China and the west in order to provide peaceful external conditions for reconstruction. He introduced *glasnost* (openness) in the media to encourage criticism of deficiencies in the economy and society; but he could not assure an

A May Day parade in Moscow, 1983 *(left)*. After the war the Communist Party became the dominant presence in Soviet society. Under Stalin, large numbers of workers and peasants entered the party. But by the 1980s it perpetuated an elite and gave few opportunities for social mobility

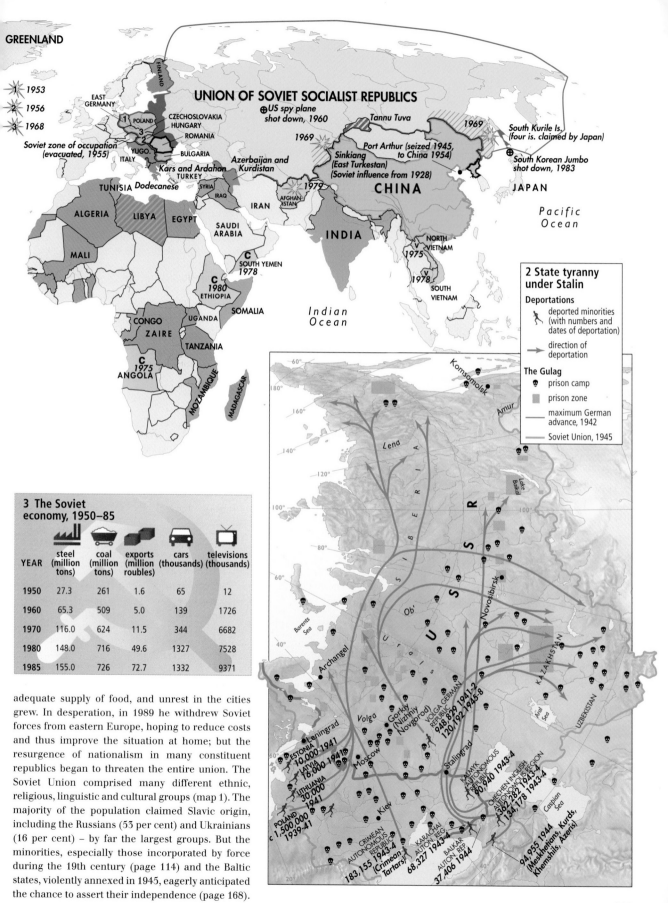

GREENLAND

⊕ 1953
⊕ 1956
⊕ 1968

UNION OF SOVIET SOCIALIST REPUBLICS

FINLAND

EAST GERMANY
POLAND
CZECHOSLOVAKIA
HUNGARY
ROMANIA
Soviet zone of occupation (evacuated, 1955)
YUGO.
ITALY
BULGARIA
Kars and Ardahan
TURKEY
Dodecanese
SYRIA
IRAQ
Azerbaijan and Kurdistan

⊕ US spy plane shot down, 1960

Tannu Tuva
1969
Port Arthur (seized 1945, to China 1954)
Sinkiang (East Turkestan) (Soviet influence from 1928)
1969
South Kurile Is, (four is. claimed by Japan)
⊕ South Korean Jumbo shot down, 1983

CHINA

JAPAN

Pacific Ocean

TUNISIA
ALGERIA
LIBYA
EGYPT
SAUDI ARABIA
IRAN
AFGHANISTAN
1979
MALI
C SOUTH YEMEN 1978
C 1980 ETHIOPIA
SOMALIA
CONGO
ZAIRE
UGANDA
TANZANIA
C 1975 ANGOLA
MOZAMBIQUE
MADAGASCAR

INDIA

Indian Ocean

NORTH VIETNAM 1975
SOUTH VIETNAM 1978

2 State tyranny under Stalin

Deportations

↟ deported minorities (with numbers and dates of deportation)

→ direction of deportation

The Gulag

☠ prison camp

▪ prison zone

— maximum German advance, 1942

— Soviet Union, 1945

3 The Soviet economy, 1950–85

YEAR	steel (million tons)	coal (million tons)	exports (million roubles)	cars (thousands)	televisions (thousands)
1950	27.3	261	1.6	65	12
1960	65.3	509	5.0	139	1726
1970	116.0	624	11.5	344	6682
1980	148.0	716	49.6	1327	7528
1985	155.0	726	72.7	1332	9371

Komsomolsk
Amur
Lena
Lake Baikal
S I B E R I A
U S S R
Novosibirsk
Ob'
KAZAKHSTAN
Urals
Barents Sea
Archangel
Aral Sea
UZBEKISTAN
Volga
Gorky (Nizhniy Novgorod)
VOLGA GERMAN REPUBLIC
948 829 1941-2
120 192 1945-8
Leningrad
ESTONIA 10,000 1941
LATVIA 16,000 1941
LITHUANIA 30,000 1941
Moscow
Stalingrad
KALMYK AUTONOMOUS REPUBLIC
90,940 1943-4
CHECHEN INGUSH AUTONOMOUS REGION
362 282 1943-4
134,178 1943-4
Kiev
POLAND c 1,500,000 1939-41
CRIMEAN AUTONOMOUS REPUBLIC 1943-4
183,155 1944 (Crimean Tartars)
KARACHAI AUTON REG 68,327 1943-4
BALKAR AUTON REP 37,406 1944
94,955 1944 (Meskhetians, Kurds, Khemshils, Azeris)
Caspian Sea

adequate supply of food, and unrest in the cities grew. In desperation, in 1989 he withdrew Soviet forces from eastern Europe, hoping to reduce costs and thus improve the situation at home; but the resurgence of nationalism in many constituent republics began to threaten the entire union. The Soviet Union comprised many different ethnic, religious, linguistic and cultural groups (map 1). The majority of the population claimed Slavic origin, including the Russians (53 per cent) and Ukrainians (16 per cent) – by far the largest groups. But the minorities, especially those incorporated by force during the 19th century (page 114) and the Baltic states, violently annexed in 1945, eagerly anticipated the chance to assert their independence (page 168).

China since 1949

The establishment of the People's Republic of China in 1949 (page 130) marked a fundamental turning point in the modern history of China. After a century of severe internal conflict and disintegration, usually provoked or exacerbated by external aggressors, China was now reunified and strongly governed by leaders who possessed a decisive vision of the society they wished to create. Whatever the excesses and failures since 1949, not least the systematic repression of much of the population, that remains a fundamental achievement.

For a time, China closely followed the Soviet model of directed economic planning and achieved modest progress in developing heavy industries and raising agricultural production. In 1958, however, the communist leader Mao Zedong became impatient and sought to mobilize the revolutionary energies of China's vast population, launching the 'Great Leap Forward'. Rural China was divided into 26,000 communes, each required to abolish private property and meet huge targets in agricultural and industrial production. Some 600,000 backyard furnaces sprang up across the countryside. The experiment proved an unmitigated disaster: production declined sharply, 20-30 million people died from starvation or malnutrition, and the project was abandoned in 1961.

This failure strengthened the hands of moderate communists who preferred a more centrally-planned, Soviet-style development. Mao responded by forming an alliance with the People's Liberation Army (PLA) and with Chinese youth who, as 'Red Guards', faithfully supported his policies. In 1966 Mao launched the Great Proletarian Cultural Revolution. Red Guards were set loose to prevent the development of 'vested interests' and careerism in party and state by establishing permanent revolution. The guards killed thousands and forcibly resettled millions. Chaos followed throughout China, forcing Mao to call on the PLA to restore order (map 1).

Mao died in 1976 and his widow Jiang Qing with three allies (later denounced as the 'Gang of Four') tried to seize power; but by this time the PLA and the elite had had enough of revolution. The 'Gang of Four' were arrested, tried and expelled from the Communist Party.

In the late 1970s Deng Xiaoping became the dominant figure in China's politics. Following the visit of United States President Nixon in 1972, which began the process of re-opening China to the capitalist West, Deng launched a policy of economic liberalization. He created special economic zones in areas bordering the foreign colonies of Hong Kong and Macao and Taiwan, and in Shanghai, with inducements to encourage foreign investment. By 1992, $36 billion had been invested. Other reforms followed: peasants were permitted to own land and, by 1984, 98 per cent did so. The communes vanished and agricultural output increased by 49 per cent in five years. Private businesses, also now permitted, grew in number from 100,000 in 1978 to 17 million in 1985 (map 2).

Economic reforms led to demands for political liberalization. In December 1986, students demonstrated for democracy in 15 cities. Deng responded

Student demonstrators in Beijing in 1989 *(right)*. Thousands of students occupied Tiananmen square for six weeks in May and June to demonstrate for greater democracy. On 3-4 June the army violently ejected the students. The death toll was later estimated at 400-800.

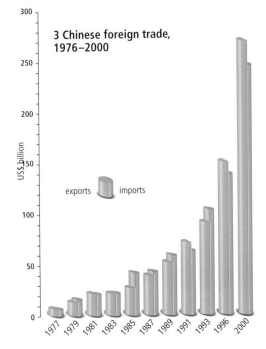

3 Chinese foreign trade, 1976–2000

exports imports

US$ billion

300
250
200
150
100
50
0

1977 1979 1981 1983 1985 1987 1989 1991 1993 1996 2000

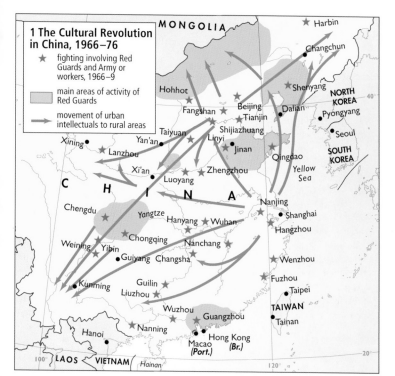

1 The Cultural Revolution in China, 1966–76

★ fighting involving Red Guards and Army or workers, 1966–9

main areas of activity of Red Guards

→ movement of urban intellectuals to rural areas

with repression: he arrested 'troublemakers' and sacked Hu Yaobang, the liberal secretary-general of the Chinese Communist Party. When Hu died in April 1989, students used the occasion to demand democracy, gathering in Beijing's Tiananmen Square, at times numbering over a million, until in June Deng sent in the PLA and the movement was ruthlessly crushed.

After the Tiananmen massacre China swiftly reassured the world that it was a stable economic partner, and most of the world obligingly ignored human rights concerns in return for a share of China's economic boom. Foreign investment soared, and so did China's foreign trade (table 3). Further economic liberalization now took place as most of China operated a 'socialist market economy'. Growth rates, which averaged 10 per cent or more for the 1980s and 1990s, were only slightly affected by the economic turmoil which hit most of the rest of east Asia in 1997–8. In 1997, Britain returned its colony of Hong Kong, which retained a degree of self-government, and two years later Portugal surrendered Macao. With growing freedom in many areas of life, the issue of democracy remained the unfinished business of China's 20th-century achievement.

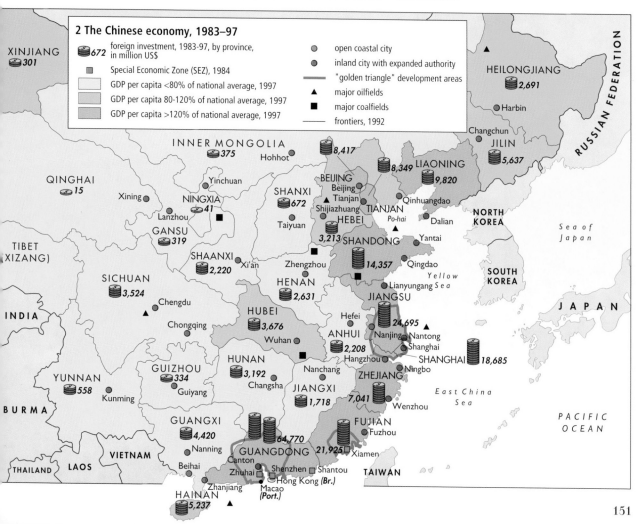

2 The Chinese economy, 1983–97

🪙 672 foreign investment, 1983-97, by province, in million US$

■ Special Economic Zone (SEZ), 1984

GDP per capita <80% of national average, 1997

GDP per capita 80-120% of national average, 1997

GDP per capita >120% of national average, 1997

● open coastal city

● inland city with expanded authority

"golden triangle" development areas

▲ major oilfields

■ major coalfields

— frontiers, 1992

Japan and Korea

In the wake of the Second World War, United States support for Japan, South Korea and Taiwan, perceived after 1948 as its first line of defence in east Asia, transformed their economies.

Japan, like Germany (page 146), ended the war with its economy in ruins: most towns and industrial plants destroyed; nearly all foreign assets lost; domestic capital run down. Moreover, the victors demanded reparations and occupied the country following its surrender. The Far East Commission, which contained representatives of all the countries that had fought Japan but remained an American enterprise, sought to demilitarize Japan and create a peaceful, democratic state. It reformed the education system (removing from the syllabus all material that had encouraged military and authoritarian values); abolished the divinity of the emperor and made the Diet (parliament) the highest political authority; established an independent judiciary and free labour unions; introduced a programme of land reform; and sought (with little success) to break up the great concentrations of corporate power. With the advance of the Chinese communists after 1948, however, the United States increasingly came to see Japan not only as the key bulwark of Western power in east Asia but also as one whose effectiveness depended on the reconstruction of its economic power. The occupation formally ended in 1951.

Japan's defeat also ended its harsh colonial rule of Korea (since 1910) and led to the peninsula's occu-

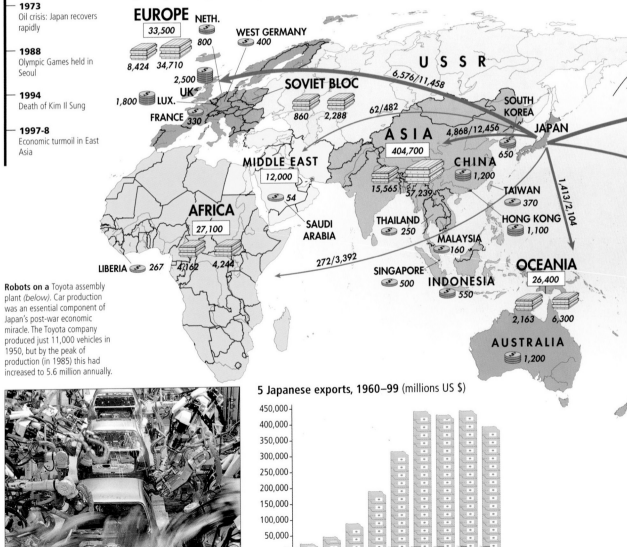

Robots on a Toyota assembly plant *(below)*. Car production was an essential component of Japan's post-war economic miracle. The Toyota company produced just 11,000 vehicles in 1950, but by the peak of production (in 1985) this had increased to 5.6 million annually.

5 Japanese exports, 1960–99 (millions US $)

pation by the victors: Japanese forces north of the 38th parallel surrendered to Soviet Russia, those in the south to the United States. The Soviets supported the establishment of a communist state in the north under Kim Il-Sung, a guerrilla leader who had spent considerable time in the Soviet Union; and the Americans retaliated by sponsoring a representative regime under Syngman Rhee, a strong anti-communist. Both new governments entertained strong ambitions to unite the country under their own rule, and in June 1950 the North attacked, pushing the South Korean and remaining United States troops back toward Pusan (map 1). The US forces counterattacked in September with a daring amphibious landing at Inchon, leading to a further offensive that promised to unify Korea. In November, however, the Chinese committed substantial forces and regained most of the north. A stalemate ensued until an armistice was signed in 1953.

The Korean War boosted the Japanese economy and initiated a period of exceptionally high economic growth – well over 10 per cent a year throughout the 1960s, and over 4 per cent annually between 1974 and 1985, faster than that of any other OECD country. A key feature of Japan's growth was its flexibility in pursuing economic objectives: in the 1950s it emphasized heavy industry, ship-building and iron and steel; in the 1960s it moved into high-technology consumer manufactures largely for export; from the 1970s it concentrated on technological innovation and higher value-added products while transferring the production of lower value-added goods overseas. Industrial production and exports soared (tables 3 and 5) and massive Japanese investment took place in Asia, Europe and North America. Yet by 2002, Japan, for so long boasting the world's strongest economy and the largest per capita GNP, had endured a decade of slow growth or recession, rising unemployment and deflation.

Korea epitomized the relative success of the communist and capitalist projects. Until 1970 North Korea had the higher GNP per capita, but by the 1990s GNP was declining at 5 per cent and the state, still communist, came close to economic and humanitarian disaster. From the mid-1960s South Korea embarked on rapid industrialization and by the 1990s boasted the world's 13th largest economy with great strengths in car manufacture, shipbuilding and semi-conductors (table 4). Its regime showed little tolerance of political dissent, however, and crushed open protest.

Although the economic turmoil that hit the east Asian economies in 1997 exposed serious structural weaknesses, particularly in the inefficient and debt-laden finance and banking sectors, the vast underlying strength of the region suggests that the Pacific Rim will remain a lynchpin of the global economic system.

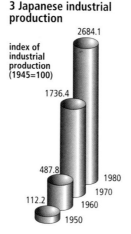

3 Japanese industrial production

index of industrial production (1945=100)

2684.1
1736.4
487.8
112.2

1950
1960
1970
1980

2 Japanese investment overseas, 1970–98

15,565 57,239 — trade with region, 1970–4 and 1985–9 (billion Yen)

6,576/3,392 — value of Japanese direct foreign investment in region, 1987/1999 (US$ million)

1,200 — value of Japanese direct foreign investment in country, 1987 (US$ million)

404,700 — workers in Japanese-affiliated companies, 1980

4 The two Koreas; per capita GNP growth, 1945–99

thousand US$

$13,300 (1999)

South Korea
North Korea

1945 1950 1960 1970 1980 1990 1999

CANADA 650

NORTH AMERICA 83,900

15,357/21,873

USA 14,700

17,170 75,190

BAHAMAS 730

CAYMAN ISLANDS 1,200

4,814/6,479

PANAMA 2,300

LATIN AMERICA 128,100

BRAZIL 230

2,024 2,372

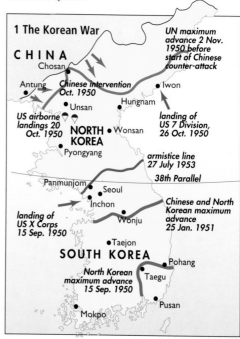

1 The Korean War

CHINA

UN maximum advance 2 Nov. 1950 before start of Chinese counter-attack

Chosan

Antung
Chinese intervention Oct. 1950

Iwon

Unsan

Hungnam

US airborne landings 20 Oct. 1950

NORTH KOREA

Wonsan

landing of US 7 Division, 26 Oct. 1950

Pyongyang

armistice line 27 July 1953

Panmunjom

38th Parallel

Seoul

Inchon

landing of US X Corps 15 Sep. 1950

Wonju

Chinese and North Korean maximum advance 25 Jan. 1951

Taejon

SOUTH KOREA

Pohang

North Korean maximum advance 15 Sep. 1950

Taegu

Pusan

Mokpo

AFTER 1947
Retreat from empire

The Western empires created in the 19th century (page 118) remained intact in 1939, though most German and Ottoman possessions had passed to Britain, France and Japan as League of Nations mandates. The United States planned to grant independence to the Philippines, acquired in 1898, and did so immediately after World War II; but none of the seven remaining European colonial powers – Britain, France, Spain, Portugal, Belgium, Italy and the Netherlands – surrendered their empires voluntarily. Only Britain even conceived of independence as the ultimate goal, albeit with continued membership of the Commonwealth, a goal already attained in 1939 by Canada, South Africa, Australia and New Zealand. The continental colonial powers thought more in terms of evolution towards a common citizenship, with their colonies as overseas parts of the metropolitan territory. Such plans were complicated, however, by the resistance of European settlers, with consequent inter-racial tensions, and by clashes between the European ideal of evolution along Western lines (in education and economic development) and the powerful Hindu, Muslim, Buddhist and Confucian cultures of the 'subject peoples'.

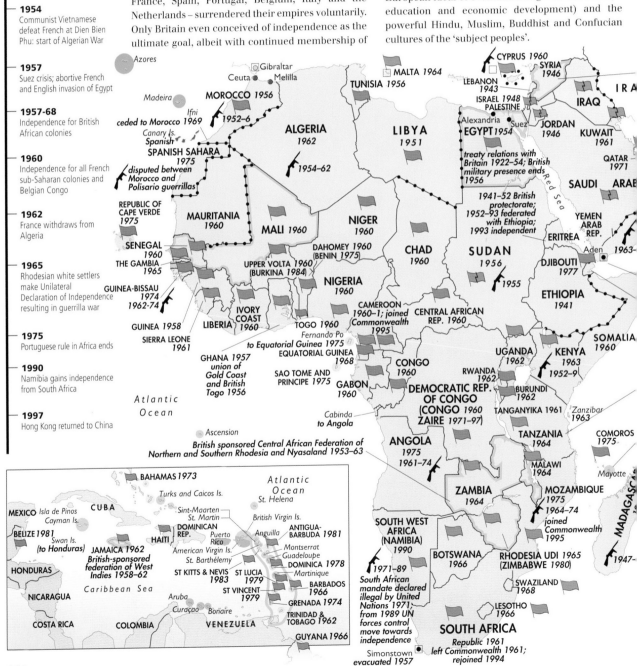

France fought stubbornly to maintain its control of Indochina (page 162), and the Netherlands struggled to contain the nationalists of Java, who had proclaimed the Indonesian Republic in 1945. Neither succeeded. Continual unrest forced Britain to grant independence to India and Pakistan (1947), followed in 1948 by Burma and Ceylon (page 162). Nevertheless Britain fought (and won) a long war against communist insurgents in Malaya, and resisted Indonesian attempts to annex Sarawak and Brunei. Only after the evacuation of Aden in 1967 did Britain abandon its presence east of Suez – save only for Hong Kong, retained until 1997, its economic success being of some benefit to Communist China.

In Africa resistance to independence was strongest in colonies with substantial white settler populations. In Algeria, with 1 million whites, a savage war of liberation occurred between 1954 and 1962; but conflict proved bitter, too, in Kenya and Rhodesia. However by 1974 all had achieved independence (page 160). By then, although Britain showed in the Falklands War (1982) its determination to fight on behalf of the few outposts still directly ruled from London, the formal structures of European imperialism had been dismantled and largely replaced by different forms of association such as the British Commonwealth or the French Community.

Mohandas Gandhi *(right)* became leader of the Indian nationalist movement in 1918, preaching non-violence *(satyragha)*. In 1922 he was imprisoned by the British authorities, but was released in 1924 on becoming president of the Indian National congress. He led a campaign to boycott British cotton imports, and in 1930 encouraged resistance to a proposed salt tax. Although he withdrew from formal politics in 1933 he remained the guiding influence of the nationalist movement, and was a key figure in the eventual negotiations for Indian independence and partition in 1946-8.

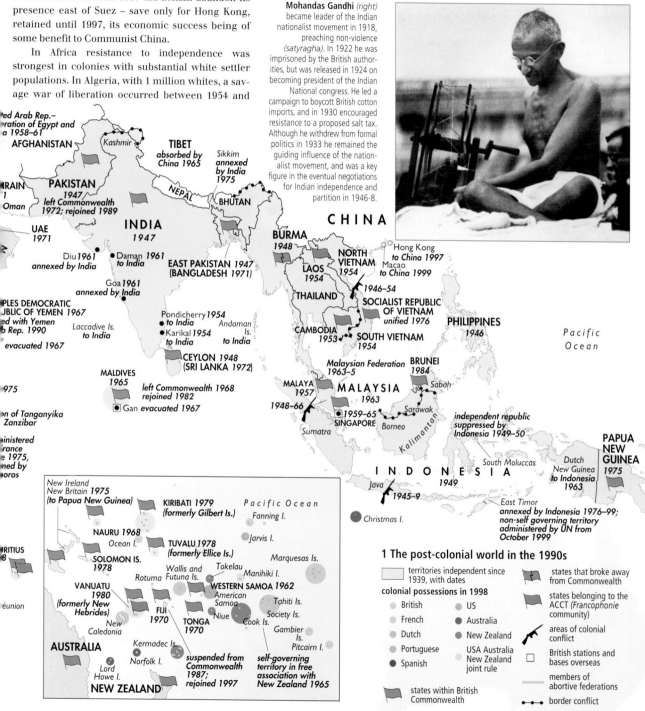

United Arab Rep.–
federation of Egypt and
Syria 1958–61

AFGHANISTAN

Kashmir

TIBET
absorbed by
China 1965

Sikkim
annexed
by India
1975

PAKISTAN
1947
left Commonwealth
1972; rejoined 1989

BAHRAIN

Oman

UAE
1971

NEPAL

BHUTAN

INDIA
1947

CHINA

Diu 1961
annexed by India

Daman 1961
to India

EAST PAKISTAN 1947
(BANGLADESH 1971)

Goa 1961
annexed by India

PEOPLES DEMOCRATIC
REPUBLIC OF YEMEN 1967
united with Yemen
Arab Rep. 1990

evacuated 1967

Laccadive Is.
to India

Pondicherry 1954
to India

Karikal 1954
to India

Andaman
Is.
to India

BURMA
1948

LAOS
1954

NORTH
VIETNAM
1954

THAILAND

CAMBODIA
1953

SOUTH VIETNAM
1954

SOCIALIST REPUBLIC
OF VIETNAM
unified 1976

1946–54

Hong Kong
to China 1997

Macao
to China 1999

PHILIPPINES
1946

Pacific
Ocean

CEYLON 1948
(SRI LANKA 1972)

MALDIVES
1965

1975

left Commonwealth 1968
rejoined 1982

Gan evacuated 1967

union of Tanganyika
and Zanzibar

administered
by France
before 1975,
claimed by
Comoros

Malaysian Federation
1963–5

MALAYA
1957

1948–66

MALAYSIA
1963

Sumatra

BRUNEI
1984

Sabah

Sarawak

1959–65
SINGAPORE

Borneo

Kalimantan

independent republic
suppressed by
Indonesia 1949–50

PAPUA
NEW
GUINEA
1975

INDONESIA
1949

Java
1945–9

South Moluccas

Dutch
New Guinea
to Indonesia
1963

East Timor
annexed by Indonesia 1976–99;
non-self governing territory
administered by UN from
October 1999

MAURITIUS
1968

Réunion

New Ireland
New Britain 1975
(to Papua New Guinea)

KIRIBATI 1979
(formerly Gilbert Is.)

Pacific Ocean

Fanning I.

NAURU 1968
Ocean I.

TUVALU 1978
(formerly Ellice Is.)

Jarvis I.

SOLOMON IS.
1978

Wallis and
Futuna Is.

Tokelau

Marquesas Is.

Manihiki I.

VANUATU
1980
(formerly New
Hebrides)

Rotuma

WESTERN SAMOA 1962

American
Samoa

Tahiti Is.

FIJI
1970

New
Caledonia

TONGA
1970

Niue

Cook Is.

Society Is.

Gambier
Is.

Pitcairn I.

AUSTRALIA

Kermadec Is.

Lord
Howe I.

Norfolk I.

suspended from
Commonwealth
1987;
rejoined 1997

self-governing
territory in free
association with
New Zealand 1965

Christmas I.

Christmas I.

NEW ZEALAND

1 The post-colonial world in the 1990s

territories independent since 1939, with dates

colonial possessions in 1998

British

French

Dutch

Portuguese

Spanish

US

Australia

New Zealand

USA Australia
New Zealand
joint rule

states within British
Commonwealth

states that broke away
from Commonwealth

states belonging to the
ACCT (Francophonie
community)

areas of colonial
conflict

British stations and
bases overseas

members of
abortive federations

border conflict

The Middle East

The Middle East has occupied world attention more consistently than any other region since 1945: Israel and its neighbours have fought four full-scale wars; Israel has invaded Lebanon twice; three Gulf wars have taken place; military coups have reinforced internal repression; refugees have fled; Western troops have intervened repeatedly.

American support for the state of Israel (founded in 1948), sponsorship of the Baghdad Pact (1955), and intervention in Lebanon (1958) alarmed the USSR and so it offered assistance to Syria, Egypt and (after 1958) Iraq. The Soviets also championed the Arab states during the Arab-Israeli war of 1967 but Israel still took and held the West Bank of the Jordan, Sinai and the Golan Heights (map 1). In 1973 an Egyptian and Syrian attack on Israel met with limited military success and opened the way for negotiations. Egypt and Israel concluded the Camp David Accords (1978) which resulted in the return of Sinai in 1982; but the Israelis refused to return the other 'occupied territories' and instead installed many Jewish settlements. Moreover in 1982, to counter Palestinian guerrilla activity, they invaded and held south Lebanon until 2000. Meanwhile, in the wake of prolonged resistance to Israeli rule in the West Bank and Gaza, which excited much outside sympathy, after extended peace talks brokered by the US (the 'Oslo accords') Israel allowed limited Palestinian self-rule from 1994-5. Although by 2002 relations with the Palestinian leadership under Yasser Arafat had collapsed completely, the death of Arafat in 2004 offered a chance to renew negotiations between Israel and the Palestinian Authority (map 1).

As open conflict between Israel and her neighbours abated, it began around the Persian Gulf. The replacement of the Shah of Iran by Ayatollah Khomeini in 1979 seemed to President Saddam Hussein of Iraq to offer the chance of territorial gain. He attacked in 1980. However, eight years of war achieved little and in 1990, in an attempt to gain resources to liquidate his war debts, Saddam invaded and annexed another neighbour, Kuwait. The United Nations, led by the US, pressured Saddam to withdraw and, when he refused, in 1991 used armed force to expel him. The invasion stopped at the Iraqi frontier and Saddam survived in power until in 2003, although the victors' economic sanctions, military 'no-fly zones' and 'weapons inspectors' prevented him from rearming. Nevertheless, in 2003 the US alleged that Iraq possessed 'weapons of mass destruction' and constituted an immediate threat to world peace: it launched a second invasion that travelled straight to Baghdad (map 2). Inadequate planning for exploiting victory led to chaos that allowed Saddam's supporters (mostly from the Sunni minority) and Muslim opponents of the West from around the world to organize resis-

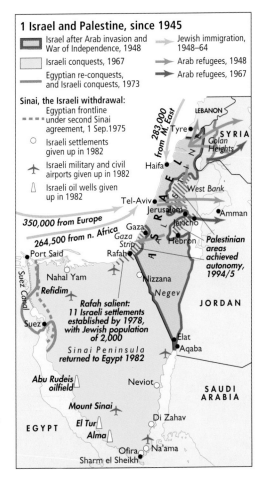

1 Israel and Palestine, since 1945

Israel after Arab invasion and War of Independence, 1948

Israeli conquests, 1967

Egyptian re-conquests, and Israeli conquests, 1973

Jewish immigration, 1948–64

Arab refugees, 1948

Arab refugees, 1967

Sinai, the Israeli withdrawal:

Egyptian frontline under second Sinai agreement, 1 Sep.1975

○ Israeli settlements given up in 1982

✈ Israeli military and civil airports given up in 1982

Israeli oil wells given up in 1982

283,000 from M. East

LEBANON

Tyre

SYRIA

Golan Heights

Haifa

West Bank

350,000 from Europe

Tel-Aviv

Jerusalem

Amman

264,500 from n. Africa

Gaza

Gaza Strip

Jericho

Hebron

Palestinian areas achieved autonomy, 1994/5

Port Said

Rafah

Nahal Yam

Nizzana

Negev

JORDAN

Refidim

Suez Canal

Suez

Rafah salient: 11 Israeli settlements established by 1978, with Jewish population of 2,000

Elat

Aqaba

Sinai Peninsula returned to Egypt 1982

Abu Rudeis oilfield

Neviot

SAUDI ARABIA

Mount Sinai

El Tur

Di Zahav

EGYPT

Alma

Ofira

Na'ama

Sharm el Sheikh

tance to the US-led occupation. Although democratic elections took place in 2004, they produced no clear winner and religious divisions among Iraq's Muslims continued to threaten the country's stability.

Islamic fundamentalism destabilized many other parts of the Muslim world (map 3). After 1979 it became a badge of hostility towards the West in Iran and towards Russia in Afghanistan, and elsewhere toward the regime in power – unless, as in Iran, that regime was an Islamic theocracy. In the 1990s Islamic fundamentalism stimulated terrorist violence from Algeria to Indonesia. Although the collapse of the Soviet Union (page 168) ended superpower rivalry in the area, the Western powers remained engaged in order to safeguard the unequalled oil supplies of the area on which their economies depended. Oil and the enormous concentrations of conventional weapons – together with attempts to develop chemical, biological and nuclear weapons – in so many antagonistic states continued to keep the Middle East at the centre of world attention.

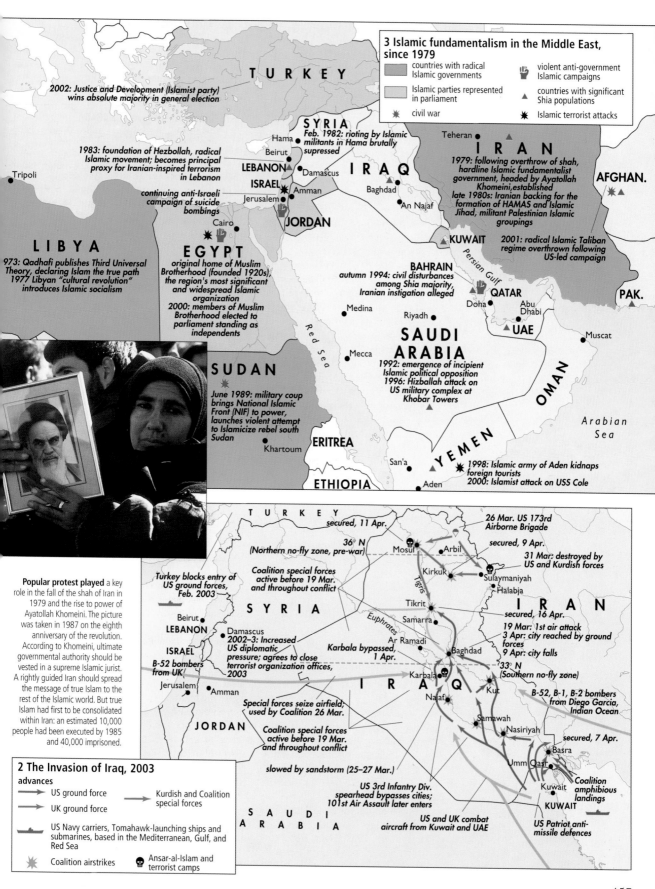

3 Islamic fundamentalism in the Middle East, since 1979

- countries with radical Islamic governments
- Islamic parties represented in parliament
- civil war
- violent anti-government Islamic campaigns
- countries with significant Shia populations
- Islamic terrorist attacks

2002: Justice and Development (Islamist party) wins absolute majority in general election

TURKEY

1983: foundation of Hezbollah, radical Islamic movement; becomes principal proxy for Iranian-inspired terrorism in Lebanon

SYRIA
Hama
Feb. 1982: rioting by Islamic militants in Hama brutally suppressed

Beirut
LEBANON
Damascus
IRAQ
Baghdad

ISRAEL
Amman
Jerusalem
JORDAN

continuing anti-Israeli campaign of suicide bombings

Cairo

IRAN
Teheran
1979: following overthrow of shah, hardline Islamic fundamentalist government, headed by Ayatollah Khomeini, established
late 1980s: Iranian backing for the formation of HAMAS and Islamic Jihad, militant Palestinian Islamic groupings

AFGHAN.

An Najaf
KUWAIT
2001: radical Islamic Taliban regime overthrown following US-led campaign

PAK.

LIBYA
1973: Qadhafi publishes Third Universal Theory, declaring Islam the true path
1977 Libyan "cultural revolution" introduces Islamic socialism

Tripoli

EGYPT
original home of Muslim Brotherhood (founded 1920s), the region's most significant and widespread Islamic organization
2000: members of Muslim Brotherhood elected to parliament standing as independents

BAHRAIN
autumn 1994: civil disturbances among Shia majority, Iranian instigation alleged

Medina
Riyadh
Doha
QATAR
Abu Dhabi
UAE
Muscat

SAUDI ARABIA
1992: emergence of incipient Islamic political opposition
1996: Hizballah attack on US military complex at Khobar Towers

Mecca

OMAN

Red Sea

SUDAN
June 1989: military coup brings National Islamic Front (NIF) to power, launches violent attempt to Islamicize rebel south Sudan

Khartoum

ERITREA

San'a

YEMEN
1998: Islamic army of Aden kidnaps foreign tourists
2000: Islamist attack on USS Cole

Aden

ETHIOPIA

Arabian Sea

Popular protest played a key role in the fall of the shah of Iran in 1979 and the rise to power of Ayatollah Khomeini. The picture was taken in 1987 on the eighth anniversary of the revolution. According to Khomeini, ultimate governmental authority should be vested in a supreme Islamic jurist. A rightly guided Iran should spread the message of true Islam to the rest of the Islamic world. But true Islam had first to be consolidated within Iran: an estimated 10,000 people had been executed by 1985 and 40,000 imprisoned.

TURKEY
secured, 11 Apr.
26 Mar. US 173rd Airborne Brigade
Mosul
Arbil
secured, 9 Apr.
36° N (Northern no-fly zone, pre-war)
31 Mar: destroyed by US and Kurdish forces
Coalition special forces active before 19 Mar. and throughout conflict
Kirkuk
Sulaymaniyah
Halabja

Turkey blocks entry of US ground forces, Feb. 2003

Beirut
SYRIA
Tikrit
IRAN
secured, 16 Apr.
19 Mar: 1st air attack
3 Apr: city reached by ground forces
9 Apr: city falls

LEBANON
Damascus
2002–3: Increased US diplomatic pressure; agrees to close terrorist organization offices, 2003
Euphrates
Samarra
Ar Ramadi

ISRAEL
B-52 bombers from UK
Jerusalem
Amman

Karbala bypassed, 1 Apr.
Baghdad
Karbala
33° N (Southern no-fly zone)

B-52, B-1, B-2 bombers from Diego Garcia, Indian Ocean

JORDAN
Najaf
Kut
Special forces seize airfield; used by Coalition 26 Mar.
Coalition special forces active before 19 Mar. and throughout conflict
Samawah
Nasiriyah
secured, 7 Apr.

slowed by sandstorm (25–27 Mar.)
Basra
Umm Qasr

US 3rd Infantry Div. spearhead bypasses cities; **101st Air Assault** later enters
Kuwait
Coalition amphibious landings

SAUDI ARABIA
US and UK combat aircraft from Kuwait and UAE
KUWAIT
US Patriot anti-missile defences

2 The Invasion of Iraq, 2003

advances

→ US ground force
→ UK ground force
→ Kurdish and Coalition special forces

⚓ US Navy carriers, Tomahawk-launching ships and submarines, based in the Mediterranean, Gulf, and Red Sea

✳ Coalition airstrikes
☠ Ansar-al-Islam and terrorist camps

Latin America since 1930

TIMELINE

1950-4
Attempted reforms in Guatemala

1955
Overthrow of Perón regime in Argentina

1959
Cuban revolution

1973
Overthrow of Allende regime in Chile

1982
The Falklands War

1982-9
Return to civilian rule in Bolivia (1982), Argentina (1983), Uruguay (1985), Chile (1989)

The Great Depression (page 138) struck Latin America a shattering blow, cutting off supplies of foreign capital and lowering the price of its primary products in the world markets. Chile's exports fell by over 80 per cent between 1929 and 1933; those of Bolivia and Peru by 75 per cent. Only oil-exporting Venezuela more or less weathered the storm. The economic collapse led to widespread disillusion with middle-class liberal or radical parties: in 1930 and 1931, 11 of the 20 republics south of the Rio Grande experienced revolutionary changes in government. Mexico, where Lázaro Cárdenas (1934-40) revived the land distribution policies of 1911 (page 112), experienced a shift to the left; but elsewhere the swing was mainly to the right. The new dictators tended to be populists, appealing directly to the masses and cooperating with organised labour. They also introduced programmes of industrialization – following Soviet or, more often, Fascist models – to reduce dependence on overseas markets and hasten economic development. Manufacturing industry received a further boost during World War II, which cut off imported consumer goods and stimulated the industrial sector. But industrialization made Latin America dependent upon imported capital goods, raw materials, technology and finance – especially from the United States – creating enormous foreign debts (map 2). Multinational corporations exploited the cheap labour of Latin America without stimulating economic development. Social tensions arose from income concentration, unemployment, lack of opportunities, and from the intrusion of foreign interests. Social revolutions were attempted but frustrated in Guatemala, Bolivia and Chile (map 1), underlining the obstacles to change in economies too narrowly based to sustain welfare programmes, where local elites were prepared to collaborate with the United States.

Cuba after 1959 attempted to achieve social change, economic growth and freedom from the United States simultaneously; but although its revolution led to greater social equality and some improvement in the lot of rural workers, it also brought a repressive regime and dependence on the Soviet Union. Moreover its attempts to spread revolution in Central and South America all failed.

In the face of revolutionary change, with some support from the upper and middle classes, the military seized power in many areas and combined political repression with economic liberalization. But by the late 1980s their policies too had largely failed and, in

A government soldier in Peru (below), guards against attacks by the Shining Path guerrillas. The Shining Path (Sendero Luminoso) was founded in 1980 by Abimael Guzmán, a philosophy professor. It adopted a mixture of Maoist political and military tactics and gained control of large areas of the central Andean highlands in the early 1990s. After Guzmán's capture in 1992, the movement fragmented and the level of its attacks diminished sharply.

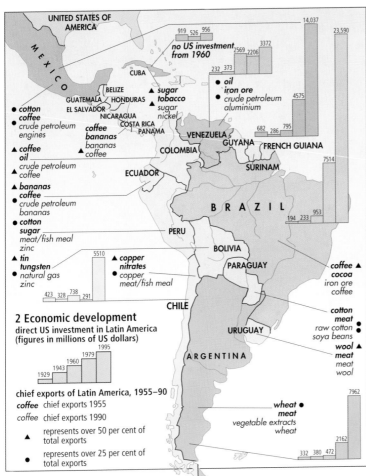

UNITED STATES OF AMERICA

MEXICO

CUBA

919 526 956

no US investment from 1960

2569 2206

3372

232 373

14,037

23,590

● oil
● iron ore
● crude petroleum
aluminium

4575

BELIZE
GUATEMALA HONDURAS
EL SALVADOR
NICARAGUA
COSTA RICA
PANAMA

● cotton
coffee
● crude petroleum
engines

coffee
bananas

▲ coffee
oil
● crude petroleum
coffee

▲ bananas
coffee
● crude petroleum
bananas

● cotton
sugar
meat/fish meal
zinc

▲ tin
tungsten
● natural gas
zinc

▲ sugar
tobacco
sugar
nickel

bananas
▲ coffee

COLOMBIA

ECUADOR

VENEZUELA
GUYANA
FRENCH GUIANA

SURINAM

682 286 795

7514

B R A Z I L

194 233 953

PERU

BOLIVIA

5510

423 328 738 291

▲ copper
nitrates
● copper
meat/fish meal

CHILE

PARAGUAY

coffee ▲
cocoa
iron ore
coffee

cotton
meat
raw cotton ●●
soya beans

wool ▲
meat
meat
wool

2 Economic development
direct US investment in Latin America (figures in millions of US dollars)

1929 1943 1960 1979 1995

URUGUAY

ARGENTINA

wheat ●
meat
vegetable extracts
wheat

7962

2162

332 380 472

chief exports of Latin America, 1955-90

coffee chief exports 1955

coffee chief exports 1990

▲ represents over 50 per cent of total exports

● represents over 25 per cent of total exports

UNITED STATES OF AMERICA

US intervention
Dominican Republic 1916-24
Grenada 1983
Cuba 1921-23, 1933, 1944, 1961
Haiti 1915-34, 1994
Panama 1903-18, 1989
Nicaragua 1912-33
Guatemala 1954
Mexico 1914

MEXICO ⊡ 5,000

▢ *Mexican revolution 1910-40*
⬡ *Zapatista revolt, 1994*

Mexico City
Puebla
Veracruz
BELIZE

Havana **CUBA** 125,000 M
⊡ 1,400
DOMINICAN REP.
PUERTO RICO (USA)

GUAT. 750 M
300 M HONDURAS
Guatemala City
Tegucigalpa

Cuban-inspired guerrilla movements 1959-68
HAITI n/a M

▢ *Guatemalan revolution 1944-54*

EL SALVADOR 125 M
▽⬡ *Military Junta 1979*
NICARAGUA 100 M
Managua
San José
COSTA RICA 1,000 M

Caribbean Sea
○ *Cuban revolution 1959*

GRENADA
Cartagena
Caracas
Port of Spain

○ *Rómulo Betancourt 1945-48, 1959-64; Carlos Andrés Pérez 1974-9*
◇ *Rafael Caldera 1969-74; Luis Herrera Campins 1979; Jaime Lusinchi 1984*
☆ *Hugo Chavez 1998–*

▢○ *Sandinista revolution 1979-90; democratization 1990*
○ *Figueres 1948*

PANAMA 500 M
Panama City
Bogotá

VENEZUELA 8,000 M
Georgetown
GUYANA 100 M
SUR.
Paramaribo
Cayenne
FR.GUIANA

○ *Liberal-Conservative Pact, 1957*

COLOMBIA 11,000 M/P

Macapá
Amazon
Manaus
Belém

○ *Getulio Vargas 1930-45; 1950-4*
☆ *João Goulart 1961-4*
▽ *Modernizing militarism 1964*

▽ *Intermittent militarism to 1978*
○ *Election of reformist government 1978*

Quito
ECUADOR 1,200 M/P
Guayaquil
Piura

Fortaleza

○ *Civilian rule 1985; democratization 1986*

☆ *Radical militarism 1968*
▢ *Sendero Luminoso from 1980*
○ *Return to civil rule 1980*
☆ *Fujimori 1990-2000*

Trujillo
3,500 M/P
PERU
Huánuco
Callao
Lima
Cuzco

B R A Z I L 7,000 M/P

Recife

Salvador (Bahía)

▢ *Bolivian revolution 1952-64*
▢ *Che Guevara (killed 1967)*
▽ *Military 1980; democratization 1982*

Arequipa
La Paz
BOLIVIA
Sucre 3,200 M/P

Brasília
Belo Horizonte

◇ *Eduardo Frei 1964-70*
▢ *Salvador Allende (Popular Unity) 1970-3*
▽ *Pinochet 1973-88*
○ *Democratization 1989*

Antofagasta
Copiapó
PARAGUAY
Asunción
São Paulo
Santos
Rio de Janeiro

▽ *Military dictatorship Stroessner 1954 Rodriguez 1989*

1 Latin America since 1945

political change in Latin America since 1945

▢ *Social revolution* Fundamental change (attempted or achieved) in economic and social structure by nationalist or Marxist movements

○ *Reformism* Moderate socio-economic change or modernization for democratic or other process

☆ *Populism* Interventionist state based on multi-class alliance for policy of development

◇ *Christian Democracy* Radical socio-economic change by Christian Democratic parties

▽ *Unreformed militarism* Military dictatorship of the right without social or modernizing programme

⬡ *Indigenous guerrilla movements* Urban guerrillas from late 1960s following failure of Cuban-inspired rural guerrillas

communism in Latin America, 1974

70,000 communist party membership

M/P loyalty (Moscow/Peking)

120,000 M
Tucumán
Córdoba
Santa Fé
Valparaíso
Santiago
Mendoza
Concepción
Valdivia
Osorno
Buenos Aires
Montevideo
Fray Bentos
Porto Alegre
Rio Grande
URUGUAY 22,000 M
Florianópolis

○ *Batllismo 1903-33*
▽ *Military 1973*
⬡ *Tupamaros*
○ *Civilian rule 1985; democratization 1986*
⬡ *Montoneros*

ARGENTINA 70,000 M
Bahía Blanca
Rawson

☆ *Juan Domingo Perón 1943-55, 1973-4*
▽ *Military 1976-83*
○ *Democratization and civilian rule 1983*

Comodoro Rivadavia
Santa Cruz
Stanley
Tierra del Fuego

● *Falkland Islands (Islas Malvinas) occupied by Argentina 1982: occupation ended by UK Task Force June 1982*

communist party status
▨ in power
▨ legal opposition
▨ illegal

the face of economic recession and popular protest, their power gradually weakened. Instead, democratic government resumed in several states of the subcontinent. In 1992 Mexico signed a free trade agreement (NAFTA) with Canada and the United States, creating the world's largest integrated trading bloc. Yet serious economic crises in Mexico in 1994-5 and in Argentina in 2001-2 highlighted the continued vulnerability of even the largest Latin American economies.

Africa since 1945

After World War II, although some French and British liberals sympathetic to African claims for advancement initiated programmes of social improvement and political reform, the need to exploit every asset in order to assist metropolitan recovery led to attempts to reassert colonial control. Nevertheless in the 1950s both Britain and France began to transfer responsibility to elected governments in their West African colonies.

In Muslim North Africa, longer-established nationalist movements received great stimulus from the overthrow of the Egyptian monarchy in 1952 and the rise to power of Gamal Abdel Nasser. In 1956 an Anglo-French-Israeli invasion failed to topple him. Meanwhile France granted independence to Tunisia and Morocco but tried to incorporate Algeria, the colony with the largest white population, into metropolitan France. This sparked a civil war that lasted until France reluctantly granted independence in 1962.

Elsewhere, white settlers strove to maintain their ascendancy. In South Africa, a Nationalist government dedicated to policies of racial separation ('apartheid') came to power; in Kenya, British troops arrived to suppress the Mau-Mau insurrection directed against the settlers; in Central Africa, a federation of Nyasaland and Rhodesia aimed to preserve white dominance. But in 1963 Kenya achieved independence and the Federation collapsed. Southern Rhodesia's white settlers created their own independent state in 1965, but had to accept black majority rule in 1980. Portugal retained its colonies longest, but in all of them guerrilla warfare eventually led to ignominious withdrawal in 1974-5.

Most of the newly independent African states possessed borders drawn by European governments in the 19th century with insufficient attention to ethnic rivalries. Soon after independence, those rivalries began to tear them apart. In 1960, tribal and regional factions in Zaire (formerly the Belgian Congo) led to demands for a federal constitution and, when these were refused, the army mutinied and the mineral rich province of Katanga seceded. United Nations intervention reunited the country in 1963, but two years later the

Nelson Mandela *(right)* joined the African National Congress in 1944 and helped to found its Youth League. In 1961, frustrated at the failure of civil disobedience to undermine apartheid, he adopted the idea of armed struggle. In 1962 he was sentenced to life imprisonment. Released in 1990, aged 72, he became leader of the ANC and, in 1994, South Africa's first president elected by universal franchise. He retired from the presidency in 1999.

army seized power and retained it for 34 years. Similarly, in Nigeria the secession of Biafra in 1967 led to a three-year civil war that restored central control, but likewise delivered power to the army. Elsewhere, ethnic violence caused enormous casualties – in the small state of Rwanda, Hutu-Tutsi violence left over 500,000 dead in 1994 – while repeated droughts (compounded by government inefficiency and corruption) caused famine and massive refugee problems in many areas of East Africa. In Algeria, from 1990 Islamic Fundamentalism challenged government control.

By the 1980s, white supremacy survived only in South Africa where the nationalist regime sought to retain its grip by draconian internal repression, by sending troops against guerrillas in neighbouring states, and by granting spurious independence to some black settlement areas set up under apartheid. Eventually, however, economic crisis and international isolation forced concessions. In 1990, the nationalists released Nelson Mandela, imprisoned leader of the banned African National Congress, and within four years the ANC's victory in the first multiracial elections in South Africa's history swept away white rule. Despite the problems of healing decades of racial tension, the ANC created a more stable political system than under white rule and preserved the most successful economy on the continent. Mandela retired in 1999. Meanwhile in Zimbabwe (formerly Rhodesia) serious racial conflict broke out.

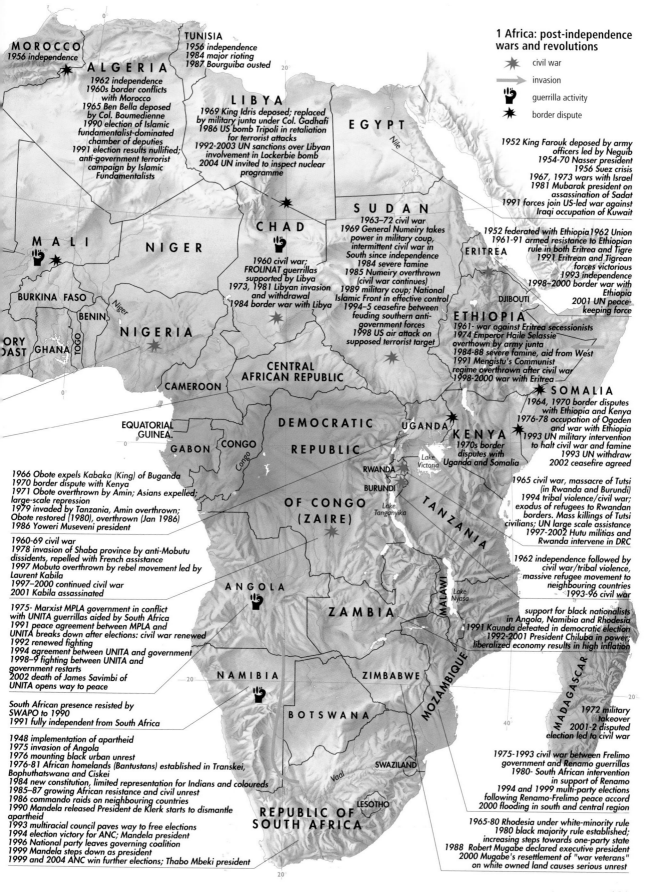

1 Africa: post-independence wars and revolutions

✸ civil war

→ invasion

✊ guerrilla activity

✴ border dispute

MOROCCO
1956 independence

ALGERIA
1962 independence
1960s border conflicts with Morocco
1965 Ben Bella deposed by Col. Boumedienne
1990 election of Islamic fundamentalist-dominated chamber of deputies
1991 election results nullified; anti-government terrorist campaign by Islamic Fundamentalists

TUNISIA
1956 independence
1984 major rioting
1987 Bourguiba ousted

LIBYA
1969 King Idris deposed; replaced by military junta under Col. Gadhafi
1986 US bomb Tripoli in retaliation for terrorist attacks
1992-2003 UN sanctions over Libyan involvement in Lockerbie bomb
2004 UN invited to inspect nuclear programme

EGYPT
1952 King Farouk deposed by army officers led by Neguib
1954-70 Nasser president
1956 Suez crisis
1967, 1973 wars with Israel
1981 Mubarak president on assassination of Sadat
1991 forces join US-led war against Iraqi occupation of Kuwait

MALI

NIGER

CHAD
1960 civil war; FROLINAT guerrillas supported by Libya
1973, 1981 Libyan invasion and withdrawal
1984 border war with Libya

SUDAN
1963–72 civil war
1969 General Numeiry takes power in military coup, intermittent civil war in South since independence
1984 severe famine
1985 Numeiry overthrown (civil war continues)
1989 military coup; National Islamic Front in effective control
1994–5 ceasefire between feuding southern anti-government forces
1998 US air attack on supposed terrorist target

ERITREA
1952 federated with Ethiopia 1962 Union
1961-91 armed resistance to Ethiopian rule in both Eritrea and Tigre
1991 Eritrean and Tigrean forces victorious
1993 independence
1998–2000 border war with Ethiopia
2001 UN peace-keeping force

DJIBOUTI

ETHIOPIA
1961- war against Eritrea secessionists
1974 Emperor Haile Selassie overthrown by army junta
1984-88 severe famine, aid from West
1991 Mengistu's Communist regime overthrown after civil war
1998-2000 war with Eritrea

BURKINA FASO

BENIN

NIGERIA

IVORY COAST

GHANA

TOGO

CAMEROON

CENTRAL AFRICAN REPUBLIC

EQUATORIAL GUINEA

GABON

CONGO

DEMOCRATIC REPUBLIC OF CONGO (ZAIRE)

UGANDA
1966 Obote expels Kabaka (King) of Buganda
1970 border dispute with Kenya
1971 Obote overthrown by Amin; Asians expelled; large-scale repression
1979 invaded by Tanzania, Amin overthrown; Obote restored (1980), overthrown (Jan 1986)
1986 Yoweri Museveni president

1960-69 civil war
1978 invasion of Shaba province by anti-Mobutu dissidents, repelled with French assistance
1997 Mobuto overthrown by rebel movement led by Laurent Kabila
1997–2000 continued civil war
2001 Kabila assassinated

KENYA
1970s border disputes with Uganda and Kenya

SOMALIA
1964, 1970 border disputes with Ethiopia and Kenya
1976-78 occupation of Ogaden and war with Ethiopia
1993 UN military intervention to halt civil war and famine
1993 UN withdraw
2002 ceasefire agreed
1965 civil war, massacre of Tutsi (in Rwanda and Burundi)
1994 tribal violence/civil war; exodus of refugees to Rwandan borders. Mass killings of Tutsi civilians; UN large scale assistance
1997-2002 Hutu militias and Rwanda intervene in DRC

RWANDA

BURUNDI

TANZANIA
1962 independence followed by civil war/tribal violence, massive refugee movement to neighbouring countries
1993-96 civil war

ANGOLA
1975- Marxist MPLA government in conflict with UNITA guerrillas aided by South Africa
1991 peace agreement between MPLA and UNITA breaks down after elections: civil war renewed
1992 renewed fighting
1994 agreement between UNITA and government
1998–9 fighting between UNITA and government restarts
2002 death of James Savimbi of UNITA opens way to peace

ZAMBIA
support for black nationalists in Angola, Namibia and Rhodesia
1991 Kaunda defeated in democratic election
1992-2001 President Chiluba in power; liberalized economy results in high inflation

MALAWI

NAMIBIA
South African presence resisted by SWAPO to 1990
1991 fully independent from South Africa

ZIMBABWE

MOZAMBIQUE
1975-1993 civil war between Frelimo government and Renamo guerrillas
1980- South African intervention in support of Renamo
1994 and 1999 multi-party elections following Renamo-Frelimo peace accord
2000 flooding in south and central region

BOTSWANA

MADAGASCAR
1972 military takeover
2001-2 disputed election led to civil war

1965-80 Rhodesia under white-minority rule
1980 black majority rule established; increasing steps towards one-party state
1988 Robert Mugabe declared executive president
2000 Mugabe's resettlement of "war veterans" on white owned land causes serious unrest

SWAZILAND

LESOTHO

REPUBLIC OF SOUTH AFRICA
1948 implementation of apartheid
1975 invasion of Angola
1976 mounting black urban unrest
1976-81 African homelands (Bantustans) established in Transkei, Bophuthatswana and Ciskei
1984 new constitution, limited representation for Indians and coloureds
1985–87 growing African resistance and civil unrest
1986 commando raids on neighbouring countries
1990 Mandela released President de Klerk starts to dismantle apartheid
1993 multiracial council paves way to free elections
1994 election victory for ANC; Mandela president
1996 National party leaves governing coalition
1999 Mandela steps down as president
1999 and 2004 ANC win further elections; Thabo Mbeki president

South and South East Asia since 1945

The history of southern Asia since independence has been dominated by three factors. First, the seizure of power by military leaders (Pakistan 1958, 1977 and 1999, Indonesia 1967), with the aim – rarely successful – of abolishing corruption and stabilizing the economy; second, the resurgence of long-standing regional, tribal and religious conflicts (Naga and Sikh unrest in India; nationalist uprisings among the Mons, Shans and other 'hill people' in Thailand and Burma); finally, intervention by the Great Powers (China and the United States in Vietnam).

Wars between states also characterized certain areas. The partition of the Indian subcontinent in 1947 left numerous points of friction between the new states of India and Pakistan (notably Kashmir, Punjab and Bengal) which erupted into war in 1965 and again in 1971 (after the secession of East Pakistan to form the separate state of Bangladesh). The potential for war became more serious after both countries developed nuclear arms in 1998, and serious clashes over Kashmir in 2002 carried the threat of nuclear confrontation. Indian forces also expelled the Portuguese from their coastal enclaves (1961), fought China over a frontier dispute (1962), and intervened in Sri Lanka to protect the Hindu Tamil minority (1986-90). Civil wars, however, proved far more common (map 1). Malaya suffered a communist insurrection (1948-60), led by ethnic Chinese; the Philippines experienced rebellions by both communists and Muslims from the 1960s; Cambodia was devastated by the civil war between the communist Khmer Rouge and its non-communist opponents; Tamils and Singhalese fought in Sri Lanka (1983-2002).

The most savage conflict, however, occurred in Vietnam (map 2). After the Japanese collapse in 1945 Ho Chi Minh established a communist regime in Hanoi while the French recreated their colonial empire in the south. In 1946 armed conflict began, continuing until a humiliating defeat at Dien Bien Phu in 1954 led the French to withdraw. Although this left Cambodia and Laos as independent states, it did not create a unified Vietnam: at the Geneva Peace Conference in 1954 Ho accepted a 'temporary' partition of the country at the 17th parallel until nationwide elections, mandated for 1956, took place. However an anti-communist regime in the south, backed by America, refused to hold elections. In 1959 Ho therefore attacked, and the US immediately provided munitions and advisers to the south, with regular troops and air strikes after 1965. Despite saturation bombing and the commitment of 500,000 US ground troops, the communists (supported by both Russia and China) held their own and launched a coordinated insurrection in numerous southern cities early in 1968 (the 'Tet offensive'). Negotiations between Hanoi and Washington began soon afterwards and in 1973 American forces withdrew. Although the US continued to supply the south on a massive scale, when the communists invaded in 1975 the south's army collapsed. Vietnam was now unified, under Hanoi, although its economy was ruined and its invasion of Cambodia in 1978 led to ostracism by the West until it withdrew in 1987.

Elsewhere in Asia, rapid development occurred. Following the path of Japan (page 152), Taiwan, Malaysia, Singapore, Thailand and eventually Indonesia achieved rapid rates of growth from the late 1960s. Even during the world recession of the

Indira Gandhi daughter of India's first premier, Nehru, was the country's prime minister from 1972 to 1977 and from 1980 to 1985. She ruled over an India torn by ethnic and religious conflict. Between 1975 and 1977 she imposed a state of emergency following her conviction for electoral malpractice. In 1985 she was assassinated by one of her Sikh bodyguards.

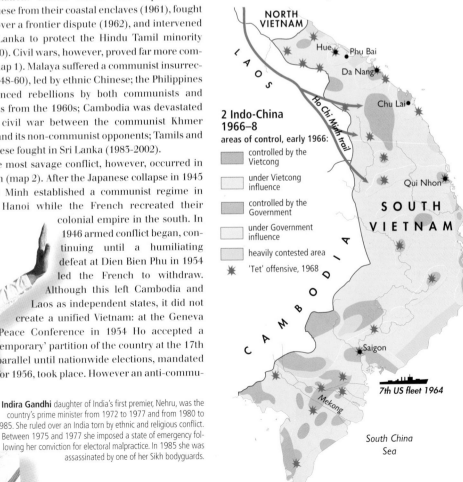

2 Indo-China 1966-8
areas of control, early 1966:

- controlled by the Vietcong
- under Vietcong influence
- controlled by the Government
- under Government influence
- heavily contested area
- ✳ 'Tet' offensive, 1968

7th US fleet 1964

NORTH VIETNAM · Hue · Phu Bai · Da Nang · Chu Lai · Qui Nhon · SOUTH VIETNAM · LAOS · Ho Chi Minh trail · CAMBODIA · Saigon · Mekong · South China Sea

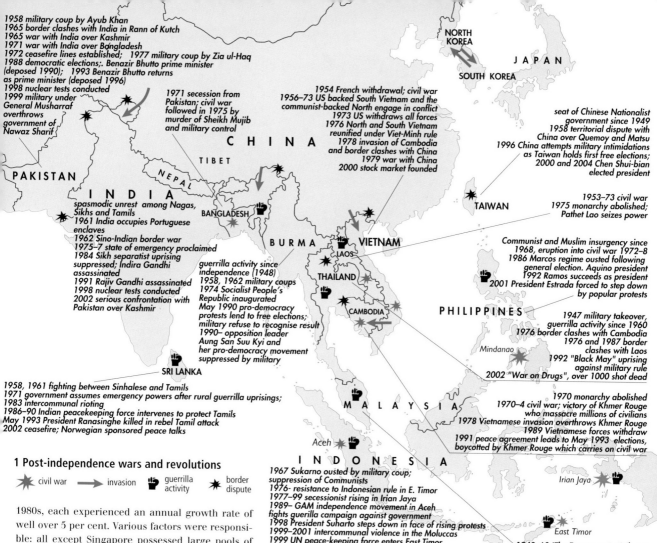

1958 military coup by Ayub Khan
1965 border clashes with India in Rann of Kutch
1965 war with India over Kashmir
1971 war with India over Bangladesh
1972 ceasefire lines established; 1977 military coup by Zia ul-Haq
1988 democratic elections;. Benazir Bhutto prime minister
(deposed 1990); 1993 Benazir Bhutto returns
as prime minister (deposed 1996)
1998 nuclear tests conducted
1999 military under
General Musharraf
overthrows
government of
Nawaz Sharif

1971 secession from
Pakistan; civil war
followed in 1975 by
murder of Sheikh Mujib
and military control

1954 French withdrawal; civil war
1956–73 US backed South Vietnam and the
communist-backed North engage in conflict
1973 US withdraws all forces
1976 North and South Vietnam
reunified under Viet-Minh rule
1978 invasion of Cambodia
and border clashes with China
1979 war with China
2000 stock market founded

seat of Chinese Nationalist
government since 1949
1958 territorial dispute with
China over Quemoy and Matsu
1996 China attempts military intimidations
as Taiwan holds first free elections;
2000 and 2004 Chen Shui-bian
elected president

PAKISTAN

CHINA

TIBET

NEPAL

INDIA

spasmodic unrest among Nagas,
Sikhs and Tamils
1961 India occupies Portuguese
enclaves
1962 Sino-Indian border war
1975–7 state of emergency proclaimed
1984 Sikh separatist uprising
suppressed; Indira Gandhi
assassinated
1991 Rajiv Gandhi assassinated
1998 nuclear tests conducted
2002 serious confrontation with
Pakistan over Kashmir

BANGLADESH

BURMA

guerrilla activity since
independence (1948)
1958, 1962 military coups
1974 Socialist People's
Republic inaugurated
May 1990 pro-democracy
protests lend to free elections;
military refuse to recognise result
1990– opposition leader
Aung San Suu Kyi and
her pro-democracy movement
suppressed by military

THAILAND

LAOS

VIETNAM

CAMBODIA

TAIWAN

1953–73 civil war
1975 monarchy abolished;
Pathet Lao seizes power

Communist and Muslim insurgency since
1968, eruption into civil war 1972–8
1986 Marcos regime ousted following
general election. Aquino president
1992 Ramos succeeds as president
2001 President Estrada forced to step down
by popular protests

PHILIPPINES

Mindanao

1947 military takeover,
guerrilla activity since 1960
1976 border clashes with Cambodia
1976 and 1987 border
clashes with Laos
1992 "Black May" uprising
against military rule
2002 "War on Drugs", over 1000 shot dead

SRI LANKA

1958, 1961 fighting between Sinhalese and Tamils
1971 government assumes emergency powers after rural guerrilla uprisings;
1983 intercommunal rioting
1986–90 Indian peacekeeping force intervenes to protect Tamils
May 1993 President Ranasinghe killed in rebel Tamil attack
2002 ceasefire; Norwegian sponsored peace talks

MALAYSIA

Aceh

1970 monarchy abolished
1970–4 civil war; victory of Khmer Rouge
who massacre millions of civilians
1978 Vietnamese invasion overthrows Khmer Rouge
1989 Vietnamese forces withdraw
1991 peace agreement leads to May 1993 elections,
boycotted by Khmer Rouge which carries on civil war

INDONESIA

Irian Jaya

East Timor

1967 Sukarno ousted by military coup;
suppression of Communists
1976- resistance to Indonesian rule in E. Timor
1977–99 secessionist rising in Irian Jaya
1989– GAM independence movement in Aceh
fights guerilla campaign against government
1998 President Suharto steps down in face of rising protests
1999–2001 intercommunal violence in the Moluccas
1999 UN peace-keeping force enters East Timor
after violence following vote in referendum for
independence from Indonesia
2002 East Timor independent

1948–60 'The Emergency'- civil war
with communist guerrillas
1975–8 Communist guerrilla activity
1981-2003 Prime Minister Mahathir Mohamad
1998 demonstrations against
Mahathir Mohamad

NORTH KOREA

SOUTH KOREA

JAPAN

1 Post-independence wars and revolutions

✦ civil war   → invasion   ✊ guerrilla activity   ✸ border dispute

1980s, each experienced an annual growth rate of
well over 5 per cent. Various factors were responsible: all except Singapore possessed large pools of
cheap labour; all created a substantial industrial base
oriented towards export markets throughout Asia,
Europe and North America; all the governments
sought to attract substantial foreign investment
through tax incentives and infrastructural development. A major part of that investment came from
Japan. Finally, political stability – Lee in Singapore;
Mahathir in Malaysia; Suharto in Indonesia – under-
pinned the economic strategy of industrial development and helped to attract foreign investment.

All these economies suffered in the economic
turmoil which hit east Asia in 1997, when a currency
crisis triggered a general crisis of confidence in the
Asian economic model. Indonesia suffered a 75 per
cent devaluation of the rupiah, again exacerbated by
a major political crisis, as the 35-year old Suharto
regime finally fell before nationwide protests. In
general the region's economies recovered far faster
than expected, although Indonesia experienced
widespread civil and ethnic unrest which threatened
to destabilize the whole country. In 2004 a tsunami
(caused by a massive earthquake) caused over
150,000 deaths and catastrophic damage in coastal
regions around the Indian Ocean (map 3).

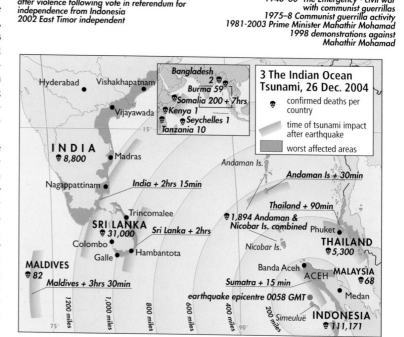

3 The Indian Ocean Tsunami, 26 Dec. 2004

☠ confirmed deaths per country
time of tsunami impact after earthquake
worst affected areas

Hyderabad   Vishakhapatnam

Bangladesh 2
Burma 59
Somalia 200 + 7hrs
Kenya 1
Seychelles 1
Tanzania 10

Vijayawada

INDIA
☠ 8,800   Madras

Nagappattinam

India + 2hrs 15min

Andaman Is.

Andaman Is + 30min

Thailand + 90min

☠ 1,894 Andaman &
Nicobar Is. combined   Phuket

Trincomalee

SRI LANKA
☠ 31,000   Sri Lanka + 2hrs

Colombo
Galle   Hambantota

Nicobar Is.

THAILAND
☠ 5,300

MALDIVES
☠ 82   Maldives + 3hrs 30min

Banda Aceh   MALAYSIA
☠ 68

ACEH   Medan

Sumatra + 15 min

earthquake epicentre 0058 GMT

Simeulue

INDONESIA
☠ 111,171

1200 miles 1,000 miles 800 miles 600 miles 400 miles 200 miles

75°   90°

1947–89
The Cold War

TIMELINE

1947
Greek Civil War: Truman Doctrine announced

1948-9
Berlin airlift

1949
NATO formed: Soviet Union detonates its first nuclear bomb

1950-3
Korean War

1955
Warsaw Pact formed

1962
Cuban missile crisis

1964-73
US intervenes militarily in Vietnam

1979
Soviet Union invades Afghanistan

1987
INF Treaty; phased elimination of intermediate range nuclear weapons

1991
Collapse of USSR; Cold War ends

The defeat of Germany, Italy and Japan and the weakening of Britain and France in World War II left the USA and USSR as the only 'superpowers'. Their ideological and political confrontation expressed itself as the Cold War. Conflict between the two had already appeared before the final victory: The Western Allies had already agreed (reluctantly) at Yalta (February 1945) to allow Soviet control of eastern Europe after the end of the war. By 1949 Stalin had developed an atomic bomb, thus ending the US monopoly of nuclear weapons. In reply, the USA built up the defence of western Europe with the formation of the North Atlantic Treaty Organization (NATO) in 1949 (page 146). In 1952 the US tested a thermo-nuclear (hydrogen) bomb; Russia followed suit in 1953.

Although it started as a conflict over central Europe, the Cold War soon developed into a global confrontation. The US saw the Korean War (1950-3: page 152) as evidence of a world-wide communist conspiracy, and American policy now became the 'containment' of Communism by a series of encircling alliances. NATO was followed by the South-East Asia Treaty Organization (SEATO) in 1954 and the Baghdad Pact (1955); the US maintained over 1400 foreign bases, including 275 bases for nuclear bombers, in 31 countries around the Soviet perimeter (map 1). As long as nuclear devices could only be delivered by aircraft, possession of these bases conferred an enormous advantage on the US. But when in the early 1960s both sides began to deploy ballistic nuclear missiles

US inspectors at a Soviet nuclear weapons site, 20 kilometres from Saratov *(right)*. Under the terms of the disarmament agreement of 1987 both sides agreed to the decommissioning of a large proportion of their nuclear stockpiles and to a system of inspections.

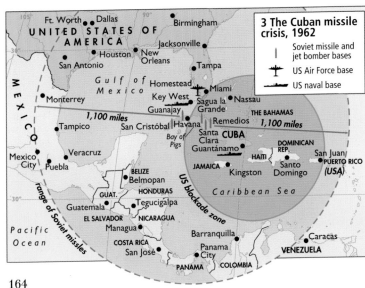

3 The Cuban missile crisis, 1962

- Soviet missile and jet bomber bases
- US Air Force base
- US naval base

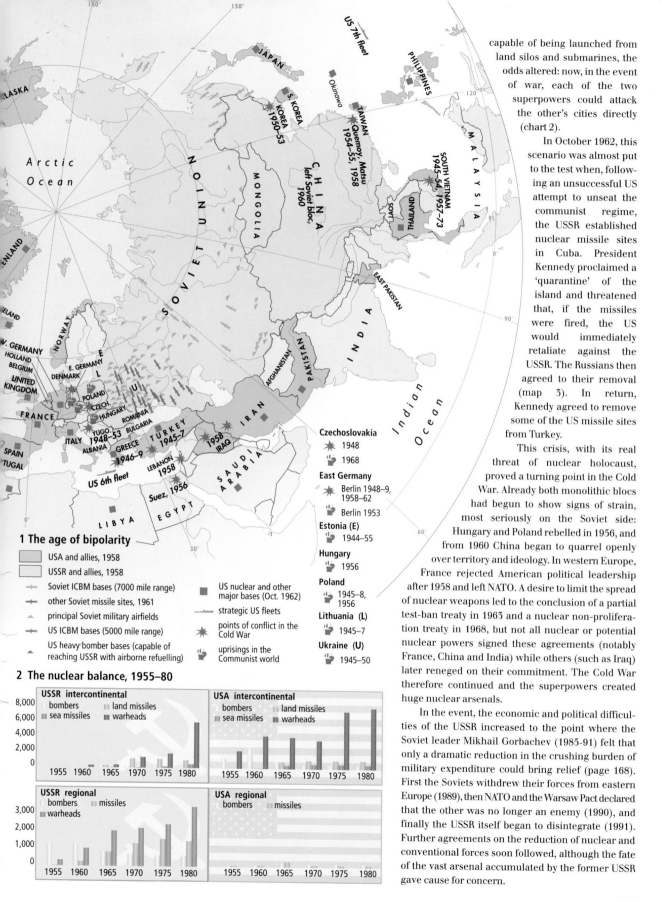

US 7th fleet

JAPAN

S. KOREA

Okinawa

S. KOREA
1950-53

TAIWAN Quemoy, Matsu
1954-55, 1958

PHILIPPINES

C H I N A
left Soviet bloc,
1960

M
A
L
A
Y
S
I
A

SOUTH VIETNAM
1945-54, 1957-73

LAOS

THAILAND

MONGOLIA

S O V I E T   U N I O N

Arctic
Ocean

ALASKA

ENLAND

ELAND

NORWAY

W. GERMANY
HOLLAND
BELGIUM
UNITED
KINGDOM

DENMARK
E. GERMANY
POLAND
CZECH.
HUNGARY

E
L
U

ROMANIA
YUGO. BULGARIA
ITALY 1948-53
ALBANIA GREECE
1946-9
TURKEY
1945-7

FRANCE

SPAIN
TUGAL

US 6th fleet

LEBANON
1958

Suez, 1956

LIBYA

EGYPT

S A U D I
A R A B I A

1958
IRAQ

IRAN

AFGHANISTAN

PAKISTAN

I N D I A

EAST PAKISTAN

I n d i a n

O c e a n

180°

150°

120°

90°

60°

30°

0°

1 The age of bipolarity

USA and allies, 1958

USSR and allies, 1958

Soviet ICBM bases (7000 mile range)

other Soviet missile sites, 1961

principal Soviet military airfields

US ICBM bases (5000 mile range)

US heavy bomber bases (capable of reaching USSR with airborne refuelling)

US nuclear and other major bases (Oct. 1962)

strategic US fleets

points of conflict in the Cold War

uprisings in the Communist world

Czechoslovakia
1948
1968

East Germany
Berlin 1948–9, 1958–62
Berlin 1953

Estonia (E)
1944–55

Hungary
1956

Poland
1945–8, 1956

Lithuania (L)
1945–7

Ukraine (U)
1945–50

2 The nuclear balance, 1955–80

USSR intercontinental
bombers land missiles
sea missiles warheads
8,000
6,000
4,000
2,000
0
1955 1960 1965 1970 1975 1980

USA intercontinental
bombers land missiles
sea missiles warheads
1955 1960 1965 1970 1975 1980

USSR regional
bombers missiles
warheads
3,000
2,000
1,000
0
1955 1960 1965 1970 1975 1980

USA regional
bombers missiles
1955 1960 1965 1970 1975 1980

capable of being launched from land silos and submarines, the odds altered: now, in the event of war, each of the two superpowers could attack the other's cities directly (chart 2).

In October 1962, this scenario was almost put to the test when, following an unsuccessful US attempt to unseat the communist regime, the USSR established nuclear missile sites in Cuba. President Kennedy proclaimed a 'quarantine' of the island and threatened that, if the missiles were fired, the US would immediately retaliate against the USSR. The Russians then agreed to their removal (map 3). In return, Kennedy agreed to remove some of the US missile sites from Turkey.

This crisis, with its real threat of nuclear holocaust, proved a turning point in the Cold War. Already both monolithic blocs had begun to show signs of strain, most seriously on the Soviet side: Hungary and Poland rebelled in 1956, and from 1960 China began to quarrel openly over territory and ideology. In western Europe, France rejected American political leadership after 1958 and left NATO. A desire to limit the spread of nuclear weapons led to the conclusion of a partial test-ban treaty in 1963 and a nuclear non-proliferation treaty in 1968, but not all nuclear or potential nuclear powers signed these agreements (notably France, China and India) while others (such as Iraq) later reneged on their commitment. The Cold War therefore continued and the superpowers created huge nuclear arsenals.

In the event, the economic and political difficulties of the USSR increased to the point where the Soviet leader Mikhail Gorbachev (1985-91) felt that only a dramatic reduction in the crushing burden of military expenditure could bring relief (page 168). First the Soviets withdrew their forces from eastern Europe (1989), then NATO and the Warsaw Pact declared that the other was no longer an enemy (1990), and finally the USSR itself began to disintegrate (1991). Further agreements on the reduction of nuclear and conventional forces soon followed, although the fate of the vast arsenal accumulated by the former USSR gave cause for concern.

Western Europe; separatism and nationalism

In 1973 the oil-producing states almost trebled cost of oil, triggering worldwide price inflation. In Europe, the crisis coincided with a general slowdown in productivity and profit growth and mounting unemployment, producing widespread labour unrest. Behind the Iron Curtain, rising oil prices caused economic performance to stagnate or decline.

In western Europe, the crisis encouraged the trend to greater economic integration. By the late 1960s, the original six members of the EEC (European Economic Community) had emerged as the economic vanguard of the continent. In 1973 Britain, Ireland and Denmark joined, followed in 1981 by Greece, in 1986 by Spain and Portugal, and in 1995 by Austria, Finland and Sweden. By the Maastricht Treaty (1991), members agreed to form a single free-trade market (renamed the EU, or European Union, in 1995) and most also agreed to introduce a single currency, the Euro, by 1999. In 2004, an additional eight countries joined the EU (though not the Eurozone) bringing the total of member states to 25 (map 1 and page 175).

The combined effects of the economic slowdown after 1973 and the realization that clinging to their pre-war authoritarian governments would push them to the margins of Europe helped reintroduce democracy to Portugal (1974) and Spain (1975). Greece also embraced democracy in 1974. But these changes paled in comparison with events in eastern Europe in the late 1980s, where the disintegration of the Soviet Union and the fall of communism in every one of its satellite states produced in its wake no less than 15 new countries (page 168). The nationalist tensions released also led to civil wars in the former Yugoslavia (page 170).

Nationalist tensions likewise continued in western Europe. Many areas achieved a measure of devolution, often on linguistic grounds (as in Belgium), while Basque separatists in Spain and Irish nationalists in Ulster used terror to try and gain autonomy. They failed, and tentative political agreements were reached in both areas in 1998, though tensions survived (map 2).

2 Western Europe: separatism and nationalism, 1945–2000

— territorial autonomy based on ethnic group, with date of autonomy

— separate administration/ autonomy for other reasons

✗ devolution rejected by referendum, with date

✓ devolution approved by referendum, with date

✊ linguistic minorities or other communities whose members have used violence in pursuit of greater autonomy or other change of political status, with areas inhabited

● ethnic or other communal based party delegated to national parliament in 1985

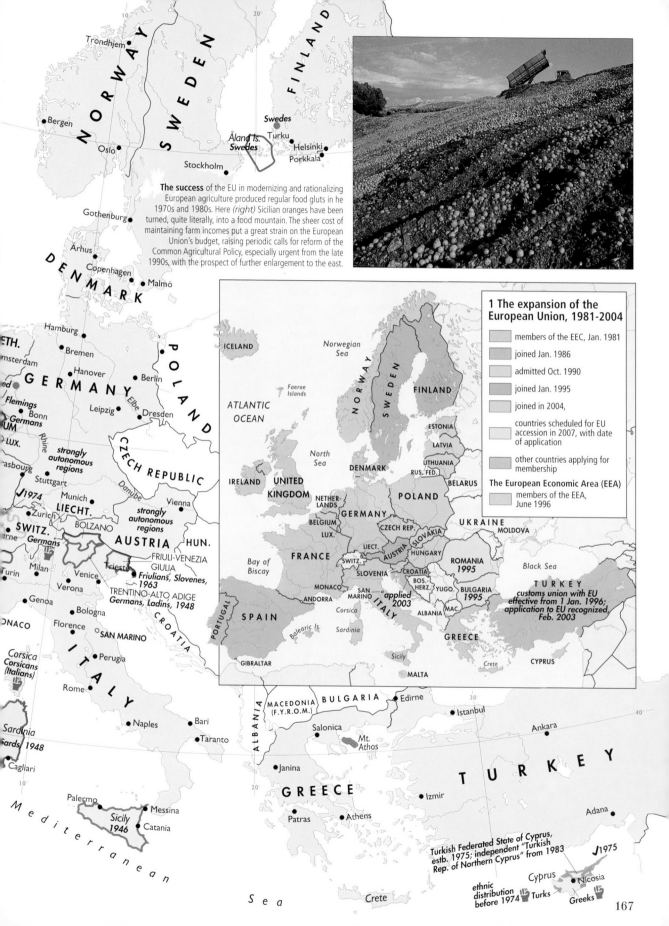

The success of the EU in modernizing and rationalizing European agriculture produced regular food gluts in he 1970s and 1980s. Here (right) Sicilian oranges have been turned, quite literally, into a food mountain. The sheer cost of maintaining farm incomes put a great strain on the European Union's budget, raising periodic calls for reform of the Common Agricultural Policy, especially urgent from the late 1990s, with the prospect of further enlargement to the east.

1 The expansion of the European Union, 1981-2004

- members of the EEC, Jan. 1981
- joined Jan. 1986
- admitted Oct. 1990
- joined Jan. 1995
- joined in 2004,
- countries scheduled for EU accession in 2007, with date of application
- other countries applying for membership

The European Economic Area (EEA)

- members of the EEA, June 1996

TURKEY customs union with EU effective from 1 Jan. 1996; application to EU recognized, Feb. 2003

applied 2003

Turkish Federated State of Cyprus, estb. 1975; independent "Turkish Rep. of Northern Cyprus" from 1983

ethnic distribution before 1974 ✊ Turks ✊ Greeks

The collapse of Communism since 1989

The collapse of the communist regimes of Eastern Europe arose directly from the changes implemented Mikhail Gorbachev, leader of the USSR (page 148). Regarding the other communist states as a drain on Soviet resources, he encouraged them to pursue economic and political reform. This policy change came at a difficult time for the Eastern bloc states, whose economic development had been adversely affected by recession in the West and by reductions in trade and aid resulting from renewed Cold War pressures. Economic modernization slowed, and provoked growing popular unrest, particularly in Poland, where a military dictatorship had arisen in 1981 to suppress the democracy movement and forestall possible Soviet military intervention.

Although few showed enthusiasm for the old regimes, popular opposition remained muted until Gorbachev pressured his communist partners to grasp the nettle of reform. Without Soviet backing, the regimes crumbled one by one: Hungary legalized opposition parties in January 1989; Poland established the first non-communist government since 1948 the following August; demonstrations ended communist rule in Czechoslovakia, East Germany and Bulgaria in November. Violence occurred only in Romania, where an army firing squad shot the fallen dictator Nicolae Ceauçescu in December (map 1).

Throughout the Eastern bloc, elections now brought to power coalition governments committed to democratic reform and economic liberalization. In the course of 1990, East Germany voted first for currency union and then for full integration with West Germany, ending the partition imposed after World War II; but other former communist countries, exposed to market pressures, soon plunged into economic decline. High unemployment and rural poverty contributed to the revival of the deep-rooted ethnic and religious conflicts that the communist regimes had papered over for 40 years. In 1993, tensions between Czechs and Slovaks produced the partition of Czechoslovakia.

Meanwhile, in the USSR, nationalist unrest grew as the Russian-dominated republics of the USSR sensed an opportunity to gain independence. The president of the Russian Republic, Boris Yeltsin, urged Gorbachev to give the Soviet republics more independence. In August 1991, a group of hard-line communists attempted a coup and, although Yeltsin suppressed the revolt, the non-Russian republics soon declared their independence. When the Ukraine staged a referendum in December 1991 that resulted in an overwhelming vote for independence, Gorbachev bowed to reality. The USSR was dissolved on 31 December, to be replaced by a Commonwealth of Independent States, co-operating on military and economic issues but no longer controlled from Moscow.

With no country left to rule, Gorbachev slipped into obscurity. Russia embraced a form of presidential democracy, with Yeltsin as its first president. In 1993, hard-line parliamentary delegates hostile to further reform tried to depose Yeltsin, but he crushed them too. Re-elected as president in 1996, Yeltsin stepped down in 1999 and power passed peacefully to Vladimir Putin. Meanwhile some republics (Belarus, Uzbekistan, Kazakhstan, Turkmenistan) maintained reformed communist governments while others adopted some form of democracy – although, as in as Ukraine in 2004, fraud marred several elections. In Russia itself the constituent republics established greater autonomy (map 2) while Chechenia sought to break away from Russia by force (page 170).

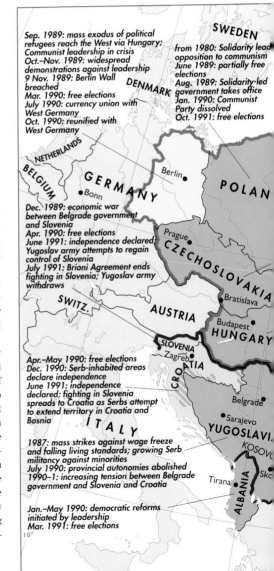

Sep. 1989: mass exodus of political
refugees reach the West via Hungary;
Communist leadership in crisis
Oct.–Nov. 1989: widespread
demonstrations against leadership
9 Nov. 1989: Berlin Wall
breached
Mar. 1990: free elections
July 1990: currency union with
West Germany
Oct. 1990: reunified with
West Germany

from 1980: Solidarity lead
opposition to communism
June 1989: partially free
elections
Aug. 1989: Solidarity-led
government takes office
Jan. 1990: Communist
Party dissolved
Oct. 1991: free elections

Dec. 1989: economic war
between Belgrade government
and Slovenia
Apr. 1990: free elections
June 1991: independence declared;
Yugoslav army attempts to regain
control of Slovenia
July 1991: Brioni Agreement ends
fighting in Slovenia; Yugoslav army
withdraws

Apr.–May 1990: free elections
Dec. 1990: Serb-inhabited areas
declare independence
June 1991: independence
declared; fighting in Slovenia
spreads to Croatia as Serbs attempt
to extend territory in Croatia and
Bosnia

1987: mass strikes against wage freeze
and falling living standards; growing Serb
militancy against minorities
July 1990: provincial autonomies abolished
1990–1: increasing tension between Belgrade
government and Slovenia and Croatia

Jan.–May 1990: democratic reforms
initiated by leadership
Mar. 1991: free elections

Map 1 (top) — labels:

FINLAND
POLAND
Murmansk
Arctic Ocean
KARELIA 74%
BELARUS
St Petersburg
NENETS
MOLDOVA
UKRAINE
CHUVASHIA 27%
Moscow
KOMI 58%
MARIYEL 47%
MORDOVIA 61%
Rostov-na-Donu
Volgograd
TATARSTAN 43%
GYEA 58%
KOMI-PERMYAK 59
UDMURTIA
KHANTY-MANSI AD
YAMALO-NENETS AD
TAYMYR AD
CHUKCHI AD
KORYAK AD
KALMYKIA 38%
a b d
EORGIA
ARM.
Yekaterinburg
BASHKORTOSTAN 59%
RUSSIAN FEDERATION
EVENKI AD
SAKHA (YAKUTIYA) 50%
Sea of Okhotsk
DAGESTAN 9%
AZER.
Caspian Sea
TURKMENISTAN
UZBEKISTAN
KAZAKHSTAN
Omsk
Novosibirsk
KHAKASSIA
ALTAY 60%
UST-ORDA BURYAT AD
TYVA 32%
BURYATIA 70%
AGA BURYAT AD
Chita
Irkutsk
JEWISH AO
Khabarovsk
IRAN
KYRGYZSTAN
AFGHANISTAN
TAJIKISTAN
MONGOLIA
CHINA
Vladivostok

a KARACHAY-CHERKESSIA 42%
b KABARDINO-BALKARIA 39%
c NORTH-OSSETIA 30%
d INGUSHETIA (from June 1992)
e CHECHENIA
} 23% combined

2 The Russian Federation, 1991–8

— the Russian Federation
constituent republics within the Russian Federation, Mar. 1992
independence declared, Nov. 1991; at war with Russia from Dec. 1994 to 1996 and from Aug. 1999

The Commonwealth of Independent States (CIS)

entered close political and economic union with Russia, 2 Apr. 1996
entered close economic union with Russia, 30 Mar. 1996
other members of the CIS
60% percentage of Russians in other members of the Russian Federation
AD autonomous district
AO autonomous oblast

In 2004 Ukraine held bitterly disputed presidential elections in which a candidate loyal to Moscow faced a challenger who favoured closer ties with the west: Viktor Yushchenko (above). Government agents apparently attempted to poison Yushchenko (hence his scarred face) and, when he lost the election, his supporters accused the government of massive electoral fraud. After several weeks of public demonstrations, Ukraine's Supreme Court ordered another election, which Yushchenko won.

Map 2 (bottom) — labels:

Baltic Sea
Tallinn
ESTONIA
Mar. 1990: Congress of Estonia formed, declares Soviet rule illegal
Mar. 1991: referendum endorses independence
Aug. 1991: independence declared
Sep. 1991: independence recognized by USSR

Riga
LATVIA
1989: mass anti-Communist demonstrations
Mar. 1991: referendum endorses independence
Aug. 1991: independence declared
Sep. 1991: independence recognized by USSR

LITHUANIA
Vilnius
IAN FED.
1989: mass anti-Communist demonstrations
Mar. 1991: independence declared
Apr.–June 1990: economic embargo imposed by USSR
Sep. 1991: independence recognized by USSR

Moscow

Minsk
BELARUS
June 1989: Popular Front founded
Aug. 1991: independence declared
Dec. 1991: founder member of Commonwealth of Independent States

RUSSIAN FEDERATION

rsaw
rom 1988: anti-government demonstrations
Nov. 1989: mass demonstrations end Communist rule
pr. 1990: new constitution dopted; becomes a federation
une 1990: free elections

rom 1987: Communist egime relaxes ontrol
ep. 1989: allows ast Germans to ravel to the West
ct. 1990: Communist ule ends peacefully
ar.–Apr. 1990: free ections

Kiev
UKRAINE
1989: opposition mass-movements emerge
Aug. 1991: independence declared
Dec. 1991: referendum endorses independence; founder member of Commonwealth of Independent States

TRANSNISTRIA
MOLDOVA
June 1989: Popular Front wins 75% of votes in election
Aug. 1991: independence declared
GAGAUZIA

OMANIA
Bucharest
Dec. 1989: mass demonstrations lead to armed uprisings and overthrow of Ceaușescu regime
June 1991: free elections
Nov. 1991: new constitution adopted

BULGARIA
ofia
Nov. 1989: President Zhivkov removed from office
June 1990: free elections
July 1991: fresh elections following adoption of new constitution

Mar. 1985: Mikhail Gorbachev becomes leader of Communist Party; initiates perestroika and glasnost, loosens Soviet control of satellite states
June 1991: Boris Yeltsin elected president of Russian Federation
Aug. 1991: hard-line Communist coup against Gorbachev fails
Nov. 1991: Communist Party declared illegal
Dec. 1991: USSR dissolved

Nov. 1988: mass demonstrations against Russification
Mar. 1991: referendum endorses independence
Apr. 1991: independence declared

Sep. 1989: economic embargo imposed by Azerbaijan
Sep. 1991: referendum endorses independence; independence declared

Jan. 1990: state of emergency declared; Soviet troops intervene
Oct. 1991: independence declared

Nov. 1991: independence declared

CHECHENIA
Grozny
GEORGIA
Sep. 1991: independence declared

AZERBAIJAN
NAGORNO-KARABAKH
ARMENIA

1 The collapse of communism, 1985–91

Soviet-dominated eastern Europe to 1989
Soviet Union to 1991
Yugoslavia to 1991
united with the Federal Republic of Germany, 1990
independent, 1991
other former communist states, 1991
de facto independent states, late 1991, on former territory of the Soviet Union, internationally unrecognized
overrun by Yugoslav army, July–Dec. 1991
borders, 1991

169

Civil wars in the communist successor states

The greatest casualty of the collapse of the communist bloc was Yugoslavia. Its six constituent republics (Serbia, Croatia, Macedonia, Bosnia-Herzegovina, Slovenia and Montenegro) were held together by an over-arching communist apparatus and the personal authority of Josip Broz Tito, the founder of communist Yugoslavia. Internal divisions appeared soon after his death in 1980, triggered by the rise of aggressive nationalism. In 1987, following the choice of Slobodan Milosevic as leader of Serbia, tensions between the republics grew stronger. Milosevic at once suppressed the Albanian minority in Kosovo, and set out to expand Serbia's influence throughout the federation.

In 1990 multi-party elections brought nationalists to the fore in Slovenia and Croatia and paved the way for their simultaneous declaration of independence in 1991. This provoked a vicious seven-month war when Serb forces intervened, allegedly to protect the ethnic Serb minority in Croatia. Another savage civil war broke out in Bosnia-Herzegovina, where Bosnian Muslims (44% of the population) and Croats (17%) demanded independence despite bitter opposition from the Bosnian Serbs (31%). Each ethnic group sought to 'cleanse' the areas under its control of all opponents until by 1993 the Serbs controlled around 70 per cent of Bosnia and besieged Sarajevo, held by the Muslim-led government. The war caused the death of at least 100,000 and displaced half of the region's 4 million inhabitants. In 1995 a renewed Serb offensive provoked NATO intervention, leading to an uneasy peace (the Dayton Accords) which left Bosnia divided between the three ethnic groups and utterly devastated by four years of war (map 1).

1 The Yugoslav civil war, 1991–5

- Croatia, June 1991
- Bosnia-Herzegovina Mar. 1992
- secured by Yugoslav army and Bosnian Serb forces by Dec. 1992
- controlled by Bosnian Croat forces, Dec. 1992
- under Bosnian government control , Dec. 1992
- Croatian advances, Jan. 1993
- Federation of Bosnia and Herzegovina advances, Oct.–Nov. 1994
- Croatian and Federation of Bosnia and Herzegovina advances, spring 1995
- Bosnian Serb advances, summer 1995
- Croatian and Federation of Bosnia and Herzegovina advances, Aug.–Oct. 1995
- overwhelmingly or largely Muslim, 1991; no significant Muslim presence by 1996
- Autonomous Province of Western Bosnia, Sep. 1993–Aug. 1994
- remained under Serb control by Dayton Agreement Nov.1995
- returned to Croatian control in Jan. 1998 under Erdut agreement of Nov. 1995
- overrun by Yugoslav army and Croatian Serb forces by Dec. 1991
- UN-designated 'safe areas'

Rijeka
Istria
Krk
Pula
Cres
Za

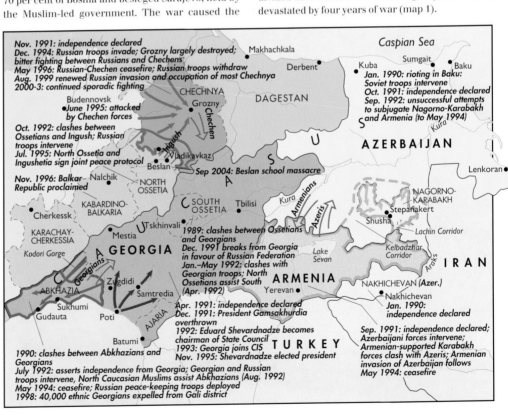

3 The Caucasus, 1988–2005

- notional extent of Georgia at independence
- advance of pro-Gamsa-khurdia forces, Oct. 1993
- Georgian advance into Abkhazia, Aug. 1992
- areas of Georgia under Abkhazian control, Oct. 1993
- evacuated by Georgia, Oct. 1994
- notional extent of Azerbaijan at independence
- Armenia at independence
- limit of Armenian control, May 1992
- Azerbaijani advance into Karabakh, Oct. 1992
- secured by Armenia and Karabakh by Nov. 1993
- Chechenia-Ingushetia at independence
- seceded from Chechenia, joined Rus. Fed., Mar. 1992
- claimed by Ingushetia, 1992
- Russian advance into Chechenia by May 1995
- mass movements of refugees
- autonomous within Russian Federation

Caspian Sea

Nov. 1991: independence declared
Dec. 1994: Russian troops invade; Grozny largely destroyed; bitter fighting between Russians and Chechens
May 1996: Russian-Chechen ceasefire; Russian troops withdraw
Aug. 1999 renewed Russian invasion and occupation of most Chechnya
2000-3: continued sporadic fighting

Makhachkala
Derbent
Kuba
Sumgait
Baku

Jan. 1990: rioting in Baku: Soviet troops intervene
Oct. 1991: independence declared
Sep. 1992: unsuccessful attempts to subjugate Nagorno-Karabakh and Armenia (to May 1994)

CHECHNYA
DAGESTAN

Budennovsk
•June 1995: attacked by Chechen forces

Grozny
Chechen

Oct. 1992: clashes between Ossetians and Ingush; Russian troops intervene
Jul. 1995: North Ossetia and Ingushetia sign joint peace protocol

Ingush
Vladikavkaz
Beslan

Sep 2004: Beslan school massacre

Nov. 1996: Balkar Republic proclaimed

Nalchik
NORTH OSSETIA

AZERBAIJAN
Lenkoran
Kura

KABARDINO-BALKARIA
Cherkessk
SOUTH OSSETIA
Tbilisi
Tskhinvali
Armenians
Azeris

1989: clashes between Ossetians and Georgians
Dec. 1991 breaks from Georgia in favour of Russian Federation
Jan.–May 1992: clashes with Georgian troops; North Ossetians assist South (Apr. 1992)

KARACHAY-CHERKESSIA
Mestia
GEORGIA
Kodori Gorge

NAGORNO-KARABAKH
Stepanakert
Shusha
Lachin Corridor
Kelbadzhar Corridor
Lake Sevan
Aroks
IRAN

Georgians
Zugdidi
Samtredia
ABKHAZIA
Sukhumi
Gudauta
Poti
AJARIA
Batumi

ARMENIA
Yerevan
NAKHICHEVAN (Azer.)
Nakhichevan

Apr. 1991: independence declared
Dec. 1991: President Gamsakhurdia overthrown
1992: Eduard Shevardnadze becomes chairman of State Council
1993: Georgia joins CIS
Nov. 1995: Shevardnadze elected president

Jan. 1990: independence declared

Sep. 1991: independence declared; Azerbaijani forces intervene; Armenian-supported Karabakh forces clash with Azeris; Armenian invasion of Azerbaijan follows May 1994: ceasefire

1990: clashes between Abkhazians and Georgians
July 1992: asserts independence from Georgia; Georgian and Russian troops intervene, North Caucasian Muslims assist Abkhazians (Aug. 1992)
May 1994: ceasefire; Russian peace-keeping troops deployed
1998: 40,000 ethnic Georgians expelled from Gali district

TURKEY

SLOVENIA
HUNGARY
CROATIA
Zagreb
Karlovac
Sisak
Osijek
Glina
Drava
Barania
Okučani
Vukovar
Prijedor
Bihać
Bosanka Krupa
Banja Luka
Sanski Most
Sava
Oraje
Bosna
UN
Ključ
Doboj
Brčko
BOSNIA-
Mrkonjić-Grad
Vrbas
Maglaj
Tuzla
Maslenica
Glamoč
Jajce
Travnik
Žepče
UN
Dinaric Alps
Donji Vakuf
Zenica
Knin
Kupres
Bugojno
Vitez
Drina
Šibenik
DALMATIA
Gornji Vakuf
Olovo
Srebrenica
UN
Livno
Kiseljak
Sarajevo
UN
Žepa
UN
Prozor
Pale
Višegrad
Split
Jablanica
HERZEGOVINA
Goražde
UN
Brač
Mostar
Hvar
YUGOSLAVIA
Korčula
Dubrovnik

S E R B I A
Novi Pazar
5km demilitarized zone established, 1999
MONTENEGRO
refugees 61,700
patriarchate of Pec
Pec
Decani
ALBANIA
main routes for weapons to KLA
Kukës
refugees 405,360
Leposavić
Kosovska Mitrovica
Podujevo
Istok
Priština
Kosovo Polje 1389
Gračanica
Vranje
K O S O V O
Gnjilane
Urosevac
Prizren
church of Bogorodica Ljeviska
Albanian guerilla – Macedonian government clashes 2001
M A C E D O N I A (F.Y.R.O.M.)
refugees 197,870
Skopje

A 50,000 Serbs

HUNGARY   ROMANIA
CROATIA   Novi Sad
BOSNIA   Belgrade
HERZE-   Kragujevac
GOVINA   S E R B I A
MONTENEGRO   Niš
Podgorica   KOSOVO
ALBANIA   Priština
MACEDONIA   Skopje

2 The war in Kosovo

→ flight of Kosovan Albanian refugees, Mar.-May 1999

✸ towns bombed by NATO forces, Mar.-June 1999

▨ KLA strongholds

⊕ sites of religous significance to Serbs

- - - NATO zone of occupatic with nationality of occupying force

→ NATO bombing raid

☠ major massacres

In 1998, conflict escalated in Serbia's province of Kosovo. Talks brokered by international mediators offered the Kosovo Albanians full autonomy within Serbia, but Milosevic objected. NATO responded with air strikes against Yugoslavia to force Belgrade to sign the peace agreement and to stop the repression of Kosovo Albanians. The Serbian security forces instead accelerated a programme of 'ethnic cleansing' against Kosovo Albanians. After more than two months of NATO bombing, Milosevic agreed to a peace plan that incorporated most of NATO's demands and a NATO-led peace implementation force entered the province (map 2).

Tensions within the Yugoslav Federation continued as the pro-western government of Montenegro sought to assert its independence from Belgrade until December 2000, when massive popular protests against presidential election fraud drove Milosevic from office. His successor, Vojislav Kostunica, made overtures to the West and promised a return to democratic rule, and in 2001 delivered Milosevic to the UN War Crimes Tribunal for trial.

The break-up of the Soviet Union, too, saw widespread ethnic and political conflict, particularly in the Caucasus region (map 3). Armenia and Azerbaijan fought over the Christian Armenian enclave of Nagorno-Karabak; Georgia fought to keep South Ossetia within her boundaries and to prevent the independence of Abkhazia. The worst conflict occurred in Chechenia, which Russian forces invaded in 1994 and 1999 to prevent secession. Russia suffered heavy casualties in both operations and, despite occupying virtually the whole province, could not stifle a vigorous Chechen guerrilla resistance or, after 2002, prevent guerrilla attacks in Russia itself.

Bosnian Muslim refugees in Han-Bila in July 1993 *(left)* at the height of the Serbian campaign against the Muslim population of the region. Thousands of Muslims were driven from their homes, tortured, imprisoned or starved to death in makeshift concentration camps. Later the most notorious perpetrators were put on trial for war crimes before the Court of Human Rights at the Hague.

171

The 21ˢᵀ-Century World

After the end of the Cold War (page 164), the superpowers began to disarm; economic development stabilized in most of the northern hemisphere; democracy spread; and armed conflicts between states decreased. Yet the absence of global confrontation did not prevent regional disputes, many of which dragged in the major powers as arbiters. In 1990, Iraq invaded Kuwait, only to be expelled by US-led coalition forces in 1991. Thereafter, tensions persisted until in 2003 a smaller US-led coalition occupied Iraq and sought to introduce democracy. In Chechenia, Russian forces fought a grim civil war against separatists, which left the region desolate and produced Chechen terrorist attacks in Russia. The largest war of all involved the states that emerged from the collapse of former Yugoslavia in 1991 (page 170).

Religious differences exacerbated many of these conflicts. Radical movements developed throughout the Islamic world, including the large Muslim communities now living and working in the West. The failure of western-style modernization encouraged many young Muslims to exalt traditional values, and to seek to destroy western 'imperialism', both by driving it out of Islamic countries, and by attacking it in its heartland. This led to civil war between Fundamentalists and Modernizers in several Muslim countries (Afghanistan, Algeria and Iran); and to attacks by terrorist groups

2 World population at the millennium

Family size and population growth

- very rapid growth (more than 5 children per family)
- intermediate growth (2.1–5 children per family)
- slow growth (fewer than 2.1 children per family)

Fastest-growing populations (% per annum)
- 4.5% 2000–5
- 4.0% 2045–50 (projection)
- 48.6 % of population under 15

Slowest-growing populations (% per annum)
- -4.5% 2000–5
- -4.0% 2045–50 (projection)

JAPAN 9 — countries with population of 50 million or more in 2000, in ranking order

JAPAN (15) — countries with population of 50 million more in 2050 (projection), in ranking o

JAPAN -13.6 — countries with projected population decrease 2000–50, with percentage

Tokyo 26.4 — cities with populations over 10 million in 2000 (with population)

Tokyo (27.2) — cities with populations over 10 million in 2050 (with projected population)

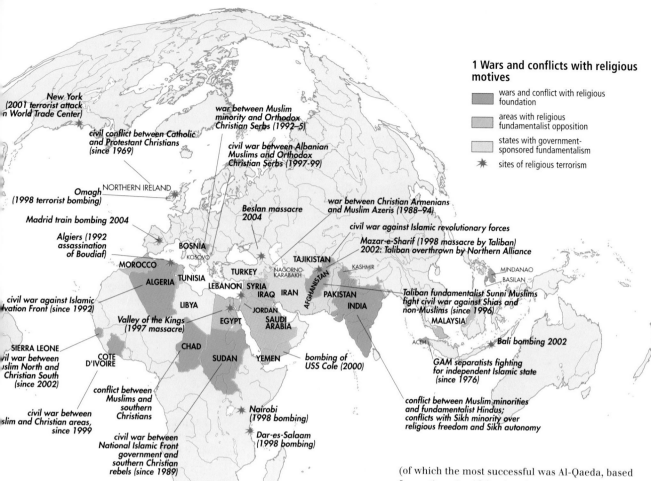

1 Wars and conflicts with religious motives

- ■ wars and conflict with religious foundation
- ■ areas with religious fundamentalist opposition
- ☐ states with government-sponsored fundamentalism
- ✳ sites of religious terrorism

New York
(2001 terrorist attack on World Trade Center)

civil conflict between Catholic and Protestant Christians (since 1969)

war between Muslim minority and Orthodox Christian Serbs (1992-5)

civil war between Albanian Muslims and Orthodox Christian Serbs (1997-99)

Omagh
(1998 terrorist bombing)

NORTHERN IRELAND

Beslan massacre 2004

war between Christian Armenians and Muslim Azeris (1988-94)

Madrid train bombing 2004

Algiers (1992 assassination of Boudiaf)

civil war against Islamic revolutionary forces

Mazar-e-Sharif (1998 massacre by Taliban) 2002: Taliban overthrown by Northern Alliance

BOSNIA
KOSOVO

TAJIKISTAN

MINDANAO
BASILAN

MOROCCO

TURKEY

NAGORNO-KARABAKH

KASHMIR

civil war against Islamic Salvation Front (since 1992)

ALGERIA   TUNISIA

LEBANON   SYRIA

IRAQ   IRAN

AFGHANISTAN   PAKISTAN

Taliban fundamentalist Sunni Muslims fight civil war against Shias and non-Muslims (since 1996)

LIBYA

JORDAN

INDIA

MALAYSIA

Valley of the Kings (1997 massacre)

EGYPT   SAUDI ARABIA

SIERRA LEONE
civil war between Muslim North and Christian South (since 2002)

COTE D'IVOIRE

CHAD

SUDAN   YEMEN

ACEH

Bali bombing 2002

bombing of USS Cole (2000)

GAM separatists fighting for independent Islamic state (since 1976)

civil war between Muslim and Christian areas, since 1999

conflict between Muslims and southern Christians

Nairobi
(1998 bombing)

conflict between Muslim minorities and fundamentalist Hindus; conflicts with Sikh minority over religious freedom and Sikh autonomy

civil war between National Islamic Front government and southern Christian rebels (since 1989)

Dar-es-Salaam
(1998 bombing)

NEW ZEALAND

Since 1981, AIDS (Auto-immune Deficiency Syndrome) has killed 19 million people world-wide, over 11 million of them in Sub-Saharan Africa, where in 2004 almost 6,000 people died every day from the disease. Over 34 million more people currently suffer from AIDS (or HIV, the virus that leads to AIDS), two-thirds of them in Sub-Saharan Africa where the death of young adults from the disease has left over 12 million orphans. Even those who do not already have the disease face a grim future.

(of which the most successful was Al-Qaeda, based for a time in Afghanistan) against pro-Western Muslim regimes (Egypt, Saudi Arabia, Morocco) as well as against the United States (2001) and Spain (2004). Religious differences also fuelled inter-communal violence in India, Indonesia, Northern Ireland and Yugoslavia, and inter-state conflicts between Iran and Iraq and between Israel and most of her Arab neighbours (map 1).

Some of the tensions in the Middle East and in south and southeast Asia arose from rapid population growth. In these areas, people under 25 sometimes made up half the total population. Indeed students and schoolchildren played a conspicuous part in protests in India, Indonesia, Burma and in Tiananmen Square in Beijing in 1989. Young South Africans, too, played a central part in achieving democracy in 1990–4. The image of the peasant-soldier typical of the liberation movements of the 1960s gave way to chilling images of pre-teenage boys with modern weapons in their hands.

Many other critical issues remained. Extreme weather events (such as prolonged droughts and catastrophic floods), acid rain, and 'global warming' all caused alarm. Above all, population growth threatened to destabilize the world system because, although in the late 1990s the growth began to slow, famine and impoverishment afflicted many overpopulated developing states (map 2). Few people entered the new millennium with complete confidence.

The Global economy

TIMELINE

1987
Single European Act for full economic union

1991
Russia begins programme of economic reforms

1992
Maastricht Treaty

1994
Mexico joins North American Free Trade Area (NAFTA)

1995
EEC becomes the European Union

1997-8
Financial crisis rocks east Asian economies

1999
European single currency (the 'euro') introduced

By the 1990s electronic communication and worldwide investment and marketing had created a genuinely global economy. Giant transnational companies dominated finance and production. However, world economic development still depended in part on the central management of key economic factors by groups of states, and on collaboration between them. Representatives of the largest industrial economies met regularly as the Group of Seven to co-ordinate financial and trade policies. Additionally, regional agreements sought to expand trade between small groups of states.

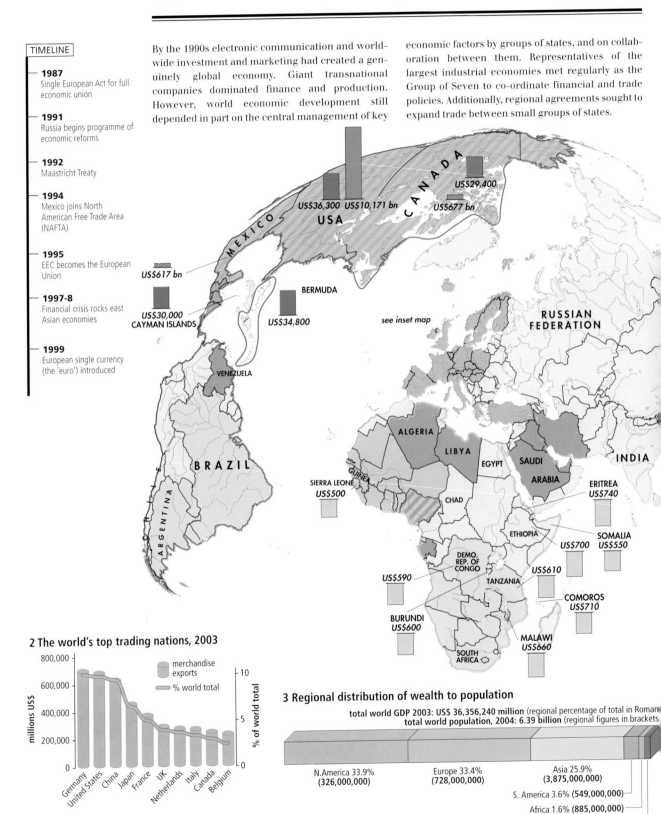

US$36,300 US$10,171 bn US$29,400 US$677 bn

USA CANADA

US$617 bn

BERMUDA

US$30,000
CAYMAN ISLANDS US$34,800

see inset map

RUSSIAN FEDERATION

VENEZUELA

ALGERIA
LIBYA
EGYPT SAUDI ARABIA INDIA

GUINEA
SIERRA LEONE
US$500 CHAD ERITREA
US$740

ETHIOPIA SOMALIA
US$700 US$550

DEMO. REP. OF CONGO
US$590 TANZANIA US$610

COMOROS
US$710

BURUNDI
US$600

MALAWI
US$660

SOUTH AFRICA

2 The world's top trading nations, 2003

- merchandise exports
- % world total

millions US$ (800,000 – 0)
% of world total (10 – 0)

Germany, United States, China, Japan, France, UK, Netherlands, Italy, Canada, Belgium

3 Regional distribution of wealth to population

total world GDP 2003: US$ 36,356,240 million (regional percentage of total in Roman
total world population, 2004: 6.39 billion (regional figures in brackets

| N.America 33.9% (326,000,000) | Europe 33.4% (728,000,000) | Asia 25.9% (3,875,000,000) |

S. America 3.6% (549,000,000)
Africa 1.6% (885,000,000)
Oceania 1.6% (33,000,000)

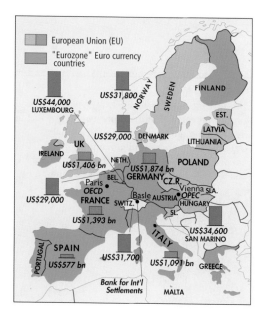

European Union (EU)

"Eurozone" Euro currency countries

US$44,000 LUXEMBOURG

US$31,800 NORWAY SWEDEN FINLAND

US$29,000 DENMARK EST. LATVIA LITHUANIA

UK IRELAND NETH. US$1,406 bn

US$1,874 bn GERMANY CZ.R. POLAND

BEL. Paris OECD Basle Vienna SLA. OPEC AUSTRIA HUNGARY

US$29,000 FRANCE SWITZ. SL.

US$1,393 bn ITALY US$34,600 SAN MARINO

PORTUGAL SPAIN US$577 bn US$31,700 US$1,091 bn GREECE

Bank for Int'l Settlements MALTA

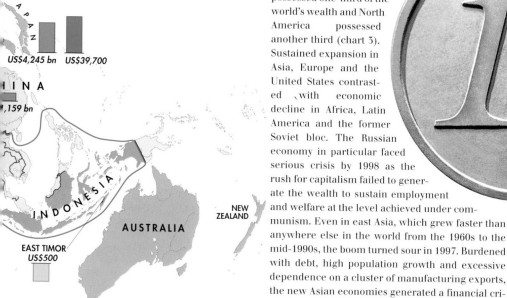

JAPAN US$4,245 bn US$39,700

CHINA ,159 bn

INDONESIA

AUSTRALIA

NEW ZEALAND

EAST TIMOR US$500

1 The world economy and economic groupings

North American Free Trade Association (NAFTA)

Common Market of the Southern Cone (Mercosur)

Central American Common Market (CACM)

Economic Community of West African States (ECOWAS)

Organization for Economic Co-operation and Development (OECD)

Organization for Petroleum Exporting Countries (OPEC)

Southern African Development Community (SADC) (note: Seychelles and Mauritius are members)

Association of South East Asian Nations (ASEAN)

Organization of American States (OAS)

African Union

10 largest economies, in US$ bn (2001)

10 largest GDP per capita (2001 PPP adjusted)

10 smallest GDP per capita (2001 PPP adjusted)

The most successful of these groupings was the European Union, which grew from the original six members of the EEC in 1957 to embrace 25 states by 2004 (page 166). Gradual economic integration culminated in 1999 with the introduction of a single currency, the euro, and the abolition of national currencies within the Eurozone in 2002. Economic groups elsewhere formed looser associations aiming to enhance regional economic integration. In 1994, for example, the USA, Canada and Mexico joined in the North American Free Trade Association (NAFTA) (map 1 and inset).

The world's top ten trading nations in 2003 provided almost two-thirds of the world's imports and exports (chart 2). A high proportion of that trade took place between the top traders, rather than trade between the developed and developing world; and an increasing proportion occurred within free-trade blocs. The fruits of the global economic success were spread very unevenly. In 2003, Europe possessed one-third of the world's wealth and North America possessed another third (chart 3). Sustained expansion in Asia, Europe and the United States contrasted with economic decline in Africa, Latin America and the former Soviet bloc. The Russian economy in particular faced serious crisis by 1998 as the rush for capitalism failed to generate the wealth to sustain employment and welfare at the level achieved under communism. Even in east Asia, which grew faster than anywhere else in the world from the 1960s to the mid-1990s, the boom turned sour in 1997. Burdened with debt, high population growth and excessive dependence on a cluster of manufacturing exports, the new Asian economies generated a financial crisis that threatened the health of the whole global economy.

Outside the growth areas, there was persistent reliance on aid and investment from the developed world, much of it supplied by the International Monetary Fund (IMF) or the Organization for Economic Co-operation and Development (OECD). The per capita Gross Domestic Product (GDP) of the poorest states in the early 21st century was less than $300, while per capita GDP in the USA was almost $27,000. For many sub-Saharan African states, aid represented more than half of the value of total GDP. This pattern of aid-dependence altered little over the 1990s, and the gulf between the poverty of the developing world and the vast wealth of the developed industrial core remained one of the unresolved issues of global economics.

A Euro coin (above). Gradual economic integration within the European Union culminated in the introduction of a single currency, the Euro, on 1 January 1999. Initially the Euro showed unexpected weakness against the dollar, but it rallied soon after Euro notes and coins became legal tender on 1 January 2002. National currencies within the Euro-zone (which did not include the United Kingdom or the eight new states that joined in 2004) ceased to exist.

The Global environment

Until the 20th century, natural changes largely determined the environment. Now, industrialization, modern communications and mass consumption have combined to produce damaging man-made environmental change. Ecological disasters have become urgent global problems.

The onset of large-scale population growth and industrialization in the 19th century (page 100), stimulated a parallel rapid increase in man-made damage to the world's environment. Before 1945, this damage was largely localized, though very visible; the spread of industry worldwide after 1945 produced new threats to the environment which, if less visible, were nonetheless more deadly. Acid rain from waste in the atmosphere destroyed forests and eroded buildings. Pollutants in rivers and seas poisoned wildlife (map 1).

High levels of carbon dioxide released from the burning of fossil fuels raised global temperatures, while other chemicals began to weaken the ozone layer in the earth's atmosphere. Between 1800 and 1900 the level of carbon dioxide in the atmosphere increased by only 4 per cent; in the 20th century it increased by 23 per cent, with most of the change

3 Radioactive fall-out from the Chernobyl accident, 1986

.·:'   pattern of fall-out

occurring since the 1950s. This raised world temperatures significantly: the 1990s were the warmest decade of the millennium.

Global warming stemmed in part from a massive increase in energy consumption, most of which consisted of fossil fuels (oil, coal and natural gas). Between 1970 and 1990 energy consumption grew by 60 per cent, despite efforts to find more efficient ways of generating power and to reduce emissions. Fossil fuels released a range of chemicals

into the atmosphere which blocked the natural loss of heat and created the so-called 'greenhouse effect', leading to a global rise in temperatures (map 2).

The search for alternative sources of energy produced other types of disaster, however. In 1986, a nuclear reactor at Chernobyl in the Ukraine exploded, spreading a cloud of radioactive waste around the world (map 3). This catastrophe was but the most spectacular of many accidents in the production of nuclear power, eventually causing a reduction in its use.

Environmental issues became a central concern of the 1990s and state action produced some positive results. In Brazil, deforestation fell from a rate of 21,000 square kilometres in 1988 to only 1000 square kilometres by 1993. At Rio de Janeiro in 1992 an assembly of world leaders agreed to reduce harmful pollutants and emissions, a decision reaffirmed at a further meeting in Kyoto in 1997. The richer states also promised to subsidize industrial and agricultural projects in the developing world that respected environmental interests. In European states, political movements developed based entirely on issues of the environment, and in 1998 the environmentalist Green Party won a share of power in Germany. The future of the world ecosystem depended on the willingness of the world's richest states to accept substantial changes in consumption patterns.

Burmah A 1979

BELIZE *CUBA*
CENTRAL AMERICA
between 33% a 50% of rainfore destroyed

VENEZUELA
Atlanti Empre 1979
COLOMBIA
COLOMBIAN CHOCO

WESTERN AMAZONIA

PERU

BRAZIL 10% of forest destroyed

BOLIVIA

CHILE

PARAGUAY

SOUTH AMERICA

ARGENTINA

URUGUAY

Metula 1974

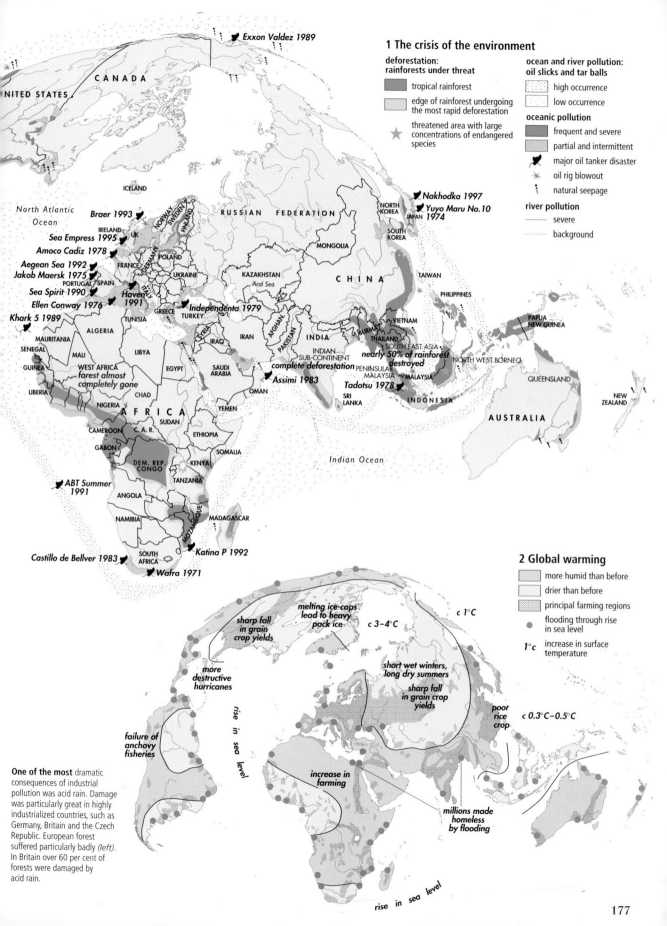

1 The crisis of the environment

deforestation: rainforests under threat

▨ tropical rainforest

▨ edge of rainforest undergoing the most rapid deforestation

★ threatened area with large concentrations of endangered species

ocean and river pollution: oil slicks and tar balls

▨ high occurrence

▨ low occurrence

oceanic pollution

▨ frequent and severe

▨ partial and intermittent

🕊 major oil tanker disaster

✳ oil rig blowout

⋮ natural seepage

river pollution

— severe

— background

Exxon Valdez 1989

CANADA

UNITED STATES

ICELAND

North Atlantic Ocean

Braer 1993

NORWAY SWEDEN FINLAND

RUSSIAN FEDERATION

IRELAND UK

Sea Empress 1995

Amoco Cadiz 1978

GERMANY POLAND

FRANCE

Aegean Sea 1992

Jakob Maersk 1975

PORTUGAL SPAIN ITALY UKRAINE KAZAKHSTAN *Aral Sea*

MONGOLIA

NORTH KOREA

JAPAN

Nakhodka 1997

Yuyo Maru No.10 1974

SOUTH KOREA

Sea Spirit 1990

Haven 1991

GREECE TURKEY

Independenta 1979

CHINA

TAIWAN

Ellen Conway 1976

Khark 5 1989

SYRIA IRAQ IRAN AFGHAN. PAKISTAN

INDIA

PHILIPPINES

TUNISIA

MAURITANIA

ALGERIA LIBYA EGYPT SAUDI ARABIA

INDIAN SUB-CONTINENT complete deforestation

BURMA VIETNAM THAILAND

SOUTH EAST ASIA *nearly 50% of rainforest destroyed*

PAPUA NEW GUINEA

SENEGAL MALI

GUINEA

LIBERIA

WEST AFRICA *forest almost completely gone*

CHAD

NIGERIA

A F R I C A

CAMEROON C. A. R.

GABON

Assimi 1983

OMAN YEMEN

SRI LANKA

Tadotsu 1978

NORTH WEST BORNEO

PENINSULAR MALAYSIA MALAYSIA

INDONESIA

QUEENSLAND

NEW ZEALAND

AUSTRALIA

Indian Ocean

SUDAN ETHIOPIA SOMALIA

DEM. REP. CONGO KENYA

ABT Summer 1991

ANGOLA TANZANIA

NAMIBIA MOZAMBIQUE MADAGASCAR

Castillo de Bellver 1983 SOUTH AFRICA *Katina P 1992*

Wafra 1971

2 Global warming

▨ more humid than before

▨ drier than before

▨ principal farming regions

● flooding through rise in sea level

1°c increase in surface temperature

melting ice-caps lead to heavy pack ice

c 1°C

sharp fall in grain crop yields

c 3–4°C

more destructive hurricanes

short wet winters, long dry summers

sharp fall in grain crop yields

poor rice crop

c 0.3°C–0.5°C

rise in sea level

failure of anchovy fisheries

increase in farming

millions made homeless by flooding

One of the most dramatic consequences of industrial pollution was acid rain. Damage was particularly great in highly industrialized countries, such as Germany, Britain and the Czech Republic. European forest suffered particularly badly *(left)*. In Britain over 60 per cent of forests were damaged by acid rain.

rise in sea level

177

Index

1 HISTORICAL PLACE NAMES

Geographical names vary with time and with language, and there is some difficulty in treating them consistently in an historical atlas, especially for individual maps within whose time span the same place has been known by different names. We have aimed at the simplest possible approach to the names on the maps, using the index to weld together the variations.

On the maps forms of names will be found in the following hierarchy of preference:

a English conventional names or spellings, in the widest sense, for all principal places and features, e.g., Moscow, Vienna, Munich (including those that today might be considered obsolete when these are appropriate to the context, e.g., Leghorn).

b Names that are contemporary in terms of the maps concerned. There are here three broad categories:

i names in the ancient world, where the forms used are classical, e.g., Latin or latinized Greek, but extending also to Persian, Sanskrit, etc.

ii names in the post-medieval modern world, which are given in the form (though not necessarily the spelling) current at the time of the map (e.g., St. Petersburg before 1914, not Leningrad).

iii modern names where the spelling generally follows that of The Times Atlas of the World, though in the interests of simplicity there has been a general omission of diacritics in spellings derived by transliteration from non-roman scripts, e.g., Sana rather than Ṣanʿāʾ.

2 THE INDEX

Where a place is referred to by two or more different names in the course of the atlas, there will be a corresponding number of main entries in the index. The variant names in each case are given in brackets at the beginning of the entry, their different forms and origins being distinguished by such words as now, later, formerly and others included in the list of abbreviations (right).

'Bizerta (anc. Hippo Zarytus)' means that the page references to that city on maps dealing with periods when it was known as Bizerta follow that entry, but the page references pertaining to it in ancient times will be found under the entry for Hippo Zarytus. Places are located generally by reference to the country in which they lie (exceptionally by reference to island groups or sea areas), this being narrowed down where necessary by location as E(ast), C(entral), etc. The reference will normally be to the modern state in which the place now falls unless (a) there is a conventional or historical name which conveniently avoids the inevitably anachronistic ring of some modern names, e.g., Anatolia rather than Turkey, Mesopotamia rather than Iraq, or (b) the modern state is little known or not delineated on the map concerned, e.g., many places on the Africa plates can only be located as W, E, Africa, etc.

Reference is generally to page number/map number (e.g. 118/1) unless the subject is dealt with over the plate as a whole, when the references have been given sub-headings where possible, e.g., Civil War 129/4. Battles are indicted by the symbol ✕.

Though page references are generally kept in numerical order, since this corresponds for the most part with chronological order, they have been rearranged occasionally where the chronological sequence would be obviously wrong, or in the interests of grouping appropriate references under a single sub-heading.

3 ABBREVIATIONS

a/c also called	form. former(ly)	obs. obsolete
AD Autonomous District	Fr. French	OT Old Testament
Alb. Albanian	f/s formerly spelled	Pers. Persian
anc. ancient	Ger. German	Pol. Polish
AR Autonomous Region	Gr. Greek	Port. Portuguese
Ar. Arabic	Heb. Hebrew	Rom. Romanian
a/s also spelled	Hung. Hungarian	Russ. Russian
ASSR Autonomous Soviet Socialist Republic	Indon. Indonesian	S South(ern)
Bibl. Biblical	Ir. Irish	s/c sometimes called
Bulg. Bulgarian	Is. Island	Som. Somali
C Century (when preceded by 17, 18, etc.)	It. Italian	Sp. Spanish
C Central	Jap. Japanese	S.Cr. Serbo-Croat
Cat. Catalan	Kor. Korean	SSR Soviet Socialist Republic
Chin. Chinese	Lat. Latin	Sw. Swedish
Cz. Czech	Latv. Latvian	Turk. Turkish
Dan. Danish	Lith. Lithuanian	Ukr. Ukrainian
Dut. Dutch	Mal. Malay	US(A) United States (of America)
E East(ern)	med. medieval	var. variant
Eng. English	mod. modern	W West(ern)
Est. Estonian	Mong. Mongolian	Wel. Welsh
f/c formerly called	N North(ern)	WW1 World War 1
Finn. Finnish	n/c now called	WW2 World War 2
	Nor. Norwegian	
	n/s now spelled	
	NT New Testament	

Aachen (*Fr.* Aix-la-Chapelle *anc.* Aquisgranum) W Germany Frankish royal residence 53/1; WW1 86/2

Abkhazia autonomous region of Georgia 170/3

Abasgia region of the Caucasus 49/1

Abyssinia (*now* Ethiopia) 111/1

Achaea (*a/s* Achaia) Roman province 37/1

Acragas (*Lat.* Agrigentum *mod.* Agrigento) Sicily Greek colony 32/1

Addis Ababa Ethiopia Italian penetration 111/1

Aden S Arabia early town 81/1; Ottoman Empire 108/1; taken by British 118/1; British base 154/1

Aden Protectorate (*successively renamed* Protectorate of South Arabia, Federation of South Arabia, People's Republic of South Yemen, People's Democratic Republic of Yemen; *now part of* United Yemen)

Admiralty Islands S Pacific Japanese attack 142/1

Adowa N Ethiopia ✕111/1

Adrianople (*anc.* Adrianopolis *mod.* Edirne) W Turkey Byzantine Empire 49/1,2; Ottoman centre 71/1; occupied by Greece 136/1

Aegospotami (*Turk.* Karaova Suyu) NW Turkey ✕33/2

Aegyptus (*mod.* Egypt) Roman province 37/1

Afars and Issas, French Territory of (*form.* French Somaliland *now* Republic of Djibouti)

Afghanistan invaded by USSR 149/1, 163/1; civil war 157/3; Islamic fundamentalism 157/3

Africa early man 12/1, 14/2; cave art 15/1; agricultural origins 17/1; early cultures 27/2; early empires 58/1; slave trade 59/2; early European voyages of discovery 79/1; European expansion and trade 80-81; 18C European trade 103/2; European penetration 111/1; colonial empires 119/2; foreign investment 1914 127/1; Japanese imports 152/2; anti-colonial resistance 154/1; modern political developments 161/1; population growth 172/2; armament imports 173/1; economic groupings 174/2; economy 174/2 environment 177/1,2

Africa (*mod.* Tunisia and Libya) conversion to Christianity 34/1, 44/1; Roman province 36/1; Byzantine province 48/1

Aga Buryat AD S Siberia in Russian Federation 169/2

Aigun NE China treaty port 95/2

Ain Jalut Palestine ✕50/2

Aix (*or* Aix-en-Provence *anc.* Aquae Sextiae) S France archbishopric 53/1; *parlement* 83/2

Ajaria autonomous district of Georgia 170/3

Ajnadain Palestine ✕51/1

Aksum early empire of E Africa 27/2

Åland Islands (*Finn.* Ahvenanmaa) SW Finland neutralized 136/1

Alaska state of USA purchase from Russia 114/1

Albania Black Death 67/1; Ottoman province 108/1; principality 125/2, 137/2; annexed by Italy 145/1; Cold War 165/1; free elections 169/1; Kosovo crisis 171/2; Kosovan refugees 171/2

Albania ancient country of Caucasus 37/1

Albany (*form.* Fort Orange) NE USA seized by English 86/2

Alemannia SW Germany part of Frankish Empire 53/1

Aleppo (*anc.* Beroea *a/c* Yamkhad *Fr.* Alep *Ar.* Halab) Syria Mitannian city 22/3; centre of European trade 103/2

Alessandria N Italy Lombard League 55/2

Aleutian Islands W Alaska to USA 114/1; attacked by Japanese 142/1; retaken by Americans 143/2

Alexandria (*Ar.* Al Iskandariyah) Egypt taken by Alexander 32/3; spread of Christianity 34/1; Roman Empire 37/1; Christian centre 45/1; Arab conquest 51/1; trade 59/2; centre of European trade 103/2

Algeria Ottoman province 70/2; French invasion 111/1; French colonization 118/1; under Vichy control 140/1; independence 154/1; Islamic fundamentalism 157/3; political development 161/1

Algiers (*Fr.* Alger *Sp.* Argel *Ar.* Al Jaza'ir *anc.* Icosium) N Algeria Ottoman rule 70/2; Habsburg Empire 93/1; Allied landing WW2 141/2

Allenstein (*Pol.* Olsztyn) W Poland acquired by Germany after plebiscite 136/1

Almanza Spain ✕83/3

Almohads Muslim dynasty and empire of North Africa 58/1

Almoravids Muslim dynasty of Morocco 58/1

Alpes Cottiae Roman province, France/Italy 36/1

Alpes Maritimae Roman province, France/Italy 36/1

Alpes Poeninae Roman province, France/Italy 36/1

Alsace (*anc.* Alsatia *Ger.* Elsass) in German Empire 55/2; acquired by French 83/2; Habsburg Empire 93/1

Alsace-Lorraine (*Ger.* Elsass-Lothringen) region of E France annexed by German Empire 116/2; ceded to France 136/1

Douala Cameroon W Africa German occupation 111/1

Dresden E Germany ✗99/2; WW2 141/2

Dristov Romania ✗56/2

Dublin (Ir. Baile Atha Cliath) Ireland Scandinavian settlement and control 54/1

Dunkirk (Fr. Dunkerque) N France fortification 83/2; WW2 140/2

Dura-Europos (mod. Salahiyeh) Syria Mithraic site 34/1; Roman Empire 37/1

Durazzo (anc. Epidamnus later Dyrrhachium mod. Durrës) Albania Byzantine Empire 49/2

Dutch East Indies (now Indonesia) early Dutch trade 80/2; early Dutch possessions 89/2; occupied by Japanese 142/1; independence 155/1 (inset)

Dutch Guiana (now Surinam) S America 87/1, 113/1

Dutch New Guinea (later West Irian n/c Irian Jaya) East Indies transferred to Indonesia 155/1

Dutch Republic (or United Provinces or Holland) in War of Spanish Succession 83/3; revolt against Spain 92/2

Dyrrhachium (earlier Epidamnus mod. Durrës It. Durazzo) Albania Roman Empire 37/1; Byzantine Empire 49/1,2

Eastern Rumelia region of Balkans Ottoman province ceded to Bulgaria 125/2

Eastern Turkestan C Asia Chinese protectorate 94/1

East Indies agricultural origins 17/1; early kingdoms 65/1; early trade 80/2; 18C European trade 103/2. See also Dutch East Indies, Indonesia

East Prussia (Ger. Ostpreussen) region of E Germany WW2 141/2; divided between Poland and Russia 169/1

East Timor independence from Indonesia 155/1

Eckmühl/Ebersberg S Germany ✗99/2

Ecuador independence 113/1; political development 159/1; economy 159/2

Edessa (mod. Urfa) SE Anatolia First Crusade 49/2

Egypt (officially Arab Republic of Egypt form. United Arab Republic Lat. Aegyptus Ar. Misr) centre of urban civilization 20/1; Old Kingdom 23/2; early settlement 27/2; campaigns of Alexander 32/3; spread of Christianity and Judaism 34/1; Arab conquest 44/1; Byzantine Empire 51/1; Fatimid Caliphate 50/2; conquered by Turks 70/2; Ottoman province 108/1; expansion into Sudan 111/1; independence 154/1; wars with Israel 156/1; Islamic fundamentalism 157/3; political development 157/3, 161/1

El Agheila Libya WW2 141/2

El Alamein Egypt ✗WW2 141/2

Elam (a/c. Susiana modern Khuzistan) ancient country of Middle East 22/3

England Scandinavian settlement 40/1; expansion of Christianity 44/1; Black Death and religious unrest 67/1; possessions in France 82/1; Reformation 91/1; WW1 133/1. See also Britain, Great Britain, United Kingdom

Ephesus (Turk. Efes) W Anatolia Greek colony 33/1; Byzantine Empire 49/1

Epidamnus (later Dyrrhachium It. Durazzo mod. Durrës) Albania Greek colony 33/1

Epirus ancient country of NW Greece 33/1; Roman province 37/1; Byzantine Empire 49/1; to Greece 125/2

Equator, Confederation of the E Brazil 113/1

Equatorial Guinea (form. Spanish Guinea a/c Rio Muni) country of W Africa independence 154/1

Eritrea region of NE Ethiopia Italian rule 108/1; Italian colony 110/2; political development 161/1

Estonia country of the Baltic acquired by Russia 85/1; Reformation 91/1; independence from Russia 136/1; constituted SSR 140/1; deportations 1941 149/2; independence 169/1

Ethiopia expansion of Christianity 34/1; 16C state 59/1; Italian invasion 111/1, 137/2; independence regained 154/1; economy 174/1

Etruscans ancient people of Italy 33/1

Eupen E Belgium ceded by Germany 136/1

Europe early man 12/1; Iron Age 15/1; agricultural origins 17/1; agricultural settlement 30/1; Hun and Avar invasions 40/1; expansion of Christianity 44/1; Viking, Magyar and Saracen invasions 54/1; Black Death 67/1; revolts and revolutions 98/1; Napoleon's empire 99/2; 19-20C alliances 124/1; foreign investment 1914 127/1; WW1 132-3; post-war territorial changes 146/1; Marshall Plan 147/3; economic blocs (EEC, EFTA, Comecon) 147/4; Japanese imports 152/2; economic blocs from 1957 167/1; collapse of Communist power 169/1; population 172/2; armaments exports 173/1; economic groupings 174/2l foreign direct investment 175/1; environment 177/1,2

European Union 167/1; 175/1 (inset)

Eylau (a/c Preussisch-Eylau now Bagrationovsk) E Prussia ✗99/2

Faeroe Islands (a/s Faroes) Norse settlement 54/1

Falkland Islands (Span. Islas Malvinas) islands of S Atlantic 113/1; war 159/1

Fanning Island C Pacific British possession 155/1 (inset)

Faroe Islands (a/s Faeroes) Norse settlement 54/1

Fars (a/c Persis, Parsa) Persia Muslim conquest 51/1

Fashoda S Sudan British/French confrontation 111/1

Fatimids Muslim dynasty of Egypt 50/2, 58/1

Federated Malay States (now Malaysia) independence 155/1

Feodosiya (a/c Kefe, Kaffa anc. Theodosia) Crimea acquired by Russia 85/1

Ferghana region of C Asia Muslim expansion 51/1

Fernando Po (Sp. Fernando Poó form. Macias Nguema Biyogo) island of Equatorial Guinea Spanish colony 111/1, 119/2; 145/1

Fez (Fr. Fès Ar. Al Fas) Morocco early trade 59/2

Fezzan (anc. Phazania) region of C Libya occupied by Italians 111/1

Fihl Palestine ✗51/1

Fiji S Pacific Melanesian settlement 27/1; British colony 119/2; independence 155/1 (inset)

Finland acquired by Russia 85/1; Reformation 91/1; WW1 133/1; independence 135/1; EU 167/1

Finns post-war migration from Karelia 146/1

Flanders (Fr. Flandre Dut. Vlaanderen) region of N Belgium Black Death 67/1; WW1 132/2

Flemings Dutch-speaking inhabitants of Belgium 166/2

Florida British rule 87/1, 104/1; annexed by USA 105/2; Depression 138/2; base for invasion of Cuba 164/3

Foix region of S France acquired by France 82/1

Foochow (a/s Fu-Chou n/s Fuzhou) SE China treaty port 95/2

Formosa (n/c Taiwan) cession to Japan 119/2; air attack by US 143/2; US bases 165/1

Fort Amsterdam (later New Amsterdam now New York) Dutch post 86/2

Fort Lamy (now N'Djamena) C Africa occupied by French 111/1

Fort William (n/c Thunder Bay) C Canada growth 120/2

Fouta Djallon (a/s Futa Jallon) W Africa early state 111/1

France (anc. Gaul Lat. Gallia) conversion to Christianity 44/1; Arab invasion 50/1; Viking and Saracen invasions 54/1; Scandinavian settlement 54/1; Black Death 67/1; 15C-16C reunification 82/1; War of Spanish Succession 83/3; administrative system under Louis XIV 83/2; Industrial Revolution 100/2; European alliances 124/1; world trade 1860-1913 127/1; WW1 132-3; EEC, NATO 165/1, 167/1; economy 174/1

Franche-Comté region of E France Habsburg Empire 93/1

Franconia (Ger. Franken) state of German Empire 55/2

French Cameroons (now part of Cameroon) W Africa independence 154/1

French Congo (a/c Middle Congo now People's Republic of the Congo) W Africa colony 111/1, 119/2

French Equatorial Africa union of French colonies 110/2

French Guiana S America 113/1

French Guinea (now Guinea) W Africa colony 111/1

French Indochina (now Cambodia, Laos and Vietnam) colonized 95/2; occupied by Japanese 123/2, 142/1; independence 155/1

French Somaliland (Fr. Côte Française des Somalis later French Territory of the Afars and Issas now Republic of Djibouti) NE Africa 110/2

French Sudan (now Mali) W Africa colony 111/1

French Territory of Afars and Issas (Djibouti)

French West Africa former union of French colonies 111/1, 119/2

Friedland (now Pravdinsk) E Prussia ✗99/2

Friedlingen W Germany ✗83/3

Fukien (n/s Fujian) province of SE China Ming province 69/1; Japanese influence 95/2, 123/2, under Nanking control 130/1; economy 151/2

Gagauzia minority area of S Moldova 169/1

Galatia country of C Anatolia Roman province 37/1

Galicia autonomous region of NW Spain 166/2

Galich (mod. Galicia) region of SW Russia Kievan principality 57/1

Gallipoli (anc. Callipolis Turk. Gelibolu) W Turkey Ottoman centre 71/1; WW1 133/1

Gambia country of W Africa British settlement 59/2; independence 155/1

Gandara (a/s Gandhara) region of E Afghanistan Indian kingdom 29/3

Gansu (f/s Kansu) province of NW China economy 1979-92 151/2

Gascony (Fr. Gascogne) region of SW France part of Frankish 50/2; province of France 83/2

Gaza Palestine Philistine city 33/1; Roman Empire 37/1; Byzantine Empire 49/1

Gaza Strip Palestine autonomy 156/1

Georgia state of S USA colony 104/1; industry 121/1; population 121/3; Depression 138/2

Georgia country of the Caucasus acquired by Russia 85/1; independent after WW1 1236/1; independence 1991 169/1

Germania Inferior province of Roman Empire 36/1

Germania Superior province of Roman Empire 36/1

Germantown E USA ✗104/1

Germany (Lat. Germania Ger. Deutschland now Federal Republic of Germany and German Democratic Republic) Hun invasion 40/1; Thirty Years' War 93/3; Reformation 91/1; Industrial Revolution 101/2; expansion in Africa 111/1; unification 111/2; colonial empire 116/2; 19C alliances 124/1; world trade 1860-1913 127/1; WW1 132-3; territorial changes after WW1 136/1; expansion 1934-41 137/2; territorial losses to Poland 146/1; Allied control zones 146/1; East and West reunited 168/1

Germany, East (German Democratic Republic or DDR) 146/1; Warsaw Pact 147/4

Middle East (*a/c* Near East) Cold War 165/1

Midway island of C Pacific US base 165/1 (inset)

Milan (*It.* Milano *anc.* Mediolanum) N Italy Lombard League 55/2

Miletus W Anatolia Mycenaean city 31/2; Greek colony 33/1; Byzantine Empire 49/1

Mindanao island of S Philippines Japanese occupation 142/1; retaken by US 143/2

Ming Empire China 69/1

Min-yüeh region of S China 39/1

Mixtec States S Mexico 24/2

Mitanni ancient kingdom of Middle East 22/3

Mocha (*Ar.* Al Mukhā) S Yemen centre of European trade 103/2

Modena (*anc.* Mutina) N Italy Lombard League 55/2; unification of Italy 117/1

Moesia region of Balkans district of Byzantine Empire 49/1

Moesiae late Roman province of Greece 37/2

Moesia Inferior Roman province of the Balkans 37/1

Moesia Superior Roman province of the Balkans 37/1

Mogadishu (*n/s* Muqdisho *It.* Mogadiscio) Somalia Muslim colony 59/1; Italian occupation 110/1

Mohács Hungary ✗70/2

Moldavia (*Turk.* Boğdan *Rom.* Moldova) region of Romania/Russia Hungarian 66/2; under Ottoman control 71/1; part of Romania 125/2; independence (Moldova) 169/1

Moluccas (*Indon.* Maluku *Dut.* Molukken *form.* Spice Islands) islands of E Indies Muslim expansion 64/2; early Portuguese trade 81/1; Dutch control 89/2

Mondovi NW Italy ✗99/2

Monemvasia (*It.* Malvasia) S Greece Byzantine Empire 49/2; Ottoman conquest 70/2

Mongol Empire 60-61

Mongolia (*form.* Outer Mongolia) nomadic pastoralism 21/1; Mongol Empire 60-61; under Han Empire 41/1; Chinese incursions under Ming 69/1; Chinese protectorate 94/1; autonomy 95/2; Russian sphere of influence 119/2; limit of Japanese expansion 123/2

Montenegro (*S. Cr.* Crna Gora) region of S Yugoslavia under Ottoman rule 108/1; 19C alliances 124/1; independent state 125/2; WW1 133/1; forms part of Yugoslavia 136/1; WW2 141/2; Kosovo crisis 171/2

Montenotte N Italy ✗99/2

Montereau N France ✗99/2

Montmirail N France ✗99/2

Montreux Switzerland 1936 conference 136/1

Montserrat island West Indies British colony 155/1 (inset)

Moravia (*Czech.* Morava *Ger.* Mähren) region of C Czechoslovakia medieval German Empire 55/2; acquired by Bohemia 66/2; Hussite influence 67/1; Reformation 91/1; Habsburg Empire 93/1; forms part of Czechoslovakia 136/1

Mordovia W Russia republic of the Russian Federation 169/2

Morea (*a/c* Peloponnese) region of S Greece Byzantine Empire 49/2; conquered by Ottomans 71/1

Morocco (*Fr.* Maroc *Sp.* Marruecos) under Almohads 50/2; Sharifian dynasties 59/2; Spanish conquest 110/2; French and Spanish protectorates 111/1, 119/2; independence 154/1; conflict with Algeria 161/1; US bases 165/1

Morotai island N Moluccas, E Indies captured by Allies 143/2

Moscow (*Russ.* Moskva) W Russia early bishopric 45/2; city of Vladimir-Suzdal 57/1; captured by Napoleon 99/2; Industrial Revolution 101/2; industrial development 134/2; Bolshevik seizure of power 135/1

Mossi early states of W Africa 59/2

Mostar Herzegovina, Yugoslavia civil war 171/2

Mosul (*Ar.* Al Mawsil) Iraq Muslim conquest 51/1; Ottoman Empire 70/2; oilfield 157/2

Mozambique (*form.* Portuguese East Africa *Port.* Moçambique) early trade 81/1; Portuguese settlement 81/1; centre of European trade 103/2; Portuguese colony 119/2; independence 154/1; political development 161/1

Mughal Empire India 63/1

Mukden Manchuria capital of Manchuria 94/1; treaty town 95/2; Japanese occupation 123/2

Muscat and Oman (*now* Oman) SE Arabia British protectorate 119/2

Muscovy early principality of W Russia 85/1

Muslims minority in Bosnia and Serbia 171/2

Mwenemutapa early state of SE Africa 59/2

Mysia ancient country of W Anatolia 33/1

Muslims minority in Bosnia and Serbia 171/2

Mysore (*now* Karnataka) region of S India district of Mughal Empire 59/1; native state 96-97

Mytilene (*a/s* Mitylene) island of Aegean ceded to Greece 125/2

Nagasaki W Japan early European trade 81/1; Dutch trade 103/2; bombed by US 143/2

Nagorno-Karabakh Caucasus 169/1, 170/3

Nakhichevan region of SW Azerbaijan 170/3

Namibia (*form.* South West Africa *earlier* German South West Africa) German colony 111/1, 119/2; independence from South Africa 154/1, 161/1

Nanking (*n/s* Nanjing) N China Ming provincial capital 65/1; treaty port 89/2; occupied by Japan 117/2; economy 143/2

Nan-yüeh early kingdom of SW China 39/1

Nan-chao tribal kingdom of SW China 47/1

Nanning S China treaty port 95/2

Nantes NW France Scandinavian settlement 54/1

Naples, Kingdom of Black Death 67/1; to Austria 83/3; Habsburg Empire 93/1; satellite of France 99/2; unification of Italy 117/1

Narbonensis (*a/c* Gallia Narbonensis) Roman province of S France 36/1

Narbonne (*anc.* Narbo) S France Muslim conquest 50/1

Nations, Battle of the (Leipzig) E Germany ✗99/2

Naucratis Egypt Greek colony 33/1

Nauru island W Pacific independence 155/1 (inset)

Navarre (*Sp.* Navarra) region of N Spain/SW France acquired by France 83/2; Habsburg Empire 93/1

Navas de Tolosa S Spain ✗50/2

Neapolis (*mod.* Napoli *Eng.* Naples) S Italy Greek colony 33/1; Roman Empire 37/1

Nepal tributary state of Chinese Empire 94/1; 95/2

Nerchinsk, Treaty of 94/1

Netherlands (*a/c* Holland *form.* Dutch Republic United Provinces) Habsburg Empire 93/1; Industrial Revolution 100/2; trade with Africa and Asia 103/2; colonial power 119/2; NATO 147/1; EU 167/1. See also Belgium, Flanders, Holland

Netherlands, Austrian (*mod.* Belgium) revolt against Emperor 98/1

Netherlands East Indies (*now* Indonesia) occupied by Japanese 142/1. See also East Indies, Borneo, Java, Moluccas, Sumatra

Netherlands, Spanish (*later* Holland *or* United Provinces; *and* Belgium) Reformation 91/1; Dutch revolt 92/2

Neustria the Frankish lands of N France 52/1

Nevis island W Indies British colony 112/1; self-government with St. Christopher 155/1 (inset)

New Amsterdam (*earlier* Fort Amsterdam *now* New York city) colonized by Dutch 86/2

New Britain island Papua New Guinea early Melanesian settlement 27/1; retaken from Japanese 143/2; to New Guinea 155/1 (inset)

New Brunswick province of E Canada joins Confederation 1120/2

New Caledonia islands S Pacific early Melanesian settlement 26/1; French colony 119/2, 155/1; US base 142/1

Newchwang Manchuria treaty port 95/2

New England NE USA British settlement 86/2

Newfoundland province of E Canada rediscovered 78/1; British colony 86/2; British settlement 87/1; joins Dominion 120/2

New France French possessions in Canada 86/2

New Granada (*mod.* Colombia) Spanish colony 87/1; vice-royalty in rebellion against Spain 99/1; 18C Atlantic economy 102/1

New Guinea (*now part of* Papua New Guinea) early settlement 27/1; Dutch/German/British control 119/2; attacked by Japanese 142/1; retaken by Allies 143/2. See also West Irian

New Hampshire state of NE USA colony 104/1; population 121/1, Depression 138/2

New Hebrides (*Fr.* Nouvelles Hébrides *now* Vanuatu) islands S Pacific early Melanesian settlement 27/1; British/French condominium 119/2; US base 142/1; independence 155/1 (inset)

New Ireland island Papua New Guinea early Melanesian settlement 26/1; occupied by Japanese 142/1

New Jersey state of E USA colony 86/2, 104/1; population 115/3; Depression 131/2

New Mexico state of SW USA ceded by Mexico 107/1; population 121/1; Depression 138/2

New Orleans S USA French/Spanish occupation 87/1

New Sarai S Russia Mongol city 60/1

New South Wales state of SE Australia settlement and development 106/1; statehood 118/1

New Spain (*mod.* Mexico, C America and Caribbean) Spanish vice-royalty 78/1; early voyages of discovery 87/1; rebellion against Spain 99/1

New Territories S China acquired by Britain 95/2

New York City (*1653-64 called* New Amsterdam *earlier* Fort Amsterdam) 86/2; industry 121/1; population 121/3; economic growth 145/1

New Zealand early Polynesian settlement 27/1; settlement and development 107/2,3

Nicaea (*mod.* Iznik) W Anatolia Mithraic site 34/1; Byzantine Empire 49/2

Nicaragua country of C America early exploration 78/1; independence 112/1; Sandinista revolution 159/1

Nicobar Islands Indian Ocean territory of British India 119/2

Nicomedia *mod.* Izmit) W Anatolia Christian centre 45/1; Byzantine Empire 49/1

Nicopolis W Greece Byzantine Empire 49/2

Niger country of W Africa French colony 111/1; independence 154/1; economy 174/1

Nigeria country of W Africa British colony 111/1, 119/2; independence 154/1; political development 161/1; economy 174/1

Nihavand (*anc.* Laodicea in Media) W Persia ✗51/1

Nineveh Mesopotamia early farming village 19/1; Assyrian Empire 22/3; Mitannian city 23/1

Ningpo (*n/s* Ningbo) E China treaty port 95/2

Ningxia (f/s Ningxia) province of N China economy 1979-92 151/2

Nippur C Mesopotamia Sumerian city 23/1

Nish (S. Cr. Niš anc. Naissus) E Yugoslavia Ottoman Empire 71/1

Nishapur (Pers. Neyshabur) W Persia Mongol conquest 61/1; Safavid conquest 63/1

Nisibis (mod. Nusaybin) E Anatolia Roman Empire 37/1

Nizhniy Novgorod (since 1932 Gorkiy) C Russia town of Vladimir-Suzdal 57/1; 1905 Revolution 115/3; Bolshevik seizure 135/1

Nomonhan (a/c Khalkin Gol) E Mongolia Russo-Japanese conflict 123/2

Nördlingen S Germany ✗93/3

Noricum Roman province of C Europe 37/1

Normandy region of N France Scandinavian settlement 54/1; French Royal domain 82/1; province of France 83/2

North Carolina state of E USA colony 86/2, 104/1; population 121/3; Depression 138/2

Northern Cook Islands (Manihiki Islands)

Northern Ireland religious divide 166/2

Northern Rhodesia (now Zambia) British colony 111/1, 119/2

North Ossetia Caucasus republic of the Russian Federation 169/2, 170/3

Northumbria early kingdom of N England 53/2

North Vietnam independence 155/1. See also Vietnam, Indo-China

North West Frontier Province N Pakistan in Indian Empire 96/2, 97/3

Norway conversion to Christianity 45/2; Black Death 67/1; Reformation 91/1; WW2 140/1, 141/2; NATO and EFTA 147/4; economy 175/1

Notium W Anatolia ✗33/2

Nova Scotia (form. Acadia) province of E Canada ceded by France 87/1; British possession 86/3, 104/1; joins Confederation 120/2; economy 120/2

Novgorod (Norse Holmegaard) NW Russia bishopric 45/2; Viking trade 57/1; WW2 141/2

Novgorod Empire NW Russia 53/2; conquered by Muscovy 851

Novgorod-Seversk early principality of W Russia 57/1

Novibazar, Sanjak of Ottoman province of Yugoslavia 124/1

Nubia region of NE Africa early settlement 27/2

Numidia Roman province of N Africa 36/1

Nupe Nigeria early Hausa state 58/1, 59/2

Nyasaland (now Malawi) British protectorate 111/1, 119/2

Oaxaca early civilization of Mexico 24/2 (inset)

Odessa S Ukraine founded 85/1; 1905 Revolution 115/3; Bolshevik seizure 135/1; WW2 141/2

Odessus (mod. Varna) Bulgaria Greek colony 33/1; Roman Empire 37/1

Offa's Dyke 53/1

Okinawa island SW Japan captured by US 143/2; reversion to Japan 163/1; US base 165/1

Olbia S Russia Greek colony 33/1

Old Calabar Nigeria 59/2

Oldenburg country of N Germany 116/2

Old Sarai S Russia Mongol city 60/1

Olmec States C Mexico 24/2

Oman region of E Arabia Muslim expansion 51/1; under Abbasid sovereignty 51/2; British sphere of influence 154/1

Ontario province of E Canada joins Confederation 120/2

Oran (Ar. Wahran) N Algeria Habsburg Empire 93/1; WW2 140/1

Orange principality of S France 83/2

Oregon state of NW USA acquired by USA 105/2; population 121/1; Depression 138/2

Orenburg (1938-57 called Chkalov) C Russia founded 85/1; Bolshevik seizure 135/1

Orissa (form. Jajnagar) region of E India district of Mughal Empire 63/1; state of modern India 97/3

Orkney islands of NE Scotland Norwegian Viking settlement 54/1

Orléanais region of C France 82/1; 83/2

Ormuz (a/s Hormuz anc. Harmozia) S Persia Portuguese control 63/1; Portuguese base 81/1

Oslo (until 1924 Kristiania a/s Christiania) Norway WW2 140/1

Otford S England ✗53/1

Ottoman Empire Mongol invasion 60/2; expansion into Europe 70-1; decline 108/1, 125/2; WW1 133/1

Oudenaarde (Fr. Audenarde) Belgium ✗83/3

Outer Mongolia (now Mongolia) Chinese protectorate 94/1; independence 131/2

Pacific Ocean early Polynesian settlement 27/1; WW2 142-43; sovereignty of islands 155/1 (inset)

Paeckche Korea early state destroyed by T'ang 47/1

Pagan C Burma Mongol attack 61/1; Buddhist site 35/1; early empire 65/1

Pakhoi S China treaty port 95/2

Pakistan independence 154/1; secession of Bangladesh 163/1; boundary dispute with India 163/1; Baghdad Pact and US alliance 165/1

Palatinate (Ger. Pfalz) historical region of W Germany Reformation 91/1; German unification 116/2

Palau (f/s Pelew) SW Caroline Islands, W Pacific occupied by US 143/2

Pale Bosnia-Herzegovina Bosnian Serb capital 171/2

Palestine (Lat. Palaestina now Israel and Jordan) Levantine cities and ports 22/1; Byzantine Empire 49/1; Ottoman province 108/1; WW2 140/1; partition between Israel and Jordan 156/1

Pamphylia ancient country of southern Anatolia 33/1, 37/1, 49/1

Panama independence 113/1; US intervention 1989 159/1; US base 165/1

Panama Canal opening 118/2

Panipat N India ✗63/1

Panmunjom Korea 1953 armistice 153/1

Pannonia C Europe Avar Kingdom 53/2

Pannonia Inferior Roman province of C Europe 37/1

Pannonia Superior Roman province of C Europe 37/1

Panticapaeum (mod. Kerch) Crimea Greek colony 33/1; Roman Empire 37/1

Papal States C Italy Black Death 67/1; Reformation 91/1; unification of Italy 117/1

Paphlagonia ancient country of N Anatolia 33/1; 49/1

Papua New Guinea SW Pacific independence 155/1. See also New Guinea

Parhae (Chin. Pohai) early Korean state 47/1

Paris N France parlement 83/2; ✗99/1; Industrial Revolution 100/2

Parma N Italy Roman Lombard League 55/2; unification of Italy 117/1

Passchendaele NW Belgium WW1✗ 132/2

Pearl Harbor Hawaii bombed by Japanese 142/1

Pechenegs tribe of Ukraine, 48/2, 56/2, 57/1

Pecsaete tribe of early England 53/1

Pegu early state of S Burma, Buddhist site 35/1; early trade 89/2

Peking (form. Mong. Khanbalik, Chin. Beijing) N China Ming capital 69/1; Japanese occupation 123/2; economy 151/2

Peloponnesian War 33/2

Peninsular War 98/2

Pennsylvania state of E USA colony 86/2, 104/1; population 121/1; Depression 138/2

Pereyaslav early principality of Ukraine 57/1

Pergamum (Gr. Pergamon Turk. Bergama) W Anatolia Roman Empire 37/1

Périgord region of C France annexed to France 82/1

Perm (1940-57 called Molotov) C Russia founded 85/1; Bolshevik seizure 135/1

Persepolis Persia taken by Alexander 32/3; Muslim conquest 51/1

Persia (now Iran) Mongol invasion 61/1; campaigns of Alexander 32/3; Zoroastrianism 34/1; attacked by White Huns 40/1; under Abbasid sovereignty 51/2; Safavid Empire 63/1; Islamic state 157/3

Persian Gulf (a/c Arabian Gulf or The Gulf) Iran-Iraq War 157/2

Peru Spanish colonization 87/1; 18C Atlantic economy 102/1; independence 113/1

Petrograd (before 1914 St. Petersburg since 1924 Leningrad) WW1 133/1; Russian Revolution 135/1

Petsamo (Russ. Pechenga) NW Russia Russian conquest from Finland 141/2

Phazania (mod. Fezzan) region of S Libya 37/1

Philadelphia E USA founded 86/2

Philippines early trade 81/1; Spanish conquest 89/2; occupied by Japanese 123/2, 142/1; retaken by Americans 143/2; independence 155/1; political development 163/1; US bases 165/1

Philippine Sea ✗143/2

Philippopolis (mod. Plovdiv Turk. Filibe) Bulgaria Byzantine Empire 49/1; Ottoman Empire 71/1

Philomelium (mod. Akşehir) C Anatolia Byzantine Empire 49/2

Phnom Penh Cambodia 65/1, 89/2; Vietnam war 162/3

Phocaea W Anatolia Greek colony 33/1

Phoenicia at time of Greeks 33/1

Phoenicians move into Africa 27/2

Phrygia ancient country of W Anatolia 33/1; Byzantine Empire 49/1

Picts early tribe of Scotland 40/1

Piedmont (It. Piemonte) region of N Italy 117/1

Pigs, Bay of Cuba CIA invasion 164/3

Pisidia ancient country of C Anatolia 49/1

Podolia region of S Ukraine acquired by Lithuania 66/2

Pohai (Kor. Parhae mod. Manchuria) NE China early state 47/1

Poitiers (anc. Limonum) C France 17C seat of intendant 77/2

Poitou region of W France province of France 83/2

Pola (mod. Pula) N Yugoslavia Roman Empire 37/1

Poland conversion to Christianity 45/2; union with Lithuania 66/2; Black Death 67/1; acquired by Russia 85/1; Reformation 91/1; revolt against Russia 98/1; WW1 133/1; WW2 140-41; territorial changes 146/1; Warsaw Pact and Comecon 138/3, 165/1; end of Communist rule 169/1

Polish Corridor 136/1

Polynesia islands of C Pacific early settlement 27/1

Pomerania (Ger. Pommern Pol. Pomorze) region of N Europe medieval German Empire 55/2; Reformation 91/1; unification of Germany 116/2

Pomerelia (Ger. Pommerellen) region of N Europe occupied by Teutonic Knights 66/2

Pondicherry (Fr. Pondichéry) SE India French enclave 97/3

Pontus district of N Anatolia 33/1; Roman province 37/1,2; Byzantine Empire 49/1

São Tomé and Príncipe islands W Africa united as independent republic 154/1

Saracens invasion of S Europe 54/1

Saragossa (*anc.* Caesaraugusta *mod.* Zaragoza) N Spain bishopric 44/1; ✗98/1; captured by French 98/1

Sarajevo C Yugoslavia captured by Ottomans 71/1; WW1 133/1; WW2 140/1; civil war 171/2

Saratoga NE USA ✗104/1

Sardinia (*It.* Sardegna) island W Mediterranean Roman empire 36/1; Byzantine Empire 48/1; Muslim conquest 50/1; Saracen attacks 54/1; Habsburg Empire 93/1; Kingdom 99/2, 117/2

Sardis (*a/s* Sardes) W Anatolia Roman Empire 37/1; Byzantine Empire 49/2

Sarkel S Russia ✗56/2

Sarmatians (*Lat.* Sarmatae) tribe of Caucasus and S Russia 33/1, 37/1

Sarmizegetusa Romania Roman Empire 37/1

Sasanian Empire Western Asia 41/1

Saudi Arabia Gulf War 157/3

Savoy (*Fr.* Savoie *It.* Savoia) region of France/Italy medieval state 55/2; Calvinism 91/1; Habsburg Empire 93/1; ceded to France 117/1

Saxon March 53/2

Saxony region of N Germany Frankish Empire 53/2; Black Death 67/1; Reformation 91/1

Scandinavia (*anc.* Scandia) Viking invasions of Europe 54/1. See also Denmark, Sweden, Norway

Scapa Flow N Scotland WW1 133/1

Schleswig-Holstein region of N Germany unification of Germany 116/2

Scotland (*anc.* Caledonia) Scandinavian settlement 54/1; Black Death 67/1; Reformation 91/1; Devolution 166/2

Scupi (*mod.* Skoplje *Mac.* Skopje *Turk.* Üsküb) Byzantine Empire 49/1

Scythians ancient tribe of S Russia 33/1

Sebastopol (*Russ.* Sevastopol) Crimea. S Russia 1905 Revolution 115/3; WW1 133/1

Sedan N France ✗116/2; WW2 140/1

Selinus (*mod.* Selinunte) Sicily Greek colony 32/1, 33/2

Seljuks Turkish Muslim dynasty of Middle East 49/2, 51/2

Senegal W Africa French colony independence 154/1

Senegambia region of W Africa source of slaves 59/2; slave trade 102/1

Seoul (*Jap.* Keijo) S Korea Korean war 153/1

Septimania ancient region of S France, part of Frankish Empire 52/2

Serbia (*now part of* Yugoslavia) country of SE Europe conversion to Christianity 45/2; Byzantine Empire 49/2; empire under Stephen Dushan 66/2; Black Death 67/1; Ottoman province 71/1; Industrial Revolution 101/2; independence 108/1; WW1 133/1; forms part of Yugoslavia 136/1; WW2 141/2; Kosovo crisis 171/2

Serdica (*a/s* Sardica *mod.* Sofia) Bulgaria Roman Empire 37/1; Byzantine Empire 49/1

Seringapatam S India ✗97/1

Sevastopol (*Eng.* Sebastopol *med. Turk.* Akhtiar) Crimea acquired by Muscovy 85/1

Seville (*Sp.* Sevilla *anc.* Hispalis) S Spain Emirate of Cordoba 50/1

Shaanxi (*f/s* Shensi) province of N China economy 1979–92 151/2

Shakas early dynasty of N India 29/4

Shanghai E China treaty port 95/2; occupied by Japanese 123/2; Nationalist control 130/1; industry 131/2; economy 151/2

Shansi (*n/s* Shanxi) province of N China Ming province 69/1; Manchu expansion 94/1; economy 151/2

Shan State(s) Burma part of India 97/3

Shandong (*f/s* Shantung) province of E China economy 1979–92 151/2

Shantou (*f/s* Swatow) S China special economic zone 151/2

Shantung (*n/s* Shandong) province of E China under Ming 69/1; Manchu expansion 94/1; Japanese influence 130/1; economy 151/2

Shanxi (*f/s* Shansi) province of N China economy 1979–92 151/2

Shensi (*n/s* Shaanxi) province of N China under Ming 69/1; Manchu expansion 94/1; economy 151/2

Shenzhen S China special economic zone 151/2

Shetland (*form.* Hjaltland) NE Scotland Norwegian settlement 54/1

Shias Muslim minority of S Iraq 147/3

Siam (*now* Thailand) spread of Buddhism 64/2; conquests 89/2; under Japanese influence 123/2; occupied by Japanese 142/1

Sian (*n/s* Xi'an) China Ming provincial capital 69/1

Siberia cave art 15/1; Russian expansion 79/2

Sichuan (*f/s* Szechwan) province of W China economy 1979–92 151/2

Sicily (*Lat. and It.* Sicilia) island C Mediterranean Greek colonization 32/1; Byzantine Empire 49/1; Saracen raids 54/1; German attacks 55/2; to Savoy 83/3; Habsburg Empire 93/1; Kingdom of the Two Sicilies annexed to Piedmont/Sardinia 117/1; WW2 141/2

Sidon (*mod.* Saïda *Ar.* Sayda) Lebanon Phoenician city 33/1; taken by Alexander 32/3

Sierra Leone country of W Africa slave trade 102/1; British settlement 111/1; British colony 119/2; independence 154/1

Sikkim country of Himalayas British protectorate 95/2 dependency of India 96/3; annexed to India 155/1

Silesia (*Ger.* Schlesien *Pol.* Śląsk) region of Germany/Poland medieval German Empire 55/2; Habsburg Empire 93/1; unification of Germany 116/2; divided between Germany and Poland 136/1

Silla (*Eng.* Korea *Kor.* Koryo) occupied by T'ang 47/1

Singapore (*earlier* Tumasik) S Malaya early trade 89/2; occupied by Japanese 142/1; independence 155/1; economy 175/1

Sinkiang (*n/s* Xinjiang) province of NW China part of Han Empire 95/2; cession of territory to Russia 95/2; economy 151/2

Sinope (*mod.* Sinop) N Anatolia Greek colony 33/1; Roman Empire 37/1; Byzantine Empire 49/1

Slovakia forms part of Czechoslovakia 136/1; occupied by Hungary in WW2 141/2

Slovenia in Yugoslavia 128/1; independence 169/1

Smolensk W Russia bishopric 45/2; principality 57/1; acquired by Lithuania 66/2; captured by Napoleon 99/2; Bolshevik seizure 135/1

Smyrna (*mod.* Izmir) W Anatolia Roman Empire 37/1; Byzantine Empire 49/1,2; Ottoman Empire 71/1; centre of European trade 103/2

Socotra island Arabian Sea acquired by Britain 119/2

Sofala Mozambique Portuguese settlement 59/2; early trade 81/1

Sofia (*anc.* Serdica *a/s* Sardica *med.* Sredets) Bulgaria Ottoman control 71/1; WW2 141/2

Sogdiana (*a/c* Sogdia, Suguda) ancient region of C Asia Chinese protectorate 46/1

Solferino N Italy ✗117/1

Solomon Islands SW Pacific British protectorate 119/2; occupied by Japanese 142/1; retaken by Allies 143/2; independence 155/1 (inset)

Somalia (*form.* British and Italian Somaliland) independence 154/1; political development 161/1

Somaliland divided between British, Italians and French 119/2

Somme river NE France WW1 offensive 124/2

Songhay (*a/s* Songhai) early empire of W Africa 58/1

Soochow E China treaty port 95/2; industry 131/2

Sopron (*Ger.* Ödenburg) Hungary to Hungary after plebiscite 136/1

Sorbs Slavic tribe of C Europe 53/2

South Africa Union 119/2; Republic 154/1; political development 161/1

South Carolina state of SE USA colony 86/2, 104/1; population 121/1; Depression 138/2

South-East Asia early civilizations 29/1; Mongol attacks 61/1; post 1945 conflicts 163/1

Southern Rhodesia (*now* Zimbabwe *f/c* Rhodesia) British colony 111/1, 119/2

South Ossetian Caucasus 170/3

South Tyrol (*Ger.* Südtirol *It.* Alto Adige) region of Austro-Hungarian Empire acquired by Italy 136/1

South Vietnam independence 155/1; war 162/3. See also Vietnam, Indo-China

South Yemen (*also called* People's Democratic Republic of Yemen *form.* Federation of South Arabia *earlier* Protectorate of South Arabia *earlier* Aden Protectorate) independence 154/1; union with north Yemen 154/1

Spa Belgium 1920 Conference 136/1

Spain (*anc.* Hispania) early invasions 40/1; conversion to Christianity 44/1; Muslim conquest 50/2; Umayyad caliphate 50/2; Reformation 91/1; War of the Spanish Succession 83/3; colonial empire 119/2; opposition to Napoleon 98/1; Industrial Revolution 100/2; 18C Atlantic economy 103/2; 19C alliances 124/1; US bases 165/1

Spanish Guinea (*now* Equatorial Guinea) W Africa colony 118/1

Spanish March 52/2

Spanish Sahara (*a/c* Western Sahara *includes* Rio de Oro) NW Africa 103/2; Spanish colony 111/1; partition between Morocco and Mauritania 154/1, 161/1

Spanish Succession, War of the 83/3

Sparta (*a/c* Lacedaemon) S Greece Peloponnesian War 33/2; Roman Empire 37/1

Spartalos N Greece ✗33/2

Sphacteria S Greece ✗33/2

Srebrenica NE Herzegovina UN safe area 171/2

Srinagar N India capital of Kashmir 97/3

Srivijaya E Indies early empire 65/1

Stalingrad (*until 1925* Tsaritsyn *since 1961* Volgograd) S Russia WW2 141/2

Stresa N Italy 1935 Conference 136/1

Styria (*Ger.* Steiermark) province of SE Austria acquired by Habsburgs 66/2; Habsburg Empire 93/1

Sudan (*form.* Anglo-Egyptian Sudan) Mahdist state 111/1; Anglo-Egyptian condominium 111/1, 119/2; independence 154/1, 161/1; Islamic fundamentalism 157/3

Sudetenland C Europe German annexation 137/2

Suez Canal N Egypt Egyptian-Israeli war 156/1

Suifen NE China treaty port 95/2

Sukhothai C Thailand Buddhist site 35/1; major political centre 65/1

Sumatra (*Indon.* Sumatera) E Indies spread of Buddhism 35/1; Dutch possession 119/2; occupied by Japanese 142/1

Sumerians ancient people of Mesopotamia 23/1

Sung Empire China Mongol conquest 61/1

Süntel N Germany ✗53/2

Surabaya (*Dut.* Soerabaja) Java trading centre 89/2; occupied by Japanese 142/1

Swabia (*Ger.* Schwaben) province of medieval German kingdom 55/2

Swakopmund SW Africa German settlement 111/1

Swatow (*n/s* Shantou) S China treaty port 95/2; Japanese occupation 123/2; 151/2

Picture credits

10 AKG Photo London; 12 Ancient Art & Architecture collection; 15 The Art Archive; 16 Chris Scarre; 18 The Art Archive; 21 Michael Holford; 23 The Art Archive; 25 Werner Forman Archive, National Museum of Anthropology, Mexico; 26 John Miles/Panos pictures; 29 Scala; 30 Ancient Art & Architecture Collection; 32 Scala; 34 Chris Scarre; 36 Scala; 38 Ancient Art & Architecture; 41 Michael Holford; 42 Werner Forman Archive; 45 AKG Photo London; 47 Werner Forman Archive, Christian Deydier, London; 48 The Art Archive; 51 The Art Archive; 52 The Art Archive; 54 Werner Forman Archive, Viking Ship Museum, Bygdoy; 57 AKG Photo London; 59 Robert Aberman; 60 Robert Harding Picture Library; 63 The Bridgeman Art Library; 65 Robert Harding Picture Library; 66 Werner Forman Archive; 69 National Palace Museum, Taiwan; 71 Sonia Halliday Photographs; 73 The Art Archive; 75 The Art Archive; 76 The Bridgeman Art Library; 79 The Art Archive; 81 South American Pictures; 82 Robert Harding Picture Library; 85 Michael Holford; 86 Thomas Gilrease Institute of American History and Art, Tulsa; 88 Tokyo National Museum; 90 AKG Photo London; 92 Beheer Collection, Gemeente Musea, Delft; 95 The Art Archive; 96 Popperfoto; 99 The Art Archive; 100 Science and Society Picture Library; 103 National Maritime Museum, Greenwich; 104 Corbis-Bettmann; 107 The Art Archive; 108 AKG Photo London; 110 The Art Archive; 112 The Art Archive; 115 Novosti (London); 116 Mary Evans Picture Library; 119 The Art Archive, Victoria and Albert Museum, Eileen Tweedy; 120 Corbis; 122 The Art Archive; 125 Jane's Information Group; 127 The Art Archive; 128 The Art Archive; 130 The Art Archive; 133 The Art Archive; 134 David King Collection; 136 Popperfoto; 139 Ullstein Bilderdienst; 142 The Art Archive; 144 STR/Reuters/Popperfoto; 147 Corbis; 148 Sygma; 150 Sygma; 152 Associated Press; 155 Hulton Getty; 156 Sygma; 158 Sygma; 160 Sygma; 162 Sygma; 164 Magnum; 165 Popperfoto; 169 Reuters/CORBIS; 171 Sygma; 173 Louise Gubb/CORBIS SABA, 175 EWI; 176 Sygma

Front cover: Franz Aberham/Getty Images